The Writer's Workplace

THE WRITER'S WORKPLACE

Building College Writing Skills

SECOND EDITION

Sandra Scarry

Hostos Community College,
City University of New York

John Scarry

Hostos Community College,
City University of New York

HARCOURT BRACE JOVANOVICH COLLEGE PUBLISHERS
Fort Worth   Philadelphia   San Diego
New York   Orlando   Austin   San Antonio
Toronto   Montreal   London   Sydney   Tokyo

Publisher	Ted Buchholz
Acquisitions Editor	Michael Rosenberg
Developmental Editor	Stacy Schoolfield
Project Editor/Text Design	Publications Development Company
Production Manager	Kathleen Ferguson
Art & Design Supervisor/Cover	Serena Barnett
Cover Design	Pat Sloan
Cover Illustration	Moira M. Cumming

Library of Congress Cataloging-in-Publication Data

Scarry, Sandra, 1946–
    The writer's workplace : building college writing skills / Sandra
Scarry, John Scarry. — 2nd ed.
       p.   cm.
    Includes index.
    ISBN 0-03-053862-9
    1. English language—Rhetoric—Problems, exercises, etc.
    2. English language—Grammar—1950—Problems, exercises, etc.
    I. Scarry, John. II. Title.
PE1413.S36   1991
808'.042—dc20   90-43023
                                                                     CIP

Copyright © 1991, 1988, 1987 by Holt, Rinehart and Winston, Inc.

All rights reserved. No part of this publication may be reproduced or transmitted in any form or by any means, electronic or mechanical, including photocopy, recording or any information storage and retrieval system, without permission in writing from the publisher.

Requests for permission to make copies of any part of the work should be mailed to: Copyrights and Permissions Department, Harcourt Brace Jovanovich, Inc., 6277 Sea Harbor Drive, Orlando, Florida 32887.

Address for editorial correspondence: Harcourt Brace Jovanovich, Inc., 301 Commerce Street, Suite 3700, Fort Worth, Texas 76102

Address for orders: Harcourt Brace Jovanovich, Inc., 6277 Sea Harbor Drive, Orlando, Florida 32887. 1-800-782-4479, or 1-800-433-0001 (in Florida)

Printed in the United States of America

1 2 3 4   085   9 8 7 6 5 4 3 2

Harcourt Brace Jovanovich, Inc.
The Dryden Press
Saunders College Publishing

For Our Students

What shall I do this year? What shall I become? What shall I learn—truly learn and know that I have learned by the time I look at these pages next year?

Lorraine Hansberry,
journal entry of August 23, 1962*

*From *To Be Young, Gifted and Black,* adapted by Robert Nemiroff (Englewood Cliffs, NJ: Prentice-Hall, 1969).

Preface

The Writer's Workplace is a complete program of grammar and writing skills for students who need steady and consistent work to build their college skills. The book explains and reinforces those skills and gives the basic writing student confidence and control while it also gives the instructor the kind of flexibility needed to work with large classes, smaller groups, and even individual students. Students who use *The Writer's Workplace* are not only working toward success in their English courses, they are making solid preparation for success in any college course that calls for the ability to write clearly and effectively.

Many of the important features in *The Writer's Workplace* have been designed to help both teacher and student as they work in the basic skills classroom. These features include:

▶ **Completeness** The book begins with a carefully constructed chapter that invites relaxed freewriting. It then introduces the student to exercises that lead to strong sentence writing, and proceeds to demonstrate the workings of excellent professional paragraphs. These related skills are designed to help the college writer achieve the goal of every English course at this level: the ability to write a well-developed college essay, a skill that is taught in the third major section of the book. At each step along the way, numerous practice exercises and writing assignments confirm what is being learned. The approach taken in *The Writer's Workplace* is unusual in that grammar *and* writing skills are taught within the pages of a single book. When you work with *The Writer's Workplace*, there is no need to use a grammar book as a supplement or to look for a basic rhetoric to teach the structure of the college essay. Everything you need for grammar skills and for writing development is contained in the book you are now holding.

▶ **Flexibility** The format of *The Writer's Workplace* allows the instructor to work on a single exercise with an entire class or to assign entire sets of exercises to groups of students. In addition, individual students who study with tutors in a lab situation can work in the book with maximum efficiency. This basic flexibility of *The Writer's Workplace* is enhanced by the separately printed annotated instructor's edition. Students may check their own answers or work under the direct supervision of the instructor or a tutor.

The book is also flexible in that a certain section may be skipped if the material of that section is not needed for a particular class, or a class might begin with a later section of the book, using the earlier chapters for review. Another major feature of the book that demonstrates its flexibility is Part II, "Mastering the Paragraph." If an instructor chooses this section as a point of departure for a class, the students could either work backward and concentrate on sentence development, or go ahead to the essay work in Part III, providing the students' abilities are strong enough.

▸ **Stimulating Content**   As students use the book, they are not only exposed to selections from the works of major, established writers as models for their own work, they are also exposed to thoughtful opinions on some of the most controversial issues facing our society today. The grammar exercises present material that deals with such current topics as AIDS, specific environmental concerns, and aspects of life in the Soviet Union today; the model paragraphs and professional essays in Parts II and III of the book are taken from the works of such well-known authors as George Orwell, Donald Murray, and James A. Michener. In addition, many of the concerns in the essay writing section of the book (Part III) deal directly with drugs, mercy killing, and the effects of modern technology on people today.

▸ New to the second edition

The many students and instructors who have used the first edition of *The Writer's Workplace* have appreciated the fact that, among the book's many features, the in-depth treatment of both grammar skills and the writing process makes for a well-balanced program that addresses the needs of both student and instructor.

In this second edition, over a third of the grammar exercises are new, with fresh content for new exercises drawn from a wide variety of sources, ranging from popular magazines to traditional reference works. Also, the book now contains several new full-length essays that are clearly accessible models for narration and persuasion. In addition, the photo unit devoted to the Lorraine Hansberry play *A Raisin in the Sun* provides expanded writing opportunities for students to demonstrate their ability to write full-length essays.

Additional features new to this second edition include:

▸ A new opening chapter, based on Anne Frank's *The Diary of a Young Girl*, that gives students opportunities for freewriting and encourages the use of a journal as part of their writing program. In addition to serving as an inviting introduction to the more structured work of the course, this chapter also provides the instructor with immediate samples of student writing.

▸ Review exercises for every chapter in Part I of the book.

▸ Stronger emphasis on verbs, with the addition of Irregular Verbs and the inclusion of the Present Perfect and Past Perfect tenses (Chapter 7).

▸ A new student essay for the chapter on "Structuring the College Essay," taking the student step-by-step through the construction and revision stages of an actual college essay.

▸ The appendix, which remains unusually extensive, has added topics on dictionary skills and look-alike and sound-alike words. The appendix is a valuable adjunct to the main parts of the book. An instructor may decide to work directly with the various sections of the appendix or assign one or more sections to individual students, as needed.

▶ A list of editing and correction symbols appears on the inside front cover of the book, enabling students to more easily understand the changes needed when an essay is returned to them.

In addition to these main features, *The Writer's Workplace* supports the work of both student and instructor by providing the following ancillary materials:

▶ A separate annotated instructor's edition of the book, with all answers included for the ease of the instructor's review. This separate edition also contains notes on teaching college grammar and composition, along with specific suggestions on using *The Writer's Workplace* in the college classroom.

▶ Computer software, *The Writing Tutor,* a grammar based tutorial software package, designed for student use in computer lab or writing lab situations.

▶ Ditto masters of additional sentence exercises, designed to strengthen student skills, as needed.

▶ An answer key with correct answers to odd-numbered exercise questions is available for students at the instructor's request.

The Writer's Workplace is the result of a great deal of cooperation and support from our colleagues at Hostos Community College and elsewhere. At Hostos our appreciation goes to Dr. Clara Velazquez, Chairperson of the English Department; Cynthia Moore, Director of the Hostos LIBRA Program; and Ralph Ranald, English Department Writing Coordinator. Our special thanks go to Vermell Blanding and John Rittershofer, who provided penetrating reviews of the first edition of the book; their insights were most valuable to us as we approached the revisions for this second edition. Beyond Hostos, our renewed thanks go to Michael Buckley for always being so available with answers to a variety of questions, and to Robert Nemiroff for his always supportive presence in matters relating to Lorraine Hansberry's *A Raisin in the Sun.*

We are grateful to the following teachers throughout the country who shared their expertise as they evaluated our manuscript for the first edition: Peter Dow Adams, Essex Community College; Kitty Chen Dean, Nassau Community College; Ann Fields, Western Kentucky University; Jan A. Geesaman, College of DuPage; Sarah H. Harrison, Tyler Junior College; Karen A. Hattaway, San Jacinto College; Barbara K. Haxby, Triton College; Alexandra G. Linett, Delaware Technical and Community College; Alfred McDowell, Bergen Community College; Diane Martin, Eastfield College; Louis Molina, Miami-Dade Community College; William C. Truckey, Lewis and Clark Community College; and Donald Wasson, University of California at Los Angeles.

We wish to thank the following colleagues for their valuable comments and sound advice on this revision: Vermell Blanding, Hostos Community College; Stanley Coberly, West Virginia University-Parkside; Robert Dees, Orange Coast College; Michael Donaghe, Eastern New Mexico State University; Carolyn Hartnett, College of the Mainland; Rosemary Hunkler, University of Wisconsin—Parkside; Evelyn Perry, Albany State College; Joanne Pinkston,

Datyona Beach Community College; John C. Presley, Central Virginia Community College; John Rittershofer, Hostos Community College; Mark Underwood, Navarro College.

Finally, we want to express our thanks to the staff at Holt, Rinehart and Winston, especially our editor Michael Rosenberg and our developmental editor Stacey Schoolfield. Their expert guidance brought together all of the elements that have gone into the making of this new edition of our book.

Contents

Discovering Ourselves as Writers: Journals and Freewriting   1
    Using the Journal to Capture our Experience   2
    Writing as Memory   3
    Writing as Fantasy   5
    Writing as Self-Analysis   7
    Looking Ahead: From Freewriting to Structure   8

PART I   DEVELOPING THE COMPLETE SENTENCE

1   Finding Subjects and Verbs in Simple Sentences   12
    Why Should we Use Complete Sentences When We Write?   12
    What is a Complete Sentence?   12
    How Do You Find the Subject of a Sentence?   13
    How Do You Find the Subject in Sentences with Prepositional Phrases?   16
    What Are the Other Problems in Finding Subjects?   20
        Sentences with a Change in the Normal Subject Position   20
        Using *there*   20
        Commands   21
        Sentences That Contain Appositive Phrases   21
    How Do You Find the Verb of a Sentence?   23
        Action Verbs   23
        Linking Verbs   24
        Helping Verbs (Also Called Auxilary Verbs)   25
    Chapter Review Exercises   27

2   Correcting the Fragment in Simple Sentences   29
    Recognizing Sentence Fragments   29
    Practice Putting a Conversation into Complete Sentences   30
    What is a Fragment?   31
    How Do You Correct a Fragment?   32
    Don't Confuse Phrases with Sentences   33
    How Many Kinds of Phrases Are There?   34
    Understanding the Uses of the Present Participle   37
    How Do You Make a Complete Sentence from a Fragment That Contains
        a Participle?   39
    Chapter Review Exercises   44

3 Combining Sentences Using Coordination — 48

- What Is Coordination? 48
- Use a Comma Plus a Coordinating Conjunction 48
- Use a Semicolon, an Adverbial Conjunction, and a Comma 53
- Use a Semicolon 58
- Chapter Review Exercises 60

4 Combining Sentences Using Subordination — 65

- What Is Subordination? 65
- Use a Subordinating Conjunction to Create a Complex Sentence 66
- Use a Relative Pronoun to Create a Complex Sentence 72
- How Do You Punctuate a Clause with a Relative Pronoun? 73
- Chapter Review Exercises 77

5 Correcting the Run-On — 82

- How Many Kinds of Run-ons Are There? 82
- How Do You Make a Complete Sentence from a Run-On? 83
- Chapter Review Exercises 92

6 Making Sentence Parts Work Together — 97

- Subject-Verb Agreement within the Sentence 97
- Special Problems in Making Verbs Agree with Their Subjects 98
- Pronoun-Antecedent Agreement 101
- Parallel Structure: Making a Series of Words, Phrases, or Clauses Balanced within the Sentence 107
- Misplaced and Dangling Modifiers 112
- Chapter Review Exercises 115

7 Solving More Problems with Verbs — 118

- What are the Principal Parts of the Irregular Verbs? 118
- Avoid Unnecessary Shift in Verb Tense 123
- What Is the Sequence of Tenses? 125
- How Do You Use the Present Perfect and the Past Perfect Tenses? 127
  - Forming the Perfect Tenses 127
  - What Do These Tenses Mean? 127
- What is the Difference between Passive and Active Voice? 129
  - How Do You Form the Passive Voice? 129
- What is the Subjunctive? 130
- Other Problems with Verbs 131
- Chapter Review Exercises 131

8 Punctuating Sentences Correctly — 134

- Eight Basic Uses of the Comma 134
- Three Uses for the Apostrophe 140
- Other Marks of Punctuation 143
  - Quotation Marks 143
  - Underlining 144
  - The Semicolon 144
  - The Colon 145
  - The Dash and Parentheses 146
- Chapter Review Exercises 148

9 Part I Review: Using All You Have Learned — 152
    Revising More Complicated Fragments and Run-Ons   152
    Editing Sentences for Errors   159

PART II   MASTERING THE PARAGRAPH

10 Working with Paragraphs: Topic Sentences and Controlling Ideas — 170
    What Is a Paragraph?   170
    What Does a Paragraph Look Like?   170
    What Is a Topic Sentence?   172
        How Can You Tell a Topic Sentence from a Title?   177
        How Do You Find the Topic in a Topic Sentence?   179
    What is a Controlling Idea?   180
        How Do You Find the Controlling Idea of a Topic Sentence?   181
        Choosing Your Own Controlling Idea   182
    Chapter Review Exercises   185

11 Working with Supporting Details — 189
    What Is a Supporting Detail?   189
    Using Examples as Supporting Details   194
    Margaret O. Hyde and Elizabeth H. Forsyth, M.D., "AIDS: An Epidemic of Fear"   195
    Avoid Restating the Topic Sentence   197
    How Do You Make Supporting Details Specific?   201

12 Developing Paragraphs: Description — 205
    What Is Description?   205
    Working with Description: Selecting the Dominant Impression   206
    Revising Vague Dominant Impressions   208
    Working with Description: Sensory Images   211
    Coherence in Description: Putting Details in Space Order   218
    Writing the Descriptive Paragraph Step by Step   224
    On Your Own: Writing Descriptive Paragraphs from Model Paragraphs   230
        A Description of a Home   230
        Charles Chaplin, *My Autobiography*
        A Description of a Person   230
        Betty Smith, *A Tree Grows in Brooklyn*
        A Description of a Time of Day   231
        John Riley, "Growing Up in Cleveland"
        A Description of a Place   232
        Betty Smith, *A Tree Grows in Brooklyn*
        A Description of a Time of Year   233
        Nan Salerno with Rosamond Vanderburgh, *Shaman's Daughter*

13 Developing Paragraphs: Narration — 234
    What Is Narration?   234
    Working with Narration: Using Narration to Make a Point   234
    Coherence in Narration: Placing Details in Order of Time Sequence   236
    Transitions and Time Order   243
    Writing the Narrative Paragraph Step by Step   245
    On Your Own: Writing Narrative Paragraphs from Model Paragraphs   251
        The Story of How You Faced a New Challenge   251
        Betty Rolin, "Hers"
        The Story of an Unpleasant Fight or Argument   252
        Albert Halper, "Prelude"

The Beginning of a Special Relationship 253
Morley Callaghan, "One Spring Night"
You Won't Believe What Happened to Me Today! 253
Berton Roueché, "Phone Call"
A Memorable Experience from Childhood 254
George Orwell, *Coming Up for Air*

14 Developing Paragraphs: Process 256

What Is Process? 256
Working with Process: Don't Overlook Any One of the Steps 257
Coherence in Process: Order in Logical Sequence 260
Transitions for Process 262
Writing the Process Paragraph Step by Step 264
On Your Own: Writing Process Paragraphs from Model Paragraphs 270
   Directional: How to Accomplish a Physical Task 270
   Betty Smith, "Moving a Piano"
   Informational: How Something Scientific Works 271
   "How to Drink the Sea," *Sweden Now*
   Directional: How to Care for Your Health 271
   "How to Get a Good Night's Sleep," *Prevention* Magazine
   Informational: How to Accomplish an Important Task 272
   "How the Hunter Wasp Establishes a Nest"
   Directional: How to Write School Assignments 272
   Donald Murray, *Write to Learn*

15 Developing Paragraphs: Comparison or Contrast 274

What Is Comparison or Contrast? 274
Working with Comparison or Contrast: Choosing the Two-Part Topic 275
Coherence in Comparison or Contrast: Two Approaches to Ordering Material 278
Working for Coherence: Using Transitions 284
Writing the Comparison or Contrast Paragraph Step by Step 288
On Your Own: Writing Comparison or Contrast Paragraphs 294
   Comparing Two Places 294
   James A. Michener, *Iberia*
   Comparing Two Cultures 295
   Brenda David, "Children of Two Nations"
   Comparing a Place Then and Now 296
   Steven Peterson, "Thirty Years Later"
   Comparing Two Approaches to a Subject 297
   "The Medical Profession and Natural Healing," *Prevention* Magazine
   Comparing Male Attitudes and Female Attitudes 297
   Richard M. Restak, "The Other Difference between Boys and Girls"

16 Developing Paragraphs: Definition, Classification, and Cause and Effect 299

What Is Definition? 299
   Writing a Paragraph Using Definition 304
What Is Classification? 305
   Writing a Paragraph Using Classification 308
What Is Cause and Effect? 309
   Looking at a Model Paragraph: Cause 309
   Writing a Paragraph Using Causes 309
   Looking at a Model Paragraph: Effect 310
   Writing a Paragraph Using Effects 310

PART III STRUCTURING THE COLLEGE ESSAY

17 Moving from the Paragraph to the Essay

    What Kinds of Paragraphs Are in an Essay? 312
    What Is a Thesis? 313
    How to Recognize the Thesis Statement 313
    Writing the Effective Thesis Statement 315
    Ways to Write an Effective Introductory Paragraph 320
        What *Not* To Say in Your Introduction 324
    Using Transitions to Move the Reader from One Idea to the Next 324
    Ways to Write an Effective Concluding Paragraph 326
        What *Not* to say in Your Conclusion 327
    A Note About Titles 328

18 The Writing Process

    What is the Process for Writing a College Essay? 329
    Understanding the Writing Process 330
        Getting the Idea 330
        A Student Essay in Progress: Getting the Idea for an Essay 331
        Gathering Information 331
        A Student Essay in Progress: Brainstorming the Topic 332
        Selecting and Organizing Details 332
        A Student Essay in Progress: Organizing the Material 332
        Writing the Rough Draft 333
        A Student Essay in Progress: The Rough Draft 333
        Revising the Rough Draft 334
        A Student Essay in Progress: Revising the Rough Draft 335
        Writing the Second Draft 336
        A Student Essay in Progress: The Second Draft 336
        Proofreading 338
        Preparing the Final Copy 338
        Checking for Errors 338

19 Writing the Narrative Essay

    Exploring the Topic 339
        The Model Essay: Taylor Caldwell, "A Tale in the Classroom" 340
        Analyzing the Writer's Strategies 343
        Suggested Topics for Writing 343
    Writing a Narrative Essay 343
        Getting the Idea 343
        Gather Information (Brainstorm or Take Notes) 344
        Select and Organize Material 345
        Write the Rough Draft 345
        Revise 348
        Write the Second Draft 348
        Proofread 348
        Prepare the Final Copy 348
        Check for Errors 348

20 Writing the Process Essay

    Exploring the Topic 349
        The Model Essay: James Beard, "Basic White Bread" 350

xvi ◀ Contents

        Analyzing the Writer's Strategies   352
        Suggested Topics for Writing   352
    Writing the Process Essay: How to . . .   352
        Get the Idea   353
        Gather Information (Brainstorm or Take Notes)   353
        Select and Organize Material   354
        Write the Rough Draft   354
        Revise   357
        Write the Second Draft   357
        Proofread   357
        Prepare the Final Copy   357
        Check for Errors   357

21 Writing the Comparison or Contrast Essay   358

    Exploring the Topic   358
        The Model Essay, Isaac Asimov, "The Computer and the Brain"   359
        Analyzing the Writer's Strategies   360
    Writing the Comparison or Contrast Essay   360
        Get the Idea   361
        Gather Information (Brainstorm or Take Notes)   361
        Select and Organize Material   362
        Write the Rough Draft   363
        Revise   365
        Write the Second Draft   365
        Proofread   365
        Prepare the Final Copy   365
        Check for Errors   365

22 Writing Persuasively   366

    What is Persuasion?   366
    Guide to Writing the Persuasive Essay   366
        The Model Essay: Dr. Howard Caplan, "It's Time We Helped Patients Die"   367
        Analyzing the Writer's Strategies   370
        Responding to the Writer's Argument   376
        The Model Essay: Robert M. Curvin, "What If Heroin Were Free?"   379
        Analyzing the Writer's Strategies   381
        Responding to the Writer's Argument   387
    Writing the Persuasive Essay: Additional Topics   390

23 From Photographs to Essays: *A Raisin in the Sun*   393

    Essay Review: Lorraine Hansberry, *A Raisin in the Sun*   394
    Narrative, Process, and Comparison or Contrast   395
    Cause and Effect, Comparison or Contrast, and Example   398
    Argumentation   401
    Example, Definition, and Cause and Effect   404

24 Writing under Pressure   407

    How to Write Well under Pressure   407
        Strategies for Answering Timed or In-Class Essay Questions   408
        Frequently Used Terms in Essay Questions   408
    Using the Thesis Statement in Timed or In-Class Essay Questions   411

APPENDICES

A Understanding Your Basic Sourcebook: The Dictionary — 416
    The Dictionary as a Working Tool 416
        Information Contained in Dictionary Entry for "gentle" 416
    One Word, Many Meanings 419
    Shades of Meaning: Denotation/Connotation 424
    Words with Special Limitations 429

B Parts of Speech — 435
    Nouns 435
    Pronouns 436
    Adjectives 436
    Verbs 436
    Adverbs 437
    Prepositions 438
    Conjunctions 438
    Interjections 439
    Study the Context 439

C Distinguishing between Words That Are Often Confused — 442
    Words That Sound Alike: Group I 442
    Words That Sound Alike: Group II 448
    Words That Sound or Look Almost Alike 456
    Words that Sound or Look Almost Alike: *sit/set; rise/raise; lie/lay* 464
    Words that Sound or Look Almost Alike: *choose/chose; lose/loose;*
        lead/led; die/dye 469
    Words that Sound or Look Almost Alike: *use/used; suppose/supposed* 470

D Solving Spelling Problems — 473
    Learning to Spell Commonly Mispronounced Words 473
    Learning to Spell -ie or -ei Words 475
    Forming the Plurals of Nouns 477
    Should the Final Consonant be Doubled? 481
    Words Ending in y 484
    Is It One Word or Two? 486
    Spelling 200 Tough Words 490
        Word List 1: Silent Letters 490
        Word List 2: Double Letters 491
        Word List 3: *-able* or *-ible* 491
        Word List 4: *de-* or *di-* 491
        Word List 5: the *-er* Sound 492
        Word List 6: *-ance* or *-ence* 492
        Word List 7: Problems with *s, c, z, x,* and *k* 492
        Word List 8: Twenty-Five Demons 493

E Capitalization — 494
    Ten Basic Rules for Capitalization 494

F Irregular Verbs — 498
    Principal Parts of Irregular Verbs 498

Index — 503

The Writer's Workplace

Introduction

Discovering Ourselves as Writers: Journals and Freewriting

"I can shake off everything if I write; my sorrows disappear, my courage is reborn. But, and that is the great question, will I ever be able to write anything great, will I ever become a journalist or a writer? I hope so, oh, I hope so very much, for I can recapture everything when I write, my thoughts, my ideals and my fantasies."
(Anne Frank, April 4, 1944)

▶ Using the journal to capture our experience

For thousands of years, people have communicated with each other through writing. Each generation of writers rediscovers the power of the written word and discovers that written language has the power to change the way we look at the world. When we carefully study a poem, we realize the power of individual words; when we read an exciting novel, the world of our imagination is expanded; and when we read an important historical document, we see the connection between ideas of the past and our lives today, and we feel the excitement of our relationship with people who have gone before us.

We are surrounded by all kinds of machines, from telephones to television, that emphasize spoken words and pictures, but the power of the written word is still primary in our lives. On a personal level, we reach out to others when we write letters or even send cards to our friends; in school, we try to get the maximum power from our words when we take an examination or write a term paper or book report. Written words are our means of communication with others, our way of persuading others, and one of our most important methods of keeping in touch with ourselves and our feelings.

One of the best known ways of communicating with ourselves while at the same time exploring the power of words is the private diary or journal. For many centuries, people all over the world have kept journals as a way of expressing themselves and of keeping in touch with their inner selves. Private diaries were kept by Japanese women a thousand years ago. In Europe during the Middle Ages, journals were kept by witches who used them to preserve ancient formulas and other forbidden knowledge. Closer to our own time, early colonists of the United States used diaries to recall their thoughts and activities as settlers of a new and challenging land. Today, people in all walks of life keep journals for all kinds of reasons. Some people simply wish to maintain a record of what they do, others want to explore themselves through the privacy of a diary they can keep at their own pace, while still others may discover the rewards of maintaining a journal after they have had to keep one as part of a high school or college course. As Tristine Rainier notes in her book, *The New Diary*, keeping a journal is "the only form of writing that encourages total freedom of expression."

One of the most famous journal writers of our century was Anne Frank, who spent the last two years of her short life hiding from Nazi persecution in a tiny secret attic in Amsterdam, Holland. Throughout her many months of hiding, Anne Frank kept a journal. After she and most of her family died in concentration camps just before the end of the war, her journal was found and published. It has become one of the best known accounts of the triumph of the human spirit in the face of brutal persecution. It was in her journal on November 7, 1942, that Anne Frank wrote: "Who besides me will ever read these letters? From whom but myself shall I get comfort?" Her diary was a great consolation to her through all her long months and years of hiding, and as she finished that November 7 entry, Anne Frank noted: "That's why in the end I always come back to my diary. That is where I start and finish . . ." Because she was able to write while in hiding, Anne Frank had a sense of freedom she otherwise could not have enjoyed.

Although Anne Frank kept a private journal, she was always aware that she not only had to express herself but she also had to have an audience for her work. For this reason, not long after she began her diary she created an imaginary friend. "I want," she wrote on June 20, 1942, "this diary to be my friend, and I shall call my friend Kitty." Anne Frank had an audience, even if it existed only in her mind. When you write, you will also be directing your words to an audience and you must be aware of that audience. For whom are you writing? What should your audience know about your subject? How much does your audience already know? If you begin your work with this awareness of audience, your writing will have a clear focus, an obvious direction, and a strong sense of purpose. You will be on your way towards accomplishment and success as a writer.

The following selections from Anne Frank's diary point out some important aspects of writing. As you read each selection, notice how the writer is careful to use very specific details; specific details make up the heart of any good piece of writing and they make the writer's work interesting and memorable. As you write your own responses to the questions that follow the selections, use as many specific details as you can. The more specific you are, the stronger and more impressive your writing will be.

▶ Writing as memory

Writing does many things for us, and among its most important accomplishments is its ability to help us recall past events. Writing can help a nation recreate its history, and it can allow an individual to recreate important personal events. Anne Frank used her diary entry for November 11, 1943, to write the history of one of her "most priceless possessions," her fountain pen. She received the pen when she was nine years old. It was a present from her grandmother, and Anne's history of her ownership of the pen shows how much she treasured it.

> The glorious fountain pen had a red leather case and was at once shown around to all my friends. I, Anne Frank, the proud owner of a fountain pen! When I was ten I was allowed to take the pen to school and the mistress went so far as to permit me to write with it.
>
> When I was eleven, however, my treasure had to be put away again, because the mistress in the sixth form only allowed us to use school pens and inkpots.
>
> When I was twelve and went to the **Jewish Lyceum**, my fountain pen received a new case in honor of the great occasion; it could take a pencil as well, and as it closed with a zipper looked much more impressive.
>
> At thirteen the fountain pen came with us to the "Secret Annexe," where it has raced through countless diaries and compositions for me.
>
> Now I am fourteen, we have spent our last year together.
>
> It was on a Friday afternoon after five o'clock. I had come out of my room and wanted to go and sit at the table to write, when I was roughly pushed on one side and had to make room for Margot and Daddy, who wanted to practice their "Latin." The fountain pen remained on the table unused while, with a sigh, its owner contented herself with a tiny little corner of the table and started rubbing beans. "Bean rubbing" is making moldy beans decent again. I swept the floor at a quarter to six and threw the dirt, together with the bad beans, into a newspaper and into the stove. A terrific flame leaped out and I thought it was grand that the fire should burn up so well when it was practically out. All was quiet again, the "Latinites" had

A type of secondary school specializing in the classics, common in most continental countries.

finished, and I went and sat at the table to clear up my writing things, but look as I might, my fountain pen was nowhere to be seen. I looked again, Margot looked, but there was not a trace of the thing. "Perhaps it fell into the stove together with the beans," Margot suggested. "Oh, no, of course not!" I answered. When my fountain pen didn't turn up that evening, however, we all took it that it had been burned, all the more as celluloid is terribly inflammable.

And so it was, our unhappy fears were confirmed; when Daddy did the stove the following morning the clip used for fastening was found among the ashes. Not a trace of the gold nib was found.

Write the history of an object that has meant a great deal to you. It could be an article of clothing you received as a gift, or it could be a souvenir you brought back from a memorable visit. Notice that when Anne Frank takes us through the history of her fountain pen she reminds us how old she was at each point in her story ("When I was eleven . . .", "When I was twelve . . ."). As you write the history of your special object, be sure to keep your audience in mind by indicating how old you were when you obtained it, how you obtained it, and how you used it. Do you still have this possession, or was it lost or destroyed?

_____
_____
_____
_____
_____
_____
_____
_____
_____
_____
_____
_____
_____
_____
_____
_____
_____

▶ Writing as fantasy

Everyone enjoys fantasy, and Anne Frank was no exception. She wrote down several of her fantasies, making the activities that took place in her imagination more real for herself—and for us. Anne Frank wrote the following excerpt in 1943. Because she was interested in movies and movie stars, she dreamed of being free of her attic hiding place and finding herself in Hollywood where she was the guest of an imaginary young star, Priscilla Lane, and her family. In her fantasy, Anne finds herself standing outside the office of an important Hollywood producer.

I joined the line and in half an hour I was inside the office. But that didn't mean it was my turn; there were still many girls ahead of me. Again I waited, this time about two hours. A bell rang—this was for me!—and bravely I stepped into the inner office, where a middle-aged man was seated behind a desk. He greeted me in a standoffish manner. Asking my name and address, he seemed surprised that I was a guest of the Lanes. Finished with those questions, he took another good look at me and asked, "I suppose that you want to be a film star?"

"Yes, sir, if I have the talent."

He pushed a button, and in walked a smartly dressed girl, who asked me, with a gesture rather than in words, to follow her. She opened a door, and the sharp light in the room made me blink my eyes. A young man behind an intricate apparatus gave me a friendlier greeting than the one I'd had before and told me to sit on a high stool. He took several pictures, then rang for the girl, and I was led back to the older man. He promised to send me word whether or not I should return to the studio.

Encouraged, I found my way back to the Lane house. A week later I received a note from Mr. Harwick (Priscilla had told me his name). He wrote that the photos had come out very well, and asked me to come to his office at three o'clock the next afternoon.

Now, armed with an invitation, I was admitted at once. Mr. Harwick asked me if I would pose for a manufacturer of tennis rackets. The job was for just one week, but after I had been told what I would be paid, I gladly consented. Mr. Harwick called the tennis man, whom I met that same afternoon.

Next day I made my appearance at a photo studio, where I was to go every day for a week. I had to change clothes in minutes; I had to stand, sit, and smile continuously; walk up and down, change clothes again, look pretty, and put on fresh make-up. At night I was so exhausted that I had to drag myself to bed. On the third day it hurt me to smile, but I felt that I must keep faith with my manufacturer.

When I came home on the evening of the fourth day, I must have looked so ill that Mrs. Lane forbade me to return to the job. She herself called the man, and got him to excuse me.

I was deeply grateful. Undisturbed, I hugely enjoyed the rest of my unforgettable vacation. As for dreams of movie stardom, I was cured. I had had a close look at the way celebrities live.

Write one of your favorite fantasies. Notice that one of the reasons Anne Frank's fantasy seems so real is that she not only uses very specific details but also quotes imaginary conversations. As you write, remember that your audience has no way of seeing your fantasy except through the specific details you use. The more details you include in your writing, the more real and convincing your fantasy will be to your reader.

Writing as self-analysis

Anne Frank kept a diary for many reasons, but one of her purposes was to better understand herself and her situation. She also used her journal to analyze her progress as a writer. On April 4, 1944, she wrote this self-portrait of herself as a writer:

> I am the best and sharpest critic of my own work. I know myself what is and what is not well written. Anyone who doesn't write doesn't know how wonderful it is; I used to bemoan the fact that I couldn't draw at all, but now I am more than happy that I can at least write. And if I haven't any talent for writing books or newspaper articles, well, then I can always write for myself.
>
> I want to get on; I can't imagine that I would have to lead the same sort of life as Mummy and Mrs. Van Daan and all the women who do their work and are then forgotten. I must have something besides a husband and children, something that I can devote myself to!
>
> I want to go on living even after my death! And therefore I am grateful to God for giving me this gift, this possibility of developing myself and of writing, of expressing all that is in me.
>
> I can shake off everything if I write; my sorrows disappear, my courage is reborn. But, and that is the great question, will I ever be able to write anything great, will I ever become a journalist or a writer? I hope so, oh, I hope so very much, for I can recapture everything when I write, my thoughts, my ideals and my fantasies.

Write a self-portrait of yourself as a writer. What are your strengths as a writer? Where do you feel you have to do the greatest amount of work to improve your writing skills? As you write your self-portrait, you might want to include some mention of your past experiences in grammar and writing classes. How have those experiences shaped your abilities and your needs as a writer?

8 ◀ Introduction

(lined writing space)

▶ **Looking ahead: from freewriting to structure**

In this chapter, your responses to Anne Frank's journal have been in the form of *freewriting,* an approach many writers use when they begin their work. Some writers keep a journal as a record of their thinking or as a place to keep ideas and suggestions for future use. Perhaps your instructor will want you to keep a journal for your present course, or perhaps you will want to keep your own private diary to help you in your work throughout the semester.

When you keep a journal, you are making an informal record of your thoughts. Much of your other writing, however, will be more formal and structured. As you work in the different chapters of this book, you will be learning very specific writing skills. You will study the different parts of a sentence and how those parts work together; you will learn about the different kinds of paragraphs and how those paragraphs are structured; and you will become familiar with the construction of a full-length essay.

As you master these skills, and as you practice your writing on a regular basis, you will be well on your way toward success in your present English course and in all of your college work. The writer who understands and practices these basic structures is the writer who will be increasingly successful—in college and beyond.

PART I
Developing the Complete Sentence

1

Finding Subjects and Verbs in Simple Sentences

▶ **Why should we use complete sentences when we write?**

If you walk up to a friend at noon and say, "Lunch?" you are expressing an idea by using a shortened form of a complete thought: you are asking your friend to join you for lunch. Even though we do not always use complete sentences in daily conversation, we usually have complete thoughts in mind. We say and hear words and phrases such as "Lunch?" every day, and these words and phrases seem to be complete thoughts because both the speaker and the listener supply the missing words in their own minds. When your friend hears you say the word "Lunch?" he or she is able to quickly understand the meaning: "Would you like to join me for lunch?"

You are free to use language in this way in casual conversation but you must use a different approach in more formal speaking and writing situations. In writing down your thoughts, you cannot assume that another person will finish your thoughts for you. Each of your written thoughts must be a complete expression of what is in your mind.

The purpose of writing is to communicate something of value to a reader. Once you understand how the parts of a complete sentence work, you will be able to focus as much attention on *what* you are saying as you devote to *how* you are saying it. Once you understand how the parts of a complete sentence work, you can take control of the sentence. You will have the power to make words work for you.

▶ **What is a complete sentence?**

A *complete sentence* must contain a subject and a verb, as well as express a complete thought.

How do you find the subject of a sentence?

To find the *subject* of any sentence, ask yourself this question: who or what is the sentence about? When you have answered this question, you have found the subject of the sentence.

──────────────── Practice ────────────────

Examine each of the following sentences and ask yourself who or what each sentence is about. Draw a line under the subject in each sentence.

1. Niki Turner ran.
2. The young girl ran.
3. She ran.
4. The streetlights glowed.
5. They illuminated the village.
6. A thought suddenly struck her.
7. Her brother and his wife would be astonished.

After you have worked with these seven sentences, study the following explanations which will give you a more thorough understanding of subjects in sentences. As you study these explanations, pay special attention to the following terms: proper and common nouns, concrete and abstract nouns, adjective, pronoun, direct object, and compound subject.

1. *Niki Turner* ran.

    Who is this sentence about? The sentence is about "Niki Turner." Words such as *Niki, Alice Walker,* and *Illinois* are called proper nouns. *Proper nouns* name particular persons, places, or things. Notice that proper nouns are always capitalized.

2. The young *girl* ran.

    Who or what is the sentence about? The sentence is about a "girl." It is a *common noun*. Most nouns are common nouns. Common nouns are not capitalized.

    Words like *the* and *young* can be put in front of nouns to describe them further. These words are called *adjectives*. (The words *the* and *a* are also known as *articles*.)

3. *She* ran.

    Who or what is the sentence about? The sentence is about "she." Words such as *she, he, it, we, I, you,* and *they* are called *pronouns*. Pronouns can be used in the place of nouns.

4. The *streetlights* glowed.

    Who or what is the sentence about? The sentence is about "streetlights." Subjects are often things rather than people. These "things" can be proper nouns or common nouns.

5. *They* illuminated the village.

   Who or what is the sentence about? The sentence is about "they." The pronoun *they* refers to a noun already mentioned. In this case the noun already mentioned is the word *streetlights* in sentence 5.

   Nouns and pronouns can be subjects of sentences, but they can also have other functions in a sentence. Do not confuse the subject noun or pronoun with other nouns or pronouns in a sentence. Remember that subjects are usually found in the early part of the sentence, before the verb. In this case the word *village* is a noun, but it is not the subject of the sentence. The noun *village* has a different function in the sentence. (It is called the *direct object* of the verb.) A noun that is the direct object in a sentence cannot be the subject.

6. A *thought* suddenly struck her.

   Who or what is the sentence about? The sentence is about "thought." The noun *thought* is an abstract noun. It cannot be seen or touched. Abstract nouns can be concepts, ideas, or qualities. Nouns like *truth, justice,* and *health* are other examples of abstract nouns. The opposite of an abstract noun is a *concrete noun* like *girl, streetlights,* or *village*. These concrete nouns can be seen and touched.

7. Her *brother* and his *wife* would be astonished.

   Who or what is the sentence about? The subject of this sentence has two nouns: *brother* and *wife*. This is called a compound subject. A *compound subject* is made up of two or more nouns joined together by *and, or, either/or,* or *neither/nor*.

   Examples: Her brother or his wife will come.

   Either her brother or his wife will come.

Guide to Finding the Subject of a Sentence

Definition: The subject of a sentence is who or what the sentence is about.

How to find the subject: Ask yourself, "Who or what is this sentence about?"

▶ Subjects usually come early in the sentence.
▶ Subjects can be modified by adjectives.
▶ Subjects can be compound.

Look for these two kinds of words as your subjects:

1. **Nouns:** the names of persons, places, or things

Common	*or*	*Proper*	*Concrete*	*or*	*Abstract*
aunt		Aunt Mary	face		loneliness
country		Nigeria	people		patriotism
watch		Timex	jewelry		time

Finding Subjects and Verbs in Simple Sentences ▸ 15

2. **Pronouns:** take the place of nouns

Personal	Indefinite	Relative	Demonstrative
I, me	one	who	this
you	each	that	that
he, him, she, her, it	some, someone, somebody, something	what	these
we, us	any, anyone, anybody, anything		those
they, them	nobody, nothing		
	everyone, everybody, everything,		
	all		
	many		
	several		

Exercise 1

Finding the Subject of a Sentence

Underline the subject in each of the following sentences. An example is done for you.

The <u>loudspeaker</u> blared.

1. The train stopped.
2. Steven Laye had arrived!
3. He was afraid.
4. Everything looked so strange.
5. The fearful man held his bag tightly.
6. The tunnel led up to the street.
7. Buses and cars choked the avenues.
8. People rushed everywhere.
9. The noise made his head ache.
10. Loneliness filled his heart.

Exercise 2

Finding the Subject of a Sentence

Underline the subject in each of the following sentences.

1. The road twisted and turned.
2. A young boy hurried along briskly.
3. He carried an important message.
4. A red-winged blackbird flew overhead.
5. Dark clouds and a sudden wind encouraged him to hurry faster.
6. His family would be elated.
7. Someone was working in the yard.

16 ◀ Developing the Complete Sentence

   8. His father called out his name.
   9. The old man tore open the envelope.
   10. The message was brief.

Exercise 3   **Finding the Subject of a Sentence**

Underline the subject in each of the following sentences.

   1. The Chicago World's Fair opened.
   2. Americans had never seen anything like it.
   3. Architects had designed a gleaming white city.
   4. The buildings and grounds were covered with heroic statues.
   5. George Ferris designed an enormous wheel 264 feet high.
   6. It could carry sixty passengers per car.
   7. The inventor George Westinghouse designed the fair's electric motors and even electric lights.
   8. Other fair inventors included Thomas Edison and Alexander Graham Bell.
   9. They all helped to make an exciting atmosphere.
   10. This fair showed people the future.

▶ **How do you find the subject in sentences with prepositional phrases?**

The sentences in Exercises 1 and 2 were short and basic. If we wrote only such sentences, our writing would sound choppy. Complex ideas would be difficult to express. One way to expand the simple sentence is to add prepositional phrases.

   Example: He put his suitcase on the seat.
   On is a preposition.
   Seat is a noun used as the object of the preposition.
   On the seat is the prepositional phrase.

A *prepositional phrase* is a group of words containing a preposition and an object of the preposition with its modifiers. Prepositional phrases contain nouns, but these nouns are *never* the subject of the sentence.

In sentences with prepositional phrases, the subject may be difficult to spot. Consider the following sentence:

   In the young man's apartment, books covered the walls.

Who or what is the sentence about?
   To avoid making the mistake of thinking that a noun in the prepositional phrase could be the subject, it is a good practice to cross out the prepositional phrase. In the sentence above, what is the prepositional phrase?

   ~~In the young man's apartment~~, books covered the walls.

With the prepositional phrase crossed out, it now becomes clear that the subject of the sentence is the noun *books*.

Finding Subjects and Verbs in Simple Sentences ▶ 17

▸ When you are looking for the subject of a sentence, do not look for it within the prepositional phrase.

You can easily recognize a prepositional phrase because it always begins with a preposition. Study the following list so that you will be able to quickly recognize all of the common prepositions.

Common Prepositions

about	below	in	since
above	beneath	inside	through
across	beside	into	to
after	between	like	toward
against	beyond	near	under
along	by	of	until
among	down	off	up
around	during	on	upon
at	except	outside	with
before	for	over	within
behind	from	past	without

In addition to these common prepositions, English has a number of prepositional combinations that together with other words also function as prepositions.

Common Prepositional Combinations

ahead of	in addition to	in reference to
at the time of	in between	in regard to
because of	in care of	in search of
by means of	in case of	in spite of
except for	in common with	instead of
for fear of	in contrast to	on account of
for the purpose of	in the course of	similar to
for the sake of	in exchange for	

Exercise 1 — Creating Sentences with Prepositional Phrases

Use each of the ten prepositions that follow to write a prepositional phrase. Then write a sentence containing that prepositional phrase. Two examples are done for you.

▸ Notice that when a prepositional phrase begins a sentence, a comma usually follows that prepositional phrase. (Sometimes, if the prepositional phrase is short, the comma is omitted.)

Preposition: before

Prepositional Phrase: *before breakfast*

Sentence: *My cousin called before breakfast.*

Preposition: between

Prepositional Phrase: between the two barns

Sentence: Between the two barns, the old Buick lay rusting.

1. Preposition: in

    Prepositional Phrase: _____

    Sentence: _____
    _____

2. Preposition: with

    Prepositional Phrase: _____

    Sentence: _____
    _____

3. Preposition: of

    Prepositional Phrase: _____

    Sentence: _____
    _____

4. Preposition: from

    Prepositional Phrase: _____

    Sentence: _____
    _____

5. Preposition: during

    Prepositional Phrase: _____

    Sentence: _____
    _____

6. Preposition: by

    Prepositional Phrase: _____

    Sentence: _____
    _____

7. Preposition: for

   Prepositional Phrase: _____

   Sentence: _____

   _____

8. Preposition: through

   Prepositional Phrase: _____

   Sentence: _____

   _____

9. Preposition: on

   Prepositional Phrase: _____

   Sentence: _____

   _____

10. Preposition: beside

    Prepositional Phrase: _____

    Sentence: _____

    _____

Exercise 2

Finding Subjects in Sentences with Prepositional Phrases

Remember that you will never find the subject of a sentence within a prepositional phrase. In each of the following sentences, cross out any prepositional phrases. Then underline the subject of each sentence. An example is done for you.

~~On the circus grounds~~, <u>Lisa</u> wandered ~~among the elephants, horses, and camels~~.

1. Young people in the circus search for travel, adventure, danger, and romance.
2. However, after a few weeks of pulling cages and sleeping on hay, most of these people get tired of the circus and go back home.
3. The art of clowning, for instance, is very serious work.
4. Today, a circus clown must graduate from Clown College in Venice, Florida.
5. The staff of Clown College looks across the country for applicants.
6. Admission to the college is not easy.
7. Only sixty people out of three thousand applicants are admitted.
8. After ten weeks of training, graduation ceremonies are held.

Developing the Complete Sentence

9. At the ceremony, the clown graduate must perform for three continuous hours.
10. In the past, clowns were not so carefully trained.

Exercise 3 — **Finding Subjects in Sentences with Prepositional Phrases**

Each of the following sentences contains at least one prepositional phrase. Cross out any prepositional phrases. Then underline the subject in each sentence. An example is done for you.

~~In every family,~~ <u>children</u> look ~~for independence~~.

1. The disappearance of sons and daughters from the lives of their parents can be devastating.
2. In their late teens and early twenties, young people often move away from home.
3. For many of them, a city offers jobs and excitement.
4. With little money and almost no experience, these young people can encounter difficulties of all kinds.
5. The fun of being independent can quickly turn into a nightmare.
6. On the other hand, young adults living with their parents often feel cheated.
7. They have no life of their own.
8. These young adults are frequently treated like children.
9. During this time, parents can be too critical.
10. From the parents' point of view, one mistake made at this time can ruin their child's life.

▶ What are the other problems in finding subjects?

Sentences with a change in the normal subject position

Some sentences begin with words that indicate that a question is being asked. Such words as *why, where, how,* and *when* give the reader the signal that a question will follow. Such opening words are not the subject. The subject will be found later on in the sentence. The following sentences begin with question words:

Why is *he* going away?
How did *he* find his sister in the city?

Notice that in each sentence the subject is not found in the opening part of the sentence.

Using *there*

The word *there* can never be the subject of a sentence.

There is a new teacher in the department.

Who or what is this sentence about? This sentence is about a teacher. *Teacher* is the subject of the sentence.

Commands

Sometimes a sentence contains a verb that gives an order:

> Go to Chicago.
>
> Help your sister.

In these sentences, the subject *you* is not written, but it is understood. This is the only case where the subject of a sentence may be left out when you write a sentence.

Sentences that contain appositive phrases

An *appositive phrase* is a group of words in a sentence that gives us extra information about a noun in the sentence. For example:

> Martin Johnson, the retired salesman, sat at his desk.

In this sentence, the words *the retired salesman* make up the appositive phrase because they give you extra information about Martin Johnson. Notice that commas separate the appositive phrase from the rest of the sentence. If you leave out the appositive phrase when you read this sentence, the thought will still be complete:

> Martin Johnson sat at his desk.

Now the subject is clear: *Martin Johnson*.

▸ When you are looking for the subject of a sentence, you will not find it within an appositive phrase.

Exercise 1 — Finding Hidden Subjects

Each of the following sentences contains an example of a special problem in finding the subject of a sentence. First cross out any prepositional phrases or appositive phrases. Then underline the subject of each sentence. An example is done for you.

> ~~In every car of the crowded train~~, <u>passengers</u> settled down ~~for the night~~.

1. In the speeding train, the child fell asleep.
2. The motion of the railroad cars made her relax.
3. The child's mother, a tired and discouraged widow, put a coat under the child's head for a pillow.
4. Outside the window, towns and cities sped by in the night.
5. Sometimes you could look into people's living rooms.
6. There was a silence in the train.
7. Why do many people choose to travel at night?
8. In most cases, children will rest quietly at night.
9. A woman with young children and heavy bags to carry often has a difficult time.
10. On the platform, an elderly man anxiously waited for the first sight of his grandson.

Exercise 2 — Finding Hidden Subjects

Each of the following sentences contains an example of a special problem in finding the subject of a sentence. First, cross out any prepositional phrases or appositive phrases. Then underline the subject of each sentence. An example is done for you.

> <u>Disneyland</u>, ~~the dream of every child~~, is a favorite destination ~~for family vacations~~.

1. There is a fantasy playland in the state of Florida.
2. Look at a map to find this child's paradise.
3. Everyone wants to visit Orlando, the location of Disneyland.
4. Where else can you see toddlers and grownups shaking hands with Mickey Mouse and Minnie Mouse?
5. In Disneyland, you are surrounded by live cartoon favorites.
6. At breakfast, lunch, and dinner, you can be surrounded by Pluto Pup, Donald Duck, and Goofy Dog.
7. The cleanliness of the place also impresses most families.
8. During the day, there are scores of attractions and activities.
9. Would you like to enjoy the cooler and less crowded evening activities?
10. In Disneyland, it is hard to tell the children from the adults.

Exercise 3 — Finding Hidden Subjects

Each of the following sentences contains an example of a special problem in finding the subject of a sentence. First cross out any prepositional phrases or appositive phrases. Then underline the subject of each sentence. An example is done for you.

> What can <u>we</u> learn ~~from the study of an ancient civilization~~?

1. Look at a map of South America.
2. Where is the ancient city of Chan Chan?
3. Here on the coastal desert of northern Peru stand the remains of this city of the kings.
4. Chan Chan, once the fabulously wealthy center of the Chimor, is situated in one of the driest, bleakest regions in the world.
5. It was the largest pre-Columbian city in South America.
6. In the ruins of this city, scientists have found fragments to piece together the mystery of the past.
7. How could this civilization have survived this hostile environment and become so advanced?
8. There the people had engineered an astonishing irrigation system.
9. Unfortunately for the Chimor, Incas captured the city in the late fifteenth century and carried away much of its wealth.
10. Later, the Spanish armies brought disease and destruction to this desert people.

Finding Subjects and Verbs in Simple Sentences ▶ 23

▶ **How do you find the verb of a sentence?**

Every sentence must have a verb. The verb has two important jobs: to show what the subject is doing, and to tell the time of that action. If a word does not perform both of these jobs, it is not the verb of the sentence.

There are three kinds of verbs to recognize:

> action verbs
> linking verbs
> helping verbs

Action verbs

Action verbs tell us what the subject is doing:

> The woman (danced.)
> She (works) with a theatrical company.

In addition to telling us what the subject does, the action verb tells us *when* the subject does the action. For example, in the first sentence above, the verb *closed* is in the past tense, while in the second sentence, the verb *dreams* is in the present tense.

▶ A good test to make sure a word really is a verb is to try to put the word into different tenses:

> *Past:* Yesterday the woman danced.
> *Present:* Today the woman dances.
> *Future:* Tomorrow the woman will dance.

Exercise 1

Finding Action Verbs

Each of the following sentences contains an action verb. Find the action verb by first underlining the subject of the sentence. Then circle the verb (the word that tells what the subject is doing). Note also the time of the action: past, present, or future. An example is done for you.

Many <u>people</u> (begin) hobbies ~~in childhood~~.

1. Some people collect very strange objects.
2. One man saves the fortunes from fortune cookies.
3. A group in Michigan often meets to discuss their spark plug collection.
4. People in Texas gather many types of barbed wire.
5. One person in New York keeps handouts from the street.
6. Arthur Fiedler hung hundreds of fire hats on pegs all around his study.
7. Tom Bloom saves "inspected by" tickets from the pockets of new clothes.
8. Collectors take pride in the possession of unusual items.
9. A collection, like odd rocks or unique automobiles, gives a person some individuality.
10. Collections keep us happy from childhood to old age.

Exercise 2   **Finding Action Verbs**

Each of the following sentences contains an action verb. Find the action verb by first underlining the subject of the sentence. Then circle the verb (the word that tells what the subject is doing). Note also the time of the action: past, present, or future. An example is done for you.

<u>Attitudes</u> ~~toward medical practices~~ often (change.)

1. Traditional Chinese medicine harnesses ancient healing techniques in the practice of "qigong."
2. Masters of this Chinese practice claim the ability to cure many diseases.
3. The master projects a mysterious force into his students.
4. The student practices for many years.
5. The hands of the Chinese qigong practitioner pound at the air above a patient.
6. Many patients respond to this invisible force.
7. Some patients sway their bodies with the power of the force.
8. Chinese success surprises Western medical authorities.
9. Some doctors conduct research in China in hopes of finding the secrets of this ancient art.
10. Other Western doctors deny the validity of this approach.

Linking verbs

A *linking verb* is a verb that joins the subject of a sentence to one or more words that describe or identify the subject. For example:

The <u>child</u> (is) a constant dreamer.
<u>She</u> (seems) distracted.
<u>We</u> (feel) sympathetic.

In each of these examples, the verb links the subject to a word that identifies or describes the subject. In the first example, the verb *is* links *child* with *dreamer*. The verb *seems* links the pronoun *she* with *distracted*. Finally, in the third example, the verb *feel* links the pronoun *we* with *sympathetic*.

Common Linking Verbs

act	feel
appear	grow
be (am, is, are, was, were, have been)	look
	seem
become	taste

Exercise 1   **Finding Linking Verbs**

Each of the following sentences contains a linking verb. Find the linking verb by first underlining the subject of the sentence. Then draw an arrow to the word or words that identify or describe the subject. Finally, circle the linking verb. An example is done for you.

<u>Dreams</u> (are) very important for many cultures.

1. My dream last night was wonderful.
2. I had become middle-aged.
3. In a sunlit kitchen with a book in hand, I appeared relaxed and happy.
4. The house was empty and quiet.
5. In the morning light, the kitchen felt cozy.
6. The brewing coffee smelled delicious.
7. The bacon never tasted better.
8. I looked peaceful.
9. I seemed to have grown calmer.
10. I felt satisfied with life.

Exercise 2

Finding Linking Verbs

Each of the following sentences contains a linking verb. Find the linking verb by first underlining the subject of the sentence. Then draw an arrow to the word or words that identify or describe the subject. Finally, circle the linking verb. An example is done for you.

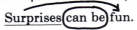

Surprises can be fun.

1. We were anxious to make the evening a success.
2. The apartment looked empty.
3. Everyone remained quiet.
4. Martha turned red at the sound of "Surprise!"
5. She seemed surprised.
6. The music sounded wonderful.
7. The food smelled delicious.
8. All of her presents were lovely.
9. The birthday party was a complete success.
10. Everyone appeared satisfied with the evening.

Helping verbs (also called auxiliary verbs)

Some verbs can be used to help the main verb express a special time or meaning.

Sentence using auxiliary verb	*Time expressed by auxiliary verb*
He **is** sleeping.	right now
He **might** sleep.	maybe now or in the future
He **should** sleep.	ought to, now or in the future
He **could have been** sleeping.	maybe in the past

Common Helping Verbs

can, could
may, might, must
shall, should
will, would
forms of the irregular verbs "be," "do," and "have."

REMEMBER that "be," "do," and "have" are also used as the main verbs of sentences. In such cases, "be" is a linking verb while "do" and "have" are action verbs. All the other helping verbs are usually used only as helping verbs.

WATCH OUT for **adverbs** that may come in between the helping verb and the main verb. *Adverbs* are words that can modify verbs, adjectives, or other adverbs. In the following sentence, the word "often" is an adverb coming between the verb phrase "can frighten."

Dreams (can) often (frighten) young children.

Exercise 1 — Finding Helping Verbs

Each of the following sentences contains a helping verb in addition to the main verb. In each sentence, first underline the subject. Then circle the entire verb phrase. An example is done for you.

~~In some writing classes~~, students (must keep) a diary of their work.

1. There could be several advantages in keeping a diary.
2. In a journal, a person can safely express true feelings without fear of criticism by family or friends.
3. Well-kept diaries have helped to give people insight into the motivations for their actions and have also been a help in dealing with change.
4. Diaries do improve a person's powers of observation: to look inwardly at one's own feelings as well as to look outwardly at actual happenings.
5. You will be able to capture your memories before they fade.
6. Important, too, would be the development of a writing style and the improvement of language skills.
7. A journal might awaken your imagination.
8. It may unexpectedly bring pleasure and satisfaction.
9. Keener observations will add to the joys of life.
10. You should seriously consider the purchase of one of those lovely fabric-bound notebooks.

Exercise 2 — Finding Helping Verbs

Each of the following sentences contains a helping verb. In each sentence, first underline the subject. Then circle the entire verb phrase. An example is done for you.

~~In this country~~, daycare (has become) an important issue.

1. How do you start a child care center?
2. First, notices can be put in local churches and supermarkets.
3. Then, you should also use word-of-mouth among your friends.
4. Many parents will need infant care during the day, after-school care, or evening and week-end care.
5. With luck, a nearby doctor may be willing to help with the local health laws and legal requirements.

6. Of course, the licensing laws in your state must be thoroughly researched.
7. Unfortunately, you could have trouble finding a low rent place for your center.
8. Any child center will depend on its ever widening good reputation.
9. In good daycare centers, parents are never excluded from meetings or planning sessions.
10. Finally, the center must be more interested in the character of its teachers than in the teachers' degrees.

▶ Chapter review exercises

Exercise 1 — Finding Subjects and Verbs in Simple Sentences

In each of the following sentences, cross out any prepositional phrases or appositive phrases. Then underline the subject and circle the complete verb. An example is done for you.

The main street ~~of Corning, New York,~~ (has been) beautifully (renovated.)

1. Older people today may recall the main street of their home town as a wonderful place forty or fifty years ago.
2. Why can't we have these old main streets back again?
3. In 1970, the National Trust for Historical Preservation began a program to bring new life to the nation's downtown areas.
4. Cities and villages needed new attitudes toward downtown areas.
5. Some local planners began a program to revitalize main streets.
6. One of the most important challenges was to convince businessmen to repair old buildings.
7. Towns quickly saw the value of making changes.
8. Citizens understood the advantages of a comfortable downtown.
9. Now many towns gladly sponsor special events and parades.
10. Will the tradition of personal service return to the American main street?

Exercise 2 — Finding Subjects and Verbs in Simple Sentences

In each of the following sentences, cross out any prepositional phrases or appositive phrases. Then underline the subject and circle the complete verb. An example is done for you.

~~In the field of writing,~~ practice is important ~~for growth~~.

1. There are several kinds of journals.
2. Which is the right one for you?
3. Your personality and interests will determine your choice.
4. Some people do not write an entry in their journal every day.

5. A growing number of people are keeping dream journals.
6. In these journals, the writer makes his or her entry first thing in the morning.
7. Otherwise, the dream might be forgotten.
8. Busy people often need to keep an activity-oriented diary.
9. Another kind of journal, the writer's journal, could benefit every college student.
10. In such a notebook, one would save for future use any interesting phrases, overheard conversations, or quotes from books and magazines.

Exercise 3

Finding Subjects and Verbs in Simple Sentences

In each of the sentences in the following paragraph, cross out any prepositional or appositive phrases. Then underline the subject and circle the complete verb.

Go West! Western Australia, one of the remaining great boom areas of the world, comprises one-third of the Australian continent. Why did people by the tens of thousands go to western Australia in the late 1800s? In 1894, Leslie Robert Menzies jumped off his camel and landed in a pile of gold nuggets. In less than two hours, this man gathered over a million dollars in gold. He eventually took six tons of gold to the bank by wheelbarrow! Kalgoorlie and Boulder, the two boom towns that grew up there, boast of the richest golden mile in the world. With all the gold seekers, this surface gold did not last very long. Now the only bands of rich ore lie more than 4,000 feet down under the ground. There are many ghost towns with their empty iron houses and run-down chicken coops.

2

Correcting the Fragment in Simple Sentences

▶ **Recognizing sentence fragments**

Once you have learned that a sentence must have a subject and a verb, and that a sentence must also express a complete thought, you are on your way to correcting one of the most frequent errors in student writing—the fragment. Although many of our daily conversations are informal and sometimes contain fragments, standard writing is always more formal and requires complete sentences.

The fragment is a major problem for many student writers. In the writer's mind, a thought may be clear; however, on paper the idea may turn out to be incomplete, missing a subject or a verb. In this section, you will improve your ability to spot incomplete sentences or fragments, and you will learn how to correct them. This practice will prepare you to avoid such fragments in your own writing. Here, for example, is a typical conversation between two people at lunchtime. It is composed entirely of fragments, but the two people speaking have no trouble understanding each other.

Ron: Had any lunch?
Jan: A sandwich.
Ron: What kind?
Jan: Ham and Swiss on rye.

If we use complete sentences to rewrite this brief conversation, the result might be the following:

Ron: Did you have any lunch yet?
Jan: Yes, I had a sandwich.
Ron: What kind of sandwich did you have?
Jan: I had a ham and Swiss sandwich on rye bread.

In the first conversation, misunderstanding is unlikely since the two speakers stand face to face, see each other's gestures, and hear the intonations of each other's voice in order to help figure out the meaning. These short phrases may be enough for communication since the speakers are using more than just words to convey their thoughts. They understand each other because each one can complete the thoughts that are in the other one's mind.

In writing, however, readers cannot be present at the scene to observe the situation for themselves. They cannot be expected to read the author's mind. Only the words grouped into sentences and the sentences grouped into paragraphs provide the clues to the meaning. Since writing often involves thoughts that are abstract and even complex, fragments cause great difficulty and sometimes total confusion for the reader.

▶ **Practice putting a conversation into complete sentences**

The following conversation is one that a couple of students might have at the start of their English class. Rewrite the conversation in complete thoughts or standard sentences. Remember the definition of a sentence.

▶ A complete sentence has a subject and a verb and expresses a complete thought.

John: Early again.
Elaine: Want to get a front row seat.
John: Your homework done?
Elaine: Nearly.
John: Think he'll give a quiz today?
Elaine: Hope not.
John: Looks like rain today.
Elaine: Better not; haven't got a bag for these new books.
John: Going to the game Saturday?
Elaine: Probably.

1. _____
2. _____
3. _____
4. _____
5. _____
6. _____
7. _____
8. _____
9. _____
10. _____

Remember, when you write in complete sentences, this writing may be somewhat different from the way you would express the same idea in everyday conversation with a friend.

Although you will occasionally spot incomplete sentences in professional writing, you may be sure the writer is using these fragments intentionally. In such cases, the fragment may capture the way a person thinks or speaks, or it may create a special effect. A student developing his or her writing skills should be sure to use only standard sentence form so that thoughts will be communicated effectively. Nearly all the writing you will do in your life—letters to friends, business correspondence, papers in school, or reports in your job—will demand standard sentence form. Fragments will be looked upon as a sign of ignorance rather than creative style!

▶ What is a fragment?

A *fragment* is a piece of a sentence.

A fragment is not a sentence for one of the following reasons:
a. The subject is missing.

>   delivered the plans to my office

b. The verb is missing.

>   the architect to my office

c. Both the subject and verb are missing.

>   to my office

d. The subject and verb are present but words do not express a complete thought.

>   the architect delivered

Exercise 1   Understanding Fragments

Each of the following groups of words is a fragment. In the blank to the right of each fragment, identify what part of the sentence could be added to make the fragment into a sentence.

a. Add a subject.
b. Add a verb.
c. Add a subject and a verb.
d. The subject and verb are already present, but needs to express a complete thought.

An example is done for you.

Fragment	**Add**
the red fox	b. verb
1. returned to the river	_____
2. a bird on the oak branch	_____

32 ◀ Developing the Complete Sentence

3. between the island and the mainland _____

4. the hawk in a soaring motion _____

5. the fishing boats on the lake _____

6. dropped like a stone into the water _____

7. the silence of the forest _____

8. carried the fish to the tree _____

9. the fisherman put _____

10. into the net _____

▶ How do you correct a fragment?

One way to correct a fragment is to add the missing part or parts.

Fragment: across the lake
Add: subject and verb
Sentence: I swam across the lake.

Exercise 2   **Making Fragments into Sentences**

Change the fragments of Exercise 1 into complete sentences by adding the missing part or parts that you have already identified.

1. returned to the river

_____.

2. a bird on the oak branch

_____.

3. between the island and the mainland

_____.

4. the hawk in a soaring motion

_____.

5. the fishing boats on the lake

_____.

6. dropped like a stone into the water

_____.

7. the silence of the forest

_____.

8. carried the fish to the tree

   _____.

9. the fisherman put

   _____.

10. into the net

    _____.

The second way to correct a fragment is to add the fragment to the sentence that preceded it or to the sentence that follows it. In other words, the fragment belongs with another sentence.

Exercise 3   **Finding Fragments That Belong to Other Sentences**

Each of the following passages contains a fragment or two. First, read each passage. Then locate the fragment in each passage. Circle the fragment and draw an arrow to the sentence to which it should be connected. An example is done for you.

Adelle assisted the dancers. She stood backstage. (Between numbers.) She helped the ballerinas change costumes.

Passage 1   Fishing is one of the oldest sports in the world. And can be one of the most relaxing. A person with a simple wooden pole and line can have as much fun as a sportsman. With expensive equipment. For busy executives, overworked teachers, and even presidents of nations. Fishing can be a good way to escape from the stress of demanding jobs.

Passage 2   The first electric car was built in 1887. Six years later, it was sold commercially. At the turn of the century, people had great faith in new technology. In fact, three hundred electric taxicabs were operating in New York City by 1900. However, electric cars soon lost their popularity. The new gasoline engine became more widely used. With our concern over pollution. Perhaps electric cars will become desirable once again.

Passage 3   Eskimos obtain most of their food from the sea. They eat seals and walruses. Whales, fish and sea birds in abundance. Eskimos boil some of their food. They eat other foods uncooked because of the scarcity of fuel. Eskimos get important vitamins and minerals. By eating every part of the animal they kill. The heart, the liver, and even the digestive tracts of the animals have great food value for the Eskimos.

▶ **Don't confuse phrases with sentences**

Fragments are usually made up of phrases. These phrases are often mistaken for sentences because they are words that go together as a group. However, they do not fit the definition of a sentence.

What Is a Phrase?

A *phrase* is a group of words that go together but that lack one or more of the elements necessary to be classified as a sentence.

▶ How many kinds of phrases are there?

In English there are six phrases you should learn to recognize. Some of them you have already studied in previous chapters.

1. **Noun phrase:** a noun plus its modifiers

    large square bricks

2. **Prepositional phrase:** a preposition plus its object and modifiers

    around our neighborhood

3. **Verb phrase:** the main verb plus its helping verbs

    is walking

    could have walked

    should have been walking

The three remaining phrases are formed from **verbs**. However, these phrases do not function as verbs in the sentence. Study carefully how to use them.

4. **Participial phrase:**

    How is the participial phrase formed?

    a. the present form of a verb ending in -ing and any other words necessary to complete the phrase

        running home

        looking very unhappy

    b. the past form of a verb usually ending in -ed and any other words necessary to complete the phrase

        greatly disappointed

        told tearfully

    How does the participial phrase function?

    Participial phrases function as **adjectives** in a sentence. Study how the above phrases could be made into complete sentences. These phrases will function as adjectives to the noun or pronoun that follows.

    Running home, the worker lost her wallet.

    Looking very unhappy, she retraced her steps.

    Greatly disappointed, she could not find it.

    Told tearfully, her story saddened her friends.

Correcting the Fragment in Simple Sentences ▶ 35

▸ Students often make the mistake of confusing a participle with a verb. When a participle is used as a verb, there *must* be a helping verb with it.

Incorrect: I running in the marathon
Correct: I *am* running in the marathon.

5. **Gerund phrase:** the present form of a verb ending in *-ing*, and any other words necessary to complete the phrase

    The gerund phrase functions as a noun.

    a. subject of the sentence:

    Running in a marathon is strenuous exercise.

    b. direct object of the sentence:

    I like *running in a marathon.*

6. **Infinitive phrase:** *to* plus the verb and any other words necessary to complete the phrase

    to pay the rent

    to walk downtown

    to have a good job

Exercise 1   Identifying Phrases

Identify each of the underlined phrases in the following sentences.

1. <u>Visiting New York</u> can be a nightmare or a thrill. _____

2. Many people love <u>to see the Broadway shows.</u> _____

3. Museums, restaurants, shopping, and the varied night life offer endless possibilities <u>for the tourist.</u> _____

4. <u>Riding the subways</u>, tourists see another side of New York. _____

5. <u>My brother Don</u> was pickpocketed on a hot and crowded, dirty subway last summer. _____

6. <u>Coming from the country</u>, he thought the prices were outrageous and the noise and traffic unbearable. _____

7. Finding a parking spot <u>may have been</u> his most frustrating experience. _____

8. <u>In addition to these problems</u>, the question of physical safety concerns most tourists. _____

9. The city <u>has begun</u> projects to clean up the Times Square area. _____

10. New York's continual fascination is the rich mix <u>of cultures and life-styles</u> from all over the world. _____

36 ◂ Developing the Complete Sentence

Exercise 2

Identifying Phrases

The following six sentences come from a paragraph by John Steinbeck. Identify each of the underlined phrases.

1. <u>At dawn</u> Cannery Row seems <u>to hang suspended</u> out of time <u>in a silvery light</u>.
2. The splashing <u>of the waves</u> <u>can be heard</u>.
3. <u>Flapping their wings</u>, the seagulls come <u>to sit</u> on the roof peaks shoulder to shoulder.
4. Cats drip <u>over the fences</u> and slither like syrup over the ground to look for fishheads.
5. <u>Silent early morning dogs</u> parade majestically.
6. No automobiles <u>are running</u> then.

1. _____
2. _____
3. _____
4. _____
5. _____
6. _____
7. _____
8. _____
9. _____
10. _____

Exercise 3

Identifying Phrases

Identify each of the underlined phrases.

1. <u>Walking near the farm</u>, I could see the growing coffee plants. _____
2. It is a very difficult job <u>to supervise a farm</u>. _____
3. <u>Growing any kind of crop</u> is a time-consuming procedure. _____
4. <u>Helped constantly</u>, crops will tend to do well. _____
5. <u>Appearing very tiny</u>, the coffee plants needed more moisture. _____
6. The plants <u>should have been watered</u> last week. _____
7. I walked through different parts <u>of the plantation</u> to see what other problems I could identify. _____
8. <u>Around the edge of the farm</u> I could see evidence of insect damage to the plants. _____
9. <u>Looking very brown</u>, the leaves showed signs of invasion by different insects.

10. Organized properly, this farm could be a source of both profit and pride. _____

▶ Understanding the uses of the present participle

The present participle causes a good deal of confusion for students working with the fragment. Because the participle can be used sometimes as a verb, sometimes as an adjective, and sometimes as a noun, you will want to be aware of which of these uses you intend.

Exercise 1   **Using the Participle in a Verb Phrase**

Below are five present participles. Use each of them as part of a verb phrase in a sentence. An example has been done for you.

Present participle: sitting
Verb phrase: is sitting
Sentence: The couple is sitting on the balcony.

1. building _____
2. crying _____
3. traveling _____
4. writing _____
5. lacking _____

Exercise 2   **Using the Participial Phrase as an Adjective**

Each of the underlined words below is a present participle. Use the word along with the phrase provided to compose sentences in which the phrase functions as an adjective. An example has been done for you.

Present participle: sitting
Participial phrase: sitting on the balcony
Participial phrase used as an adjective phrase in the sentence: Sitting on the balcony, the couple enjoyed the moonlight.

1. Building a house

_____

_____

2. Crying over the broken vase

_____

_____

38 ◂ **Developing the Complete Sentence**

3. Traveling in Mexico

   _____
   _____

4. Hastily writing the letter

   _____
   _____

5. Lacking the courage to tell the truth

   _____
   _____

Exercise 3   **Using the Participial Phrase as a Noun (Gerund)**

Each of the underlined words below is a present participle. Use the word along with the phrase provided as a noun phrase in a sentence. An example has been done for you.

            Present participle: sitting
            Participial phrase: sitting on the balcony
Participial phrase used as a
   noun phrase in a sentence: Sitting on the balcony is relaxing.

1. Building a house

   _____
   _____

2. Crying over the broken vase

   _____
   _____

3. Traveling in Mexico

   _____
   _____

4. Hastily writing the letter

   _____
   _____

5. Lacking the courage to tell the truth

   _____

▶ How do you make a complete sentence from a fragment that contains a participle?

Fragment: he talking in his sleep

1. Add a helping verb to the participle:

    He is talking in his sleep.

2. Change the participle to a different form of the verb:

    He talks in his sleep.

3. Use the participle as an adjective, being sure to provide a subject and verb for the sentence:

    Talking in his sleep, he muttered something about his boss.

4. Use the participle as a noun:

    Talking in his sleep revealed his innermost thoughts.

Exercise 1 Correcting the Fragment That Contains a Participle

Make four complete sentences from each of the following fragments. Use the following example as your model.

Fragment: using the back stairway

    a. He is using the back stairway.
    b. He uses the back stairway.
    c. Using the back stairway, he got away without being seen.
    d. Using the back stairway is not a good idea.

1. moving out of the house

    a. _____
    b. _____
    c. _____
    d. _____

2. talking on the telephone

    a. _____
    b. _____
    c. _____
    d. _____

3. driving the car down Highway 60

   a. _____
   b. _____
   c. _____
   d. _____

Exercise 2

Correcting the Fragment That Contains a Participle

The following passage is made up of fragments containing participles. Rewrite the passage using complete sentences. Use any of the correction methods discussed above.

I walking through the deserted rooming house. Poking around in piles of junk. The brick walls crumbling. Two children playing in the dismal hallways. Waiting for someone to restore the house to its former glory.

_____
_____
_____
_____
_____

Exercise 3

Correcting the Fragment That Contains a Participle

The following passage contains four fragments containing participles. Circle the fragments and correct them in one of the four ways discussed.

At last taking the driving test. I felt very nervous. My mother was sitting in the back seat. All my papers sitting on the front seat. The inspector got into the car and sat on my insurance form. He looked rather sour and barely spoke to me. Trying not to hit the curb. I parallel parked surprisingly well. I managed to get through all the maneuvers. Now tensely waiting for the results.

_____
_____
_____
_____
_____
_____

Correcting the Fragment in Simple Sentences ▸ 41

Exercise 1

Correcting Fragments

Rewrite each fragment so that it is a complete sentence.

1. early morning a time of peace in my neighborhood

2. the gray mist covering up all but the faint outlines of nearby houses

3. the shapes of cars in the streets and driveways

4. to sit and look out the window

5. holding a steaming cup of coffee

6. the only sound the rumbling of a truck

7. passing on the highway a quarter-mile away

8. children all in their beds

9. no barks of dogs

10. in this soft, silent dreamworld

Exercise 2

Correcting Fragments

Each of the following groups of words is a phrase. First, name each phrase. Second, make each phrase into a complete sentence.

1. hanging in clusters over the doorways

    Name of phrase: _____

    Sentence: _____

2. from other parts of the city

   Name of phrase: _____

   Sentence: _____

   _____

3. to earn a living

   Name of phrase: _____

   Sentence: _____

   _____

4. for children of my age and younger

   Name of phrase: _____

   Sentence: _____

   _____

5. making candy of various kinds

   Name of phrase: _____

   Sentence: _____

   _____

6. to sit outside

   Name of phrase: _____

   Sentence: _____

   _____

7. at the bottom of the hill

   Name of phrase: _____

   Sentence: _____

   _____

8. shaping the dough into donkeys and clowns

   Name of phrase: _____

   Sentence: _____

   _____

Correcting the Fragment in Simple Sentences ▶ 43

9. into the oven on a wooden spatula with a long handle for a quick baking

   Name of phrase: _____

   Sentence: _____

   _____

10. walking up and down the block

    Name of phrase: _____

    Sentence: _____

    _____

Exercise 3 **Correcting Fragments**

Each of the following groups of words is a phrase. First, name each phrase. Second, make each phrase into a complete sentence.

1. for people of this generation

   Name of phrase: _____

   Sentence: _____

   _____

2. to watch

   Name of phrase: _____

   Sentence: _____

   _____

3. in the ring

   Name of phrase: _____

   Sentence: _____

   _____

4. hitting each other

   Name of phrase: _____

   Sentence: _____

   _____

5. at each sound of the bell

   Name of phrase: _____

Sentence: _____

_____

6. supported by the ropes

   Name of phrase: _____

   Sentence: _____

   _____

7. to conduct the fight

   Name of phrase: _____

   Sentence: _____

   _____

8. the screaming fans

   Name of phrase: _____

   Sentence: _____

   _____

9. by the second round

   Name of phrase: _____

   Sentence: _____

   _____

10. knocked unconscious

    Name of phrase: _____

    Sentence: _____

    _____

▶ Chapter review exercises

Exercise 1   Recognizing and Correcting the Fragment

Each of the following passages contains a fragment. Underline the fragment, and on the lines beneath each passage, rewrite the passage so that it is composed of complete sentences.

Correcting the Fragment in Simple Sentences ▶ 45

1. The moon rose high in the sky. All of us worked quickly to pitch the tent. Then making a fire.

   Revised passage: _____

   _____

   _____

2. Raising the drinking age to twenty-one saves the lives of all drivers. The drinkers and the nondrinkers. Every state should raise the drinking age to twenty-one.

   Revised passage: _____

   _____

   _____

   _____

3. Companies do a lot of research before they name a new product. Based on the results of a market research team. The company makes its final selection.

   Revised passage: _____

   _____

   _____

4. The day of my eighteenth birthday, reservations made at a fine restaurant. My father came home early from work.

   Revised passage: _____

   _____

   _____

5. Francie loved to see her mother grind the coffee. Her mother would sit in the kitchen with the coffee mill clutched between her knees. Grinding away with a furious turn of her left wrist. The room filled up with the rich odor of freshly ground coffee.

   Revised passage: _____

   _____

   _____

   _____

Exercise 2 — Recognizing and Correcting the Fragment

The following paragraph contains fragments. Read the paragraph and circle each fragment. Then rewrite the paragraph being sure to use only complete sentences.

We called it our house. It was only one room. With about as much space as a tent. Painted in a pastel color with a red tiled roof. The front window reaching nearly from the sidewalk to the roof. We could look up and down the street. Sitting indoors on the window seat. Our kitchen was a small narrow area. With the brick stove and two benches to serve as shelves. Three steel bars and a short piece of lead pipe from a scrap heap to make a grate.

Exercise 3 — Recognizing and Correcting the Fragment

The following paragraph is written incorrectly with fragments. Read the paragraph and circle each fragment. Then rewrite the paragraph being careful to use only complete sentences.

That afternoon the street was full of children. Taking a shower in the rain. Soaping themselves and rushing out into the storm. To wash off the suds. In a few minutes, it was all over. Including the rubdown. The younger children took their showers naked. Teetering on the tips of their toes and squealing to one another. The stately coconut palm in one corner of the patio. Thrashed its branches high over the dripping children bouncing on the cobblestones.

Correcting the Fragment in Simple Sentences

3

Combining Sentences Using Coordination

So far you have worked only with the simple sentence. If you go back and read a group of these sentences, such as on page 15, you will see that writing only simple sentences would result in a choppy style. Also, you would have trouble trying to express more complicated ideas.

You will therefore want to learn how to combine sentences. You can do this by using particular marks of punctuation and special connecting words called conjunctions. The two major ways of joining sentences together are called coordination and subordination.

▶ What is coordination?

You can use **coordination** whenever you have two sentences that are related and that contain ideas of equal importance. There are three ways to combine such sentences. All three ways result in a new kind of sentence called a **compound sentence**. Before you study these three methods, however, it is important to understand the term independent clause. The *independent clause* is a group of words that could be a simple sentence. In a compound sentence we could say we are combining simple sentences, or we could say we are combining independent clauses. Don't let the term confuse you. *Independent* means that the words could stand alone as a sentence, and *clause* means that there is a subject and a verb. *IC* will mean "independent clause" in the work that follows.

▶ Use a comma plus a coordinating conjunction

The first way to combine independent clauses is to use a comma plus a coordinating conjunction.

IC	, and	IC
He spoke forcefully	, and	I felt compelled to listen.

Combining Sentences Using Coordination ▸ 49

Connectors: Coordinating Conjunctions

and	***Used in Pairs***
but	either . . . or
or, nor	neither . . . nor
for (meaning "because")	not only . . . but also
yet	
so	

Practice

In each of the following compound sentences, draw a single line under the subject and draw two lines under the verb for each independent clause. Then circle both the coordinating conjunction and the comma. The following example has been done for you.

The <u>speaker</u> <u><u>rose</u></u> to his feet, (and) the <u>room</u> <u><u>became</u></u> quiet.

1. The audience was packed, for this was a man with an international reputation.
2. He could have told about all his successes, but instead he spoke about his disappointments.
3. His words were electric, so the crowd was attentive.
4. I should have brought a tape recorder, or at least I should have taken notes.

Did you find a subject and verb for both independent clauses in each sentence?
    Now that you understand the structure of a compound sentence, you need to think about the meanings of the different coordinating conjunctions and how they can be used to show the relationship between two ideas, each idea being given equal importance.

Meaning of Coordinating Conjunctions

to add an idea:	and
to add an idea when the first clause is in the negative:	nor
to contrast two opposing ideas:	but, yet
to introduce a reason:	for
to show a choice:	or
to introduce a result:	so

Exercise 1   Combining Sentences Using Coordinating Conjunctions

Each of the following examples contains two simple sentences that could be related with a coordinating conjunction. Decide what relationship the second sentence has to the first, and then select the conjunction that will make sense. An example is done for you.

   She broke her arm.
   She couldn't play in the finals.

50 ◀ Developing the Complete Sentence

Relationship of 2nd sentence to 1st: <u>result</u>
Conjunction that introduces this meaning: <u>so</u>
New compound sentence:

She broke her arm, **so** she couldn't play in the finals.

1. Mr. Watson is kind and patient.
   His brother is sharp and nagging.
   Relationship of 2nd sentence to 1st: <u>CONTRAST</u>
   Conjunction that introduces this meaning: <u>Mr. Watson is kind and patient, but his brother is sharp and nagging.</u>

2. The two men are having great difficulty.
   They are trying to raise a teenager.
   Relationship of 2nd sentence to 1st: <u>The two men</u>
   Conjunction that introduces this meaning: <u>the two men are ~~trying~~ having great difficulty, for they are trying to raise a teenager</u>

3. Young Michael has no family of his own.
   He feels angry and alone.
   Relationship of 2nd sentence to 1st: _____
   Conjunction that introduces this meaning: <u>Young Michael has no family of his own, so he feels angry and alone</u>

4. Michael hasn't been doing well in school.
   He isn't involved in any activities outside school.
   Relationship of 2nd sentence to 1st: _____
   Conjunction that introduces this meaning: <u>Michael hasn't been ~~doing~~ well in school, and he isn't involved in any activities outside school</u>

Combining Sentences Using Coordination ▶ 51

5. Mr. Watson encouraged Michael to do volunteer work at the hospital.
   This might show Michael the satisfaction of helping other people.

   Relationship of 2nd sentence to 1st: _____

   Conjunction that introduces this meaning: Mr. Watson encouraged Michael to do volunteer work at the hospital, for this might show Michael the satisfaction of helping...

6. Mr. Watson's brother wanted Michael to spend more time on his homework.
   He also wanted him to get a job that would bring in some money to help with expenses.

   Relationship of 2nd sentence to 1st: _____

   Conjunction that introduces this meaning: _____

   _____
   _____
   _____

7. Michael liked going to the hospital.
   He was doing something important.

   Relationship of 2nd sentence to 1st: _____

   Conjunction that introduces this meaning: _____

   _____
   _____
   _____

8. He didn't earn any money.
   He liked helping people.

   Relationship of 2nd sentence to 1st: _____

   Conjunction that introduces this meaning: _____

   _____
   _____
   _____

9. Michael now wants to have a career working in a hospital.
   He will have a reason to work harder in school.

   Relationship of 2nd sentence to 1st: _____

Conjunction that introduces this meaning: _____

_____

_____

_____

10. Mr. Watson thinks the hospital work was a good idea.
    His brother has to agree.

    Relationship of 2nd sentence to 1st: _____

    Conjunction that introduces this meaning: _____

    _____

    _____

    _____

Exercise 2 **Combining Sentences Using Coordinating Conjunctions**

For each example, add a second independent clause using the given coordinating conjunction. Be certain that your new sentence makes sense.

1. Jessica Tandy is my favorite female actress, and _____

   _____

2. I loved the movie *Driving Miss Daisy*, but _____

   _____

3. Either I go to a movie on Friday night, or _____

   _____

4. I wish I could have dinner first in a fine restaurant, but _____

   _____

5. The weather this Friday night is supposed to be cold and wet, so _____

   _____

6. My friend Craig cannot go with me, for _____

   _____

7. I can't borrow my father's car, nor _____

   _____

8. Not only are the beverages there too expensive, _____

   _____

9. It would be nice to own a video machine, for _____

10. Watching videos at home is cheap, yet _____

Exercise 3 — Combining Sentences Using Coordinating Conjunctions

Now you are ready to work with coordinating conjunctions in a more difficult context. Each of the following examples is a compound sentence with the comma and the coordinating conjunction missing. Study the relationship between the two independent clauses to determine which conjunction will best show the relationship between the two sentences. Don't forget to add the comma.

1. Some farmers in the United States are prosperous **, but** others are going bankrupt.
2. Hundreds are losing their farms **, so** certain banks are refusing to make any further loans.
3. Some of the government farm programs have not been successful **, nor** has the public been able to do anything to help.
4. These farmers feel neglected **, so** they are protesting to the government.
5. Some people think the farmers are themselves to blame **, for** they went too heavily into debt in recent years.
6. The world has an increased need for farm products **, but** the government pays farmers not to grow food.
7. The government has cooperated with farmers for years **, but** the farmers are in more difficulty than ever before.
8. Angry farmers watch their land and machinery being sold at auction **, and** they can do nothing about it.
9. All of us need farm products **, so** we should be concerned about these problems.
10. In the future, fewer people will become farmers **, so** the problem is likely to become increasingly serious.

▶ Use a semicolon, an adverbial conjunction, and a comma

A second way to combine independent clauses is to form the compound sentence by using a semicolon, an adverbial conjunction, and a comma.

IC	; therefore,	IC
I had worked hard	; therefore,	I expected results.

54 ◂ Developing the Complete Sentence

Another set of conjunctions that have meanings similar to the common coordinating conjunctions are called **adverbial conjunctions** (or conjunctive adverbs). These connecting words will give the compound sentence you write more emphasis. They may also sound slightly more formal to you than the shorter conjunctions *and* and *but*. The punctuation for these connectors is somewhat more complex.

Connectors: Frequently Used Adverbial Conjunctions

Addition (and)	**Alternative (or)**	**Result (so)**
In addition	instead	accordingly
also	otherwise	consequently
besides		hence
furthermore		therefore
likewise		thus
moreover		
Contrast (but)	**Emphasis**	**To Show Time**
however	indeed	meanwhile
nevertheless	in fact	
nonetheless		

Practice

In each of the following compound sentences, draw a single line under the subject and draw two lines under the verb for both independent clauses. Then circle the semicolon, adverbial conjunction, and comma. For example:

The jet was the fastest way to get there; moreover, it was the most comfortable.

1. The restaurant is always too crowded on Saturdays; nevertheless, it serves the best food in town.
2. The land was not for sale; however, the house could be rented.
3. The lawsuit cost the company several million dollars; consequently, the company went out of business a short time later.
4. The doctor told him to lose weight; furthermore, she insisted he also stop smoking.

Exercise 1   Combining Sentences Using Adverbial Conjunctions

Combine each pair of sentences below to make a compound sentence. Use a semicolon, an adverbial conjunction, and a comma. Be sure the conjunction you choose makes sense in the sentence. For example:

Two simple sentences: Our family would like to purchase a computer.

We must wait until prices come down further.

Compound sentence: Our family would like to purchase a computer; however, we must wait until prices come down further.

Combining Sentences Using Coordination ▶ 55

1. Most people have preferred to write with a pen or pencil.

   The computer is quickly becoming another favorite writing tool.

   _____

   _____

2. Computers provide a powerful way to create and store pieces of writing.

   They will become even more important in the future. (Show result.)

   _____

   _____

3. Some people do not like the idea of using electronics to create words.

   They should realize that the modern typewriter is also an electronic tool. (Show contrast.)

   _____

   _____

4. Computers have already revolutionized today's offices.

   No modern business can afford to be without them. (Show emphasis.)

   _____

   _____

5. Many schools are using computers in the classroom.

   These same schools are helping students prepare for their working careers. (Add an idea.)

   _____

   _____

6. The prices of many computers are coming down these days.

   More and more people see that owning a computer is a real possibility. (Show result.)

   _____

   _____

7. Some children know more about computers than many adults.

   Some children are teaching the adults how to operate computers. (Add an idea.)

   _____

   _____

56 ◀ Developing the Complete Sentence

8. Professional writers have become enthusiastic about the use of computers.

   There are still some writers who will use only a ballpoint pen. (Show contrast.)

   _____
   _____

9. The electronic revolution has just begun.

   The nation faces a great challenge to keep up with that revolution. (Show result.)

   _____
   _____

10. We have many technological aids to writing.

    Let us not forget that the source for all our ideas is the human brain. (Show contrast.)

    _____
    _____

Exercise 2 Combining Sentences Using Adverbial Conjunctions

Combine each pair of sentences below to make a compound sentence. Use a semicolon, an adverbial conjunction, and a comma. Be sure the conjunction you choose makes sense in the sentence. For example:

Two simple sentences: Our family would like to purchase a computer.
We must wait until prices come down further.

Compound sentence: Our family would like to purchase a computer; however, we must wait until prices come down further.

1. She doesn't like her job anymore.

   She cannot find another job that pays as well.

   _____; nevertheless, _____
   _____

2. The office is clean and spacious.

   The people with whom she works are very kind.

   _____
   _____

Combining Sentences Using Coordination ▸ 57

3. The work is very repetitious and boring.
   She finds herself looking at her watch twenty times a day.

   _____

   _____

4. Her best qualities are carefulness and industriousness.
   Her problem is that she wants to have some excitement and challenge.

   _____

   _____

5. She long ago learned everything about the job.
   She now has no sense of growth or personal satisfaction.

   _____

   _____

6. Even doctors sometimes grow tired of their jobs.
   They have invested too much time and energy to change careers.

   _____

   _____

7. One solution could be the establishment of regular retraining programs.
   It seems a shame for a person with years of experience in one field to leave it all behind for something new.

   _____

   _____

   _____

8. Society would lose the benefit of their expertise.
   Individuals would lose the chance to be at the top of their fields.

   _____

   _____

9. Some large companies move employees around every few years.
   Workers seem energized by new surroundings and people.

   _____

   _____

10. Perhaps every ten years we should all switch jobs.
    We had better make the best of our situations.

    _____

    _____

Exercise 3   Combining Sentences Using Adverbial Conjunctions

For each example, add the suggested adverbial conjunction and another independent clause that will make sense. Remember to punctuate correctly.

1. (however) We were told not to leave the building _____
   _____

2. (therefore) I hadn't done the homework very carefully _____
   _____

3. (otherwise) He accepted the job he was offered _____
   _____

4. (instead) Matthew doesn't like office work _____
   _____

5. (in fact) The running shoes are expensive _____
   _____

6. (furthermore) The doctor advised my father to stop smoking _____
   _____

7. (consequently) The hurricane struck last night _____
   _____

8. (meanwhile) I worked feverishly for days on the report _____
   _____

9. (nevertheless) The young singer was nervous _____
   _____

10. (moreover) The car is the fastest way to get to work _____
    _____

▶ Use a semicolon

The third way to combine two independent clauses is to use a semicolon.

IC	;	IC
He arrived at ten	;	He left at midnight.

This third method of combining sentences is used less often. No connecting word is used. The semicolon takes the place of the conjunction.

Two independent clauses: Last year I read F. Scott Fitzgerald's *The Great Gatsby.*

Tonight I saw the movie version of his *Tender Is the Night.*

Compound sentence: Last year I read F. Scott Fitzgerald's *The Great Gatsby;* tonight I saw the movie version of his *Tender Is the Night.*

The semicolon was used in this example to show that the content of both sentences is closely related and therefore belongs together in one sentence.

When sentences are combined by using a semicolon, the grammatical structure of each sentence is often similar:

The women pitched the tents; the men cooked the dinner.

Exercise 1

Combining Sentences Using the Semicolon

For each of the independent clauses below, add your own independent clause that is a related idea with a similar grammatical structure. Join the two clauses with a semicolon. An example has been done for you.

Independent clause: He wrote the speech.
Compound sentence: He wrote the speech; she gave it.

1. The apartment was light and airy.

   _____

   _____

2. Shoppers were pushing grocery carts down the aisles.

   _____

   _____

3. I plan to learn two foreign languages.

   _____

   _____

4. I tried to explain.

   _____

   _____

5. Many teenagers spend hours listening to rock music.

   _____

   _____

Exercise 2 — Combining Sentences Using the Semicolon

Below are five independent clauses. Combine each one with an independent clause of your own to make a compound sentence. Connect the two clauses with a semicolon. Be sure to construct independent clauses that are related in their grammatical structure as well as in their ideas. An example has been done for you.

Independent clause: The guests are putting on their coats.

Compound sentence: The guests are putting on their coats; the cab is at the door.

1. The pickup truck was filled with old furniture.
   _____
   _____

2. Children played in the streets.
   _____
   _____

3. We expected them to understand.
   _____
   _____

4. The older men wore ties.
   _____
   _____

5. She hoped her boyfriend would soon call.
   _____
   _____

▶ **Chapter review exercises**

Exercise 1 — Combining Sentences Using Coordination

Combine each pair of sentences below to make a compound sentence. Choose from the three methods you have studied in this chapter. Be sure that the conjunctions you choose clearly show the relationships between the ideas.

1. For some people, mathematics is a necessary evil.
   To others, mathematics provides a lifetime of challenge and fun.
   _____
   _____

2. The Westinghouse Scholarship is a major national competition.
   Teachers encourage their most outstanding math students to enter it.

3. Students have to come up with a new theory.
   They must find a new application of an already existing theory. (Hint: show a choice.)

4. Bram Boroson is a semifinalist in the contest this year.
   He is also a National Merit semifinalist.

5. Math can be very satisfying.
   Unlike in the humanities, there is usually only one correct answer.

6. Some people can have a special talent for math.
   These same people can be very ordinary in language skills.

7. Physics demands math skill.
   Engineering also involves a great deal of mathematical ability.

8. Many schools form math teams to compete in area contests.
   Other schools encourage interest in math with math clubs.

9. Some schools suffer from a lack of good science and math teachers.
   These people have found better-paying jobs in industry.

62 ◀ Developing the Complete Sentence

10. Our future may depend on finding and adequately paying good teachers.
American students may continue to trail behind those of many other countries in math and science ability.

_____

_____

Exercise 2 **Combining Sentences Using Coordination**

Combine each pair of sentences below to make a compound sentence. Choose from the three methods you have studied in this chapter. Be sure that the conjunctions you choose clearly show the relationships between the ideas.

1. The large rain forests of Africa and South America are in danger.
   They can never be replaced.

   _____

   _____

2. The varieties of insects and animals in the rain forest are enormous.
   Their destruction means the loss of the world's greatest biological laboratory.

   _____

   _____

3. Many countries are cutting down their rain forests every year.
   The world's natural resources are steadily decreasing.

   _____

   _____

4. Scientists are concerned about the loss of animal and plant species in the rain forest.
   They are trying to slow down this destruction.

   _____

   _____

5. The governments of the world should be concerned about the loss of the rain forests.
   They are not actively trying to stop the developers.

   _____

   _____

6. The rain forests could be a valuable source of medical knowledge.
   The forests are also an invaluable source of timber and other products.

   _____

   _____

7. Most people in our country have never seen a rain forest.
   They find it difficult to imagine how beautiful it is.

   _____

   _____

8. Rain forests appear to be fertile.
   They actually have very poor soil for growing crops.

   _____

   _____

9. Many animals of the rain forest have not yet been studied by scientists.
   Many plants may still hold the secret to medical cures.

   _____

   _____

10. Some countries pride themselves in the cutting down of their rain forests.
    Most scientists are deeply disturbed by this monumental destruction of nature.

    _____

    _____

Exercise 3   Combining Sentences Using Coordination

Below are five simple sentences. Using each sentence as an independent clause, construct a compound sentence. Use each of the three possible methods at least once.

1. The beach was crowded. (Add an idea.)

   _____

   _____

2. The first apartment had no bedroom. (Show a contrast.)

   _____

   _____

3. January had been bitterly cold. (Show a result.)

_____

_____

4. The young model wore dark glasses. (Introduce a reason.)

_____

_____

5. The community waited for news. (Show time.)

_____

_____

4

Combining Sentences Using Subordination

▶ What is subordination?

When you use coordination to combine sentences, the ideas in both the resulting clauses are given equal weight. However, ideas are not always equally important. *Subordination* is the method used to combine sentences whose ideas are not equally important. Subordination allows you to show which idea is the main idea.

The sentence that results when two sentences are combined using subordination is called a **complex sentence**. We identify the two or more ideas that are contained within this complex sentence by calling them **clauses**. The main idea clause is called the **independent clause**. It could stand alone as a simple sentence. The less important idea is called the **dependent clause** because even though this clause has a subject and a verb, it is dependent on the rest of the sentence for its meaning. Consider the following clauses:

>*Independent clause:* That girl will leave soon.
>
>*Dependent clause:* If that girl will leave soon . . .

Notice that both clauses in the examples above have a subject and a verb. (The subject is *girl* and the verb phrase is *will leave.*) The difference is that the dependent clause has an additional word. *If* is a special kind of connecting word that makes the clause "dependent" on an additional idea. A dependent clause does not make sense by itself. The thought is not complete. Below is the same dependent clause with an independent clause added to it.

>If that girl will leave soon, I can finish my homework.

Now the thought is complete.

In your work with sentences, you will want to be comfortable writing sentences with dependent clauses. For this you will need to practice using two kinds of "connecting" words: subordinating conjunctions and relative pronouns. First, practice using subordinating conjunctions.

Use a subordinating conjunction to create a complex sentence

Following is a list of subordinating conjunctions. These connecting words signal the beginning of a dependent clause. Be sure to learn them. It is a good idea to memorize them.

Connectors: Common Subordinating Conjunctions

after	if, even if	unless
although	in order that	until
as, as if	provided that	when, whenever
as long as, as though	rather than	where, wherever
because	since	whether
before	so that	while
even though	though	

Function of Subordinating Conjunctions

To introduce a *condition*:   if, even if, as long as, provided that, unless (after a negative independent clause)

    I will go *as long as* you go with me.
    I won't go *unless* you go with me.

To introduce a *contrast*:   although, even though, though

    I will go *even though* you won't go with me.

To introduce a *cause*:   because, since

    I will go *because* the meeting is very important.

To show *time*:   after, before, when, whenever, while, until (independent clause is negative)

    I will go *whenever* you say.
    I won't go *until* you say it is time.

To show *place*:   where, wherever

    I will go *wherever* you send me.

To show *purpose*:   in order that, so that

    I will go *so that* I can hear the candidate for myself.

You have two choices of how to write the complex sentence. You can begin with the dependent clause, or you can begin with the independent clause.

First way:	DC	,	IC
Example:	If Barbara leaves	,	we can finish our homework.

	IC	DC
Second way:		
Example:	We can finish our homework	if Barbara leaves.

▶ The comma is used when you begin a sentence with a dependent clause. No comma is used when you begin the sentence with the independent clause. Your ear will help you remember this rule because when a sentence begins with a dependent clause, you can hear a pause at the end of that dependent clause. This is where the comma belongs. When a sentence begins with the independent clause, there is no pause, and therefore no comma.

―――――― **Practice** ――――――

Here are three pairs of sentences. Combine each pair by using a subordinating conjunction. Write the sentence two different ways. First, begin the sentence with the dependent clause and use a comma. Second, begin the sentence with the independent clause and do not use any comma.

1. (Use *since*.) The librarian took too many coffee breaks.
   The boss fired him.

   a. _____

   b. _____

2. (Use *after*.) He won the wrestling match.
   He went out to celebrate.

   a. _____

   b. _____

3. (Use *when*.) Donna returned from Europe this spring.
   The family was excited.

   a. _____

   b. _____

Exercise 1   Recognizing Dependent and Independent Clauses

In the blank to the side of each group of words, write the letters *IC* if the group is an independent clause (a complete thought) or *DC* if the group of words is a dependent clause (not a complete thought even though it contains a subject and a verb).

_____ 1. while the photographer was getting ready

_____ 2. before the show began

_____ 3. I seldom go to the movies by myself

_____ 4. even if it rains

_____ 5. the Monopoly game lasted five hours

_____ 6. whenever I see you

_____ 7. since I did not take the medicine

_____ 8. I spent the day in bed

_____ 9. when I was sitting on the crosstown bus

_____ 10. until the day he died

Exercise 2

Recognizing Dependent and Independent Clauses

In the blank to the side of each group of words, write the letters *IC* if the group is an independent clause (a complete thought) or *DC* if the group of words is a dependent clause (not a complete thought even though it contains a subject and a verb).

_____ 1. when his back was turned

_____ 2. he stared at his watch angrily

_____ 3. even though I offered to walk with him

_____ 4. this was a new development

_____ 5. I was so astonished

_____ 6. unless I acted at once

_____ 7. after my brother arrived

_____ 8. I had to be very quiet

_____ 9. sometimes I pinched him

_____ 10. as he lay sleeping

Exercise 3

Recognizing Dependent and Independent Clauses

In the blank to the side of each group of words, write the letters *IC* if the group is an independent clause (a complete thought) or *DC* if the group of words is a dependent clause (not a complete thought even though it contains a subject and a verb).

_____ 1. William Faulkner was a regional writer

_____ 2. he was born near Oxford, Mississippi

_____ 3. where he lived and died

_____ 4. even if he used the dialect of the area

_____ 5. some of his books share the same characters and themes

_____ 6. because Faulkner devoted many pages to greed, violence, and meanness

_____ 7. until the year he died

_____ 8. he won the Nobel Prize in 1950

_____ 9. when he became one of America's greatest writers

_____ 10. although Faulkner departed from the traditional style of prose

Exercise 1

Using Subordinating Conjunctions

Use each of the following subordinating conjunctions to compose a complex sentence. An example has been done for you.

> ***Subordinating conjunction:*** after
>
> ***Complex:*** After the game was over, we all went out for pizza.

Remember that a complex sentence has one independent clause and at least one dependent clause. Every clause must have a subject and a verb. Check your sentences by underlining the subject and verb in each clause.

▸ Can you explain why the following sentence is not a complex sentence?

After the game, we all went out for pizza.

After the game is a prepositional phrase. *After,* in this case, is a preposition. It is not used as a subordinating conjunction to combine clauses.

1. as if

_____

_____

2. before

_____

_____

3. until

4. although

5. because (Begin with the independent clause. Traditional English grammar frowns on beginning a sentence with *because*. Ask your instructor for his or her opinion.)

Exercise 2 **Combining Sentences Using Subordination**

Combine each pair of sentences using subordination. Look back at the list of subordinating conjunctions if you need to.

1. He was eating breakfast.
   The results of the election came over the radio.
   WHILE HE WAS EATING BREAKFAST, THE RESULTS OF THE ELECTION CAME OVER THE RADIO.

2. The town council voted against the plan.
   They believed the project was too expensive.
   BECAUSE THE TOWN COUNCIL VOTED AGAINST THE PLAN, THEY BELIEVED THE PROJECT WAS TOO EXPENSIVE

3. I will see Maya Angelou tonight.
   She is speaking at the university this evening.

4. The worker hoped for a promotion.
   Not one person in the department had received a promotion last year.

5. The worker hoped for a promotion.
   He made sure all his work was done accurately and on time.

Exercise 3

Combining Sentences Using Subordination

Rewrite the following paragraph using subordination to combine some of the sentences wherever you feel it would be effective. Discuss your choices with your classmates. You might want to discuss places where coordination might be a good choice.

At the present time, the United States recycles 10 percent of its trash. It burns another 10 percent. The remaining 80 percent is used as landfill. Over the next few years, many of our landfills will close. They are full. Some of them are leaking toxic wastes. Some parts of the Northeast already truck much of their trash to landfills in Pennsylvania, Ohio, Kentucky, and West Virginia. The garbage continues to pile up. The newspapers print stories about it every week. Trash is not a very glamorous subject. People in every town talk about the problem. One magazine, called *Garbage,* is printed on recycled paper. No town ever before gathered together information about garbage. The town of Lyndhurst, New Jersey, began what is the world's only garbage museum. One landfill now has a restaurant on its premises. Another landfill displays some of its unusual garbage. It displays these objects like trophies. We really want to solve the garbage problem. We must change our "buy more and throw everything old away" mentality.

Use a relative pronoun to create a complex sentence

Often sentences can be combined with a relative pronoun.

Common Relative Pronouns

who whose whom	refers to people
which	refers to things
that	refers to people and/or things

Two simple sentences: The researcher had a breakthrough.
He was studying diabetes.

These sentences are short and choppy. To avoid this choppiness, a writer could join these two related ideas with a relative pronoun.

Combining sentences with a relative pronoun: The researcher who was studying diabetes had a breakthrough.

Now join a third idea to the sentence: (use *which*).

Third idea: He reported the breakthrough to the press.

Remember to put the relative pronoun directly after the word it relates to.

Incorrect: The researcher, which he reported to the press, had a breakthrough.

The relative pronoun and its clause *who was studying diabetes* refers to the *researcher*, not to a *breakthrough*. The relative pronoun *which* and its clause *which he reported to the press* does refer to *breakthrough*. This clause will follow the noun *breakthrough*.

Correct: The researcher *who was studying diabetes* had a breakthrough, *which he reported to the press.*

---Practice 1---

Combine each of the three pairs of sentences into one complex sentence by using a relative pronoun. Do not use commas. An example is done for you.

First sentence: That woman created the flower arrangement.
Second sentence: She visited us last weekend.
Combined sentence: That woman who visited us last weekend created the flower arrangement.

1. The chemistry lab is two hours long.
   I attend that chemistry lab.

   Combined: _____

   _____

2. The student assistant is very knowledgeable.
The student assistant is standing by the door.

Combined: _____

_____

3. The equipment was purchased last year.
The equipment will make possible some important new research.

Combined: _____

_____

▶ How do you punctuate a clause with a relative pronoun?

Punctuating relative clauses can be tricky because there are two types of relative clauses:

1. Those that are basic to the meaning of the sentence:

   Never eat fruit *that isn't washed first.*

   The basic meaning of the sentence is not "never eat fruit." The relative clause is necessary to restrict the meaning. This clause is called a **restrictive clause** and does not use commas to set off the clause. *Note:* The pronoun "that" is usually in this category.

2. Those that are not basic to the meaning of the sentence:

   Mother's fruit salad, *which consisted of grapes, apples, and walnuts,* was delicious.

   In this sentence, the relative clause is not basic to the main idea. In fact, if the clause were omitted, the main idea would not be changed. This clause is called a **nonrestrictive clause**. Commas are required to indicate the information is nonessential. *Note:* The pronoun "which" is usually in this category.

_____ Practice 2 _____

Choose whether or not to insert commas in the following sentences. Use the following examples as your models.

   The man *who is wearing the Hawaiian shirt* is the bridegroom.

The bridegroom can only be identified by his Hawaiian shirt. Therefore, the relative clause *who is wearing the Hawaiian shirt* is essential to the meaning. No commas are necessary.

   Al, *who was wearing a flannel shirt,* arrived late to the wedding.

The main idea is that Al was late. What he was wearing is not essential to that main idea. Therefore, commas are needed to set off this nonessential information.

1. The poem that my classmate read in class was very powerful.
2. The teacher who guided our class today is my favorite college professor.

74 ◂ Developing the Complete Sentence

3. The biology course which met four times a week for two hours each session was extremely demanding.
4. You seldom learn much in courses that are not demanding.
5. My own poetry which has improved over the semester has brought me much satisfaction.

Now you are ready to practice joining your own sentences with relative pronouns, being careful to punctuate carefully. The following exercises ask you to insert a variety of relative clauses into simple sentences.

Exercise 1   Combining Sentences Using Relative Pronouns

Add a relative clause to each of the following ten sentences. Use each of the possibilities at least once: who, whose, whom, which, that. Be sure to punctuate correctly. An example has been done for you.

Simple sentence: The leader was barely five feet tall.
Complex sentence: The leader, who was always self-conscious about his height, was barely five feet tall.

1. The president _____
   asked his advisors for help.

2. His advisors _____
   met with him in his office.

3. The situation _____
   was at a critical point.

4. Even his vice president _____
   appeared visibly alarmed.

5. Stacked on the table, the plans _____
   _____ looked impressive.

6. The meeting _____
   began at 2 o'clock.

7. Every idea _____
   was examined in great detail.

8. Several maps _____
   showed the area in question.

9. One advisor _____
   was vehemently opposed to the plan.

10. Finally the group agreed on a plan of action _____
    _____.

Exercise 2 **Combining Sentences Using Relative Pronouns**

Combine the following pairs of sentences using a relative pronoun.

1. Stress can do a great deal of harm.
   We experience stress every day.

   _____
   _____

2. People often use food to help them cope.
   Some people work long hours at demanding jobs.

   _____
   _____

3. The practice of eating to cope with stress is often automatic.
   The practice of eating to cope often goes back to childhood.

   _____
   _____

4. Foods can actually increase tension.
   People turn to foods in times of stress.

   _____
   _____

5. Sweet foods are actually not energy boosters.
   Sweet foods are popular with people who need a lift.

   _____
   _____

6. Another substance is caffeine.
   People use other substances to get an energy boost.

   _____
   _____

7. One of the biggest mistakes people make is to use alcohol as an aid to achieving calm.
   Alcohol is really a depressant.

   _____
   _____

8. People should eat three light meals a day and two small snacks.
   People want to feel a sense of calm.

   _____

   _____

9. Getting enough protein is also important in keeping an adequate energy level.
   An adequate energy level will get you through the day.

   _____

   _____

10. Most important is to eat regularly so you will avoid binges.
    Binges put on pounds and drain you of energy.

    _____

    _____

Exercise 3 — Combining Sentences Using Relative Pronouns

Combine the following pairs of sentences using a relative pronoun.

1. Murray, Kentucky, is a Norman Rockwell painting come to life.
   It is in the middle of America's heartland.

   _____

   _____

2. You will soon notice the blue, clean lakes.
   They are bustling with activity.

   _____

   _____

3. A quarter million acres of water surround the town.
   This water is perfect for sailing, water-skiing, fishing, and relaxing.

   _____

   _____

4. Scouting enthusiasts enjoy the National Scouting Museum.
   The museum has exhibits visitors can touch.

   _____

   _____

5. The same museum has a large collection of paintings by Norman Rockwell. His work reflects the surrounding landscape.

6. Murray State University is an important part of local life. The University often has inexpensive concerts and other activities.

7. The Homeplace is a working farm. It shows the way families lived a century ago.

   The Homeplace that shows the way families lived a century ago is a working farm

8. The Homestead also puts on old-fashioned weddings. *where* The wedding parties are made up of actors and actresses in beautiful antique attire.

   The Homestead also puts on

9. People can see herds of buffalo. People like to see rare sights.

10. At the end of the day, you can enjoy the local cooking. Murray is famous for its local cooking.

▶ Chapter review exercises

Exercise 1

Combining Sentences with a Subordinating Conjunction or a Relative Pronoun

Combine each of the following pairs of sentences using either a subordinating conjunction or a relative pronoun. Be sure the word you choose makes sense in the sentence.

78 ◀ Developing the Complete Sentence

1. People have been fascinated for centuries by the problem of stuttering.
   Modern science is only beginning to understand some of the underlying causes of the problem.

   _____

   _____

   _____

   _____

2. For some people stuttering disappears by itself.
   For others, stuttering continues into adulthood.

   _____

   _____

   _____

3. Stutterers usually keep their affliction.
   They seek professional help.

   _____

   _____

4. Many stutterers lose their impediment when they sing or whisper.
   Under stress the impediment becomes worse.

   _____

   _____

   _____

5. Stutterers become unable to speak when they appear in public or when they find themselves on the phone.
   They try to avoid such situations.

   _____

   _____

   _____

6. You see a stutterer reciting the pledge of allegiance with a whole class.
   That same person is usually tongue-tied when called on by a teacher.

   _____

   _____

   _____

   _____

7. It is true that there is some psychological basis for stuttering.
   It is true that psychologists have not been able to solve the problem.

   _____

   _____

8. All kinds of scientists have looked at the problem from all different angles.
   There is no single answer to stuttering.

   _____

   _____

9. Stuttering runs in families.
   Children of such families have greater chances of becoming stutterers.

   _____

   _____

10. You hear someone say he or she knows the causes of stuttering.
    You know that person cannot be speaking scientifically.

    _____

    _____

Exercise 2

Combining Sentences with a Subordinating Conjunction or a Relative Pronoun

Combine each of the following pairs of sentences using either a subordinating conjunction or a relative pronoun.

1. I live alone with two dogs.
   They sleep on the braided rug in my bedroom.

   _____

   _____

2. The police stood by the door.
   They blocked our entrance.

   _____

   _____

3. She wore high heels.
   They made marks in the wooden floor.

   _____

   _____

80 ◂ Developing the Complete Sentence

4. My aunt is a tyrant.
   Her name is Isabel.

   _____

   _____

5. Her outfit was classy.
   Her hair was dirty and unattractive.

   _____

   _____

6. The interviewer did not smile.
   He discovered we had a friend in common.

   _____

   _____

7. I had a test the next day.
   I stayed up to watch a Betty Grable movie.

   _____

   _____

8. The skater fell and broke his arm.
   He was trying to skate backward.

   _____

   _____

9. For a moment her face glowed with pleasure.
   Her face was usually serious.

   _____

   _____

10. I was thinking.
    The toast burned.

    _____

    _____

Exercise 3   Combining Sentences Using Coordination and Subordination

Now you are ready to have some fun! James Thurber, a famous American humorist, wrote a magazine article that gave a portrait of a man named Doc Marlowe. Below are some simple sentences made from one of his paragraphs. Look over the sentences, and then rewrite the paragraph combining sentences wherever you think it would improve the meaning and style. Your instructor can provide Thurber's original version although there is certainly more than one way to revise it. Don't be afraid to change the wording slightly to accommodate the changes you want to make.

I met Doc Marlowe at old Mrs. Willoughby's rooming house. She had been a nurse in our family. I used to go and visit her over week-ends sometimes. I was very fond of her. I was about eleven years old then. Doc Marlowe wore scarred leather leggings and a bright-colored bead vest. He said he got the vest from the Indians. He wore a ten-gallon hat with kitchen matches stuck in the band, all the way around. He was about six feet four inches tall, with big shoulders, and a long, drooping mustache. He let his hair grow long, like General Custer's. He had a wonderful collection of Indian relics and six-shooters. He used to tell me stories of his adventures in the Far West. His favorite expressions were "Hay, boy!" and "Hay, boy-gie!" He used these the way some people now use "Hot dog!" or "Doggone!" I thought he was the greatest man I had ever seen. He died. His son came in from New Jersey for the funeral. I found out something. He had never been in the Far West in his life. He had been born in Brooklyn.

5

Correcting the Run-On

A teenager came home from school with a long face.

Daughter: I had a terrible day.
Mother: What happened?
Daughter: Well, to start with my hair looked terrible <u>and then</u> the science teacher called on me to give my oral report <u>and</u> I was counting on having another day at least to <u>get</u> ready for it <u>and</u> when I got to English class I realized I had left my <u>purse</u> in science class <u>and</u> I didn't have time to go back and get it <u>and</u> to top <u>it</u> off Mrs. Edmunds gave us a surprise quiz on our reading assignment.
Mother: <u>And</u> I thought my day was bad!

This is probably typical of many conversations you have had at one time or another. In telling about a series of events, we sometimes join the events together as if they were one long thought. A problem arises when you want to write down these events in acceptable writing form. Writing ideas down as if they are all one thought without any punctuation to help the reader is not acceptable. Such a sentence as the one above is called a **run-on**. You cannot combine independent clauses without some kind of punctuation.

▶ How many kinds of run-ons are there?

The Different Kinds of Run-On Sentences

1. *The fused run-on:* two or more independent clauses that run together without any punctuation

    I met Diana again we were happy to see each other.

2. *The comma splice:* two or more independent clauses that run together with only a comma

    I met Diana again, we were happy to see each other.

82

> **3.** *The "and" run-on;* two or more independent clauses that run together with a coordinating conjunction but no punctuation
>
>   I met Diana again and we were happy to see each other.

▶ **How do you make a complete sentence from a run-on?**

> ### Guide for Correcting Run-Ons
>
> **1.** Make two simple sentences with end punctuation:
>
>   I met Diana again. We were happy to see each other.
>
> **2.** Make a compound sentence using one of the three methods of coordination:
>
>   I met Diana again, and we were happy to see each other.
>
>   I met Diana again; furthermore, we were happy to see each other.
>
>   I met Diana again; we were happy to see each other.
>
> **3.** Make a complex sentence using subordination:
>
>   When I met Diana again, we were happy to see each other.
>
>   We were happy to see each other when I met Diana again.

Exercise 1   **Recognizing and Correcting Run-Ons**

The following story is written as one sentence. Rewrite the story, making sure to correct the run-on sentences. Put a period at the end of each complete thought. You may have to omit some of the words that loosely connect the ideas, or you may want to use coordination and subordination. Remember to make each new sentence begin with a capital letter.

    Well, to start with my hair looked terrible <u>and then</u> the science teacher called on me to give my oral report <u>and</u> I was counting on having another day at least to get ready for it <u>and when</u> I got to English class I realized I had left my purse in science class <u>and</u> I did not have time to go back and get it <u>and</u> to top it off, Mrs. Edmunds gave us a surprise quiz on our reading assignment.

_____

_____

_____

_____

_____

_____

Exercise 2

Recognizing and Correcting Run-Ons

The following story is written as one sentence. Rewrite the story, making sure to correct the run-on sentences. Put a period at the end of each complete thought. You may have to omit some of the words that loosely connect the ideas, or you may want to use coordination and subordination. Remember to make each new sentence begin with a capital letter.

My best friend is accident-prone if you knew her you'd know that she's always limping, having to write with her left hand or wearing a bandage on her head or ankle, like last week for example she was walking down the street minding her own business when a shingle from someone's roof hit her on the head and she had to go to the emergency ward for stitches, then this week one of her fingers is purple because someone slammed the car door on her hand sometimes I think it might be better if I didn't spend too much time with her you know her bad luck might be catching!

Exercise 3

Recognizing and Correcting Run-Ons

The following story is written as one sentence. Rewrite the story, making sure to correct all run-on sentences. Put a period at the end of each complete thought. You may have to omit some of the words that loosely connect the ideas, or you may want to use coordination and subordination. Remember to make each new sentence begin with a capital letter.

One morning, not too early, I will rise and slip downstairs to brew the coffee and no baby will wake me up and no alarm clock will rattle my nerves and the weather will be so warm that I will not have to put on my coat and hat to go out for the paper there will be no rush I will go to the refrigerator and take out eggs and sausage the bathroom will be free so I will be able to take a shower with no one knocking on the door and I will not have to run up and down the stairs first looking for someone's shoes and then for someone's car keys I will leisurely fix my hair and pick out a lovely suit to wear the phone might ring and it will be a friend who would like to have lunch and share the afternoon with me money will be no problem maybe we'll see a movie or drive to the nearby city to visit a museum and the countryside will be beautiful and unspoiled my life will seem fresh and promising.

Exercise 1   **Revising Run-Ons**

Each of the following examples is a run-on. Supply four possible ways to revise each run-on. Use the guide on page 83 if you need help.

1. Intelligence tests for children are not always useful they are a basic tool for measurement in most schools.

   Two simple sentences:

   _____

   _____

   _____

   Two kinds of compound sentence:

   a. _____

   _____

   b. _____

   _____

   Complex sentence:

   _____

   _____

2. Many people are opposed to gambling in all its forms they will not even buy a lottery ticket.

   Two simple sentences:

   _____

   _____

   _____

   Two kinds of compound sentence:

   a. _____

   _____

   b. _____

   _____

   Complex sentence:

   _____

   _____

3. Public transportation is the major problem facing many of our cities little is being done to change the situation.

   Two simple sentences:

   _____

   _____

   _____

   Two kinds of compound sentence:

   a. _____

   _____

   b. _____

   _____

   Complex sentence:

   _____

   _____

4. Travel is a great luxury one needs time and money.

   Two simple sentences:

   _____

   _____

   _____

   Two kinds of compound sentence:

   a. _____

   _____

   b. _____

   _____

   Complex sentence:

   _____

   _____ *Although,*

5. The need for proper diet is important in any health program, all the junk food on the grocery shelves makes it hard to be consistent.

   Two simple sentences:

   _____

   _____

Developing the Complete Sentence

Two kinds of compound sentence:

a. _____
_____

b. _____
_____

Complex sentence:
_____
_____

Exercise 2   Revising Run-Ons

Each of the following examples is a run-on. Supply four possible ways to revise each run-on. Use the guide on page 83 if you need help.

1. The airline has begun its new route to the islands everyone is looking forward to flying there.

    Two simple sentences:
    _____
    _____

    Two kinds of compound sentence:

    a. _____
    _____

    b. _____
    _____

    Complex sentence:
    _____
    _____

2. The movie begins at nine o'clock let's have dinner before the show.

    Two simple sentences:
    _____
    _____

    Two kinds of compound sentence:

    a. _____
    _____

Correcting the Run-On ▶ 89

b. _____
_____

Complex sentence:
_____
_____

3. The studio audience screamed at the contestant they wanted her to try for the big prize.

Two simple sentences:
_____
_____

Two kinds of compound sentence:

a. _____
_____

b. _____
_____

Complex sentence:
_____
_____

4. The baby covered his eyes he thought he could disappear that way.

Two simple sentences:
_____
_____

Two kinds of compound sentence:

a. _____
_____

b. _____
_____

Complex sentence:
_____
_____

90 ◀ Developing the Complete Sentence

5. He might be admitted to the university he could always go to the local community college.

   Two simple sentences:
   _____
   _____

   Two kinds of compound sentence:

   a. _____
   _____

   b. _____
   _____

   Complex sentence:
   _____
   _____

Exercise 3 — Revising Run-Ons

Each of the following examples is a run-on. Supply four possible ways to revise each run-on. Use the guide on page 83 if you need help.

1. The people stood on the street waiting for the bank to open it was their last chance to cash a check before Monday.

   Two simple sentences:
   _____
   _____

   Two kinds of compound sentence:

   a. _____
   _____

   b. _____
   _____

   Complex sentence:
   _____
   _____

2. We didn't start our trip until noon it was pouring.

   Two simple sentences:
   _____
   _____

Two kinds of compound sentence:

a. _____

b. _____

Complex sentence: _____

3. Learning a skill on the job is very satisfying a work situation can be just as valuable as a classroom.

Two simple sentences: _____

Two kinds of compound sentence:

a. _____

b. _____

Complex sentence: _____

4. After many years, women finally won the right to vote now the struggle for equal rights is found in other areas besides politics.

Two simple sentences: _____

Two kinds of compound sentence:

a. _____

b. _____

92 ◀ Developing the Complete Sentence

Complex sentence:

_____

_____

5. Mrs. Brighton takes in student lodgers every year she likes to have people in the house.

Two simple sentences:

_____

_____

Two kinds of compound sentence:

a. _____

_____

b. _____

_____

Complex sentence:

_____

_____

▶ **Chapter review exercises**

Exercise 1   Editing for Run-Ons

Rewrite the following paragraph, correcting all three kinds of run-on sentences.

    In 1990, John Ehrlichman drove 600 miles in Russia talking to ordinary citizens, Soviet workers were quick to talk about their everyday troubles. The dismal state of the economy was evident everywhere. Cars waited for hours in line to get gasoline people were lined up at stores to buy anything the stores might be happening to sell that day. It's a way of life to the people in the Soviet Union. Russians are deeply distressed for the privileged hierarchy still enjoys fine housing and imported delicacies while the masses cope with grinding shortages. Doctors work in old facilities and they have little medicine or basic equipment like antibiotics or disposable syringes. Meat is very scarce even if a farmer is very productive, 25 percent of his food spoils en route. The United States feeds all its people with 2 million farmers, Russia can't feed its people with 24 million farmers and 4 million bureaucrats to tell the farmers what to do. At one factory where Ehrlichman visited, he was told to be careful where he walked because the ground was saturated with sulfuric acid and it would eat up his shoes. In other places, he could see pipes discharging untreated waste chemicals into the marshlands and rivers. The city of Novgorod hopes its sister city, Rochester, New York, will help Novgorod obtain instruments to test the purity of the air, they cannot enforce pollution laws without such equipment.

Exercise 2

Editing for Run-Ons

Rewrite the following paragraph, correcting all run-on sentences.

In laboratory experiments, scientists have discovered a diet which extends the life of their animals up to 50 percent or more. This diet prevents heart disease, diabetes, and kidney failure and it greatly retards all types of cancer. It even slows down the aging process of cataracts, gray hair, and feebleness. Staying on this diet keeps the mind flexible and the body active to an almost biblical old age! These rats, fish, and worms stay very slim, they are fed a diet of necessary vitamins and nutrients, but only 65 percent of the calories of the animal's normal diet. Every creature fed this restricted diet has had a greatly extended life span. Richard Weindruch, a gerontologist at the National Institute on Aging in Bethesda, Maryland, says the results of caloric restriction is spectacular. Gerontologists have tried many things to extend life but this is the only experiment that works every time in the lab. Animals who received enough protein, vitamins, and minerals to prevent malnutrition survived to a grand old age and it does not seem to matter whether they eat a diet composed largely of fats or carbohydrates. Researchers warn against people undertaking this diet too hastily, it is easy to become malnourished. Dr. Roy Walford is a pioneer in the field from the University of California he believes humans could live to an extraordinarily advanced age if they were to limit their caloric intake.

Exercise 3

Editing Run-Ons

Rewrite these ten run-on sentences correctly in the form of a finished paragraph.

1. This spring, like all springs, homeowners want a perfect lawn so they will apply millions of pounds of chemical pesticides to their lawns.
2. Some officials are issuing new warnings about these lawn insecticides and weedkillers for many homeowners are careless when they apply these chemicals.
3. Pesticide use has been associated with some illnesses among homeowners, and pesticides have clearly been responsible for the killing of many songbirds and waterfowl.
4. Diazinon is a highly toxic insecticide that killed thousands of ducks and Canadian geese this is the very same pesticide most widely used on lawns.
5. Every time this pesticide is applied, it threatens the health of birds many people believe it causes disabling illnesses for human beings as well.
6. Reports from around the country are beginning to be heard, they link feeling terrible with the fact that a neighbor had the lawn sprayed the day before.
7. Sellers of pesticides defend their use, when used according to the labels, they say there are no adverse affects to health or the environment.
8. However, we all know many people never read the labels, even the Environmental Protection Agency admits they know very little about the health effects for families using these products.
9. Commercial lawn-care companies have created a $1.5 billion dollar business, they have often misled the public about the safety of these pesticides.
10. Recently, a Buffalo lawn-care company showed an ad with a baby on the lawn, the ad implied that a baby could safely play on a lawn treated with their pesticide.

96 ◄ Developing the Complete Sentence

6

Making Sentence Parts Work Together

For your sentences to be logical, all parts of the sentence must agree. A verb must agree in number with its subject; a pronoun must agree with the noun to which it refers; and verb tenses and persons must be consistent.

Since most of us have problems with agreement in our writing, you should work through this chapter carefully so that you will be able to look for these trouble spots in your own writing.

▶ Subject-verb agreement within the sentence

A verb must agree with its subject in **number**.

he		I	
she		you	
it	sleeps	we	sleep
any singular noun		they	
		plural noun	

Example: The baby *sleeps*.　　　　*Example:* The babies *sleep*.

▶ Remember that a verb that goes with a singular noun or pronoun needs an *s*.

——————————— Practice ———————————

Underline the correct verb in the following sentences.

1. The dog (bark, barks).
2. It (wake, wakes) up the neighborhood.
3. The neighbors (become, becomes) very angry.
4. People (deserve, deserves) a quiet Sunday morning.
5. I (throws, throw) an old shoe at the dog.

98 ◀ Developing the Complete Sentence

▶ Special problems in making verbs agree with their subjects

1. The subject is not always the noun closest to the verb. Remember, do not look for the subject within a prepositional phrase.

    The hairline <u>cracks</u> ~~in the engine~~ (*present*) a serious threat to the passengers' lives.

2. These indefinite pronouns take a singular verb:

    Indefinite Pronouns
    one, nobody, nothing, none
    anyone, anybody, anything
    everyone, everybody, everything
    someone, somebody, something
    either, neither
    each, another

    For example:

    Neither of my parents *is* able to attend the ceremony.

    ▶ The indefinite pronoun *both* takes a plural verb.

    Both of *my* parents *are* able to attend the ceremony.

3. When a pair of conjunctions is used, the verb agrees with the subject closer to the verb.

    Pairs of Conjunctions
    neither . . . nor
    either . . . or
    not only . . . but also

    For example:

    Neither the textbook nor my lecture *notes explain* the meaning of the term "tidal wave."

    Textbook and *notes* together make up the compound subject. Since *notes* is closer to the verb, the verb agrees with *notes*.

4. In some sentences the subject can come after the verb. In these cases, be sure that the verb agrees with the subject.

    Here *is* the *surprise* I promised you.
    Who *were* the *people* with you last night?

5. A group noun in American English usually takes a singular verb if the group acts as a unit. (The test is to substitute the word *it* in place of the group noun.)

    The town *council is planning* a Fourth of July celebration.

    In this sentence, the council is acting as a unit. "It" is planning a celebration. Therefore, the verb is singular.

A group noun takes a plural verb if the members of the group act as individuals. (The test is to substitute the word *they* for the group noun and see if it sounds right.)

The town *council are preparing* their speeches for this event.

In this sentence, the council members are individually preparing speeches. *They* substitutes for the group noun in this sentence. Since the individuals are acting separately, the verb is plural.

Common Group Nouns

audience	family
class	group
committee	jury
council	number
crowd	team

6. The verbs *do* and *be* are often troublesome. Remember that standard English uses *s* for the third person singular.

The Verb to do

Singular **Plural**

I do   we
you do   you (plural) } do
he   they
she } does
it

In some parts of our country, it is common to hear people say, "He *don't* have the proper tools with him." This is not standard English.

The Verb to be (Past Tense)

Singular **Plural**

I was   we
you were   you } were
he   they
she } was
it

Practice

Underline the verb that agrees with the subject.

1. He (doesn't, ~~don't~~) study in the library anymore.
2. We (~~was~~, were) hoping to find him there.
3. The library (doesn't, ~~don't~~) close until eleven o'clock.
4. (~~Was~~, Were) you late tonight?
5. And (doesn't, ~~don't~~) care if you say until closing time.

Exercise 1   Making the Subject and Verb Agree

In the blanks next to each sentence, write the subject of the sentence and the correct form of the verb. An example has been done for you.

	Subject	Verb
The eleven proposals for the development of a new building at Columbus Circle (has, have) been submitted to the city.	proposals	have

1. The price of airline tickets to England (has, have) remained fairly reasonable. — PRICE / HAS
2. His decision (**requires**, require) a lot of thought. — DECISION
3. She (**doesn't**, don't) know the answers to any of the test questions. — SHE
4. Either the elevator operator or the security guard (see, **sees**) every visitor. — OPERATOR/GUARD
5. The committee (agree, **agrees**) to the fund-raising projects for this year. — committee
6. Potato chips and soda (makes up, **make up**) most of her diet. — CHIPS / SODA
7. One of the people in the audience (**is**, are) my brother. — ONE
8. There (was, **were**) two raccoons sleeping in the barn last night. — raccoons
9. Posted on the bulletin board (was, **were**) the assignments for the week. — assignments
10. Everyone (**takes**, take) the test on Monday. — EVERYONE

Exercise 2

Making the Subject and Verb Agree

In the blanks next to each sentence, write the subject of the sentence and the correct form of the verb.

	Subject	Verb

1. Included in the **price** of the trip (**was**, **were**) five **nights** in a lovely hotel and all meals.
2. **Nobody** in the family (**knows**, know) how to swim.
3. **Jerry** and **Craig** (works, **work**) well together.
4. The **number** of essay questions on the state exam (**seems**, seem) to be increasing.

5. Where (is, are) the wrapping paper for these packages?

6. In the entire building there (is, are) only two windows.

7. Either the fruit pies or that chocolate cake (looks, look) like the best choice for your picnic.

8. Performing in public (makes, make) me nervous.

9. One of my most favorite shows (is, are) *The Fantasticks*.

10. The book for the report (doesn't, don't) have to be from the reading list.

Exercise 3

Making the Subject and Verb Agree

Using your own words and ideas, complete each of the following sentences. Be sure that the verb in each sentence agrees with the subject of each sentence. Use the verbs in the present tense.

1. Our team _____

2. The box of chocolates _____

3. Both of my sisters _____

4. The effects of his pay cut on his family _____
   _____

5. Where is _____

6. Not only the teacher but also the students _____
   _____

7. The jury _____

8. Each of the contestants _____

9. Do you think there is _____

10. The table of contents in that book _____

▶ **Pronoun-antecedent agreement**

1. A pronoun must agree in number (singular or plural) with any other word to which it refers. The following sentence contains a pronoun-antecedent disagreement in number:

   Everyone worked on *their* final draft.

The problem in this sentence is that "everyone" is a singular word, but "their" is a plural pronoun. You may have often heard people use the plural pronoun "their" to refer to a singular subject. In fact, the above sentence may sound correct, but it is still a mistake in formal writing. Here are two approaches a writer might take to correct this sentence:

Everyone worked on *his* final draft.

Although you may encounter this approach in current writing, it is unpopular because it is widely considered a sexist construction.

Everyone worked on *his/her* final draft.

This form is technically correct, but if it is used several times it sounds awkward and repetitious.

The best solution is to revise such a construction so that the antecedent is plural:

All the students worked on *their* final drafts.

Another problem with pronoun-antecedent agreement in number occurs when a demonstrative pronoun (*this, that, these, those*) is used with a noun. That pronoun must agree with the noun it modifies:

Singular: this kind, that type

Incorrect: These *kind* of shoes hurt my feet.
Correct: This *kind* of shoe hurts my feet.

Plural: these kinds, those types

Incorrect: Those *type* of cars always need oil.
Correct: Those *types* of cars always need oil.

Practice 1

Rewrite each of the following sentences so that the pronoun agrees with its antecedent in *number*.

1. Everyone should bring their suggestions to the meeting.

   _____

2. This sorts of clothes are popular now.
   these sorts, this sort

3. There was not anyone who knew what they were doing.

   _____

4. If the bird watchers hope to see anything, one must get up early.
   they

5. These type of book appeals to me.
   this

2. Pronouns must also agree with their antecedents in **person**. The following sentence contains a pronoun-antecedent disagreement in person:

> When mountain climbing, *one* must maintain *your* concentration at all times.

When you construct a piece of writing, you choose a "person" to whom you direct your words. (In this book, the authors chose the word "you.") Some teachers ask students not to choose the first person ("I") because they believe such writing sounds too personal. Other teachers warn students not to use "you" because it is too casual. Whatever guidelines your teacher gives you, the important point is to be consistent in person.

Here are the correct possibilities for the above sentence:

> When mountain climbing, *one* must maintain *one's* concentration at all times.
>
> When mountain climbing, *you* must maintain *your* concentration at all times.
>
> When mountain climbing, *I* must maintain *my* concentration at all times.
>
> When mountain climbing, *we* must maintain *our* concentration at all times.

―――――― Practice 2 ――――――

Correct each of the following sentences so that the pronoun agrees with its antecedent in *person*.

1. I enjoy math exams because you can show what you know.
2. When I took geometry, we discovered that frequent review of past assignments helped make the course seem easy.
3. People always need to practice your skills in order not to forget them.
4. Math games can be fun for one if you have a spirit of curiosity.
5. When studying math, you must remember that we have to "use it or lose it."

3. The antecedent of a pronoun should not be *missing, ambiguous,* or *repetitious*.

   a. **Missing antecedent:** In Florida, *they* have many beautifully developed retirement areas.

   Possible revision: Florida has many beautifully developed retirement areas.

   Explanation: In the first sentence, who is *they*? If the context has not told us that *they* refers to the government or to the developers, then the antecedent is missing. The sentence should be rewritten in order to avoid *they*.

   b. **Ambiguous antecedent:** Margaret told Lin that *she* needed to earn one thousand dollars during the summer.

   Possible revision: Margaret said that Lin needed to earn one thousand dollars during the summer.

Explanation: In the first example, *she* could refer to either Margaret or Lin. The sentence should be revised in a way that will avoid this confusion.

c. **Repetitious pronoun and antecedent:** The newspaper article, *it* said that Earth Day, 1990, reestablished man's commitment to the earth.

Possible revision: The newspaper article said that Earth Day, 1990, reestablished man's commitment to the earth.

Explanation: The subject should be either *article* or if there is already an antecedent, *it*. Using both the noun and the pronoun results in needless repetition.

Practice 3

Rewrite the following sentences so that the antecedents are not *missing, ambiguous,* or *repetitious.*

1. The biologist asked the director to bring back his microscope.

2. In the report, it says that the number of science and engineering students seeking doctoral degrees has fallen fifty percent since the mid-sixties.

3. At the laboratory, they said the research had run into serious difficulties.

4. The testing equipment was accidentally dropped onto the aquarium, and it was badly damaged.

5. I don't watch the 10 o'clock news anymore because they have become too slick.

Exercise 1   Making Pronouns and Antecedents Agree

Each of the following sentences contains errors with pronouns. Revise each sentence so that pronouns agree with their antecedents and so that there are no missing, ambiguous or repetitious antecedents.

1. His father mailed him his high school yearbook.

2. No one wants their income reduced.

3. When a company fails to update its equipment, they often pay a price in the long run.

4. The woman today has many more options open to them than ever before.

5. Everybody knows their own strengths best.

6. Each of the workers anticipates their summer vacation.

7. If the campers want to eat quickly, each one should help themselves.

8. These sort of bathing suits look ridiculous on me.

9. On the application, it says you must pay a registration fee of thirty-five dollars.

10. The doctor said that those type of diseases are rare here.

Exercise 2

Making Pronouns and Antecedents Agree

Each of the following sentences may contain an error with pronouns. Revise each sentence so that pronouns agree with their antecedents, and so that there are no missing, ambiguous or repetitious antecedents. If a sentence is correct, mark a C on the line provided.

1. The teacher suggested to the parent that he might have been too busy to have noticed the child's unhappiness.

2. The county submitted their proposal for the bridge repairs.

3. We all rushed to our cars because you had to wait for the thunderstorm to stop.

4. A young person does not receive enough advice on how they should choose their career.

5. These type of watches are very popular.

6. People were taken forcibly from our homes.

7. No one brought their books today.

8. The college it is holding homecoming weekend on October 5.

9. They call it the "Hoosier" state.

10. Anyone who fails the final will be unlikely to get his or her diploma.

Exercise 3 — Making Pronouns and Antecedents Agree

Each of the following sentences contains an error in pronoun-antecedent agreement. Revise each sentence so that pronouns agree with their antecedents, and so that there are no missing, ambiguous or repetitious antecedents.

1. Let me tell you a story that one shivers to tell.

2. In April, Sheila went with her friend Melissa to the motor vehicle bureau where she passed her driver's test.

3. Later that month, Sheila asked her mother if she could run an errand.

4. Sheila drove to an unfamiliar town where they had never been before.

5. The radio it reported the driving was dangerous due to both rain and fog.

6. On a dark rainswept and unfamiliar road, Sheila did not see a stop sign; the car coming through the intersection from another direction didn't have time to stop. He killed my friend.

7. I believe Sheila was a good driver, but the police didn't agree with it.

8. The doctor told Sheila's parents that they did everything possible to save her.

9. Everyone feels the shock of their loss.

10. The police say those type of accidents are unfortunately very common with inexperienced drivers.

▶ Parallel structure: making a series of words, phrases, or clauses balanced within the sentence

Which one of the following sentences achieves a better sense of balance?

His favorite hobbies are playing the trumpet, listening to jazz, and to go to concerts.

His favorite hobbies are playing the trumpet, listening to jazz, and going to concerts.

If you have selected the second sentence, you have made the better choice. The second sentence uses parallel structure to balance the three phrases in the series (playing, listening, and going). By matching each of the items in the series with the same *-ing* structure, the sentence becomes easier to understand and more pleasant to read. You can make words, phrases, and even sentences in a series parallel:

1. Words in a series should be the same parts of speech.

    Incorrect: The town was small, quiet, and the atmosphere was peaceful.
    (The series is composed of two adjectives and one clause.)
    Correct: The town was small, quiet, and peaceful.
    (*Small, quiet,* and *peaceful* are adjectives.)

2. Phrases in a series should be the same kind of phrase (infinitive phrases, prepositional phrases, verb phrases, noun phrases, participial phrases).

    Incorrect: Her lost assignment is in her closet, on the floor, and the clothes are hiding it.
    (two prepositional phrases and one clause)

Correct: Her lost assignment is in her closet, on the floor, and under a pile of clothes.

(three prepositional phrases beginning with *in, on,* and *under*)

3. Clauses in a series should be parallel.

Incorrect: One clerk polished the antique spoons; they were placed into the display case by the other clerk.

Correct: One clerk polished the antique spoons; the other clerk placed them in the display case.

―――――――――― Practice ――――――――――

Each of the following sentences has an underlined word, phrase, or clause that is not parallel. Make the underlined section parallel.

1. My favorite armchair is lumpy, worn out, and <u>has dirt spots everywhere</u>.

2. She enjoys reading novels, studying the flute, and <u>also sews her own clothes</u>.

3. He admires teachers who make the classroom an exciting place and <u>willingly explaining material more than once</u>.

Exercise 1   Revising Sentences for Parallel Structure

Each of the following sentences needs parallel structure. Underline the word, phrase, or clause that is not parallel and revise it so that its structure will balance with the other items in the pair or series. An example has been done for you.

Incorrect: The best leather comes from Italy, from Spain, and <u>is imported from Brazil</u>.

Correct: The best leather comes from Italy, from Spain, and <u>from Brazil</u>.

1. Winter in Chicago is very windy and has many bitterly cold days.

2. I would prefer to fix an old car than watching television.

3. George is a helpful neighbor, a loyal friend, and dedicated to his children.

4. The apartment is crowded and without light.

5. The dancer is slender and moves gracefully.

6. The nursery was cheerful and had a lot of sun.

7. My friend loves to play chess, to read science fiction, and working out at the gym.

8. For homework today I must read a chapter in history, do five exercises for Spanish class, and working on my term paper for political science.

9. The painting reveals the artist's talent and it is imaginative.

10. The cars race down the track, turn the corner at great speed, and then they are heading for the home stretch.

Exercise 2

Revising Sentences for Parallel Structure

Each of the following sentences needs parallel structure. Underline the word, phrase, or clause that is not parallel and revise it so that its structure will balance with the other items in the pair or series.

1. The dog had to choose between jumping over the fence or he could have dug a hole underneath it.

2. She disliked going to the beach, hiking in the woods, and she didn't care for picnics, either.

3. As I looked down the city street, I could see the soft lights from restaurant windows, I could hear the mellow sounds of a night club band, and carefree moods of people walking by.

4. The singers have been on several road tours, have recorded for two record companies, and they would also like to make a movie someday.

5. They would rather order a pizza than eating their sister's cooking.

6. I explained to the teacher that my car had broken down, my books had been stolen, and I left my assignment pad home.

7. That night the prisoner was sick, discouraged, and she was filled with loneliness.

8. As the truck rumbled through the street, it suddenly lurched out of control, smashed into a parked car, and then the truck hit the storefront of my uncle's hardware store.

9. The teacher is patient, intelligent, and demands a lot.

10. He was determined to pass the math course, not only to get his three credits but also for a sense of achievement.

Exercise 3 **Revising Sentences for Parallel Structure**

Each of the following sentences needs parallel structure. Underline the word, phrase, or clause that is not parallel and revise it so that its structure will balance with the other items in the pair or series.

1. The first-grade teacher told us that our child was unruly, mischievous, and talked too much.

2. The dog's size, its coloring, and whenever it barked reminded me of a wolf.

3. Carol is not only very talented, but she is also acting kindly to everyone.

4. He dried the dishes; putting them away was the job of his wife.

5. Jordan would rather travel and see the world than staying home and reading about other places.

6. For weeks he tried to decide if he should major in chemistry, continue with accounting, or to take off a year.

7. Her depression was a result of the loss of her job, the breakdown of her marriage, and a teenage daughter who was a problem.

8. She must either cut back on her expenses, or selling her car.

9. His office is without windows, on the fourth floor, and you have to go down a dark hallway to get there.

10. He went through four years of college, one year of graduate school, and he has spent one year teaching seventh-grade science.

▶ Misplaced and dangling modifiers

Modifiers are words or groups of words that function as adjectives or adverbs. Single-word adjectives usually precede the words they modify while adjective phrases or clauses usually follow the words they modify. If the modifier is put in the wrong place, or if the modifier appears to modify the wrong word or none at all, the sentence will be confusing or even humorous.

Misplaced modifier: The salesperson sold the used car to the customer *that needed extensive body work.*

Did the *customer* need *body work?*

Revised: The salesperson sold the used car *that needed extensive body work* to the customer.

Dangling modifier: *Working on the car's engine,* the dog barked all afternoon.

Who worked on the engine? Was it the dog?

Revised: *While working on the car's engine,* I heard the dog barking all afternoon.

(By changing the subject to *I,* the modifying phrase *While working on the car's engine* now modifies a logical subject.)

Exercise 1   Revising Misplaced or Dangling Modifiers

Revise each sentence so there is no dangling modifier.

1. Victor fed the dog wearing his tuxedo.

2. Visiting Yellowstone National Park, Old Faithful entertained us by performing on schedule.

3. Hoping to see the news, the television set was turned on and all ready by seven o'clock.

4. A woodpecker was found in Cuba that had been considered extinct.

5. After running over the hill, the farm was visible in the valley below.

6. The truck caused a traffic jam, which was broken down on the highway, for miles.

7. Hanging from the ceiling in my bedroom, I saw three spiders.

8. After wiping my glasses, the redbird flew away.

9. Howling without a stop, I listened to the neighbor's dog all evening.

10. After painting my room all afternoon, my cat demanded her dinner.

Exercise 2 — Revising Misplaced or Dangling Modifiers

Revise each sentence so there is no dangling modifier.

1. Leaping upstream, we fished most of the day for salmon.

2. At the age of ten, my family took a trip to Washington, D.C.

3. Skimming every chapter, my biology textbook made more sense.

4. Running up the stairs, the train had already left for Philadelphia.

5. Working extra hours last week, my salary increased dramatically.

6. We watched a movie in the theater for which we had paid five dollars.

7. Dressed in a Dracula costume, I thought my son looked perfect for Halloween.

8. Last week while shopping, my friend's purse was stolen.

9. While eating lunch outdoors, our picnic table collapsed.

10. Our car is in the parking lot with two bags of groceries unlocked.

Chapter review exercises

Exercise 1 Making Sentence Parts Work Together

Each sentence has a part that does not work with the rest of the sentence. Find the error and correct it.

1. A new medical study of thousands of Chinese show[s] new connections between diet and health.

2. Eating a lot of animal protein, the researchers found Western people have many health problems.

3. A person who lives in one place for a long time and who eats the same food all the time make perfect subjects for a study on diet.

4. ~~A~~ Chinese ~~person~~ [people] eat[s] very few dairy products, but they get calcium in other ways.

5. They believe ~~we~~ [they] should eat mostly vegetables.

6. One of the many results of the study ~~are~~ [is] an awareness of better eating habits.

7. ~~Those~~ Chinese who eat the most protein also have the highest rates of serious illnesses like heart disease, diabetes, and suffer~~ing~~ from cancer.

8. ~~A~~ [diets] rich diet while children are small increase[s] the risk of developing cancer later in life.

9. One of the most interesting findings ~~are~~ [is] that obesity is related more to what people eat than how much they eat.

10. These type[s] of studies have long-range value for the study of diet and health.

Exercise 2 Making Sentence Parts Work Together

Each sentence has a part which does not work with the rest of the sentence. Find the error and correct it.

1. My family need[s] to buy a car.

2. Neither a new car nor a leased car seem[s] to be a good value.

3. When car shopping, one should always do ~~your~~ their best to find a bargain.

4. Good used cars are sometimes advertised for sale in the newspapers ~~which~~ that are hard to find.

5. A car shopper must always take into account the mileage on the odometer, the condition of the engine, and is ~~the body rusty or not~~ rust on the body.

6. A good engine and transmission ~~are~~ is very important because ~~it is~~ they are so expensive to replace.

7. The car ~~it~~ should be taken to a good mechanic for an evaluation.

8. ~~In~~ several states, ~~they~~ have laws to regulate the sales of used cars.

9. For example, a dealer or a private owner ~~are~~ is not allowed to tamper with the odometer.

10. Every customer should have the right to some type of guarantee on the car~~s~~ ~~they~~ we buy~~s~~.

Exercise 3 **Making Sentence Parts Work Together**

Read the following paragraph. Look for errors in agreement, parallel structure, and misplaced or dangling modifiers. Then rewrite your corrected version on the lines provided.

Cowboys became important in the United States after the Civil War who lived on large ranches in Texas, Montana, and other Western States. One of the traditional names for cowboys are "cowpokes" although they prefer to be called "cowhands." The equipment for cowboys came into use because of ~~his~~ their many practical needs. The wide-brimmed cowboy hat served as a bucket to hold water, as a sort of whip to drive cattle, and ~~waving~~ to wave to other cowboys a few hills away. Cowboys began to wear tight trousers because they did not want loose pants to catch in bushes as they chased cattle. The rope is a cowboy's most important tool since they use it to catch cattle, pull wagons, tie up equipment, and even ~~killing~~ kill snakes. The famous roundup, which takes place twice a year, ~~are~~ is important because cattle are separated, classified, and selected for market. When cowboys get together for such a roundup, they often hold a rodeo as a celebration. Rodeos give cowboys opportunities to compete in riding bareback, wrestling steer, and ~~to rope~~ roping calves.

_____

_____

7

Solving More Problems with Verbs

Since every sentence contains at least one verb, and this verb can take one of many forms, it is worth a good deal of your time and effort to understand these many forms and uses. So far in this book, you have learned to recognize verbs (Chapter 1), to use them to make participial and gerund phrases (Chapter 2), and to make them agree with their subjects (Chapter 6). In this chapter, you will study several other areas that often cause difficulty for writers:

>   Irregular Verbs
>   Verb Tense Consistency
>   Sequence of Verb Tenses
>   Present Perfect and Past Perfect Tenses
>   Active and Passive Voice
>   The Subjunctive

▶ What are the principal parts of the irregular verbs?

The English language has more than one hundred verbs that do not form the past tense or past participle with the usual *-ed* ending. Their forms are irregular. When you listen to children aged four or five, you often hear them utter expressions such as "Yesterday I *cutted* myself." Later on, they will learn that the verb "cut" is unusual, and they will change to the irregular form, "Yesterday I *cut* myself." The best way to learn these verbs is to listen to how they sound. Pronounce them out loud over and over until you have learned them. If you find that you don't know a particular verb's meaning, or you cannot pronounce a verb and its forms, ask your instructor for help. Most irregular verbs are very common words that you will be using often in your writing and speaking. You will want to know them well.

Solving More Problems with Verbs ▸ 119

Practicing 50 irregular verbs

These are the three principal parts of irregular verbs:

Simple Form	***Past Form***	***Past Participle***
(also called **Infinitive Form**)		(used with perfect tenses after, "has," "have," or "will have" or with passive voice after the verb "to be.")

I. 8 Verbs that do not change their forms

(Notice they all end in *-t* or *-d*)

Simple Form	***Past Form***	***Past Participle***
bet	bet	bet
cost	cost	cost
cut	cut	cut
fit	fit	fit
hit	hit	hit
hurt	hurt	hurt
quit	quit	quit
spread	spread	spread

II. 2 Verbs that have the same simple present form and the past participle

Simple Form	***Past Form***	***Past Participle***
come	came	come
become	became	become

─────── Practice 1 ───────

Fill in the correct form of the verb in the following sentences.

(cost) 1. Last year the tuition for my education <u>cost</u> seven percent more than the year before.

(quit) 2. I <u>have quit</u> trying to guess my expenses for next year.

(spread) 3. The message <u>has spread</u> that college costs continue to spiral.

(hit) 4. Most parents <u>have been hit</u> with large tax increases.

(become) 5. Financing a child's higher education <u>has become</u> a difficult task.

III. 20 Verbs that have the same simple past form and past participle

Simple Form	***Past Form***	***Past Participle***
bend	bent	bent
lend	lent	lent
send	sent	sent
spend	spent	spent

Simple Form	Past Form	Past Participle
creep	crept	crept
keep	kept	kept
sleep	slept	slept
sweep	swept	swept
weep	wept	wept
teach	taught	taught
catch	caught	caught
bleed	bled	bled
feed	fed	fed
lead	led	led
speed	sped	sped
bring	brought	brought
buy	bought	bought
fight	fought	fought
think	thought	thought
seek	sought	sought

──────── Practice 2 ────────

Fill in the correct form of the verb in the following sentences.

(buy)　　1. Last year the school district _bought_ new Chemistry texts.

(spend)　2. Some parents felt they had _spent_ too much money on these new books.

(bleed)　3. They claimed the taxpayers were being _bleed_ dry.

(keep)　　4. These parents argued that the school should have _kept_ the old books.

(think)　 5. The teachers _thought_ the old books were worn out.

IV. 20 Verbs that have all different forms

Simple Form	Past Form	Past Participle
blow	blew	blown
fly	flew	flown
grow	grew	grown
know	knew	known
throw	threw	thrown
begin	began	begun
drink	drank	drunk
ring	rang	rung
shrink	shrank	shrunk
sink	sank	sunk
sing	sang	sung
spring	sprang	sprung
swim	swam	swum
bite	bit	bitten (or bit)

Solving More Problems with Verbs ▸ 121

Simple Form	Past Form	Past Participle
hide	hid	hidden (or hid)
drive	drove	driven
ride	rode	ridden
stride	strode	stridden
rise	rose	risen
write	wrote	written

―――― Practice 3 ――――

Fill in the correct form of the verb in the following sentences.

(sing) 1. Last night, the tenor _sang_ "The Flower Song" from <u>Carmen</u>.

(grow) 2. Over the past few performances, his audiences <u>have</u> _grown_.

(begin) 3. I first _began_ to enjoy his singing when I heard his voice on the radio last spring.

(hide) 4. I <u>have</u> never _hidden_ my admiration for the tenor voice.

(know) 5. Famous tenors like Enrico Caruso, John McCormack, and Luciano Pavarotti <u>are</u> _known_ all over the world.

Exercise 1   Knowing the Irregular Verb Forms

Supply the past form or the past participle for each verb in parentheses.

Ever since men _began_ (begin) to write, they <u>have</u> _written_ (write) about the great mysteries in nature. For instance, no one _knew_ (know) why the dinosaurs had disappeared. Scientists now <u>have</u> _bet_ (bet) on one strong possibility. That possibility is that sixty-five million years ago, a six-mile-wide chunk of rock _hit_ (hit) the earth and _threw_ (throw) up a thick cloud of dust. The dust _kept_ (keep) the sunlight from the earth; therefore, certain life forms disappeared. Some scientists <u>have</u> _thought_ (think) that this could also <u>have</u> _shrunk_ (shrink) the earth's animal population by as much as seventy percent. Other scientists are not so sure that this is the answer. They believe time <u>has</u> _hidden_ (hide) the real reason for the disappearance of the dinosaurs.

Developing the Complete Sentence

Exercise 2 — Knowing the Irregular Verb Forms

Supply the past form or the past participle for each verb in parentheses.

Medical researchers have _____(seek)_____ a cure for the common cold, but so far they have _____(fight)_____ without success. The cold virus has _____(spread)_____ throughout the world and the number of cold victims has _____(rise)_____ every year. Past experience has _____(teach)_____ us that people who have _____(drink)_____ plenty of liquids and taken aspirin get over colds more quickly than those who do not, but this is not a good enough remedy. Some people believed that if you _____(feed)_____ a fever, you starved a cold, but recent research has _____(lead)_____ to a disclaimer of this belief. It has _____(cost)_____ a lot of time and effort in the search for a vaccine, but so far the new knowledge has not _____(bring)_____ a cure.

Exercise 3 — Knowing the Irregular Verb Forms

Rewrite the following paragraph in the past tense.

The jockey drives his pickup truck to the race track. He strides into the stalls where the horses are kept. His head swims with thoughts of the coming race. He springs into the saddle and rides to the starting gate. The whistle blows and the horses fly out of the gate. They speed around the first turn. The crowd grows tense, and excitement spreads as the horses near the finish line.

_____
_____
_____
_____
_____
_____
_____
_____

Solving More Problems with Verbs ▶ 123

▶ Avoid unnecessary shift in verb tense

Do not shift verb tenses as you write unless you intend to change the time of the action.

Shifted tense: The customer *asked* (past tense) for the prescription, but the pharmacist *says* (present tense) that the ingredients *are being ordered* (present continuous passive voice).

Revised: The customer *asked* (past tense) for the prescription, but the pharmacist *said* (past tense) that the ingredients *were being ordered* (past continuous passive voice).

Exercise 1 — Correcting Unnecessary Shift in Verb Tense

Each sentence has an unnecessary shift in verb tense. Revise each sentence so that the tense remains consistent.

1. After I complete that writing course, I took the required history course.

   _____

   _____

2. In the beginning of the movie, the action was slow; by the end, I am sitting on the edge of my seat. [*was*]

   _____

   _____

3. The textbook gives the rules for writing a bibliography, but it didn't explain how to do footnotes. [*doesn't*]

   _____

   _____

4. While working on her report in the library, my best friend lost her note cards and comes to me for help.

   _____

   _____

5. The encyclopedia gave several pages of information about astronomy, but it doesn't give anything about "black holes."

   _____

   _____

6. The invitation requested that Juan be at the ceremony and that he will attend the banquet as well.

7. This is an exciting book, but it had too many characters.

8. The senator was doing just fine until along comes a younger and more energetic politician with firm support from the middle class.

9. At the end of *Gulliver's Travels,* the main character rejects the company of people; he preferred the company of horses.

10. My sister arrives, late as usual, and complained that her dinner was cold.

Exercise 2 — Correcting Unnecessary Shift in Verb Tense

The following paragraph contains unnecessary shifts in verb tense. Change each incorrect verb to its proper form.

The writer Willa Cather (1873–1947) grew up in Red Cloud, Nebraska, at a time when many parts of the United States were still undeveloped. In 1890 she went to college in Lincoln, Nebraska, when it was still a small town; the university is made up of only a few buildings. After graduating, she tried teaching and writing in Pittsburgh, but in New York she becomes a real success, doing magazine work and writing fiction. Later, she traveled to other parts of the country to find inspiration for her novels and short stories. She visits the Southwest to get inspiration for her novel *The*

Solving More Problems with Verbs ▸ 125

Song of the Lark, and she went to New Mexico to find material for one of her most popular books, *Death Comes for the Archbishop.* Her most famous book is *My Antonia,* a novel that told about life in the American West. In that book we see both a portrait of America and a picture of Willa Cather's own mind.

Exercise 3 **Correcting Unnecessary Shift in Verb Tense**

The following paragraph contains unnecessary shifts in verb tense. Change each incorrect verb to its proper form.

Charles Dickens was a nineteenth-century author whose work is well known today. One of the reasons Dickens remained so popular is that so many of his stories are available not only as books but also as movies, plays, and television productions. We all knew from our childhood the famous story of Uncle Scrooge and Tiny Tim. Often we saw a television version of *The Christmas Carol* at holiday time. If we have never read the story of Oliver Twist in book form, we might see the musical *Oliver!* Also, there was a movie version of *Great Expectations.* Many students still studied *A Tale of Two Cities* in high school. No matter how many adaptations of Dickens's books we see, people seem to agree that there was no substitute for the books themselves. At first, the vocabulary seemed hard to understand, but if we concentrate on the story and read a chapter or two every day, we will find ourselves not only comprehending these wonderful stories but loving the richness of Dickens's use of language.

▸ What is the sequence of tenses?

The term *sequence of tenses* refers to the proper use of verb tenses in complex sentences (sentences that have an independent clause and a dependent clause). The guide on page 126 shows the relationship between the verb in the independent clause (IC) and the verb in the dependent clause (DC).

126 ◀ Developing the Complete Sentence

Sequence of Tenses

| Independent Clause | Dependent Clause | Time of the DC in Relation to the IC |

If the tense of the independent clause is in the present (He *knows*), here are the possibilities for the dependent clause.

	that she *is* right.	at the same time
He knows	that she *was* right.	earlier
	that she *will be* right.	later

If the tense of the independent clause is in the past (he *knew*), here are the possibilities for the dependent clause.

	that she *was* right.	same time
He knew	that she *had been* right.	earlier
	that she *would be* right.	later

If the independent clause is in the future (he *will tell*), here are the possibilities for the dependent clause.

	if she *goes*.	same time
He will tell us	if she *has gone*.	earlier
	if she *will go*.	later

Practice

In each of the following sentences, choose the correct verb tense for the verb in the dependent clause. Use the guide above if you need help.

1. The program <u>will only continue</u> after the coughing and fidgeting _____.
   (to stop)

2. Since he was poor and unappreciated by the music world when he died in 1791, Mozart <u>did not realize</u> the importance that his music _____ in the twentieth century.
   (to have)

3. Dad <u>will tell</u> us tonight if he _____ a new car next month.
   (to buy)

4. Albert Einstein <u>failed</u> the entrance exam at the Swiss Federal Institute of Technology because he _____ a very disciplined student.
   (to be) + never

5. Einstein only <u>studied</u> subjects that he _____.
   (to like)

Solving More Problems with Verbs ▸ 127

6. Cancer researchers <u>think</u> it's likely that a cure for most cancers _____ found.
   (to be) + soon

7. We <u>know</u> that science _____ now close to finding a cure for leukemia.
   (to be)

8. The interviewer <u>felt</u> that the young woman _____ more than she was telling him.
   (to know)

9. The doctor went into the operating room. She <u>hoped</u> that the operation _____ out all right.
   (to turn)

10. The doctor came out of the operating room. She <u>said</u> that the operation _____ well.
    (to go)

▸ How do you use the present perfect and the past perfect tenses?

Forming the perfect tenses

Present perfect tense: "has" or "have" + past participle of the main verb
has worked
have worked

Past perfect tense: "had" + past participle of the main verb
had worked

What do these tenses mean?

The *present perfect tense* describes an action that *started in the past and continues to the present time.*

Jennifer *has worked* at the hospital for ten years.

This sentence indicates that Jennifer began to work at the hospital ten years ago and is still working there now.

Examine the following time line. What does it tell you about the present perfect tense?

```
                          present
                     (moment of speaking)
      past                    |                          future
             x x x x x x x x x
_____
          10 years       still | working
            ago                | now
```

Other example sentences of the present perfect tense:

She *has studied* violin since 1980.

I *have* always *appreciated* his generosity.

The **present perfect tense** can also describe an action that has just taken place, or where the exact time of the action in the past is indefinite.

Has Jennifer *found* a job yet?

Jennifer *has* (just) *found* a new job in Kansas City.

Have you ever *been* to San Diego?

Yes, I *have been* there three times.

If the time were definite, you would use the simple past:

Jennifer *found* a new job yesterday.

Yes, I *was* there last week.

The *past perfect tense* describes an action that occurred before another activity or another point of time in the past.

```
                        present
                  (moment of speaking)
past                                              future
     first action   second action
     in the past   in the past
          x             x
_____|_____
```

Jennifer *had worked* at the hospital for ten years *before* she *moved* away.

In this sentence, there are two past actions: Jennifer "worked," and Jennifer "moved." The action that took place first is in the past perfect (*had worked*). The action that took place later, and was also completed in the past, is in the simple past (*moved*).

```
                        present
                  (moment of speaking)
past                                              future
     first action   second action
     in the past   in the past
     x x x x x x x x x
_____|_____
     had worked      moved
```

Other example sentences using the **past perfect tense**:

I *had* just *finished* when the bell *rang*.

He *said* that Randall *had told* the class about the experiment.

He *had provided* the information *long before* last week's meeting.

Practice

Complete each of the following sentences by filling in each blank with either the present perfect tense or past perfect tense of the verb given.

1. Yolanda told us that she _____ in Fort Worth
   (live)
   before she moved to Mexico City.

2. Mexico City _____ visitors for many years.
   (fascinate)

3. This city _____ the third largest city in the
(become)

world, and people _____ it grow larger every year.
(watch)

4. The suburbs of the city _____ old villages that
(overwhelm)

_____ peacefully since the days of the Aztecs.
(exist)

5. Today, Mexico City _____ a computer controlled
(build)

subway system to deal with its huge transportation problem.

▶ What is the difference between passive and active voice?

In **active voice**, the subject does the acting:

The committee made the decision.

In **passive voice**, the subject is acted upon:

The decision was made (by the committee).

The subject *decision* in the second sentence did nothing. In other words, the subject is passive. It did no acting. It was acted upon. Writers may use passive voice to avoid naming the actor. In fact, the actor may not always be known. Consider this sentence:

Somebody shot John F. Kennedy in 1963.

This sentence is in the active voice. Such a sentence emphasizes the subject *somebody*. The writer may not want to emphasize the actor in this case.

The passive voice, on the other hand, would allow a writer to emphasize the importance of the person or thing acted upon. Consider the following sentence:

John F. Kennedy was shot in 1963.

Such a sentence in the passive voice allows a writer to stress the importance of the person or event acted upon—in this case, John F. Kennedy.

How do you form the passive voice?

Subject acted upon	+ verb "to be"	+ past participle	+ "by" phrase (optional)
The race	was	won	(by the runner)
The fish	was	cooked	(by the chef)
The books	are	illustrated	(by the artists)

In general, remember that writers avoid the passive voice if the active voice sounds more direct, economical, or forceful.

◀ Developing the Complete Sentence

――――――――――― **Practice** ―――――――――――

Fill in the following chart by making all sentences on the left active voice and all sentences on the right passive voice. Then discuss with your classmates and instructor why you might choose the active voice or the passive voice in each case.

Active Voice   *Passive Voice*

1. _____   1. The wrong number was dialed by the child by mistake.

2. _____   2. The sweater was crocheted very carefully by my grandmother.

3. The tornado struck Cherry Creek last spring.   3. _____

4. The wind blew the leaves across the yard.   4. _____

5. _____   5. In the 60s, platform shoes were worn by many fashionable young men and women.

▶ What is the subjunctive?

Recognize the three circumstances in which the verb does not agree with the subject.

1. Unreal conditions using *if* or *wish*

   <u>If he were</u> my teacher, I would be pleased.
   <u>I wish he were</u> my teacher.

2. Clauses starting with *that* after verbs such as *ask, request, demand, suggest, order, insist,* or *command*

   I demand <u>that she work harder.</u>
   Sullivan insisted <u>that Jones report on Tuesday.</u>

Solving More Problems with Verbs ▸ 131

3. Clauses starting with *that* after adjectives expressing urgency, as in *it is necessary, it is imperative, it is urgent, it is important,* and *it is essential*

It is necessary that she wear a net covering her hair.
It is essential that John understand the concept.

───────────── Practice ─────────────

In the following sentences, circle the subjunctives (the subjects and verbs that do not agree). Underline the word or phrase that determines the subjunctive. An example has been done for you.

Truman suggested that the country adopt the Marshall Plan in 1947.

1. When President Roosevelt died in 1945, the law required that Vice President Truman take over immediately.
2. It was essential that President Truman act quickly and decisively.
3. Truman must have wished that he were able to avoid using the atomic bomb to bring an end to World War II.
4. He felt it was necessary that the United States help Europe recover from the destruction of World War II.
5. President Truman always insisted that other countries be economically strong.

▸ **Other problems with verbs**

Do not use more than one modal auxiliary (*can, may, might, must, should, ought*) with the main verb.

Incorrect: Matt shouldn't ought to sell his car.
Correct: Matt ought not to sell his car.
or
Matt shouldn't sell his car.

Do not use *should of, would of,* or *could of* to mean *should have, would have,* or *could have*

Incorrect: Elana would of helped you if she could of.
Correct: Elana would have helped you if she could have.

▸ **Chapter review exercises**

Exercise 1   Solving Problems with Verbs

Revise each of the following sentences to avoid problems with verbs.

1. He hadn't ought drive so fast.

_____

2. The officer said that the motorist drove through a red light.

_____

132 ◀ Developing the Complete Sentence

3. I wish I was a senior.
   _____

4. She sung for a huge crowd Saturday night.
   _____

5. I was shook up by the accident.
   _____

6. The map was studied by the motorist. (use active voice)
   _____

7. My father ask me last night to help him build a deck.
   _____

8. I should of kept the promise I made.
   _____

9. I insist she keeps her records on her side of the room.
   _____

10. The ship sunk off the coast of Florida.
    _____

Exercise 2

Solving Problems with Verbs

Some of the verbs in the following paragraph are incorrect. Find the errors and correct them.

When the day arrived, my mother was jubilant. We drive to the synagogue. My aunt Sophie and her daughters comes with us. Once in the temple, the women were not allowed to sit with the men. They had to go upstairs to their assigned places. I was ask to keep my hat on and was given a shawl to wear which I seen before. I was suppose to watch for the rabbi to call me. My turn finally come. I was brung to a table in the front. There I read from the Bible in Hebrew. I knew I could of read louder, but I was nervous. My mother had said that if I was good, she would be especially proud of me, so I done my best. Afterward, I was took by my mother and other relatives to a fine kosher restaurant where we celebrated. I receive a fine gold watch.

Exercise 3 — Solving Problems with Verbs

Some of the verbs in the following paragraph are incorrect. Find the errors and correct them.

I ~~knowed~~ [knew] I was in big trouble in chemistry when I took a look at the midterm exam. My semester should ~~of~~ [have] been a lot better. The first week I had my new textbook, I ~~lend~~ [lent] it to a friend who lost it. Then I ~~catched~~ [caught] a cold and ~~miss two~~ [missed] classes. When I finally start [started] off for class, I missed the bus and walked into the classroom half an hour late. The teacher scowls [scowled] at me and ask [asked] to speak to me after class. I use [used] to always sit in the front row so I could see the board and hear the lectures, but since I ~~am~~ [was] late, I ~~have~~ [had] to take a seat in the last row. I wish I was able [were] to start this class over again the right way. No one had ought to have such an unlucky start in any class.

8

Punctuating Sentences Correctly

▶ **Eight basic uses of the comma**

Many students feel very uncertain about when to use the comma. The starting point is to concentrate on a few basic rules. These rules will cover most of your needs.

The tendency now in English is to use fewer commas than in the past. There is no one perfect complete set of rules on which everyone agrees. However, if you learn these basic eight, your common sense will help you figure out what to do in other cases. Remember that a comma usually signifies a pause in a sentence. As you read a sentence out loud, listen to where you pause within the sentence. Where you pause is often your clue that a comma is needed. Notice that in each of the examples for the following eight uses, you can pause where the comma is placed.

I. **Use a comma to separate items in a series.**

> I was angry, fretful, and impatient.
>
> I was dreaming of running in the race, finishing among the top ten, and collapsing happily on the ground.

▶ A series means more than two items.
▶ Some writers omit the comma before the *and* that introduces the last item.

> I was angry, fretful and impatient.

▶ When an address or date occurs in a sentence, each part is treated like an item in a series. A comma is put after each item, including the last:

> I lived at 428 North Monroe Street, Madison, Wisconsin, for many years.
>
> I was born on August 18, 1965, in the middle of a hurricane.

▸ A group of adjectives may not be regarded as a series if some of the words "go together." You can test by putting *and* between each item. If it doesn't work, then don't use commas.

> I carried my *old, dark green* coat.
>
> I took the *four black spotted* puppies home.
>
> I rode in his *new red sports* car.

───────── Practice 1 ─────────

In each of the following sentences, insert commas wherever they are needed.

1. Problems with the water supply of the United States, Europe, Canada and other parts of the world are growing.
2. Water is colorless, tasteless, odorless and free of calories.
3. You will use on an average day twenty-four gallons of water for flushing, thirty-two gallons for bathing and washing clothes and twenty-five gallons for other uses.
4. It took 120 gallons of water to create the eggs you ate for breakfast, 3,500 gallons for the steak you might eat for dinner, and over 60,000 gallons to produce the steel used to make your car.
5. On November 14, 1977, officials discovered a major body of polluted water in Oswego, New York.

II. Use a comma along with a coordinating conjunction to combine two simple sentences (also called independent clauses) into a single compound sentence. (See Chapter 3 on coordination.)

> The house was on fire, but I was determined not to leave my place of safety.

Be careful that you use the comma with the conjunction only when you are combining sentences. If you are combining only words or phrases, no comma is used.

> I was safe but not happy.
>
> My mother and father were searching for me.
>
> I was neither in class nor at work.

───────── Practice 2 ─────────

In each of the following sentences, insert commas wherever they are needed.

1. The most overused bodies of water are our rivers but they continue to serve us daily.
2. American cities developed understandably next to rivers and industries followed soon after in the same locations.
3. The people of the industrial age can try to clean the water they use or they can watch pollution take over.
4. The Great Lakes are showing signs of renewal yet the struggle against pollution there must continue.
5. Many people have not yet been educated about the dangers to our water supply nor are all our legislators fully aware of the problem.

III. Use a comma to follow introductory words, expressions, phrases, or clauses.

   A. Introductory words (such as *yes, no, oh, well*)

      Oh, I never thought he would do it.

   B. Introductory expressions (transitions such as *as a matter of fact, finally, secondly, furthermore, consequently*)

      Therefore, I will give you a second chance.

   C. Introductory phrases

      Long prepositional phrase: In the beginning of the course, I thought I would never be able to do the work.

      Participial phrase: Walking on tiptoe, the young mother quietly peeked into the nursery.

      Infinitive phrase: To be quite honest, I don't believe he's feeling well.

   D. Introductory dependent clauses beginning with a subordinating conjunction (See Chapter 4.)

      When the food arrived, we all grabbed for it.

Practice 3

In each of the following sentences, insert commas wherever they are needed.

1. To many people from the East, the plans to supply more water to the western states seem unnecessary.
2. However, people in the West know that they have no future without a good water supply.
3. When they entered Salt Lake Valley in 1847, the Mormons found dry soil that needed water before crops could be grown.
4. Confidently, the new settlers dug ditches that brought the needed water.
5. Learning from the past, modern farmers are trying to cooperate with nature.

IV. Use commas surrounding a word, phrase, or clause when the word or group of words interrupts the main idea.

   A. Interrupting word

      We will, however, take an X ray.

   B. Interrupting phrase

      Prepositional phrase: I wanted, of course, to stay.

      Appositive phrase: Ann, the girl with the red hair, has a wonderful sense of humor.

C. Interrupting clause:

He won't, I think, try that again.

Ann, who has red hair, has a wonderful sense of humor.

▸ Sometimes the same word can function differently.

She came to the dance; however, she didn't stay long.

In this sentence, *however* is used to combine independent clauses.

She did, however, have a good time.

In this sentence, *however* interrupts the main idea.

▸ Sometimes the same clause can be used differently.

Ann, who has red hair, has a wonderful sense of humor.

In this sentence, *who has red hair* interrupts the main idea of the sentence and so commas are used.

That girl who has red hair is my sister Ann.

The clause *who has red hair* is part of the identity of "that girl." This clause does not interrupt the main idea but is necessary to and part of the main idea. Therefore, no commas are used.

Practice 4

In each of the following sentences, insert commas wherever they are needed.

1. Some parts of our country I believe do not have ample supplies of water.
2. The rocky soil of Virginia for example cannot absorb much rainwater.
3. Johnstown, Pennsylvania an industrial city of 48,000 is situated in one of the most flood-prone valleys of America.
4. It is not therefore a very safe place to live.
5. The Colorado which is one of our longest rivers gives up most of its water to farmers and cities before it can reach the sea.

V. **Use a comma around nouns in direct address.**

I thought, Maria, that I saw your picture in the paper.

Practice 5

In each of the following sentences, insert commas wherever they are needed.

1. Dear your tea is ready now.
2. I wonder Jason if the game has been canceled.
3. Dad could I borrow five dollars?
4. I insist sir on speaking with the manager.
5. Margaret is that you?

VI. Use a comma in numbers of one thousand or larger.

1,999
1,999,999,999

Practice 6

In each of the following numbers, insert commas wherever they are needed.

1. 4876454
2. 87602
3. 156439600
4. 187000
5. 10000000000000

VII. Use a comma to set off exact words spoken in dialogue.

"Let them," she said, "eat cake."

▸ The comma as well as the period is always placed inside the quotation marks.

Practice 7

In each of the following sentences, insert commas wherever they are necessary.

1. "I won't" he insisted "be a part of your scheme."
2. He mumbled "I plead the Fifth Amendment."
3. "I was told" the defendant explained "to answer every question."
4. "This court case" the judge announced "will be televised."
5. "The jury" said Al Tarvin of the press "was hand-picked."

VIII. Use a comma where it is necessary to prevent a misunderstanding.

Before eating, the cat prowled through the barn.

Practice 8

In each of the following sentences, insert commas wherever they are needed.

1. Kicking the child was carried off to bed.
2. To John Russell Baker is the best columnist.
3. When you can come and visit us.
4. Whoever that is is going to be surprised.
5. Skin cancer seldom kills doctors say.

Punctuating Sentences Correctly   139

Exercise 1 — Using the Comma Correctly

In each of the following sentences, insert commas wherever they are needed.

1. The penguins that live in an area of South Africa near the coast, are an endangered species.
2. One breeding ground for these penguins, tiny Dassen Island, is northwest of Cape Town.
3. Today, fewer than sixty thousand penguins can be found breeding on this island.
4. At one time, seabirds that stole the penguins' eggs were the only threat to the funny-looking birds.
5. Now human egg collectors, not to mention animals that simply take the eggs, are constantly reducing the penguin population.
6. However, the worst threat to the penguins is oil pollution.
7. If a passing tanker spills oil, many penguins can die.
8. In 1971, an oil tanker, the *Wafra*, spilled thousands of gallons of oil off the coast of southern Africa.
9. Whenever there is an oil spill near this area, the number of healthy penguins declines.
10. The ideal situation, of course, is to make the oil tankers take a completely different route.

Exercise 2 — Using the Comma Correctly

In each of the following sentences, insert commas wherever they are needed.

1. Abraham Lincoln was born on February 12 1809 in Kentucky.
2. In December 1816 after selling most of their possessions the Lincoln family moved to Indiana.
3. During their first weeks in Indiana the family hunted for food drank melted snow and huddled together for warmth.
4. After a little formal education Lincoln worked on a ferryboat on the Ohio River.
5. The first large city that Lincoln visited was New Orleans an important center of trade in 1828.
6. Among the 40000 people Lincoln found himself with on that first visit there were people from all the states and several foreign countries.
7. New Orleans also showed Lincoln the luxury that such a city could offer including fancy clothes gleaming silverware expensive furniture and imported china and glassware.
8. As a result of this visit Lincoln may have compared the log cabin of his childhood with the wealthy houses of this big city.
9. A few years later Lincoln became a merchant but the loss of all his money left him in debt for over ten years.
10. We should be grateful that Lincoln who started off in a commercial career turned his attention to politics.

140 ◀ Developing the Complete Sentence

Exercise 3   Using the Comma Correctly

In each of the following examples, insert commas wherever they are needed.

1. The Hope Diamond is one of the most famous if not the most famous gems in the world.
2. Mined in India the diamond reached Europe in 1668 along with the story that there was a curse on the stone.
3. The curse or so the legend goes is that bad fortune followed the diamond because it had been stolen from a temple in India.
4. The curse may be true since nearly all of its owners including Marie Antoinette of France a French actress who was shot to death and an American woman whose children were killed in accidents have met with tragedy.
5. Well if we cannot share in the history of the Hope Diamond we can see it in the Smithsonian Institution in Washington, D.C.
6. Other gems not as famous have served people throughout history as payments for ransom as bribes and as lavish wedding presents.
7. One of the most famous mines in South America is in Colombia where an emerald mine started in 1537 is still being worked today.
8. Some gems are difficult to find but as the earth's crust changes rough stones may find their way into streams rivers and other bodies of water where they may be found.
9. In several parts of the world notably Africa and South America the greatest number of diamonds emeralds amethyst topaz and other precious and semiprecious stones are to be found.
10. We could travel to these places if we had the time the money and the interest but we can see the most famous not to mention the most infamous stones in the Smithsonian in Washington D.C.

▶ Three uses for the apostrophe

I. To form the possessive:

A. Add *'s* to singular nouns:

the pen of the teacher   = the teacher's pen
the strategy of the boss = the boss's strategy
the work of the week   = the week's work

Watch out that you choose the right noun to make possessive. Always ask yourself *who* or *what* possesses something. In the sentences above, the teacher possesses the pen, the boss possesses the strategy, and the week possesses the work.

Note these unusual possessives:

Hyphenated words: mother-in-law's advice
Joint possession: Lucy and Desi's children
Individual possession: John's and Steve's ideas

B. Add *'s* to irregular plural nouns that do not end in *-s*.

> the hats of the children = the children*'s* hats
> the harness for the oxen = the oxen*'s* harness

C. Add *'s* to indefinite pronouns:

> everyone's responsibility
> somebody's wallet

Indefinite Pronouns

anyone	everyone	no one	someone
anybody	everybody	nobody	somebody
anything	everything	nothing	something

Possessive pronouns in English (his, hers, its, ours, yours, theirs, whose) do *not* use an apostrophe.

Whose key is this?
The key is *his*.
The car is *theirs*.

D. Add an apostrophe only to regular plural nouns ending in *-s*.

> the coats of the ladies = the ladies' coats
> the store of the brothers = the brothers' store

▸ A few singular nouns ending in the *s* or *z* sound are awkward-sounding if another *s* sound is added. You may in these cases drop the final *s*. Let your ear help you make the decision.

> Jesus' robe *not* Jesus's robe

II. To form certain plurals in order to prevent confusion, use *'s*.

Numbers: 100's
Letters: *a*'s and *b*'s
Years: 1800's or 1800s
Abbreviations: Ph.D.'s
Words referred to in a text: He uses too many *and*'s in his writing.

▸ Be sure *not* to use the apostrophe to form a plural in any case other than these.

III. To show where letters have been omitted in contractions, use an apostrophe.

cannot = can't
should not = shouldn't
will not = won't (the only contraction that changes its spelling)
I am = I'm
she will = she'll

142 ◂ Developing the Complete Sentence

Exercise 1 — Using the Apostrophe

Fill in each of the blanks below using the rules you have just studied for uses of the apostrophe.

1. rays of the sun — the _____ rays
2. sleeve of the dress — the _____ sleeve
3. width of the feet — the _____ width
4. the house of Antony and Maria (joint possession) — _____ house
5. the idea of nobody — *nobody's* idea
6. The book belongs to him. — The book is *his*.
7. in the century of 1700 — in the _____
8. That is her opinion. — *That's* her opinion.
9. shirts for boys — *boys* shirts
10. the cover of the book — the *book's* cover

Exercise 2 — Using the Apostrophe

Fill in each of the blanks below using the rules you have just studied for uses of the apostrophe.

1. clarity of the ice — the _____ clarity
2. the flight of the geese — the _____ flight
3. the work of Ann and Chris (individual possession) — _____ work
4. the plan of someone — _____ plan
5. The drums belong to her. — The drums are _____.
6. the terrible year of two — the terrible _____
7. We cannot leave yet. — We _____ leave yet.
8. the leaves of the tree — the _____ leaves
9. the cheese of the farmers — the _____ cheese
10. the life-style of my brother-in-law — my _____ life-style

Exercise 3 — Using the Apostrophe

Fill in each of the blanks below using the rules you have just studied for uses of the apostrophe.

1. the engine of the train   the _____ engine
2. the spirit of the class   the _____ spirit
3. the center for women   the _____ center
4. the wish of everybody   _____ wish
5. The toys belong to them.   The toys are _____
6. The child mixes up *b* and *d*.   The child mixes up his _____.
7. I will not leave this house.   I _____ leave this house.
8. the grain of the wood   the _____ grain
9. the story of the owners   the _____ story
10. the policies of Ridge School and Orchard School (individual possession)   _____ policies

▶ Other marks of punctuation

Quotation marks

Use quotation marks as follows.

A. For a direct quotation:

"Please," I begged, "don't go away."

Not for an indirect quotation:

I begged her not to go away.

B. For material copied word for word from a source:

According to *Science* magazine, "In an academic achievement test given to 600 sixth-graders in eight countries, U.S. kids scored last in mathematics, sixth in science, and fourth in geography."

C. For titles of shorter works such as short stories, one-act plays, poems, articles in magazines and newspapers, songs, essays, and chapters of books:

"A Modest Proposal," an essay by Jonathan Swift, is a masterpiece of satire.

"The Lottery," a short story by Shirley Jackson, created a sensation when it first appeared in the *New Yorker*.

D. For words used in a special way:

> "Duckie" is a term of affection used by the British, the way we would use the word "honey."

Underlining

Underlining is used in handwriting or typing to indicate a title of a long work such as a book, full-length play, magazine, or newspaper. (In print, such titles are put in italics.)

> ***In print:*** Many famous short stories have first appeared in the *New Yorker*.
>
> ***In type or handwriting:*** Many famous short stories have first appeared in the New Yorker.

Practice 1

In each of the following sentences, insert quotation marks wherever they are needed.

1. The Gift of the Magi is one of the short stories contained in O. Henry's book *The Four Million*.
2. Franklin Delano Roosevelt said, We have nothing to fear but fear itself.
3. The president told his cabinet that they would have to settle the problem in the next few days.
4. Punk is a particular form of rock music.
5. She read the article Trouble in Silicon Valley in last February's *Newsweek*.

If these five sentences were handwritten or typed, which words would have to be underlined?

The semicolon

Use the semicolon as follows.

A. To join two independent clauses whose ideas and sentence structure are related:

> He decided to consult the map; she decided to ask the next pedestrian she saw.

B. To combine two sentences using an adverbial conjunction:

> He decided to consult the map; however, she decided to ask the next pedestrian she saw.

C. To separate items in a series when the items themselves contain commas:

> I had lunch with Linda, my best friend; Mrs. Zhangi, my English teacher; and Jan, my sister-in-law.

Notice in the last example that if only commas had been used, the reader might think six people had gone to lunch.

Practice 2

In each of the following sentences, insert a semicolon wherever needed.

1. One of the best ways to remember a vacation is to take numerous photos one of the best ways to recall the contents of a book is to take notes.
2. The problem of street crime must be solved otherwise, the number of vigilantes will increase.
3. The committee was made up of Kevin Corey, a writer Anita Lightburn, a professor and T. P. O'Connor, a politician.
4. The bank president was very cordial however, he would not approve the loan.
5. Robots are being used in the factories of Japan eventually they will be common in this country as well.

The colon

Use the colon as follows.

A. After a *complete* sentence when the material that follows is a list, an illustration, or an explanation:

 1. A list:

 Please order the following items: five dozen pencils, twenty rulers, and five rolls of tape.

Notice that in the sentence below, no colon is used because there is not a complete sentence before the list.

 The courses I am taking this semester are Freshman Composition, Introduction to Psychology, Art Appreciation, and Survey of American Literature.

 2. An explanation or illustration:

 She was an exceptional child: At seven she was performing on the concert stage.

B. For the salutation of a business letter:

 To whom it may concern:
 Dear Madam President:

C. In telling time:

 We will eat at 5:15.

D. Between the title and subtitle of a book:

 Plain English Please: A Rhetoric

Practice 3

In each of the following sentences, insert colons where they are needed.

1. Three pianists played in New York on the same weekend Andre Watts, Claudio Arrau, and Jorge Bolet.
2. The official has one major flaw in his personality greed.
3. The restaurant has lovely homemade desserts such as German chocolate layer cake and baked Alaska.
4. The college offers four courses in English literature Romantic Poetry, Shakespeare's Plays, The British Short Story, and The Modern Novel.
5. Arriving at 615 in the morning, Marlene brought me a sausage and cheese pizza, soda, and a gallon of ice cream.

The dash and parentheses

The comma, dash, and parentheses can all be used to show an interruption of the main idea. The particular form you choose depends on the degree of interruption.

Use the dash for a less formal and more emphatic interruption of the main idea.

> He came—I thought—by car.
>
> She arrived—and I know this for a fact—in a pink Cadillac.

Use the parentheses to insert extra information that some of your readers might want to know but that is not at all essential for the main idea. Such information is not emphasized.

> Johann Sebastian Bach (1685–1750) composed the "Preludes and Fugues."
>
> Plea bargaining (see page 28) was developed to speed court verdicts.

Practice 4

Insert dashes or parentheses wherever needed.

1. Herbert Simon is and I don't think this is an exaggeration a genius.
2. George Eliot her real name was Mary Ann Evans wrote *Silas Marner*.
3. You should in fact I insist see a doctor.
4. Unemployment brings with it a number of other problems see the study by Brody, 1982.
5. Mass media television, radio, movies, magazines, and newspapers are able to transmit information over a wide range and to a large number of people.

Punctuating Sentences Correctly ▶ 147

Exercise 1

Other Marks of Punctuation

In each of the following sentences, insert marks of punctuation wherever they are needed.

1. To measure crime, sociologists have used three different techniques official statistics, victimization surveys, and self-report studies.
2. The Bells is one of the best-loved poems of Edgar Allan Poe.
3. The lake this summer has one major disadvantage for swimmers seaweed.
4. E. B. White wrote numerous essays for adults however, he also wrote a few very popular books for children.
5. Tuberculosis also known as consumption has been nearly eliminated by medical science.
6. The Victorian Period 1837–1901 saw a rapid expansion in industry.
7. He promised me I know he promised that he would come to my graduation.
8. Do you know what the expression *déjà vu* means?
9. She wanted to go to the movies he decided to stay home and see an old film on his new video cassette recorder.
10. She has the qualifications needed for the job a teaching degree, a pleasant personality, two years' experience, and a love of children.

Exercise 2

Other Marks of Punctuation

In each of the following sentences, insert marks of punctuation wherever they are needed.

1. Many young people have two feelings about science and technology awe and fear.
2. Mr. Doyle, the realtor Mrs. White, the bank officer and Scott Castle, the lawyer are the three people to help work out the real estate transaction.
3. The book was entitled English Literature The Victorian Age.
4. I decided to walk to school, she said, because the bus fare has been raised again.
5. She brought a bathing suit, towel, sunglasses and several books to the beach.
6. The conference I believe it is scheduled for sometime in January will focus on the development of a new curriculum.
7. The song Memories comes from the Broadway show Cats.
8. The complex lab experiment has these two major problems too many difficult calculations and too many variables.
9. The mutt that is to say my dog is smarter than he looks.
10. Violent crime cannot be reduced unless the society supports efforts such as strengthening the family structure, educating the young, and recruiting top-notch police.

Exercise 3 — Other Marks of Punctuation

In each of the following sentences, supply marks of punctuation wherever they are needed.

1. Star Wars is the popular term for the development of atomic weapons for use in space.
2. Remember, the doctor told the patient, the next time I see you I want to see an improvement in your condition.
3. The student's short story Ten Steps to Nowhere appeared in a collection entitled The Best of Student Writing.
4. The report stated specifically that the company must if it wanted to grow sell off at least ten percent of its property.
5. The foreign countries she visited are Mexico, Israel, and Morocco.
6. My father enjoyed spending money my mother was frugal.
7. These students made the high honor roll David Hyatt, Julie Carlson, and Erica Lane.
8. The scientist showed the class a glass of H_2O water and asked them to identify the liquid.
9. He said that he would give us an extension on our term papers.
10. The work was tedious nevertheless, the goal of finding the solution kept him motivated.

▶ Chapter review exercises

Exercise 1 — Editing for Correct Punctuation

Read the following paragraph and insert the following marks of punctuation wherever they are needed.

a. commas to separate items in a series
b. comma with coordinating conjunction to combine sentences
c. comma after introductory words, phrases, or clauses
d. commas around words that interrupt main idea
e. comma to set off spoken words
f. parentheses
g. quotation marks
h. underlining titles of full-length works of art
i. semicolon
j. apostrophe

Will Rogers 1879–1935 is often remembered as the cowboy philosopher.

He was born on November 4 1879 on a ranch near Oologah Oklahoma.

After two years in a military academy he left school and became a cowboy in the Texas Panhandle. Then he drifted off to Argentina later he turned up in South Africa as a member of Texas Jacks Wild West Circus. He was one of the best ropers of all times but his real talent was his ability as a writer. He became famous for his homespun humor and his shrewd timely comments on current events. His comments on the news appeared in 350 daily newspapers. He always began a performance by saying All I know is what I read in the papers. This saying became a byword in the 1920s. Rogers married Betty Blake an Arkansas school teacher in 1908 and together they had four children. Although he started his motion picture career in 1918 it was not until 1934 that he made his first appearance in a stage play Ah, Wilderness by Eugene O'Neill. Unfortunately Rogers was killed the next year in a plane crash near Point Barrow Alaska on his way to the Orient.

Exercise 2

Editing for Correct Punctuation

Read the following paragraph and insert the following marks of punctuation wherever they are needed.

a. commas to separate items in a series
b. comma with coordinating conjunction to combine sentences
c. comma after introductory words, phrases, or clauses
d. comma around words that interrupt main idea
e. comma in numbers of one thousand or larger
f. parentheses
g. quotation marks
h. underlining titles of full-length works of art
i. semicolon
j. colon
k. apostrophe

Albert Schweitzer was a brilliant German philosopher physician musician clergyman missionary and writer on theology. Early in his career he based his philosophy on what he called reverence for life. He felt a deep sense of obligation to serve mankind. His accomplishments as a humanitarian were great consequently he was awarded the Nobel Peace Prize in 1952. Before Schweitzer was 30 he had won an international reputation as a writer on theology as an organist and authority on organ building as an interpreter of the works of Johann Sebastian Bach and as an authority on Bachs life. When he became inspired to become a medical missionary he studied medicine at the university in Strasbourg Germany. He began his work in French Equatorial Africa now called Gabon in 1913 where his first consulting room was a chicken coop. Over the years he built a large hospital where thousands of Africans were treated yearly. He used his $33000 Nobel prize money to expand the hospital and set up a leper colony in fact he even designed all the buildings. One of Schweitzers many famous books which you might like to find in the library is entitled Out of My Life and Thought. His accomplishments were so many music medicine scholarship theology and service to his fellow man.

Exercise 3 — Editing for Correct Punctuation

Read the following paragraph and insert the following marks of punctuation wherever they are needed.

a. commas to separate items in a series
b. comma with coordinating conjunction to combine sentences
c. comma after introductory words, phrases, or clauses
d. commas around words that interrupt main idea
e. quotation marks
f. underlining titles of full-length works of art
g. apostrophe
h. semicolon

Valentines Day is celebrated on February 14 as a festival of romance and affection. People send their sweethearts greeting cards that ask Won't you be my Valentine? Children like to make their own valentines from paper doilies red construction paper bright foils and wallpaper samples.

These customs probably came from an ancient Roman festival called Lupercalia which took place every February 15. The festival honored Juno the Roman goddess of women and marriage and Pan the god of nature. Young men and women chose partners for the festival by drawing names by chance from a box. After exchanging gifts they often continued to enjoy each others company long after the festival and many were eventually married. After the spread of Christianity churches tried to give Christian meaning to the pagan festival. In 496 the Pope changed the Lupercalia festival of February 15 to Saint Valentines Day on February 14 but the sentimental meaning of the old festival has remained to the present time. Saint Valentine is believed to be a priest who was jailed for aiding the persecuted Christians. People believe he cured the jailkeepers daughter of blindness. According to the book Popular Antiquities which was written in 1877 people were observing this holiday in England as early as 1446. One account tells of young men wearing the names of their ladies on their sleeves for several days. The expression He wears his heart on his sleeve probably came from this custom. In the United States Valentines Day became popular in the 1800s at the time of the Civil War. Many of the valentines of that period were hand painted and today their beautiful decorative qualities make them collectors items.

9

Part I Review: Using All You Have Learned

▶ **Revising more complicated fragments and run-ons**

By now, you have learned to recognize the basic fragment or run-on error in your writing. You have worked with revising fairly uncomplicated sentences so that they are correct.

This chapter presents sentences that are more complicated. Even though a sentence may have more than one dependent clause and several phrases, you must always remember that the sentence must have an independent clause with a subject and verb. For example:

> When my family finally went on a vacation which was to take us across Canada by train, we never guessed that my three younger brothers would come down with the chicken pox on the second day.

Cross out all dependent clauses and phrases. Can you find the independent clause? What is the subject? What is the verb? *We never guessed* is the independent clause. All other parts of the sentence are dependent clauses that include many prepositional phrases.

The following exercises require mastery of all the skills you have learned in this unit on the sentence. See if you can now revise these more complicated sentences to rid them of fragments and run-ons.

Exercise 1   **Correcting More Complicated Fragments and Run-Ons**

Read each example on the following page. If you think the example is a complete sentence, place a C beside the number of the sentence. If you think the example is not correct, revise it so that the sentence is complete. Use the methods you have studied for coordination and subordination.

Part I Review: Using All You Have Learned   153

1. Tokyo and New York, two of the largest cities in the world, but they have very different histories.

2. While New York was still a small city in the 1700s, Tokyo was the largest city in the world its only rival was Peking in China.

3. Now in the twentieth century, New York the dominant urban center, Tokyo catching up in the last twenty years.

4. The time of greatest growth for both cities began with the twentieth century.

5. Tokyo, the capital of a rapidly industrializing nation, New York with immigrants coming from all over Europe.

6. Originally New York had immigrants mostly from Europe now Latin America and Asia are other major sources of immigrant populations.

7. Tokyo faces an uncertain economic future also a natural disaster in the form of earthquakes.

154 ◂ Developing the Complete Sentence

8. The average citizen of Tokyo does not even think of earthquakes this disaster nevertheless will most certainly come to this city in the next few decades.

   _____
   _____
   _____
   _____

9. Visitors from Tokyo often say that they feel at home in New York the same dense populations and the same fast pace are found in both cities.

   _____
   _____
   _____
   _____

10. Although Tokyo may be more expensive than New York and New York may have more crime the two most exciting cities in the world today.

    _____
    _____
    _____
    _____

Exercise 2   Correcting More Complicated Fragments and Run-Ons

Read each example. If you think the example is a complete sentence, place a C beside the number of the sentence. If you think the example is not correct, revise it so that the sentence is complete. Use the methods you have studied for coordination and subordination.

1. Dinner in India is an experience that Western people find very strange things we take for granted are not always available there.

   _____
   _____
   _____
   _____

2. Whenever you eat an Indian meal you are not given anything to drink it is not considered appropriate to drink a beverage with a meal.

   _____
   _____
   _____
   _____

3. Indian food is eaten with the right hand, you pick up a piece of bread or some rice and scoop up some food.

4. However, when water for rinsing the fingers is given to you at the end of the meal.

5. Because Indian food is so spicy and there are so many different pickles and relishes that are served with nearly every meal.

6. Indians serve plain yogurt with their meals in order to comfort the mouth after spicy foods have been eaten.

7. The habit of chewing betel leaves and betel nuts aiding digestion and sweeten the breath.

8. Breakfast in India, unlike breakfast in the United States.

9. For breakfast, people in India eat dishes of rice and lentils in addition a special lentil soup is part of their first meal of the day.

10. Often trying different kinds of food but sometimes thinking the best meal of all is a good juicy steak.

Exercise 3

Correcting More Complicated Fragments and Run-Ons

Read each example. If you think the example is a complete sentence, place a C beside the number of the sentence. If you think the example is not correct, revise it so that the sentence is complete. Use the methods you have studied for coordination and subordination.

1. Because the Golden Gate Bridge has been freshly painted with a color that blends beautifully with the color of the sunset.

2. The roses which are in full bloom in Golden Gate Park.

3. On Fisherman's Wharf, a few men are sitting together talking about the days when the fish were plentiful they caught so many that they thought the supply would never run out.

4. Some people, thinking that the famous cable cars of San Francisco are noisier now that they have been repaired.

Part I Review: Using All You Have Learned ▸ 157

5. If you visit San Francisco and you are planning some trips into the surrounding countryside.

_____

_____

_____

6. Since the city itself has not only cable cars but also buses and trolleys that make up one of the easiest-to-use public transportation systems in the country.

_____

_____

_____

7. San Francisco is an easy place to see two or three days will permit you to enjoy most of the city's highlights.

_____

_____

_____

8. On a weekend everyone trying to see Fisherman's Wharf, Nob Hill, the Union Square shopping district, and North Beach.

_____

_____

_____

9. You can now take a tour of the famous Alcatraz prison where prisoners once spent many years behind bars tourists now walk at leisure.

_____

_____

_____

_____

10. For a taste of the local history, you could visit Fort Point, a fortress built during the Civil War to guard the entrance to the bay.

_____

_____

_____

Exercise 4 **Correcting More Complicated Fragments and Run-Ons**

Read each example. If you think the example is a complete sentence, place a C beside the number of the sentence. If you think the example is not correct, revise it so that the sentence is complete. Use the methods you have studied for coordination and subordination.

1. In 1985 hundreds of people waiting for organ transplants.

2. All the people who need transplants are desperate they only have a certain time left to live.

3. In recent years, a number close to one thousand people who have needed transplants.

4. In spite of the appeals for organ transplants, very few people donate their organs.

5. Every state is in need of organ donors, some states need more than others.

6. Since organs are in so much demand, all over the world and for large sums of money.

7. A group that has special problems are those who need kidney transplants and they are afraid that if other treatment fails they will have no hope.

8. In 1985 when it was discovered that some people were selling their kidneys to wealthy people in need of them.

9. A whole new area of medical, legal, and ethical problems.

10. The need for closer government regulation of organ sales, transplants, and research.

▶ Editing sentences for errors

In the following exercises, you will find all types of sentence problems that you have studied in Part I. If you think an example is correct, mark it with a *C*. If you think there is an error, correct the error so that the sentence is correct.

Major Sentence Errors
Fragments
Run-ons
Incorrect punctuation
Sentence parts that do not work together

Exercise 1 — Editing Sentences for Errors

The following examples contain sentence errors studied in Part I. If you think an example is a complete and correct sentence, mark it with a *C*. If the example has an error, correct it. An example has been done for you.

Incorrect: A group of Gypsies who now live in Ireland.
Correct: A group of Gypsies now live in Ireland.
or
A group of Gypsies, who now live in Ireland, make their living by repairing pots and pans.

1. Gypsies now living in many countries of the world.

2. The international community of scientists agree that these Gypsies originally came from India thousands of years ago. (Hint: Look at subject and verb.)

3. After the original Gypsies left India they went to Persia there they divided into groups.

4. One branch of Gypsies went west to Europe the other group decided to go east.

5. In the Middle Ages 476–1453 some Gypsies lived in a fertile area of Greece called Little Egypt.

6. Gypsies often found it hard to gain acceptance in many countries. Because of their wandering life-style.

7. Although the Gypsies needed the protection from the pope in Rome.

8. In the year 1418 when large bands of Gypsies passed through Hungary and Germany where the emperor offered them his protection.

9. Between the fifteenth and eighteenth centuries, every country of Europe had Gypsies however not every one of those countries enjoyed having them as guests.

10. Today Gypsy families may be found from Canada to Chile living much as his ancestors did thousands of years ago.

Exercise 2

Editing Sentences for Errors

The following examples contain sentence errors studied in Part I. If you think an example is a complete and correct sentence, mark it with a C. If the example has an error, correct it. An example has been done for you.

Incorrect: The idea of travel by stagecoach in the Old West a very romantic idea for most of us today was often dangerous and uncomfortable for people a century ago.

Correct: The idea of travel by stagecoach in the Old West (a very romantic idea for most of us today) was often dangerous and uncomfortable for people a century ago.

1. The typical stagecoach provided fifteen inches of bench space for each of six nine or twelve passengers.

2. The stagecoach carried mail and baggage in covered compartments they carried additional goods and passengers on the roof.

3. Since robbers often attacked the stagecoaches.

4. Drivers tried to travel as rapidly as possible nevertheless the average stagecoach seldom went more than nine miles an hour.

5. Stagecoach operators often found that replacement teams of horses were not always available when they stopped to change teams.

6. If a coach was weighed down and the horses were tired something that happened fairly often the passengers would be asked to walk behind the coach in order to lighten the load.

7. When passengers stopped at relay stations they often would have twenty-five to forty minutes to order and eat a meal.

8. Each meal could cost as much as a dollar a very high price for those days.

9. Obtaining fresh water was often a real problem in fact passengers sometimes had to walk over a mile from the stagecoach to get a drink at a rest stop.

10. Stagecoach passengers of a hundred years ago were hungry uncomfortable and often in danger however they had to put up with all of the inconvenience because there was no other ways to travel.

Exercise 3 Editing Sentences for Errors

The following examples contain sentence errors studied in Part I. If you think an example is correct, mark it with a C. If the example has an error, correct it. An example has been done for you.

Incorrect: Science fiction writers have created magic rays that can destroy entire cities, but in recent years a magic ray in the form of laser beams have become scientific fact.

Correct: Science fiction writers have created magic rays that can destroy entire cities, but in recent years a magic ray in the form of laser beams has become scientific fact.

1. The laser beam a miracle of modern science already has many practical uses in today's world.

2. Laser beams are narrow, highly concentrated beams of light that burns brighter than the light of the sun.

3. They have found many possible military uses for the laser, but they are hoping it can be converted into constructive channels.

4. Movie audiences saw the laser beam at work in *Goldfinger* when the villain used a laser against James Bond.

5. The possibility of making a laser was first described in 1958 and two years later in California the first laser beam was created.

6. Since they are so precise, laser beams are used in medicine to help make a specific diagnosis and to perform operations such as repairing delicate retinas and the removal of cancerous tumors. (*Hint:* parallel construction.)

Part I Review: Using All You Have Learned ▶ 165

7. In the area of communication, laser beams with the ability to carry thousands of telephone conversations at once, or transmit all of the information in a twenty-volume encyclopedia in a fraction of a second.

8. Lasers are also used to help in the building of bridges and tunnels, it helps make sure that both ends meet properly.

9. The word laser comes from the words "light amplification by stimulated emission of radiation."

10. The future uses of the laser seems endless, and it is up to us whether we want to use this invention for war or for peaceful purposes.

Exercise 4   Editing Sentences for Errors

The following examples contain sentence errors studied in Part I. If you think the example is a complete and correct sentence, mark it with a C. If the example has an error, correct it. An example has been done for you.

Incorrect: Most of us buy our food in stores, people in more than one part of the world still hunt for their food.

Correct: While most of us buy our food in stores, people in more than one part of the world still hunt for their food.

Developing the Complete Sentence

1. For the Eskimos of Alaska, hunting for whales are important in the economy of the people.

2. Among the Eskimos, a good hunter one of the most respected members of the community.

3. In the spring, the Eskimos who know that the whaling season is about to begin set up camps to prepare for the hunt.

4. The arrival of some Eskimos from faraway places just to be present at the hunt.

5. Children are excused from school for as long as six weeks they help with the work of the camp.

6. While the men go out in their boats, the women and children stay in camp cooking meals and to take care of the dog teams.

7. Sometimes a period of several days go by with no success for the boat crews.

8. Eventually, the people in the camps hear the shouts of the boat crews a whale has been caught.

9. Eskimos use every part of the captured whales the blubber is used for fuel, the meat is eaten, and the internal organs are fed to the dogs.

10. Because the Eskimos are careful hunters and only kill what they use.

Exercise 5

Editing Sentences for Errors

The following examples contain sentence errors studied in Part I. If you think an example is a complete and correct sentence, mark it with a C. If the example has an error, correct it. An example has been done for you.

Incorrect: Although there are many tricks that we would like to teach our pets.

Correct: Although there are many tricks that we would like to teach our pets, few of us have the time and patience required for a training program.

1. Porpoises also known as dolphins are amazing animals.

2. Among their many tricks they can play baseball and basketball jump through hoops ring bells and raise flags.

3. Porpoises are able to use a kind of radar to find objects it cannot see.

4. The wonderful ability of porpoises to imitate human speech.

5. A movie and a television series with a real porpoise named Flipper.

6. Trained porpoises now do tricks for thousands of people, who are in zoos and marinelands from Florida to Hawaii.

7. Because they like to ride in the waves made by the boat.

8. The first step in training a porpoise is to observe their natural behavior.

9. Porpoises have always been helpful and friendly toward humans indeed stories of their good relationships with people go back thousands of years.

10. If you throw a ball to a porpoise he will probably throw it back to you.

PART II

Mastering the Paragraph

10

Working with Paragraphs: Topic Sentences and Controlling Ideas

▶ **What is a paragraph?**

A *paragraph* is a group of sentences written to develop one main idea. A paragraph may stand by itself as a complete piece of writing, or it may be a section of a longer piece of writing, such as an essay.

There is no single rule to tell you how long a paragraph should be, but if a paragraph is too short, the reader will feel that basic information is missing. If the paragraph is too long, the reader will be bored or confused. An effective paragraph is always long enough to develop the main idea that is being presented. A healthy paragraph usually consists of at least six sentences and no more than ten or twelve sentences. You have undoubtedly read paragraphs in newspapers that are only one sentence long, but in fully developed writing one sentence is usually not an acceptable paragraph.

▶ **What does a paragraph look like?**

Some students come to college not accustomed to using standard paragraph form. Study the following paragraph to observe standard form. Margins, indentation, and complete sentences are the essential parts of paragraph form.

This paragraph is taken from the essay "A Cold-Water Flat" by Elizabeth Pollet:

First word indented

Consistent margin of at least one inch on each side.

I got the job. I worked in the bank's city collection department. For weeks I was like a mouse in a maze: my feet scurried. Every seventh day I received thirteen dollar bills. It wasn't much. But, standing beside the pneumatic tube, unloading the bundles of mail that pelted down and distributing them according to their texture, size, and color to my superiors at their desks, I felt humble and useful.

Blank space after the final word.

Working with Paragraphs: Topic Sentences and Controlling Ideas ▶ 171

Exercise 1   **Standard Paragraph Form**

Write the following six sentences in standard paragraph form. As you write, use margins, indentation, and complete sentences. Each sentence must begin with a capital letter and end with a period, question mark, or exclamation point.

1. In the large basement of the school, thirty families huddled in little groups of four or five.
2. Volunteer workers were busy carrying in boxes of clothing and blankets.
3. Two Red Cross women stood at a long table sorting through boxes to find sweaters and blankets for the shivering flood victims.
4. One heavyset man in a red woolen hunting jacket stirred a huge pot of soup.
5. Men and women with tired faces sipped their steaming coffee and wondered if they would ever see their homes again.
6. Outside the downpour continued.

_____

_____

_____

_____

_____

_____

_____

_____

_____

_____

_____

_____

Exercise 2   **Standard Paragraph Form**

Write the following seven sentences in standard paragraph form. As you write, use margins, indentation, and complete sentences. Each sentence must begin with a capital letter and end with a period, question mark, or exclamation point.

1. Friday afternoon I was desperate to get my English homework finished before I left the campus.
2. The assignment was due on Monday, but I really wanted my weekend free.
3. As I sat at the table in the library, I could see dictionaries and other reference books on the nearby shelves.

4. I felt in a good mood because I knew that if I had to find some information for my assignment, it would be available to me.
5. The only worry I had was whether or not I would be interrupted by my friends who might stop by, wanting to chat.
6. Luckily I worked along with no interruptions and was able to finish my work by five o'clock.
7. My weekend was saved!

_____
_____
_____
_____
_____
_____
_____
_____
_____
_____
_____
_____
_____
_____

▶ What is a topic sentence?

A *topic sentence* is the sentence in a paragraph that states the main idea of that paragraph. It is the most general sentence of the paragraph. All the other sentences of the paragraph serve to explain, describe, extend, or support this main-idea sentence.

Most paragraphs you read will begin with the topic sentence. However, some topic sentences come in the middle of the paragraph; others come at the end. Some paragraphs have no stated topic sentence at all; in those cases, the main idea is implied. Students are usually advised to use topic sentences in all their work in order to be certain that the writing has a focus and develops a single idea at a time. Whether you are taking an essay exam in a history course, doing a research paper for a sociology course, or writing an essay in a freshman composition course, thoughtful use of the topic sentence will always

Working with Paragraphs: Topic Sentences and Controlling Ideas ▶ 173

bring better results. Good topic sentences help both the writer and the reader to think clearly about the main points.

Below are two paragraphs. Each paragraph makes a separate point, which is stated in its topic sentence. In each of these paragraphs, the topic sentence happens to be first. Read the paragraphs and notice how the topic sentence is the most general sentence; it is the main idea of each paragraph. The other sentences explain, describe, extend, or support the topic sentence.

Model Paragraph 1

I went through a difficult period after my father died. I was moody and sullen at home. I spent most of the time in my bedroom listening to music on the radio, which made me feel even worse. I stopped playing soccer after school with my friends. My grades in school went down. I lost my appetite and seemed to get into arguments with everybody. My mom began to look worried, but I couldn't bring myself to participate in an activity with any spirit. It seemed life had lost its joy for me.

Model Paragraph 2

Fortunately, something happened that spring that brought me out of my depression. My uncle, who had been crippled in the Vietnam War, came to live with us. I learned many years later that my mother had asked him to come and live with us in the hope that he could bring me out of myself. I, on the other hand, was told that it was my responsibility to help my uncle feel at home. My mother's plan worked. My uncle and I were both lonely people. A friendship began that was to change both our lives for the better.

Exercise 1 — Finding the Topic Sentence of a Paragraph

Each of the following five paragraphs contains a topic sentence that states the main idea of the paragraph. Find which sentence best states the main idea and underline it. The topic sentence will not always be the first sentence of the paragraph.

1. Mountains of disposable diapers are thrown into garbage cans every day. Tons of yogurt containers, soda cans, and other plastic items are discarded without so much as a stomp to flatten them out. If the old Chevy is not worth fixing, tow it off to sit with thousands of others on acres of fenced-in junkyards. Radios, televisions, and toasters get the same treatment because it is easier and often less expensive to buy a new product than to fix the old one. Who wants a comfortable old sweater if a new one can be bought on sale? No thought is given that the new one will soon look like the old one after two or three washings. <u>We are the great "Let's junk it" society!</u>

2. <u>The airshaft was a horrible invention.</u> Even with the windows tightly sealed, it served as a sounding box and you could hear everybody's business. Rats scurried around the bottom. There was always the danger of fire. A match absently tossed into the airshaft by a drunken teamster under the impression that he was throwing it into the yard or street would set the house afire in a moment. There were vile things cluttering up the bottom. Since this bottom couldn't be reached by man (the windows being too small to admit

the passage of a body), it served as a fearful repository for things that people wanted to put out of their lives. Rusted razor blades and bloody cloths were the most innocent items.

3. Anything can happen at a county agricultural fair. It is the perfect human occasion, the harvest of the fields and of the emotions. To the fair come the man and his cow, the boy and his girl, the wife and her green tomato pickle, each anticipating victory and the excitement of being separated from his money by familiar devices. It is at a fair that man can be drunk forever on liquor, love, or fights; at a fair that your front pocket can be picked by a trotting horse looking for sugar, and your hind pocket by a thief looking for his fortune.

4. This was one of the worst situations I had ever been in. There was a tube in my nose that went all the way to the pit of my stomach. I was being fed intravenously, and there was a drain in my side. Everybody came to visit me, mainly out of curiosity. The girls were all anxious to know where I had gotten shot. They had heard all kinds of tales about where the bullet struck. The bolder ones wouldn't even bother to ask: they just snatched the cover off me and looked for themselves. In a few days, the word got around that I was in one piece.

5. On hot summer days, the only room of the house that was cool was the sunporch. My mother brought all her books and papers and stacked them up on the card table. There she would sit for hours at a stretch with one hand on her forehead trying to concentrate. Baby Kathleen would often sit in her playpen beside her, throwing all her toys out of the pen or screeching with such a piercing high pitch that someone would have to come and rescue mom by giving the baby a cracker. Father would frequently bring in cups of tea for everyone and make mother laugh with his Irish sense of humor. It was there I would love to curl up on the wicker sofa (which was too short for my long legs even at twelve) and read one of the forty or fifty books I had bought for ten cents each at a local book fair. The sounds of neighborhood activities—muted voices, a back door slamming, a dog barking—all these were a background that was friendly yet distant. During those summer days, the sunporch was the center of our lives.

Exercise 2 Finding the Topic Sentence of a Paragraph

Each of the following five paragraphs contains a sentence that states the main idea of the paragraph. Find which sentence best states the main idea and then underline it. In these paragraphs, the topic sentence will not always be the first sentence.

1. Last evening at a party, a complete stranger asked me, "Are you a Libra?" Astrology is enjoying increasing popularity all across the United States. My wife hurries every morning to read her horoscope in the paper. At the local stores, cards, books, T-shirts, and other useless astrological products bring fat profits to those who have manufactured them. Even some public officials, like the British royal family, are known to consider the "science" of astrology before scheduling an important event.

2. Travelers to the United States have usually heard about the wonders of Niagara Falls and the Grand Canyon. They are not always so aware that an

impressive variety of other sights awaits them in this country. The spectacular beauty of the Rocky Mountains and the wide majesty of the Mississippi River are sure to please the tourist. The green hills and valleys of the East are a contrast to the purple plains and dramatic skies of the West. The sandy beaches of the southern states are becoming increasingly popular. Even the area of the Great Lakes becomes a center of activity for boating, fishing, and swimming throughout the summer months.

3. When you remember something, your brain uses more than one method to store the information. You have short-term memory, which helps you recall recent events; you have long-term memory, which brings back items that are further in the past; and you have deep retrieval, which gives you access to long-buried information that is sometimes difficult to recall. Whether these processes are chemical or electrical, we do not yet know, and much research remains to be done before we can say with any certainty. The brain is one of the most remarkable organs, a part of the body that we have only begun to investigate. It will be years before we even begin to understand all its complex processes.

4. Some of the homes were small with whitewashed walls and thatched roofs. We were eager to see how they were furnished. The living rooms were simple, often with only a plain wooden table and some chairs. The tiny bedrooms usually had room for only a single bed and a small table. Occasionally, a bedroom would be large enough to also have a stove made of richly decorated tiles. Visiting these houses was an experience that would always stay in our memory. All of the windows held boxes for flowers so that even in the dark of winter there was the promise of a blaze of colors in the spring.

5. Advertisements that claim you can lose five pounds overnight are not to be trusted. Nor are claims that your luck will change if you send money to a certain post office box in a distant state. You should also avoid chain letters you receive in the mail that promise you large amounts of money if you will cooperate and keep the chain going. Many people are suspicious of the well-publicized million-dollar giveaway promotions that seem to offer enormous cash prizes, even if you do not try the company's product. We should always be suspicious of offers that promise us something for little or no effort or money.

Exercise 3

Finding the Topic Sentence of a Paragraph

The topic sentence is missing in each of the following five paragraphs. Read each paragraph carefully and in the space provided write the letter of the best topic sentence from the four possible answers that follow each paragraph.

1. Topic sentence: _____

    The men own little more than spears and boomerangs. The women have containers made of wood or bark. They grind their grass seeds with a stone and have no more than a simple stick to dig up tubers and small creatures. These people have never learned to weave cloth for clothes, to make pottery for cooking, or to use animals to help carry their belongings.

    a. Aborigine women have very few tools with which to work.

    b. The poorest people in the world.

    c. The Aborigines of Australia have very few material possessions.

d. Aborigines can survive in the deserts of central Australia where no other people can live unless they bring their own food with them.

2. Topic sentence: _____

Actually, this idea is far from the truth. The Aborigines have been able to survive for centuries in the harsh environment of the desert because their minds are highly trained in the knowledge of food sources. Since they have no means for storing food, their entire attention must be directed toward the daily search for food. From the youngest child to the oldest member of the tribe, food gathering is the top priority. The Aborigines possess a profound understanding of the life around them.

a. In the earliest years, children are taught when foods ripen, where foods are to be found, when animals hibernate and reproduce, and where water is likely to be found.

b. The Aborigines' in-depth knowledge of the environment around them.

c. The interior of Australia is arid and inhospitable to human beings.

d. Many observers have mistakenly thought that the Aborigines, with so few tools, must have a lower intelligence than other peoples.

3. Topic sentence: _____

To catch the larger creatures—kangaroos, wallabies, and emus—the men often have to make long journeys in the cold of winter or the blazing heat of summer. The women, laden with the children and the camp gear, travel in a more or less straight line from one stopping place to the next, gathering vegetable foods, fruits, and small creatures on the way. The men often return empty-handed at the end of the day, for the desert animals are wary and difficult to capture, but the women always bring in some food. Sometimes it is not much, nor particularly tasty, but it is usually enough to keep the family going until the hunters are more successful.

a. The Aborigines are very industrious, working the entire day.

b. The labor of food-gathering is fairly equally divided between the men and the women.

c. Aboriginal men face the difficult task of finding food for their families.

d. Food-gathering among the Aborigines.

4. Topic sentence: _____

A full knowledge of the secret and ceremonial life of the tribe is possessed only by these elders. It is they who maintain the ancient laws, agree on the punishment of law-breakers, and decide when the rituals, on which the social and philosophical life of the tribe depends, will be performed. It is not, therefore, the task of a professional or priestly class to preserve the traditional myths and their associated rituals, but a number of groups of fully initiated men, each group being responsible for memorizing myths, songs, and rites belonging to their family territories, and for passing them on, unaltered, to the succeeding generation.

a. The government of these people is in the hands of the well-informed old men, not the physically active youths.

b. Passing on traditions to the next generation of Aborigines.

c. Aboriginal myths and rituals must be memorized since there is no written language.

d. The Aboriginal government is successful in getting its people to live together in harmony.

5. Topic sentence: _____

Greek tales tell of how the gods and demigods of Olympia created the volcanoes, mountains, and coastline of the Mediterranean. Sagas from Scandinavia record how gods made the universe. Myths of the Australian Aborigines tell what life was like when the world was young. They refer to this time as the "Dreamtime." Dreamtime heroes created everything in the Aborigines' daily life. Besides explaining the origin of the world about them, these myths from ancient civilizations governed the life of the people with a rich philosophy and stimulated the cultural development.

a. The myths of ancient Greece are similar to other ancient myths.

b. The myths of the Australian Aborigines are comparable to those of other ancient civilizations.

c. The myths of Greece have influenced the literature, drama, and art of the Western world for over two thousand years.

d. The myths of ancient times are accepted as absolute truth and an answer to all the questions of living.

How can you tell a topic sentence from a title?

The topic sentence works like a title by announcing to the reader what the paragraph is about. However, keep in mind that the title of an essay or book is usually a single word or short phrase, whereas the topic sentence of a paragraph must *always* be a complete sentence.

Title: Backpacking in the mountains
Topic sentence: Backpacking in the mountains last year was an exciting experience.
Title: The stress of college registration
Topic sentence: College registration can be stressful.

Exercise 1   **Distinguishing a Topic Sentence from a Title**

Each of the following ten examples is either a title or a topic sentence. In each of the spaces provided, identify the example by writing *T* or *TS*.

___T___   1. The benefits of a college education

___T___   2. The outstanding achievements of aviator Charles Lindbergh

___TS___   3. The Carter administration faced two major problems

___T___   4. The basis of the Arab-Israeli Conflict

___TS___   5. The Japanese diet is perhaps the healthiest diet in the world

___T___   6. The astounding beauty of the Rocky Mountains at dusk

Mastering the Paragraph

___T___ 7. The finest sports car on the market

___TS___ 8. Fast-food restaurants are popular with families having small children

___T___ 9. The expense of maintaining a car

___TS___ 10. Maintaining a car is expensive

Exercise 2 — Distinguishing a Topic Sentence from a Title

Each of the following ten examples is either a title or a topic sentence. In each of the spaces provided, identify the example by writing T or TS.

___TS___ 1. Dreams can be frightening

___T___ 2. The advantages of getting a job after high school

___TS___ 3. *On Golden Pond* was an unusual movie because it portrayed the unpopular subject, growing old, but it still was a commercial success

___T___ 4. The home of my dreams

___TS___ 5. Walking on the beach at sunset calms me down after a stressful day at work

___TS___ 6. Making your own clothes requires great patience as well as skill

___T___ 7. Selecting the right camera for an amateur

___TS___ 8. Finding the right place to study was my most difficult problem at college

___T___ 9. The worst bargain of my life

___TS___ 10. The old car I bought from my friend's father turned out to be a real bargain

Exercise 3 — Distinguishing a Topic Sentence from a Title

Each of the following ten examples is either a title or a topic sentence. In each of the spaces provided, identify the example by writing T or TS.

___T___ 1. How to make friends at college and still have time to study

_____ 2. As the computer becomes a common working tool, typing will be an even more important skill to learn than it has been before

_____ 3. The disadvantages of living alone

_____ 4. The fight to keep our neighborhood park

Working with Paragraphs: Topic Sentences and Controlling Ideas ▸ 179

_____ 5. The peacefulness of a solitary weekend at the beach

_____ 6. Our investigation into the mysterious death of Walter D.

_____ 7. The flea market looked promising

_____ 8. The two main reasons why divorce is common

_____ 9. The single life did not turn out to be as glamorous as I had hoped

_____ 10. The increasing popularity of board games

How do you find the topic in a topic sentence?

To find the topic in a topic sentence, ask yourself this question: What is the topic the writer is going to discuss? Below are two topic sentences. The topic for the first topic sentence is underlined. Underline the topic in the second example.

<u>Backpacking in the mountains last year</u> was an exciting experience.

College registration can be stressful.

Exercise 1 Finding the Topic in the Topic Sentence

Find the topic in each of the following topic sentences. For each example, ask yourself this question: What is the topic the writer is going to discuss? Then underline the topic.

1. <u>Remodeling an old house</u> can be frustrating.
2. <u>College work</u> demands more independence than high school work.
3. <u>A well-made suit</u> has three easily identified characteristics.
4. <s><u>Growing up near a museum</u></s> had a profound influence on my life.
5. <u>My favorite room in the house</u> would seem ugly to most people.
6. <u>A student who goes to school full time and also works part time</u> has to make careful use of every hour.
7. One of the disadvantages <u>of skiing</u> is the expense.
8. <u>Spanking</u> is the least successful way to discipline a child.
9. <u>An attractive wardrobe</u> does not have to be expensive.
10. Of all the years in college, <u>the freshman year</u> is usually the most demanding.

Exercise 2 Finding the Topic in the Topic Sentence

Find the topic in each of the following topic sentences. For each example, ask yourself this question: What is the topic the writer is going to discuss? Then underline the topic.

1. To my surprise, the basement had now been converted into a small studio apartment.
2. Of all the presidents, Abraham Lincoln probably enjoys the greatest popularity.

3. Scientists cannot yet explain how an identical twin often has an uncanny knowledge of what the other twin is doing or feeling.
4. If you don't have a car in the United States, you have undoubtedly discovered that public transportation is in a state of decay.
5. When we met for dinner that night, I was shocked at the change that had come over my friend.
6. According to the report, current tax laws greatly benefit those who own real estate.
7. Charles Chaplin, the famous movie actor, had a tragic childhood.
8. As we rode into town, the streets seemed unusually empty.
9. IBM offers its employees many long-term benefits.
10. Many people claim that clipping coupons can save them as much as 30 percent of their food bill.

Exercise 3 — Finding the Topic in the Topic Sentence

Find the topic in each of the following topic sentences. For each example, ask yourself this question: What is the topic the writer is going to discuss? Then underline the topic.

1. Taking care of a house can easily be a full-time job.
2. Many of the daytime television shows are wasting people's time.
3. One of the undisputed goals in teaching is to be able to offer individualized instruction.
4. Whether it's a car, a house, or a college, bigger isn't always better.
5. Violence on television is disturbing to most child psychologists.
6. In today's economy, carrying at least one credit card is probably advisable.
7. Much highway advertising is not only ugly but also distracting for the driver.
8. Choosing a lifelong career involves a complicated process of making many decisions.
9. In recent years we have seen a dramatic revival of interest in quilting.
10. The grading system of the state university is quite different from that of the small liberal arts college in my hometown.

▶ What is a controlling idea?

Every topic sentence contains not only the topic but also a controlling idea. This *controlling idea* tells us the attitude the writer has taken toward the topic. For example, in the topic sentence "Backpacking in the mountains last year was an exciting experience," the topic is "backpacking" and the controlling idea is that this backpacking trip was "exciting." Another person on the same trip might have had another attitude toward the trip. The person might have found the trip exhausting or boring. A single topic can therefore have any number of possibilities for development since the writer can choose from a limitless number of controlling ideas, depending on his or her attitude.

How do you find the controlling idea of a topic sentence?

When you look for the controlling idea in a topic sentence, ask yourself this question: What is the writer's attitude toward the topic?

In each of the following examples, the topic is underlined and the controlling idea is circled.

<u>Sealfon's Department Store</u> is my (favorite) store in town.
<u>Sealfon's Department Store</u> is (too expensive) for my budget.

Exercise 1 — Finding the Controlling Idea

Below are ten topic sentences. For each sentence, underline the topic and circle the controlling idea.

1. Vigorous exercise is a good way to reduce the effect of stress on the body.
2. Buffalo and Toronto differ in four major ways.
3. Television violence causes aggressive behavior in children.
4. Athletic scholarships available to women are increasing.
5. Caffeine has several adverse effects on the body.
6. Julia Child, a famous gourmet cook, is an amusing personality.
7. Training a parakeet to talk takes great patience.
8. Baby-sitting for a family with four preschool children was the most difficult job I've ever had.
9. The hours between five and seven in the morning are my most productive.
10. The foggy night was spooky.

Exercise 2 — Finding the Controlling Idea

Below are ten topic sentences. For each sentence, underline the topic and circle the controlling idea.

1. Piano lessons turned out to be a disaster.
2. The training of Japanese policemen is quite different from American police training.
3. An Olympic champion has five distinctive characteristics.
4. The candidate's unethical financial dealings will have a negative impact on this campaign.
5. A bicycle ride along the coast is a breathtaking trip.
6. The grocery store is another place where people waste a significant amount of money every week.
7. Being an only child is not as bad as people think.
8. Rewarding children with candy or desserts is an unfortunate habit of many parents.
9. A childhood hobby often develops into a promising career.
10. The writing of a dictionary is an incredible process.

Exercise 3 — Finding the Controlling Idea

Below are ten topic sentences. For each sentence, underline the topic and circle the controlling idea.

1. Learning to type takes more practice than talent.
2. Shakespeare's plays are difficult for today's students because English has undergone many changes since the sixteenth century.
3. Atlanta, Georgia, is one of the cities in the Sunbelt that is experiencing significant population growth.
4. Half a dozen new magazines totally devoted to health are enjoying popularity with the public.
5. The importance of good preschool programs for children has been sadly underestimated.
6. The disposal of toxic wastes has caused problems for many manufacturers.
7. Censorship of school textbooks is a controversial issue in most towns.
8. How to make salt water drinkable by an inexpensive method has been a difficult problem for decades.
9. Developing color film is more complicated than developing black and white.
10. The cloudberry is one of the rare berries of the world.

Choosing your own controlling idea

Teachers often assign one general topic on which all students must write. Likewise, when writing contests are announced, the topic is generally the same for all contestants. Since very few people have exactly the same view or attitude toward a topic, it is likely that no two papers would have the same controlling idea. There could be as many controlling ideas as there are people to write them. The secret of writing a good topic sentence is to find the controlling idea that is right for you.

Exercise 1 — Choosing Controlling Ideas to Write Topic Sentences

Below are two topics. For each topic, think of three different possible controlling ideas, and then write a different topic sentence for each of these controlling ideas. An example is done for you.

Topic: My mother

Three possible controlling ideas:
1. Unusual childhood
2. Silent woman
3. Definite ideas about alcohol

Three different topic sentences:
1. My mother had a most unusual childhood.
2. My mother is a very silent woman.
3. My mother has definite ideas about alcohol.

1. **Topic:** My father

   First controlling idea: _____

   First topic sentence: _____

   _____

   Second controlling idea: _____

   Second topic sentence: _____

   _____

   Third controlling idea: _____

   Third topic sentence: _____

   _____

2. **Topic:** California

   First controlling idea: *OVERCROWDED*

   First topic sentence: *CALIFORNIA IS OVERCROWDED.*

   _____

   Second controlling idea: *GREAT PLACE*

   Second topic sentence: *CALIFORNIA IS A GREAT PLACE TO LIVE.*

   _____

   Third controlling idea: *NICE PEOPLE*

   Third topic sentence: *CALIFORNIA HAS A LOT OF NICE PEOPLE*

Exercise 2 — Choosing Controlling Ideas to Write Topic Sentences

Below are two topics. For each topic, think of three different possible controlling ideas, and then write a different topic sentence for each of these controlling ideas. An example is done for you.

Topic: My mother

Three possible controlling ideas:
1. Unusual childhood
2. Silent woman
3. Definite ideas about alcohol

Three different topic sentences:
1. My mother had a most unusual childhood.
2. My mother is a very silent woman.
3. My mother has definite ideas about alcohol.

1. **Topic:** Thanksgiving

    First controlling idea: _____

    First topic sentence: _____
    _____

    Second controlling idea: _____

    Second topic sentence: _____
    _____

    Third controlling idea: _____

    Third topic sentence: _____
    _____

2. **Topic:** Working in a nursing home

    First controlling idea: _____

    First topic sentence: _____
    _____

    Second controlling idea: _____

    Second topic sentence: _____
    _____

    Third controlling idea: _____

    Third topic sentence: _____
    _____

Exercise 3 — Choosing Controlling Ideas to Write Topic Sentences

Below are two topics. For each topic, think of three different possible controlling ideas, and then write a different topic sentence for each of these controlling ideas. An example is done for you.

Topic: My mother

Three possible controlling ideas:
1. Unusual childhood
2. Silent woman
3. Definite ideas about alcohol

Three different topic sentences:
1. My mother had a most unusual childhood.
2. My mother is a very silent woman.
3. My mother has definite ideas about alcohol.

1. **Topic:** Miss America

    First controlling idea: _____

    First topic sentence: _____

    _____

    Second controlling idea: _____

    Second topic sentence: _____

    _____

    Third controlling idea: _____

    Third topic sentence: _____

    _____

2. **Topic:** Junk food

    First controlling idea: _____

    First topic sentence: _____

    _____

    Second controlling idea: _____

    Second topic sentence: _____

    _____

    Third controlling idea: _____

    Third topic sentence: _____

    _____

▶ Chapter review exercises

Exercise 1 — Further Practice Writing the Topic Sentence

Develop each of the following topics into a topic sentence. In each case, the controlling idea is missing. First, decide on an attitude you might take toward the topic. Then use the attitude you have chosen to write your topic sentence. When you are finished, underline your topic and circle your controlling idea. Be sure your topic sentence is a complete sentence and not a fragment. An example has been done for you.

Topic: My brother's car accident

Controlling idea: Tragic results

Topic sentence: My brother's car accident had (tragic results) for the entire family.

1. **Topic:** Teaching a child good manners

   Controlling idea: _____

   Topic sentence: _____
   _____

2. **Topic:** Two years in the army

   Controlling idea: _____

   Topic sentence: _____
   _____

3. **Topic:** Making new friends

   Controlling idea: _____

   Topic sentence: _____
   _____

4. **Topic:** The old woman

   Controlling idea: _____

   Topic sentence: _____
   _____

5. **Topic:** Going on a diet

   Controlling idea: _____

   Topic sentence: _____
   _____

Exercise 2 — Further Practice Writing the Topic Sentence

Develop each of the following topics into a topic sentence. In each case, the controlling idea is missing. First, decide on an attitude you might take toward the topic. Then use the attitude you have chosen to write your topic sentence. When you are finished, underline your topic and circle your controlling idea. Be sure your topic sentence is a complete sentence and not a fragment.

1. **Topic:** Compact cars

   Controlling idea: _____

   Topic sentence: _____
   _____

Working with Paragraphs: Topic Sentences and Controlling Ideas ▶ 187

2. **Topic:** Vegetarians

   Controlling idea: _____

   Topic sentence: _____

   _____

3. **Topic:** My hometown

   Controlling idea: _____

   Topic sentence: _____

   _____

4. **Topic:** Writing essays

   Controlling idea: _____

   Topic sentence: _____

   _____

5. **Topic:** Subways

   Controlling idea: _____

   Topic sentence: _____

   _____

Exercise 3 — Further Practice Writing the Topic Sentence

Develop each of the following topics into a topic sentence. In each case, the controlling idea is missing. First, decide on an attitude you might take toward the topic. Then use the attitude you have chosen to write your topic sentence. When you are finished, underline your topic and circle your controlling idea. Be sure your topic sentence is a complete sentence and not a fragment.

1. **Topic:** Computer programming

   Controlling idea: _____

   Topic sentence: _____

   _____

2. **Topic:** Jewelry fashions

   Controlling idea: _____

   Topic sentence: _____

   _____

3. **Topic:** Zoos

   Controlling idea: _____

   Topic sentence: _____

   _____

4. **Topic:** Motorcycles

   Controlling idea: _____

   Topic sentence: _____

   _____

5. **Topic:** Homework

   Controlling idea: _____

   Topic sentence: _____

   _____

11
Working with Supporting Details

▸ What is a supporting detail?

A **supporting detail** is a piece of evidence used by the writer to make the controlling idea of the topic sentence convincing to the reader.

Once you have constructed your topic sentence with its topic and controlling idea, you are ready to move on to supporting your statement with details. These details will convince your readers that what you are claiming in the topic sentence is believable or reasonable.

As you choose these supporting details, realize that the readers do not necessarily have to agree with your point of view. However, your supporting details must be good enough so that your readers will at least respect your attitude. Your goal is to educate your readers. Try to make them experts on the subject you are writing about. The quality and number of your supporting details will determine how well you do this. If you have enough details, and if your details are specific enough, your readers will feel they have learned something new about the subject. This is always a satisfying experience.

It is also true that specific details tend to stay in readers' minds much better than general ideas. The fact that 70,000 people died of the Hong Kong flu in 1968 in the United States is much more effective and memorable than a statement saying only that the Hong Kong flu killed many people.

Finally, specific details make a piece of writing more fun to read. When the reader has concrete objects, particular people, or recognizable places to hang on to, the contents of the writing become a pleasure to read.

The following paragraph, taken from an essay about the richness of American Indian languages, contains a topic sentence with several good supporting details.

> Unlike solid rock, languages are remarkably adaptable, easily borrowing or coining new words as circumstances change. The horse, unknown when the Spanish landed, soon took on a central role among the tribes, and words for the horse and its many uses were introduced. One device

was to borrow some form of the Spanish word *caballo*. Another was to invent a descriptive term. Indians of eastern New York State used a word meaning "one rides its back"; in the western part the word for horse means "it hauls out logs." Presumably these were the first uses of horses seen in the two areas. Among the Kwakiutl of British Columbia a steamboat was "fire on its back moving in the water." To the Tsimshian of the same area, the word for rice was "looking like maggots."

Notice that the topic sentence gives us the topic (language) and the writer's attitude toward the topic (remarkably adaptable). Each of the sentences that follow this topic sentence is a supporting detail that convinces us that the controlling idea is a reasonable attitude. The writer provides more than one example and chooses these examples from more than one Indian tribe. This wide range makes the topic sentence convincing and, of course, more interesting.

--- Practice ---

Using the lines given, copy the exact topic sentence for the paragraph above. Then, in your own words, give each of the details for each of the supporting sentences. Be prepared to discuss how each of the supporting sentences supports or explains the controlling idea contained in the topic sentence.

Topic sentence: _____
_____
_____

First supporting detail: _____
_____
_____

Second supporting detail: _____
_____
_____

Third supporting detail: _____
_____
_____

Exercise 1 — Finding the Topic Sentence and Supporting Details

For each of the two paragraphs below, divide the sentences into topic sentence and supporting details.

1. Saturday afternoon was a blessed time on the farm. First of all, there would now be no mail in till Monday afternoon, so that no distressing business letters could reach us till then, and this fact in itself seemed to close the

whole place in, as within an enceinte [a circular enclosure]. Secondly, everybody was looking forward to the day of Sunday, when they would rest or play all the day, and the Squatters could work on their own land. The thought of the oxen on Saturday pleased me more than all other things. I used to walk down to their paddock at six o'clock, when they were coming in after the day's work and a few hours' grazing. To-morrow, I thought, they would do nothing but graze all day.

From Isak Dinesen,
Out of Africa

Topic sentence: _____

_____

First supporting detail: _____

_____

Second supporting detail: _____

_____

Third supporting detail: _____

_____

2. More people watched the Superbowl than watched Neil Armstrong's walk on the moon. Fifteen percent of all television programs produced are sports programs. Professional football games have a yearly attendance of over ten million spectators and both baseball leagues together draw over three million spectators every year. In one year, North American spectators spent over $300 million for tickets to sports events. There probably is not a person in the United States who does not recognize a picture of Muhammad Ali, and who cannot identify a picture of the soccer star Pélé? The popularity of sports is enormous.

Adapted from Ronald W. Smith and Andrea Fontana,
Social Problems

Topic sentence: _____

_____

First supporting detail: _____

_____

Second supporting detail: _____

_____

Third supporting detail: _____

_____

192 ◀ Mastering the Paragraph

Fourth supporting detail: _____

_____

_____

Exercise 2   Finding the Topic Sentence and Supporting Details

For each of the two paragraphs below, divide the sentences into topic sentence and supporting details.

1. Hilda takes an enormous amount of space, though so little time, in my adolescence. Even today, her memory stirs me; I long to see her again. She was three years older than I, and for a short while all I wanted to look like, sound like, dress like. She was the only girl I knew who told me I wrote excellent letters. She made a plaster cast of my face. She had opinions on everything. She took a picture of me, at sixteen, which I have still. She and I were nearly killed, falling off a hillside road in her small car. Hilda was so full of life, I cannot believe her dead.

From Han Suyin,
A Mortal Flower

Topic sentence: _____

_____

First supporting detail: _____

_____

Second supporting detail: _____

_____

Third supporting detail: _____

_____

Fourth supporting detail: _____

_____

Fifth supporting detail: _____

_____

Sixth supporting detail: _____

_____

2. A steadily accumulating body of evidence supports the view that cancers are caused by things that we eat, drink, breathe, or are otherwise exposed to. That evidence is of three kinds. First, the incidence of many types of cancers differs greatly from one geographic region of the world to another. Second,

when groups of people permanently move from one country to another, the incidence of some types of cancer changes in their offspring. For example, when Japanese move to this country, the relatively high rate of occurrence of stomach cancer they experience in Japan falls so that their children experience such cancer only a fifth as frequently, the same incidence as other Americans. Orientals have low incidence of breast cancer, but when they come to the United States, it increases sixfold. Third, we are becoming aware of an increasing number of chemical pollutants in air and water and food that have proven to be cancer-producing.

From Mahlon B. Hoagland,
The Roots of Life

Topic sentence: _____

_____

First supporting detail: _____

_____

Second supporting detail: _____

_____

Third supporting detail: _____

_____

_____

Exercise 3   Finding the Topic Sentence and Supporting Details

For each of the two paragraphs below, divide the sentences into topic sentence and supporting details.

1. Pollen consists of small grains produced by a flower's anthers. Each grain contains sex cells which, when fused with an egg, will lead to the creation of a new plant. In plants favoured by bees, the grains are usually prickly and coated with fatty substances so that they are easily caught up by the bee when it visits a flower. Pollen grains contain protein, fats, and carbohydrates, as well as vitamins and minerals, and are a nourishing source of food for many animals apart from bees.

From Lennart Nillson,
Nature Magnified

Topic sentence: _____

_____

First supporting detail: _____

_____

Second supporting detail: _____

_____

Third supporting detail: _____

_____

_____

2. ^TS^ The airshaft was a horrible invention. Even with the windows tightly sealed, it served as a sounding box and you could hear everybody's business. Rats scurried around the bottom. There was always the danger of fire. A match absently tossed into the airshaft by a drunken teamster under the impression that he was throwing it into the yard or street would set the house afire in a moment. There were vile things cluttering up the bottom. Since this bottom couldn't be reached by man (the windows being too small to admit passage of a body), it served as a fearful repository for things that people wanted to put out of their lives. Rusted razor blades and bloody cloths were the most innocent items. Once Francie looked down into the airshaft. She thought of what the priest said about Purgatory and figured it must be like the airshaft bottom only on a larger scale. When Francie went into the parlor, she passed through the bedrooms shuddering and with her eyes shut.

From Betty Smith,
A Tree Grows in Brooklyn

Topic sentence: _____

_____

First supporting detail: _____

_____

Second supporting detail: _____

_____

Third supporting detail: _____

_____

Fourth supporting detail: _____

_____

▶ Using examples as supporting details

An example is a very specific illustration or piece of evidence that supports a writer's point of view. Examples make general ideas more concrete and therefore easier to comprehend and remember. When you use examples in your writing, you are convincing your reader that what you are saying is true and worthy of belief. Often, when you use examples to support your ideas, you will find yourself providing further examples to help your reader see your examples more clearly. If you are writing about cars, you may find yourself using Ford, Dodge, Buick, and Honda to illustrate your points. However, to make your points even more concise, you could find yourself referring to a Ford Bronco Wagon, a Dodge Caravan, a Buick Skylark, and a Honda Accord. The more precise your examples, the more clearly your reader will be able to see what you mean—and therefore the more memorable your writing will be.

Examples may be given in more than one way. They may appear as lists of specific items to illustrate a particular point, or they may be written as extended examples. Extended examples include lengthy descriptions or stories that can be an entire paragraph long. A good piece of writing is filled with both kinds of examples that work together to create a well-developed, convincing whole. As you read the following essay, look for the different kinds of examples that show the extent to which the fear of AIDS has affected our society.

Margaret O. Hyde and Elizabeth H. Forsyth, M.D., "AIDS: An Epidemic of Fear"

1 Some people are so frightened by AIDS that they shun all homosexuals. Many customers have changed hairdressers because they suspected that the ones they frequented were gay. They now insist on women doing their hair. Actresses have refused to be made up by men who might be homosexual. One couple visiting New Orleans was so concerned about the numerous gay waiters in the French Quarter restaurants that they stopped going out to eat. They bought food in supermarkets and ate it in their hotel room. A woman who was given a book purchased at a gay-lesbian book store called the store and asked if she could safely open the package without getting AIDS. Even people who do not think they know a homosexual person have expressed fear of the disease. All of these people were acting on unfounded fears.

2 The epidemic of fear has been evident in many places. Some television technicians refused to work on a program in which an AIDS patient was to be interviewed. Fourteen people asked to be excused from jury duty in the trial of a man who had AIDS and was accused of murder. The sheriff's deputies who had to walk with this murder suspect were so concerned about contracting the disease that they wore rubber gloves and other protective clothing when they escorted him into the courtroom.

3 There have been reports that funeral homes refused to handle the bodies of AIDS patients without using elaborate precautions. In one case, it was alleged that a funeral home charged a family an extra two hundred dollars for the gloves and gowns used to handle an AIDS patient's body, and another funeral home tried to sell a family an expensive "germ-free" coffin. A Baltimore man, Don Miller, who is concerned about the rights of homosexuals, reported that he called ninety-nine funeral homes to see what response they gave when he told them he had AIDS and was making funeral arrangements in advance. Ten refused to deal with him, and about half of them said they would require special conditions such as no embalming and/or a sealed casket. Some groups have been working toward establishing guidelines for embalming and burying people who had AIDS.

4   Children with AIDS and those whose parents have AIDS have been the victims of the epidemic of fear that spread throughout the country. Prospective foster parents often shy away from children whose mothers died from infectious diseases because of AIDS, even though the children do not have the disease. For example, one little boy lived at Jackson Memorial Hospital in Miami, Florida, for two years after he was born because his mother had AIDS before she died. He showed no indication of having the virus.

5   While some babies die quickly after birth, others live well into school age. In a number of places, hospitals have begun day care programs for children with AIDS, and a California monastery has opened its doors to unwanted infants born with AIDS who might otherwise have to spend their lives in hospitals. For many children with AIDS, life outside the hospital is one in which they are shunned by friends, neighbors, and even relatives because of the fear that still surrounds the disease.

6   Controversies about whether or not children with AIDS should be permitted to attend school have reached far and wide. The case of Ryan White of Russiaville, Indiana, was well publicized. A hemophiliac, he contracted AIDS from a blood transfusion he received in December 1984. At one point, Ryan was forced to monitor classes at home by telephone because of a restraining order obtained by parents of the other children. In the fall of 1986, Ryan started school with his class for the first time in two years, after the parents who fought his return dropped their lawsuit because of legal costs. Ryan's school had been picketed in the past, but by 1986, some students just took the attitude that they did not mind his being in school as long as he did not sit near them. Ryan was assigned his own bathroom and was given disposable utensils in the cafeteria, even though scientists believe this precaution to be unnecessary. School staff members were instructed in handling any health emergencies that arose.

7   In New York City, when school opened in late August of 1985, the fear of AIDS created a great deal of excitement. Whether or not a child who had AIDS could attend public school in New York City was determined by a panel made up of health experts, an educator, and a parent. One child with AIDS had been attending school for three years and was identified only as a second grader. The child was said to have been born with AIDS but was in good health, the disease being in remission. She had received all the inoculations necessary for school admission, and had recovered from a case of chicken pox, managing to fight off this childhood illness uneventfully.

8   In Hollywood, many people were near hysteria after Rock Hudson's announcement that he was suffering from AIDS. Some actresses who had kissed people with AIDS were especially concerned, while others refused to work with anyone considered to be gay. After one actor became sick, make-up artists burned the brushes they had used on him. But Hollywood stars have been outstanding in their support of care for persons with AIDS and research on AIDS. Shortly before he died, Rock Hudson sent a brief message to a benefit dinner, "I am not happy that I am sick. I am not happy that I have AIDS. But if that is helping others, I can, at least, know that my own misfortune has had some positive worth."

9   Only through education and further research can one strike a balance between fear of the disease, sensible precautions, and concern for people who suffer from AIDS. Fear makes people "block out" information. We

need more campaigns which emphasize the lack of danger from casual contact since polls show that people are simply not listening.

Exercise 1   **Finding Examples**

Analyze each of the paragraphs from the essay "AIDS: An Epidemic of Fear." What kind(s) of examples can you find in each paragraph?

Exercise 2   **Finding Examples**

Find a newspaper or magazine article on a current topic or other subject of interest to you. Examine the article for paragraphs containing lists of examples and paragraphs containing extended examples. Specifically, how has the writer made the article interesting and memorable through the use of examples?

▶ Avoid restating the topic sentence

One of your most important jobs as you write a paragraph is recognizing the difference between a genuine supporting detail and a simple restatement of the topic sentence. The following is a poor paragraph with all its sentences merely restatements of the topic sentence.

> The wedding day was the highest point in a girl's life—a day to which she looked forward all her unmarried days and to which she looked back for the rest of her life. All the events of the day were unlike any other day in her life before or after. Everyone would remember this day. Each event was unforgettable. The memories would last a lifetime. A wedding was the beginning of living "happily ever after."

By contrast, this paragraph, "From Popping the Question to Popping the Pill" by Margaret Mead, has good supporting details:

> The wedding day was the highest point in a girl's life—a day to which she looked forward all her unmarried days and to which she looked back for the rest of her life. The splendor of her wedding, the elegance of dress and veil, the cutting of the cake, the departure amid a shower of rice and confetti, gave her an accolade of which no subsequent event could completely rob her. Today people over fifty years of age still treat their daughter's wedding this way, prominently displaying the photographs of the occasion. Until very recently, all brides' books prescribed exactly the same ritual they had prescribed fifty years before. The etiquette governing wedding presents—gifts that were or were not appropriate, the bride's maiden initials on her linen—was also specified. For the bridegroom the wedding represented the end of his free, bachelor days, and the bachelor dinner the night before the wedding symbolized this loss of freedom. A woman who did not marry—even if she had the alibi of a fiancé who had been killed in war or had abilities and charm and money of her own—was always at a social disadvantage while an eligible bachelor was sought after by hostess after hostess.

Exercise 1 Distinguishing a Supporting Detail from a Restatement of the Main Idea

Each of the following topic sentences is followed by four additional sentences. Three of these additional sentences contain acceptable supporting details, but one of the sentences is simply a restatement of the topic sentence. In the space provided, identify each sentence as SD for *supporting detail* or R for *restatement*.

1. I am surprised at myself when I think how neat I used to be before I started school full time.

   _____ a. In my closet, I had my clothes arranged in matching outfits with shoes, hats, and even jewelry to go with them.

   ___R___ b. I always used to take great pride in having all my things in order.

   _____ c. If I opened my desk drawer, compartments of paper clips, erasers, staples, pens, pencils, stamps, and rulers greeted me without one lost penny or safety pin thrown in out of place.

   _____ d. On top of my chest of drawers sat a comb and brush, two oval frames with pictures of my best friends, and that was all.

2. Iceland has a very barren landscape.

   _____ a. One-tenth of the island is covered by ice.

   _____ b. Not one forest with magnificent trees is to be found.

   ___R___ c. Nature has not been kind to the people of Iceland.

   _____ d. Three-fourths of the island is uninhabitable.

3. Until recently, books have been the most important method of preserving knowledge.

   ___R___ a. Without books, much of the knowledge of past centuries would have been lost.

   _____ b. Leonardo da Vinci kept notebooks of his amazing inventions and discoveries.

   _____ c. During the Middle Ages, monks spent their entire lives copying books by hand.

   _____ d. The Library of Congress in Washington, D.C., obtains a copy of every book published in the United States.

4. Most people no longer wonder whether cigarette smoking is bad for their health.

   _____ a. Following the evidence from over 30,000 studies, a federal law requires that cigarette manufacturers place a health warning to all smokers on their packages.

Working with Supporting Details ▸ 199

_____ b. Studies have shown that smoking presently causes nearly 80 percent of lung cancer deaths in this country.

____R_____ c. Few authorities today have any doubts about the connection between cigarette smoking and poor health.

_____ d. We know that 30 percent of the deaths from coronary heart disease can be attributed to smoking.

5. When the Mexican earthquake struck in 1985, scientists and city planners learned a great deal about the kinds of buildings that can survive an earthquake.

_____ a. Buildings that had foundations resting on giant rollers suffered very little damage.

_____ b. Buildings that were made only of adobe material simply fell apart when the earthquake struck.

_____ c. Many of the modern buildings were designed to vibrate when earthquakes occur, so these received the least amount of shock.

____R_____ d. After the earthquake was over, officials realized why some buildings were destroyed while others suffered hardly any damage at all.

Exercise 2

Recognizing a Supporting Detail from a Restatement of the Main Idea

Each of the following topic sentences is followed by four additional sentences. Three of these additional sentences contain acceptable supporting details, but one of the sentences is simply a restatement of the topic sentence. In the space provided, identify each sentence as *SD* for *supporting detail* or *R* for *restatement*.

1. In the last thirty years, the number of people living alone in the United States has increased by 400 percent.

   _____ a. People are living alone because the number of divorces has dramatically increased.

   _____ b. Many young people are putting off marriage until they are financially more secure or emotionally ready.

   ____R_____ c. More and more Americans are finding themselves living alone.

   _____ d. An increasing percentage of our population is the age group over sixty-five, among whom are many widows and widowers.

2. More and more people are realizing the disadvantages of using credit cards too often.

   ____R_____ a. People should think twice before using their cards.

   _____ b. Interest rates on credit cards have been rising at an alarming rate.

_____ c. Credit cards make it possible to buy on impulse, rather than plan a budget carefully.

_____ d. Many credit card companies charge an annual fee for the privilege of using cards.

3. The evidence of health problems among people living near Love Canal in upstate New York has been dramatic.

_____ a. In a professional analysis done by Buffalo scientist Beverly Paigen, out of 245 homes, she found 34 miscarriages, 18 birth defects, 19 nervous breakdowns, 10 cases of epilepsy, and high rates of hyperactivity and suicide.

_____ b. On October 4, 1978, a little boy suffering with nosebleeds, headaches, and dry heaves died of kidney failure; he often played in the polluted creek behind his house.

_____ c. Ann Hillis's first baby was born so badly deformed that doctors could not determine the sex of the child.

___R___ d. The story of Love Canal is filled with human tragedy.

4. Since World War II, the status of women in Japan has changed.

_____ a. In 1947, women won the right to vote.

___R___ b. The women's position in Japanese society has altered over the past thirty-five years.

_____ c. Many Japanese women now go on to higher education.

_____ d. Women can now own property in their own name and seek divorce.

5. Certain factors which cannot be changed have been shown to contribute to heart attacks and stroke.

_____ a. Three out of four heart attacks and six out of seven strokes occur after the age of sixty-five, so age is definitely a factor.

___R___ b. Heart attacks and strokes have many causes, some of which we can do nothing about.

_____ c. Black Americans have nearly a 45 percent greater risk of having high blood pressure, a major cause of heart attacks and strokes.

_____ d. Men are at greater risk than women in their chance of suffering from cardiovascular disease.

▶ How do you make supporting details specific?

Students often write paragraphs that are made up only of general statements. When you read such paragraphs, you doubt the author's knowledge and you suspect that the point being made may have no basis in fact. Here is one such paragraph that never gets off the ground.

> Doctors are terrible. They cause more problems than they solve. I don't believe most of their treatments are necessary. History is full of the mistakes doctors have made. We don't need all those operations. We should never ingest all those drugs doctors prescribe. We shouldn't allow them to give us all those unnecessary tests. I've heard plenty of stories that prove my point. Doctors' ideas can kill you.

Here is another paragraph on the same topic. This topic is much more interesting and convincing because the general statements throughout the essay have been changed to supporting details.

> Evidence shows that "medical progress" has been the cause of tragic consequences and even death for thousands of people. X-ray therapy was thought to help patients with tonsillitis. Now many of these people are found to have developed cancer from these X-rays. Not so long ago, women were kept in bed for several weeks following childbirth. Unfortunately, this cost many women their lives since they developed fatal blood clots from being kept in bed day after day. One recent poll estimates that 30,000 people each year die from the side effects of drugs that were prescribed by doctors. Recently, the Center for Disease Control reported that 25 percent of the tests done by clinical laboratories were done poorly. All this is not to belittle the good done by the medical profession, but to impress on readers that it would be foolish to rely totally on the medical profession to solve all our health problems.

This second paragraph is much more likely to be of real interest. Even if you would like to disprove the author's point, it would be very hard to dismiss these supports, which are based on facts and information that can be researched. Because the author sounds reasonable, you can respect him even if you have a different position on the topic.

In writing effectively, the ability to go beyond the general statement and get to the accurate pieces of information is what counts. A writer tries to make his or her reader an expert on the subject. Readers should go away excited to share with the next person they meet the surprising information they have just learned. A writer who has a statistic, a quotation, an anecdote, a historical example, or a descriptive detail has the advantage over all other writers, no matter how impressive these writers' styles may be.

Good writing, therefore, is filled with supporting details that are specific, correct, and appropriate for the subject. Poor writing is filled with generalizations, stereotypes, vagueness, untruths, and even sarcasm and insults.

Exercise 1   Creating Supporting Details

Below are five topic sentences. Supply three supporting details for each one. Be sure each detail is specific and not general or vague.

1. Your first semester in college can be overwhelming.

   a. _____
   b. _____
   c. _____

2. Clothing is a bad investment of your money.

   a. _____
   b. _____
   c. _____

3. Dr. Kline is an easy teacher.

   a. _____
   b. _____
   c. _____

4. It is difficult to stop eating junk food.

   a. _____
   b. _____
   c. _____

5. My sister is the sloppiest person I know.

   a. _____
   b. _____
   c. _____

Exercise 2   Creating Supporting Details

Below are five topic sentences. Supply three supporting details for each one. Be sure each detail is specific and not general or vague.

1. December has become a frantic time at our house.

   a. _____
   b. _____
   c. _____

2. My best friend can often be very immature.

   a. HE PREFURES CORN POPS OVER FRUIT LOOPS

   b. HE SLEEPS WITH A NIGHTLITE

   c. HIS MOTHER WALKS HIM TO SCHOOL

3. Each sport has its own peculiar injuries associated with it.

   a. _____

   b. _____

   c. _____

4. My car is on its "last wheel."

   a. _____

   b. _____

   c. _____

5. Watching too much television has serious effects on family life.

   a. PARENTS SPEND LESS TIME COMPLAINING ABOUT THIER DEADEND JOBS

   b. KIDS SPEND LESS TIME ON THE STREETS

   c. _____

Exercise 3

Creating Supporting Details

Below are five topic sentences. Supply three supporting details for each one. Be sure each detail is specific and not general or vague.

1. Maintaining a car is a continual drain on one's budget.

   a. _____

   b. _____

   c. _____

2. Traveling by train has several advantages over traveling by car.

   a. _____

   b. _____

   c. _____

3. Last year I redecorated my bedroom.

   a. _____

   b. _____

   c. _____

4. Washington, D.C., is the best city for a family vacation.

   a. _____

   b. _____

   c. _____

5. The amateur photographer needs to consider several points when selecting a camera.

   a. _____

   b. _____

   c. _____

12

Developing Paragraphs: Description

▶ **What is description?**

Description is one of the basic building blocks of good writing. When you are able to write an effective description of a person, an object, a place, or even an idea, you are in control of your writing. Good description also makes you able to control what your reader sees and does not see.

The key to writing a good description is the choice of the **specific details** you will use. Specific details make your descriptions real and help your reader remember what you have written. A careful writer always pays special attention to specific details in any piece of writing.

A second important aspect of good description is the use of **sensory images.** Sensory images are details that relate to your sense of sight, smell, touch, taste, or hearing. When you use at least some of these five senses in your descriptive writing, your reader will be able to relate directly to what you are saying. Sensory images also help your reader remember what you have written.

A third important aspect of good description is the **order** in which you place the details you have chosen. The combination of specific details, sensory images, and the order in which you present these details and impressions will help your reader form a **dominant impression** of what you are describing.

The following example of descriptive writing shows all of the elements of a good description. As you read this description of a typical neighborhood delicatessen, note the specific details and the sensory images the writer uses. After you have read the whole description, ask yourself what dominant impression the writer wanted us to have of the place.

The delicatessen was a wide store with high ceilings which were a dark brown color from many years of not being painted. The rough wooden shelves on both sides of the store were filled from floor to ceiling with cans of fruits and vegetables, jars of pickles and olives, and special imported canned fish. A large refrigerator case against one wall was always humming loudly from the effort of keeping milk, cream, and several cases of soda and beer cool at all times. At the end of the store was the main counter with its cold cuts, freshly made salads, and its gleaming white metal scale on top. Stacked beside the scale today were baskets of fresh rolls and breads which gave off an aroma that contained a mixture of onion, caraway seed, and pumpernickel. Behind the scale was the friendly face of Mr. Rubino, who was in his store seven days a week, fourteen hours or more each day. He was always ready with a smile or a friendly comment, or even a sample piece of cheese or smoked meat as a friendly gesture for his "growing customers," as he referred to us kids in the neighborhood.

▸ Working with description: selecting the dominant impression

When you use a number of specific, sensory images as you write a description, you should do more than simply write a series of sentences that deal with a single topic. You should also create a dominant impression in your reader's mind. Each individual sentence that you write is part of a picture that becomes clear when the reader finishes the paragraph.

For example, when you describe a place, the dominant impression you create might be of a place that is warm, friendly, or comfortable; or it could be a place that is formal, elegant, or artistic. When you write a description of a person, your reader could receive the dominant impression of a positive, efficient person who is outgoing and creative, or of a person who appears to be cold, distant, or hostile. All the sentences should support the dominant impression you have chosen.

Here is a list for you to use as a guide as you work through this unit. Picking a dominant impression is essential in writing the descriptive college paragraph.

Possible Dominant Impressions for Descriptions of Place

crowded	cozy	inviting	cheerful	dazzling
romantic	restful	dreary	drab	uncomfortable
cluttered	ugly	tasteless	unfriendly	gaudy
stuffy	eerie	depressing	spacious	sunny

Possible Dominant Impressions for Descriptions of People

creative	angry	independent	proud	withdrawn
tense	shy	aggressive	generous	sullen
silent	witty	pessimistic	responsible	efficient
snobbish	placid	bumbling	bitter	easygoing

Exercise 1 — Selecting the Dominant Impression

Each of the following places could be the topic for a descriptive paragraph. First, the writer must decide on a dominant impression. Fill in each blank to the right of the topic with an appropriate dominant impression. Use the guide above if you need help.

Developing Paragraphs: Description ▶ 207

Topic	Dominant Impression
1. A high school gym on prom night	_____
2. Your barber or hairdresser's shop	_____
3. The room where you are now sitting	_____
4. The grocery store nearest you	_____
5. A hardware store	_____
6. The post office on Saturday morning	_____
7. An overcrowded waiting room	_____
8. San Francisco in the spring	_____
9. The home of your best friend	_____
10. The kitchen in the morning	_____

Exercise 2   **Selecting the Dominant Impression**

Each of the following persons could be the topic for a descriptive paragraph. First, the writer must decide on a dominant impression. Fill in each blank to the right of the topic with an appropriate dominant impression. Use the guide on page 206 if you need help.

Topic	Dominant Impression
1. An actor or actress being interviewed on television	WITTY
2. An old woman in a nursing home	CRABBY
3. A librarian	IRROGANT
4. A bank clerk on a busy day	EFFICIENT
5. A farmer	EASYGOING
6. A politician running for office	PROUD
7. A cab driver	AGGRESSIVE
8. A shoe salesman	AGGRESSIVE
9. A bride	TENSE
10. A soldier just discharged from the service	CHEERFUL

208 ◂ Mastering the Paragraph

Exercise 3 Selecting the Dominant Impression

Choose your own dominant impression for each of the following persons or places. In the space following each example, write the dominant impression you have chosen.

Topic	Dominant Impression
1. A city park	_____
2. A favorite aunt or uncle	_____
3. A large department store at Christmas	_____
4. A truck driver	_____
5. A school cafeteria	_____
6. A nurse	_____
7. A used-car salesman	_____
8. A beach in the late afternoon	_____
9. A movie theater on Friday evening	_____
10. A student late for class	_____

▸ **Revising vague dominant impressions**

Certain words in the English language have become so overused that they no longer have any specific meaning for a reader. Careful writers avoid these words because they are almost useless in descriptive writing. Here is a list of the most common overused words:

> good, bad
> nice, fine, okay
> normal, typical
> interesting
> beautiful

The following paragraph is an example of the kind of writing that results from the continued use of vague words:

> I had a typical day. The weather was nice and my job was interesting. The food for lunch was okay; supper was really good. After supper I saw my girlfriend, who is really beautiful. That's when my day really became fun.

Notice that all of the details in the paragraph are vague. The writer has told us what happened, but we cannot really see any of the details that are mentioned. This is because the writer has made the mistake of using words that have lost much of their meaning.

Developing Paragraphs: Description ▸ 209

———————— Practice ————————

Rewrite this vague paragraph you have just read. Replace the vague words with details that are more specific.

_____
_____
_____
_____
_____
_____
_____
_____
_____
_____
_____
_____
_____
_____
_____
_____
_____
_____

The next group of exercises will give you practice in recognizing and eliminating overused words.

Exercise 1 — Revising Vague Dominant Impressions

In each of the spaces provided, change the underlined word to a more specific dominant impression. An example has been done for you.

    Vague: The tablecloth was beautiful.

    Revised: The tablecloth was of white linen with delicate blue embroidery.

1. The sky was beautiful. _____

2. The water felt nice. _____

3. Walking along the beach was fun. _____

4. The storm was bad. _____

5. The parking lot was typical. _____

6. The main street is interesting.   _____

7. The dessert tasted good.   _____

8. My brother is normal.   _____

9. Our house is fine.   _____

10. My job is okay.   _____

Exercise 2 — Revising Vague Dominant Impressions

In each of the spaces provided, change the underlined word to a more specific dominant impression.

1. It was a really nice date.   WARM
2. The window display was beautiful.   CONVINCING
3. The boat ride was fine.   _____
4. The circus was fun.   CHEERFUL
5. The lemonade was awful.   SOUR
6. The play was bad.   _____
7. His new suit looked okay.   _____
8. The dance class was fine.   INFORMATIVE
9. Her new watch was nice.   INFORMATIVE
10. It was a good lecture.   INFORMATIVE

Exercise 3 — Revising Vague Dominant Impressions

In each of the spaces provided, change the underlined word to a more specific dominant impression.

1. It was a normal Friday evening.   _____
2. It was an interesting ride through the country.   _____
3. She sang in a very normal voice.   _____
4. The cook served a very typical dinner.   _____
5. The customer bought a nice hat to go with her dress.   _____
6. Roberta told us she had read two good books.   _____
7. She married a fine young pilot.   _____

8. Our trip to the discount store was <u>okay</u>. _____

9. It was a <u>bad</u> interview. _____

10. The couple went to a <u>typical</u> resort last weekend. _____

▶ Working with description: sensory images

One of the basic ways all good writers communicate experiences to their readers is by using sense impressions. We respond to writing that makes us *see* an object, *hear* a sound, *touch* a surface, *smell* an odor, or *taste* a flavor. When a writer uses one or more of these sensory images in a piece of writing, we tend to pay more attention to what the writer is saying, and we tend to remember the details of what we have read.

For example, if you come across the word *door* in a sentence, you might or might not pay attention to it. However, if the writer tells you it was a *brown wooden* door that was *rough to the touch* and that *creaked loudly* when it opened, you would hardly be able to forget it. The door would stay in your mind because the writer used sensory images to make you aware of it.

Practice

The following sentences are taken from the description of Mr. Rubino's delicatessen, a description that you read on pages 205–206. Notice how in each sentence the writer uses at least one sensory image to make the details of that sentence remain in our minds. As you read each of the sentences, identify the physical sense the writer is appealing to by the use of one or more sensory images.

1. A large refrigerator case against one wall was always humming loudly from the effort of keeping milk, cream, and several cases of soda and beer cool at all times.

    Physical sense: _____

2. Stacked on top of the counter were baskets of fresh rolls and breads which gave off an aroma that contained a mixture of onion, caraway seed, and pumpernickel.

    Physical sense: _____

3. He was always ready with a sample piece of cheese or smoked meat as a friendly gesture.

    Physical sense: _____

When you use sensory images in your own writing, you will stimulate your readers' interest, and these images created in their minds will be remembered.

Mastering the Paragraph

Exercise 1 — Recognizing Sensory Images

Each of the following paragraphs contains examples of sensory images. Find the images and list them in the spaces provided.

    I knew how a newspaper office should look and sound and smell—I worked in one for thirteen years. The paper was the *New York Herald Tribune,* and its city room, wide as a city block, was dirty and disheveled. Reporters wrote on ancient typewriters that filled the air with clatter; copy editors labored on coffee-stained desks over what the reporters had written. Crumpled balls of paper littered the floor and filled the wastebaskets—failed efforts to write a good lead or a decent sentence. The walls were grimy—every few years they were painted over in a less restful shade of eye-rest green—and the atmosphere was hazy with the smoke of cigarettes and cigars. At the very center the city editor, a giant named L. L. Engelking, bellowed his displeasure with the day's work, his voice a rumbling volcano in our lives. I thought it was the most beautiful place in the world.

From William Zinsser,
Writing with a Word Processor

Sensory Images

Sight: _____

_____

_____

Sound: _____

_____

Smell: _____

_____

Exercise 2 — Recognizing Sensory Images

Each of the following paragraphs contains examples of sensory images. Find the images and list them in the spaces provided.

    The lake ice split with a sound like the crack of a rifle. Thick slabs of ice broke apart, moving ponderously, edge grinding against edge, upthrusting in jagged peaks, the green-gray water swirling over half-submerged floes. In an agony of rebirth, the splitting and booming of the ice reverberated across the thawing land. Streams raced toward the lake, their swift currents carrying fallen branches and undermining overhanging banks of earth and softened snow. Roads became mires of muck and slush, and the meadows of dried, matted grass oozed mud.

From Nan Salerno with Rosamond Vanderburgh,
Shaman's Daughter

Developing Paragraphs: Description ▶ 213

Sensory Images

Sight: _____
_____
_____

Sound: _____
_____

Touch: _____
_____

Exercise 3

Recognizing Sensory Images

Each of the following paragraphs contains examples of sensory images. Find the images and list them in the spaces provided.

    In the waiting room there were several kerosene stoves, placed about to warm the shivering crowd. The stoves were small black chimneys with nickel handles. We stood around them rubbing hands and watching our clothes steam. An American lady, in a slicker, like the men, and rubber boots up to her knees kept bringing bowls of soup and shiny tin cups with hot coffee. Whatever she said to us and whatever we said to her neither understood, but she was talking the language of hot soup and coffee and kindness and there was perfect communication.

From Ernesto Galarza,
Barrio Boy

Sensory Images

Sight: _____
_____
_____

Sound: _____
_____

Touch: _____
_____

Taste: _____
_____

Smell: _____
_____

Mastering the Paragraph

Exercise 1 **Creating Sensory Images**

Each of the following topic sentences contains an underlined word that names a physical sense. For each topic sentence write three sentences that give examples of sensory images. For example, in the first sentence the sensory image of hearing in the vicinity of a hospital could be explained by writing sentences that describe ambulance sirens, doctors being called over loudspeaker systems, and the voices of people in the waiting room.

1. I knew I was walking past the hospital emergency room from the sounds I could <u>hear</u>.

   Three sentences with sensory images:

   a. _____

   b. _____

   c. _____

2. I can't help stopping in the bakery every Sunday morning because the <u>smells</u> are so good.

   Three sentences with sensory images:

   a. _____

   b. _____

   c. _____

3. The best part of my vacation last year was the <u>sight</u> that greeted me when I got up in the morning.

   Three sentences with sensory images:

   a. _____

   b. _____

   c. _____

Developing Paragraphs: Description ▶ 215

4. Our team won the game because we fans kept *showing* the players our support.

   Three sentences with sensory images:

   a. THE FANS SHOUTED & CHEERED AT THE TOP OF THEIR LUNGS

   b. THEY HELD UP BRIGHT RED BANNERS

   c. THEY SHOT OFF SPECTACULAR FIREWORKS DURING HALFTIME.

5. Thanksgiving makes me always think of the delicious <u>tastes</u> of my grandmother's Thanksgiving dinner.

   Three sentences with sensory images:

   a. _____

   b. _____

   c. _____

Exercise 2 — Creating Sensory Images

Each of the following topic sentences contains an underlined word that names a physical sense. For each topic sentence write three sentences that give examples of sensory images.

1. It is a luxury to wear clothing made with natural fibers because the <u>feeling</u> is quite different from polyesters.

   Three sentences with sensory images:

   a. _____

   b. _____

   c. _____

2. I knew the garbage strike had gone on for a long time when I had to <u>hold my nose</u> walking down some streets.
   Three sentences with sensory images:

   a. _____

   b. _____

   c. _____

3. A lake in the summertime is a relaxing place to be because the <u>sounds</u> you hear all day are so subdued.
   Three sentences with sensory images:

   a. _____

   b. _____

   c. _____

4. As the child walked through the field, she <u>touched</u> the different plants.
   Three sentences with sensory images:

   a. _____

   b. _____

   c. _____

5. Fred drives a very old car, but you can <u>see</u> it is in good condition.
   Three sentences with sensory images:

   a. _____

   b. _____

Developing Paragraphs: Description ▶ 217

c. _____

Exercise 3 — Creating Sensory Images

Each of the following topic sentences contains an underlined word that names a physical sense. For each topic sentence write three sentences that give examples of sensory images.

1. Going to a disco is an overwhelming experience because of the different sounds you <u>hear</u> there.

    Three sentences with sensory images:

    a. *People were talking loudly over the music.*

    b. *The loud obnoxious music was extremely annoying.*

    c. *Drink glasses clanging together were also very loud.*

2. My friend Bill says he loves the <u>feel</u> of the chocolate, the nuts, and the coconut when he eats that candy bar.

    Three sentences with sensory images:

    a. _____

    b. _____

    c. _____

3. I could <u>see</u> that the old woman standing on the corner was very poor.

    Three sentences with sensory images:

    a. _____

    b. _____

    c. _____

4. When you visit a delicatessen you want to taste a great many things at once.
   Three sentences with sensory images:

   a. _____

   b. _____

   c. _____

5. I could see from her reaction that the coffee was too hot.
   Three sentences with sensory images:

   a. _____

   b. _____

   c. _____

▶ Coherence in description: putting details in space order

In descriptive paragraphs, the writer often chooses to arrange supporting details according to space. With this method, you place yourself at the scene and then use a logical order such as moving from nearby to farther away, right to left, or top to bottom. Often you move in such a way that you save the most important detail until last in order to achieve the greatest effect.

In the paragraph on the delicatessen given on pages 205–206, the writer first describes the ceilings and walls of the store, then proceeds to the shelves and large refrigerator, and ends by describing the main counter of the deli with its owner, Mr. Rubino, standing behind it. The ordering of details has been from the outer limits of the room to the inner area, which is central to the point of the paragraph. A description of a clothes closet might order the details differently. Perhaps the writer would begin with the shoes standing on the floor and finish with the hats and gloves arranged on the top shelf, an arrangement that goes from the ground up.

Here is a paragraph from Ernesto Galarza's autobiography, *Barrio Boy*. The writer is describing the one-room apartment where he and his family lived in Mazatlán, Mexico.

> The floor was of large square bricks worn smooth and of grey mortar between. The ceiling was the underside of the tile resting on beams that

pointed from back to front. Families who had lived there before had left a helter-skelter of nails, bolts, and pegs driven into the walls. The kerosene lamp hung from a hook on the center beam.

Notice that the writer begins with a description of the floor, then gives us an idea of what the ceiling is like, and ends with a detailed picture of the walls. We are able to follow the writer through the description because there is a logic or plan. No matter which method of space order you choose in organizing details in a descriptive paragraph, be sure the results allow your reader to see the scene in a logical order.

Exercise 1

Working for Coherence: Using Space Order

Each of the following topic sentences is followed by four descriptive sentences that are out of order. Put these descriptive sentences in order by placing the number 1, 2, 3, 4, or 5 in the space provided before each sentence.

1. The Statue of Liberty, now completely restored, is a marvel to visitors from all over the world.

   (*Order the material from bottom to top.*)

   __3__ With current restoration finished, the crown continues to be used as a place where visitors can get a good view of New York Harbor.

   __1__ The granite base of the statue was quarried and cut many miles from New York City and then taken by boat to Bedloe's Island, where the statue was built.

   __5__ The torch has been repaired and will now be illuminated by outside lights, not lights from inside the torch itself.

   __4__ The seven spikes that rise above the crown represent the seven seas of the world.

   __2__ The body was covered with sheets of copper that was originally mined on an island off the coast of Norway.

2. The old wallet lay on the nightstand.

   (*Order the material from the outside to the inside.*)

   __3__ A clear plastic insert held photographs and necessary items such as a driver's license and credit cards.

   __5__ The secret compartment, which could hold extra money for emergencies, was visible when a small flap of leather was turned up.

   __4__ Behind the photographs and other papers was a small pocket for postage stamps.

   __1__ The rich brown leather of the wallet, worn smooth from years of hard use, faintly showed the owner's name stamped in gold.

   __2__ The wallet seemed to double in size when it was opened, and the color inside was a lighter brown.

3. The young woman was a teen of the eighties.

   (*Order the material from top to bottom.*)

   __3__ She wore an oversized sweater that she had borrowed from her father.

   __5__ Her shoes were white tennis sneakers.

   __2__ Her dangling earrings, which were red and green, matched her outfit.

   __1__ Her short blond hair was clean and feathered attractively.

   __4__ Her jeans, which were the latest style, had a faint paisley print.

4. My aunt's kitchen is a very orderly place.

   (*Order the material from near to far.*)

   __2__ As usual, in the center of the table sits a vase with a fresh yellow daffodil.

   __3__ Nearby on the refrigerator, a magnet holds the week's menu.

   __1__ Sitting at the kitchen table, I am struck by the freshly pressed linen tablecloth.

   __4__ Looking across the room through the stained glass doors of her kitchen cupboards, I can see neat rows of dishes, exactly eight each, matching the colors of the tablecloth and wallpaper.

5. The dashboard of most cars has a standard order.

   (*Order the material from the left to the right.*)

   __4__ The radio, which the driver can reach with his or her right hand without stretching too far, is a standard item in most cars today.

   __5__ Another item on the typical dashboard, usually right in front of the passenger's seat, is the glove compartment.

   __1__ The dashboard of a car contains the instruments needed to operate the car, beginning with the directional signals and light switches often located to the left of the steering wheel.

   __3__ Just to the right of the steering wheel are the controls for the heating vents.

   __2__ The main instrument panel directly in front of the driver indicates the mileage driven, the speed the car is going, and the condition of the battery.

Exercise 2

Working for Coherence: Using Space Order

Each of the following topic sentences could be expanded into a fully developed paragraph. In the spaces provided, give the appropriate supporting details for the topic sentence. Be sure to give your supporting details in a particular order. That is, the details should go from top to bottom, from outside to inside, from close to far, or around the area you are describing.

1. The airport terminal was as busy inside as it was outside.

   a. _____

   b. _____

   c. _____

   d. _____

2. The cafeteria is a large and often deserted area of our school.

   a. _____

   b. _____

   c. _____

   d. _____

3. The picnic area was shady and inviting.

   a. _____

   b. _____

   c. _____

   d. _____

222 ◀ Mastering the Paragraph

4. The motel lobby was obviously once very beautiful, but it was beginning to look shabby.

   a. _____

   b. _____

   c. _____

   d. _____

5. The night I had tickets to see my favorite rock group perform was a night to remember.

   a. _____

   b. _____

   c. _____

   d. _____

Exercise 3   Working for Coherence: Using Space Order

Each of the following topic sentences could be expanded into a fully developed paragraph. In the spaces provided, give the appropriate supporting details for the topic sentence. Be sure to give your supporting details in a particular order. That is, the details should go from top to bottom, from outside to inside, from close to far, or around the area you are describing.

1. The shopping mall was supposed to be restful, but the noise and the bright lights gave me a headache.

   a. _____

   b. _____

Developing Paragraphs: Description ▸ 223

    c. _____

    d. _____

2. The swimming pool looked like a fish tank crowded with exotic fish.

    a. _____

    b. _____

    c. _____

    d. _____

3. We took our final examination in the chemistry laboratory.

    a. _____

    b. _____

    c. _____

    d. _____

4. The pizza shop is so tiny that people are not likely to stay and eat.

    a. _____

    b. _____

    c. _____

    d. _____

5. The bus was filled with a strange assortment of people.

   a. _____
   _____

   b. _____
   _____

   c. _____
   _____

   d. _____
   _____

▶ Writing the descriptive paragraph step by step

To learn a skill with some degree of ease, it is best to follow a step-by-step approach so that various skills are isolated. This will ensure that you are not missing a crucial point or misunderstanding a part of the whole. There certainly are other ways to go about writing an effective paragraph, but here is one method you can use to get good final results. You will learn that writing, like most skills, can be developed by using a logical process.

Steps for Writing the Descriptive Paragraph

1. Study the given topic, and then plan your topic sentence, especially the dominant impression.
2. List at least ten details that come to your mind when you think about the description you have chosen.
3. Then choose the five or six most important details from your list. Be sure these details support the dominant impression.
4. Put your list in order.
5. Write one complete sentence for each of the details you have chosen from your list.
6. Write a concluding statement that offers some reason for describing this topic.
7. Finally, copy your sentences into standard paragraph form.

Exercise 1 — Writing the Descriptive Paragraph Step by Step

The following exercise will guide you through the construction of a descriptive paragraph. Start with the suggested topic. Use the seven steps to help you work through each stage of the writing process.

Topic: A place you have lived

1. Topic sentence: _____
   _____

Developing Paragraphs: Description ▸ 225

2. Make a list of possible supporting details.

   a. _____   f. _____

   b. _____   g. _____

   c. _____   h. _____

   d. _____   i. _____

   e. _____   j. _____

3. Circle the five or six details you believe are the most important for the description.

4. Put your final choices in order by numbering them.

5. Using your final list, write at least one sentence for each detail you have chosen.

   a. _____
   _____

   b. _____
   _____

   c. _____
   _____

   d. _____
   _____

   e. _____
   _____

   f. _____
   _____

   g. _____
   _____

6. Write a concluding statement. _____
   _____
   _____

7. Copy your sentences into standard paragraph form.
   _____
   _____

226 ◂ Mastering the Paragraph

_____
_____
_____
_____
_____
_____
_____
_____
_____
_____
_____
_____
_____
_____
_____
_____

Exercise 2 **Writing the Descriptive Paragraph Step by Step**

The following exercise will guide you through the construction of a descriptive paragraph. Start with the suggested topic. Use the seven steps to help you work through each stage in the writing process.

Topic: A person you admire

1. Topic sentence: _____
   _____

2. Make a list of possible supporting details.

   a. _____   f. _____

   b. _____   e. _____

   c. _____   h. _____

   d. _____   i. _____

   e. _____   j. _____

3. Circle the five or six details you believe are the most important for the description.

Developing Paragraphs: Description ▸ 227

4. Put your choices in order by numbering them.
5. Using your final list, write at least one sentence for each detail you have chosen.

   a. _____
   _____

   b. _____
   _____

   c. _____
   _____

   d. _____
   _____

   e. _____
   _____

   f. _____
   _____

   g. _____
   _____

6. Write a concluding statement. _____
   _____
   _____
   _____

7. Copy your sentences into standard paragraph form.

_____
_____
_____
_____
_____
_____
_____
_____
_____

Exercise 3 Writing the Descriptive Paragraph Step by Step

The following exercise will guide you through the construction of a descriptive paragraph. Start with the suggested topic. Use the seven steps to help you work through each stage of the writing process.

Topic: A treasured possession.

1. Topic sentence: _____
   _____

2. Make a list of possible supporting details.

   a. _____   f. _____
   b. _____   g. _____
   c. _____   h. _____
   d. _____   i. _____
   e. _____   j. _____

3. Circle the five or six details you believe are the most important for the description.
4. Put your final choices in order by numbering them.
5. Using your final list, write at least one sentence for each detail you have chosen.

   a. _____
      _____

   b. _____
      _____

Developing Paragraphs: Description   229

c. _____

d. _____

e. _____

f. _____

g. _____

6. Write a concluding statement. _____

7. Copy your sentences into standard paragraph form.

On your own: writing descriptive paragraphs from model paragraphs

A description of a home

ASSIGNMENT 1: Write a paragraph in which you describe a house or room that you remember clearly. Choose your dominant impression carefully and then make your sensory images support that impression. You may want to include in your description the person who lives in the house or room. Notice, in the model paragraph from Charles Chaplin's *My Autobiography,* the importance of the last sentence, in which the writer gives his paragraph added impact by naming the person who lives in the room he has described.

Model Paragraph

It was dark when we entered his bungalow, and when we switched on the light I was shocked. The place was empty and drab. In his room was an old iron bed with a light bulb hanging over the head of it. A rickety old table and one chair were the other furnishings. Near the bed was a wooden box upon which was a brass ashtray filled with cigarette butts. The room allotted to me was almost the same, only it was minus a grocery box. Nothing worked. The bathroom was unspeakable. One had to take a jug and fill it from the bath tap and empty it down the flush to make the toilet work. This was the home of G. M. Anderson, the multimillionaire cowboy.

Ten suggested topics

1. A student's apartment
2. A vacation cottage
3. A dormitory
4. The house of your dreams
5. Your bedroom
6. A kitchen
7. The messiest room you ever saw
8. The strangest room you ever saw
9. A house you will never forget
10. A house that did not fit the character of the person living there

A description of a person

ASSIGNMENT 2: Describe a person you have observed more than once. If you saw this person only once, indicate the details that made him or her stay in your mind. If you choose to describe a person with whom you are more familiar, select the most outstanding details that will help your reader have a single, dominant impression. In the model paragraph, from Betty Smith's novel *A Tree Grows in Brooklyn,* Francie, the main character, sees an old man sitting in a bakery; his appearance leads her to describe him to herself in detail.

Model Paragraph

Francie stared at the man. She played her favorite game, figuring out about people. His thin tangled hair was the same dirty gray as the stubble standing on his sunken cheeks. Dried spittle caked the corners of his mouth. He yawned. He had no teeth. She watched, fascinated and revolted, as he closed his mouth, drew his lips inward until there was no mouth, and made his chin come up to almost meet his nose. She studied his old coat with the padding hanging out of the torn sleeve seam. His legs were sprawled wide in helpless relaxation and one of the buttons was missing from his grease-caked pants opening. She saw that his shoes were battered and broken open at the toes. One shoe was laced with a much-knotted shoestring, and the other with a bit of dirty twine. She saw two thick dirty toes with creased gray toenails.

Ten suggested topics

1. An elderly relative
2. A hard-working student
3. An outstanding athlete
4. A loyal friend
5. An overworked waitress
6. A cab driver
7. A fashion model
8. A gossipy neighbor
9. A street vendor
10. A rude salesperson

A description of a time of day

ASSIGNMENT 3: Write a paragraph in which you describe the sights, sounds, and events of a particular time of day in a place you know well. In the model paragraph that follows, the writer has chosen to describe an especially busy time of day, namely, the morning hours, when activity can be frantic in a household.

Model Paragraph

I remember the turmoil of mornings in our house. My brothers and sisters rushed about upstairs and down trying to get ready for school. Mom would repeatedly tell them to hurry up. Molly would usually scream down from her bedroom, "What am I going to do? I don't have any clean underwear!" Amy, often in tears, sat at the kitchen table still in her pajamas trying to do her math. Paul paced back and forth in front of the mirror angrily combing his unruly hair which stuck up in all directions while Roland threatened to punch him if he didn't find the pen he had borrowed the night before. Mother was stuffing sandwiches into bags while she sighed, "I'm afraid there isn't anything for dessert today." No one heard her. Then came the yelling up the stairs, "You should have left ten minutes ago." One by one, these unwilling victims were packed up and pushed out the door. Mother wasn't safe yet. Somebody always came back frantic and desperate. "My flute, Mom, where's my flute, quick! I'll get killed if I don't have it today." Every crisis apparently meant the difference between life and death. Morning at our house was like watching a troop preparing for battle. When they had finally gone, I was left in complete silence while my mother slumped on a chair at the kitchen table. She paid no attention to me.

Ten suggested topics

1. A Saturday filled with errands
2. The dinner hour at my house
3. Lunchtime in a cafeteria
4. A midnight raid on the refrigerator
5. Christmas morning
6. TGIF (Thank God It's Friday)
7. Getting ready to go out on a Friday night
8. My Sunday-morning routine
9. Coming home from school or work
10. Watching late-night movies

A description of a place

ASSIGNMENT 4: Write a paragraph in which you describe a place you know well or remember clearly. The model paragraph that follows is from the novel *A Tree Grows in Brooklyn* and describes one of the stores that the main character, Francie Nolan, would visit often. The description is very effective because the writer, Betty Smith, has selected specific, colorful details that tend to stay in the reader's mind.

Model Paragraph

One of Francie's favorite stores was the one which sold nothing but tea, coffee, and spices. It was an exciting place of rows of lacquered bins and strange, romantic, exotic odors. There were a dozen scarlet coffee bins with adventurous words written across the front in black China ink: Brazil! Argentine! Turkish! Jafa! Mixed Blend! The tea was in smaller bins: beautiful bins with sloping covers. They read: Oolong! Formosa! Orange Pekoe! Black China! Flowering Almond! Jasmine! Irish Tea! The spices were in miniature bins behind the counter. Their names marched in a row across the shelves: cinnamon—cloves—ginger—all-spice—ball nutmeg—curry—pepper corns—sage—thyme—marjoram. All pepper when purchased was ground in a tiny pepper mill.

Ten suggested topics

1. A large department store
2. A delicatessen
3. A coffee shop
4. A pizza parlor
5. A shoe store
6. A shopping mall
7. A lively street corner
8. A college bookstore
9. A gymnasium
10. A student lounge

A description of a time of year

ASSIGNMENT 5: Write a paragraph in which you describe a particular time of year. Make sure that all of the details you choose relate specifically to that time of year. In the model paragraph that follows, from the novel *Shaman's Daughter* by Nan Salerno and Rosamond Vanderburgh, the description of a lake just emerging from the grip of winter is a vivid picture of a natural phenomenon.

Model Paragraph

The lake ice split with a sound like the crack of a rifle. Thick slabs of ice broke apart, moving ponderously, edge grinding against edge, upthrusting in jagged peaks, the green-gray water swirling over half-submerged floes. In an agony of rebirth, the splitting and booming of the ice reverberated across the thawing land. Streams raced toward the lake, their swift currents carrying fallen branches and undermining overhanging banks of earth and softened snow. Roads became mires of muck and slush, and the meadows of dried, matted grass oozed mud.

Ten suggested topics

1. A winter storm
2. A summer picnic
3. Summer in the city
4. A winter walk
5. Jogging in the spring rain
6. Sunbathing on a beach
7. Signs of spring in my neighborhood
8. The woods in autumn
9. Ice skating in winter
10. Halloween night

13

Developing Paragraphs: Narration

▶ What is narration?

Narration is the oldest and best-known form of verbal communication. It is, quite simply, the telling of a story. Every culture in the world, past and present, has used narration to provide entertainment as well as information for the people of that culture. Since everyone likes a good story, the many forms of narration, such as novels, short stories, soap operas, and full-length movies, are always popular.

The following narrative paragraph, taken from Helen Keller's autobiography, tells the story of this young girl's realization that every object has a name. The paragraph shows the enormous difficulties faced by a seven-year-old girl who was unable to see, hear, or speak.

The morning after my teacher came she led me into her room and gave me a doll. The little blind children at the Perkins Institution had sent it and Laura Bridgman had dressed it; but I did not know this until afterward. When I had played with it a little while, Miss Sullivan slowly spelled into my hand the word "d-o-l-l." I was at once interested in this finger play and tried to imitate it. When I finally succeeded in making the letters correctly, I was flushed with childish pleasure and pride. Running downstairs to my mother I held up my hand and made the letters for doll. I did not know that I was spelling a word or even that words existed; I was simply making my fingers go in monkey-like imitation. In the days that followed I learned to spell in this uncomprehending way a great many words, among them *pin, hat, cup* and a few verbs like *sit, stand,* and *walk.* But my teacher had been with me several weeks before I understood that everything has a name.

▶ Working with narration: using narration to make a point

At one time or another you have met a person who loves to talk on and on without making any real point. This person is likely to tell you everything that happened in one day, including every cough and sideways glance. Your reaction to the seemingly needless and endless supply of details is probably one of fatigue and hope for a quick getaway. This is not narration at its best! A good story is almost always told to make a point: it can make us laugh, it can make us understand, or it can change our attitudes.

When Helen Keller tells the story of her early experiences with her teacher, she is careful to use only those details that are relevant to her story. For example, the doll her teacher gave her is an important part of the story. Not only does this doll reveal something about Helen Keller's teacher and her other friends, but it also reveals the astounding fact that Helen began to understand that objects have names. We see the beginning of Helen's long struggle to communicate with other people.

Exercise 1

Using Narration to Make a Point

Each of the following examples is the beginning of a topic sentence for a narrative paragraph. Complete each sentence by providing a controlling idea that could be the point for the story.

1. Since my family is so large (or small), I have had to learn to _____

2. When I couldn't get a job, I realized _____

3. After going to the movies every Saturday for many years, I discovered _____

4. When I arrived at the room where my business class was to meet, I found _____

5. When my best friend got married, I began to see that _____

Exercise 2

Using Narration to Make a Point

Each of the following examples is the beginning of a topic sentence for a narrative paragraph. Complete each sentence by providing a controlling idea that could be the point for the story.

1. When I looked more closely at the man, I realized that _____

2. When the president finished his speech, I concluded that _____

[Handwritten note in margin: TOPIC OPINION POINT]

3. By the end of the movie, I decided that _____
   _____

4. After I changed the course as well as the teacher, I felt _____
   _____

5. When I could not get past the office secretary, I realized that _____
   _____

Exercise 3 **Using Narration to Make a Point**

Each of the following examples is the beginning of a topic sentence for a narrative paragraph. Complete each sentence by providing a controlling idea that could be the point for the story.

1. When the art teacher tore up my sketches in front of the class, I decided
   _____
   _____

2. When there were no responses to my ad, I concluded _____
   _____

3. After two days of trying to sell magazine subscriptions, I knew _____
   _____

4. After I had actually performed my first experiment in the lab, I understood
   _____
   _____

5. The first time I tried to cook a dinner for a group of people, I found out
   _____
   _____

▶ Coherence in narration: placing details in order of time sequence

Ordering details in a paragraph of narration usually follows a time sequence. That is, you tell what happened first, then next, and next, until finally you get to the end of the story. An event could take place in a matter of minutes or over a period of many years.

In the following paragraph, the story takes place in a single day. The six events that made the day a disaster are given in the order in which they happened. Although some stories flash back to the past or forward to the future, most use the natural chronological order of the events.

Developing Paragraphs: Narration ▶ 237

My day was a disaster. First, it had snowed during the night, which meant I had to shovel before I could leave for work. I was mad that I hadn't gotten up earlier. Then I had trouble starting my car, and to make matters worse, my daughter wasn't feeling well and said she didn't think she should go to school. When I eventually did arrive at school, I was twenty minutes late. Soon I found out the secretary had forgotten to type the exam I was supposed to give my class that day. I quickly had to make another plan. By three o'clock, I was looking forward to getting my paycheck. Foolish woman! When I went to pick it up, the girl in the office told me that something had gone wrong with the computers. I would not be able to get my check until Tuesday. Disappointed, I walked down the hill to the parking lot. There I met my final defeat. In my hurry to park the car in the morning, I had left my parking lights on. Now my battery was dead. Even an optimist like me had the right to be discouraged!

Exercise 1

**Working for Coherence:
Using Details in Order of Time Sequence**

Each of the topics below is followed by five supporting details. These supporting details are not given in any order. Order the events according to time sequence by placing the appropriate number in the space provided.

1. A fight in my apartment building

    __3__ Some of the neighbors became so frightened that they called the police.

    __1__ The man and the woman began to fight around six o'clock.

    __4__ When the police came, they found the couple struggling in the kitchen.

    __2__ The neighbors heard the man's voice shouting angrily.

    __5__ There were no arrests, but the police warned both individuals not to disturb the peace again.

2. A night patrol

    __5__ Their uniforms were soaking wet from hours in the rain.

    __2__ The captain ordered the soldiers to prepare for a special night patrol.

    __3__ Grumbling, the men got up and dressed in the dark.

    __4__ As they marched in single file through the woods, it began to rain.

    __1__ The captain barked his orders to the men who were sleeping in the barracks.

3. An important invitation

    __5__ On the day of the party Louise asked her boss if she could leave an hour or two early in order to have time to get ready.

Mastering the Paragraph

_1_ When Louise was invited to the party, she was very excited.

_4_ Four days before the party, she finally got up enough nerve to call Bob and ask him to go with her.

_3_ One week before the party she bought a new dress even though she could not afford one.

_2_ Still holding the invitation, she searched through her closet, but all her dresses looked so dull and unfashionable.

4. The driving test

_2_ She had her last lesson with Mr. Johnson on Saturday morning.

_5_ As she ate breakfast that morning, Melinda read the driver's manual one more time because she knew it was her last chance to review.

_1_ Melinda's driving test was scheduled for Monday morning.

_3_ On Sunday afternoon her father gave her some advice on what to be careful of when she took her road test.

_6_ As her mother drove her to the motor vehicle bureau, Melinda tried to relax and not think about the test.

_4_ The night before her test, Melinda had phone calls from two friends who wished her good luck.

5. Making up my mind

_4_ By the time I saw the dean for final approval of the change, I knew I had made the right decision.

_5_ When I registered for my new courses for the next semester, I knew that I was doing what I should have done all along.

_1_ I spent the summer of my sophomore year thinking about the career I really wanted to follow.

_6_ I suppose the experience taught me that you should always make a change in your life after you have thought it through completely.

_2_ When I finally did decide to change majors, my friends acted as though I had decided to change my citizenship.

_3_ When I told my favorite professor about my change of mind, he was very supportive, even though I had begun my major with him.

Developing Paragraphs: Narration ▸ 239

Exercise 2   Working for Coherence:
                    Using Details in Order of Time Sequence

Each of the following topics is followed by supporting details. These supporting details are not in any order. Place a number in the space provided before each sentence to show the order according to time sequence.

1. From the life of Amelia Earhart, pioneer aviator and writer

   __1__ Amelia Earhart was born in Atchison, Kansas, in 1897.

   __3__ Toward the end of World War I, she worked as a nurse's aide.

   __2__ When she was sixteen, her family moved to St. Paul, Minnesota.

   __5__ Four years after her history-making flight across the Atlantic, she made her solo flight across that same ocean.

   __4__ After learning to fly in the early 1920s, she became, in 1928, the first woman to cross the Atlantic, although on that trip she was a passenger and not a pilot.

   __6__ Three years after her solo Atlantic flight, she became the first person to fly from Hawaii to California.

   __7__ On her last flight, in 1937, she was lost at sea; no trace of her was ever found.

2. From the life of Sojourner Truth, crusader, preacher, and the first black woman to speak out against slavery

   __1__ Sojourner Truth began life as a slave when she was born in 1797, but she was set free in 1827.

   __2__ She was forty-six when she took the name of Sojourner Truth.

   __6__ She was received by Abraham Lincoln in the White House the year before that president was assassinated.

   __7__ She spent her final years giving lectures throughout the North.

   __3__ In 1850 she traveled to the West, where her speeches against slavery and for women's rights drew large crowds.

   __5__ At the beginning of the Civil War she was active in gathering supplies for the black regiments that were fighting in the war.

   __4__ Not long after her first trip west, she settled in Battle Creek, Michigan.

3. From the life of Theodore Roosevelt, president, explorer, naturalist, and writer

   __1__ Theodore Roosevelt was born in New York City in 1858; he went to college at the age of eighteen.

   __4__ He ran for mayor of New York in 1886, but lost.

_5_ Two years before the turn of the century, he was elected governor of New York State.

_2_ Six years before he was defeated for mayor of New York City, he married.

_3_ Just one year before he tried to become mayor of New York, he was appointed president of that city's Police Board.

_6_ In 1904 he began work on the Panama Canal.

_7_ In 1905 he was awarded the Nobel Peace Prize for his part in bringing about peace between Russia and Japan.

4. From the life of Helen Keller, activist for handicapped people, writer, and lecturer

_1_ Helen Keller was born in 1880.

_5_ She entered Radcliffe College in 1900.

_4_ Shortly after she began to work with her tutor, she could spell out 300 words.

_2_ When she was less than two years of age, a fever led to the loss of her vision and hearing.

_6_ She published *The Story of My Life* when she was twenty-two.

_3_ When she was seven years old, she met Anne Sullivan, who became her tutor.

_7_ She graduated with honors after four years in college.

5. From the life of Thomas Edison, inventor

_1_ Thomas Edison was born in Ohio in 1847. He was not good in school, but he read widely.

_3_ As a teenager, he started a profitable business selling newspapers and candy on passenger trains.

_2_ By the age of ten, he had developed a deep interest in chemistry.

_7_ During World War I, he conducted research on torpedoes and submarine periscopes.

_4_ In 1863 he became a telegraph operator; five years later he went to work for Western Union.

_5_ When he was thirty years old, he invented the phonograph.

_6_ In 1879 he made it possible for the light bulb to be a commercially practical product.

Developing Paragraphs: Narration ▶ 241

Exercise 3

Working for Coherence:
Using Details in Order of Time Sequence

Each of the following topics is followed by supporting details. These supporting details are not in any order. Place a number in the space provided before each sentence to show the order according to time sequence.

1. The novel *Frankenstein* by Mary Shelley

   __4__ The monster turns on Victor Frankenstein and kills his younger brother, William.

   __2__ While at college in Ingolstadt, Victor Frankenstein learns the secret of creating life.

   __9__ Victor Frankenstein chases the monster to the frozen North, where he dies and the monster escapes.

   __8__ In revenge, the monster kills Victor Frankenstein's new bride.

   __3__ By raiding butcher shops and medical labs, Victor Frankenstein is able to make an eight-foot monster and give it life.

   __5__ Suspicious after discovering his brother, Victor Frankenstein tries to find the monster; when he finds him, the monster demands that he make a mate for him.

   __1__ Victor Frankenstein was born in Geneva, Switzerland, and from an early age had a deep interest in science.

   __6__ If Victor Frankenstein agrees, the monster and his bride will go to South America, never to be seen again; if he refuses, the monster will continue to kill people at random.

   __7__ Victor Frankenstein agrees, but at the last moment destroys the monster's mate.

2. The novel *The Time Machine* by H. G. Wells

   __3__ The Eloi hide his time machine and refuse to give it back.

   __4__ He travels thirty million years into the future, but he finds only a barren landscape.

   __1__ The Time Traveler goes forward in time and finds himself in a strange country where everyone is a vegetarian—animals have become extinct. The people of this land are the Eloi, who are soft and sensual; because the world is at peace, there is no need to struggle and people have lost their strength.

   __2__ The Eloi live in the year 802,701.

   __5__ He returns to the present.

3. The novel *Great Expectations* by Charles Dickens

   _6_ Pip realizes Miss Havisham has had nothing to do with his inheritance.

   _1_ Pip, an orphan, is raised by a blacksmith, Joe Gargery, and his sister.

   _3_ After his adventure with the convict, Pip works in a mansion near his home for a Miss Havisham, a crazed old woman who still wears the wedding dress she wore on the day her bridegroom failed to show up for the wedding.

   _2_ One day, Pip sees a stranger in the marshes near his home. The man asks Pip to bring him food and a filing iron—he is an escaped convict.

   _4_ Pip is contacted by a lawyer, who tells him that a nameless person has arranged for him to go to London, all expenses paid, to begin life as a gentleman.

   _5_ On his twenty-first birthday, Pip receives a visitor; it is the convict, Abel Magwitch, whom he had helped years before—it is he who has given Pip the money.

4. The story *Gulliver's Travels* by Jonathan Swift

   _2_ He helps Lilliput in a war with a neighboring country. However, he has a disagreement with the emperor, leaves the country, and sails back to England.

   _3_ On his way to his native country, the ship is blown off course and Gulliver is captured by giants. He is put on show. After two years in the country of the Brobdingnag, he escapes and returns to England.

   _1_ Lemuel Gulliver finds himself shipwrecked on the shore of a strange country and he wakes up to find himself held to the ground by hundreds of small ropes. This is Lilliput, the land of small humans, and this is his first adventure.

   _4_ Perhaps his most famous voyage is to the land of the Houyhnhnms, intelligent horses who are the masters of the Yahoos, humanlike creatures who also live in that country.

5. The novel *1984* by George Orwell

   _2_ Julia and Winston are arrested together by the thought police.

   _3_ Winston is tortured; he confesses.

   _1_ In the society of Oceania, Winston Smith is a worker at the Ministry of Truth, where he revises historical facts to suit the needs of the ruling party.

_____ At work, Winston meets Julia and they have a love affair, something forbidden by the authorities.

_____ Winston finally accepts Big Brother, the ruler of Oceania who is never seen.

▶ Transitions and time order

Writers who deal with time order in their work find themselves using words and phrases to help their readers get from one part of their work to another. These words and phrases are called **transitions**, and they are an important tool for every writer. Here is the Helen Keller paragraph you studied earlier, but this time printed with each of the transitional words and phrases in boldface.

The morning after my teacher came she led me into her room and gave me a doll. The little blind children at the Perkins Institution had sent it and Laura Bridgman had dressed it; but I did not know this **until afterward**. When I had played with it **a little while**, Miss Sullivan slowly spelled into my hand the word "d-o-l-l." I was **at once** interested in this finger play and tried to imitate it. When I **finally** succeeded in making the letters correctly, I was flushed with childish pleasure and pride. Running downstairs to my mother I held up my hand and made the letters for doll. I did not know that I was spelling a word or even that words existed; I was simply making my fingers go in monkey-like imitation. **In the days that followed** I learned to spell in this uncomprehending way a great many words, among them *pin, hat, cup* and a few verbs like *sit, stand,* and *walk*. But my teacher had been with me **several weeks** before I understood that everything has a name.

Notice how the time transitions used in this paragraph make the order of events clear. "*The morning after* my teacher came" gives the reader the sense that the action of the story is being told day by day. The second sentence contains information about the doll that Helen Keller admits that she did not learn about until later—*afterward*. The writer then tells us that when she played with the doll *a little while*, she suddenly—*at once*—became interested in the connection between an object and the word for that object. This realization was one of the central lessons in young Helen Keller's education, and it became the starting point for all of her later learning. She uses two more transitional phrases to tell us about the beginning of this education: *In the days that followed*, we learn, she mastered a great many words, although it took her *several weeks* before she learned the even more important concept that everything had a name.

Helen Keller has used time words and phrases to give us an idea of how long it took her to reach these important realizations in her life. Her use of transitions helps to make her meaning clear.

Mastering the Paragraph

Exercise 1 — Working with Transitions

Using the transitions given in the list below or using ones you think of yourself, fill in each of the blanks in the following student paragraph.

at once	later, later on	after a little while
immediately	now, by now	first, first of all
soon afterward	finally	then
suddenly	in the next moment	next

    I arrived at Aunt Lorinda's in the middle of a heat wave. It was 105 in the shade and very humid. Aunt Lorinda as usual greeted me with the list of activities she had scheduled for the day. _____ we went to the attic to gather old clothes for the Salvation Army. I nearly passed out up in the attic. Sweat poured down my face. Aunt Lorinda, in her crisp cotton sundress, looked cool and was obviously enjoying herself. "If you see something you want, take it," she said graciously. "It's so nice of you to give me a hand today. You're young and strong and have so much more energy than I." _____ her plans included the yard work. I took off my shirt and mowed the lawn while my eighty-year-old aunt trimmed hedges and weeded the flower beds. _____ it was time to drive into the dusty town and do errands. Luckily, Auntie stayed behind to fix lunch and I was able to duck into an air-conditioned coffee shop for ten minutes' rest before I dropped off the old clothes at the Salvation Army. I wasn't anxious to find out what help I could be to my aunt in the afternoon. I hoped it wouldn't be something like last year when I had to put a new roof on the old shed in the backyard. I could feel the beginning of a painful sunburn.

Exercise 2 — Working with Transitions

Below is a narrative paragraph from the famous story "The Overcoat" by Nikolai Gogol. Make a list in the spaces provided of all the transitions of time that give order to the paragraph.

    In the meantime Akakii Akakiievich walked along feeling in the most festive of moods. He was conscious every second of every minute that he had a new overcoat on his shoulders, and several times even smiled slightly because of his inward pleasure. In reality he was a gainer on two points: for one, the overcoat was warm; for the other, it was a fine thing. He did not notice the walk at all and suddenly found himself at the Bureau; in the porter's room he took off his overcoat, looked it over, and entrusted it to the particular care of the doorman. None knows in what manner everybody in the Bureau suddenly learned that Akakii Akakiievich had a new overcoat, and that the **negligee** was no longer in existence. They all immediately ran out into the vestibule to inspect Akakii Akakiievich's new overcoat. They fell to congratulating him, to saying agreeable things to him, so that at first he could merely smile, and in a short time became actually embarrassed. And when all of them, having besieged him, began telling him that the new overcoat ought to be baptized and that he ought, at the least, to get up an evening party for them, Akakii Akakiievich was utterly at a loss, not

any piece of informal clothing

knowing what to do with himself, what answers to make, nor how to get out of inviting them. It was only a few minutes later that he began assuring them, quite simple-heartedly, that it wasn't a new overcoat at all, that it was just an ordinary overcoat, that in fact it was an old overcoat. Finally one of the bureaucrats—some sort of an Assistant to a Head of a Department actually—probably in order to show that he was not at all a proud stick and willing to mingle even with those beneath him, said: "So be it, then; I'm giving a party this evening and ask all of you to have tea with me; today, appropriately enough, happens to be my birthday."

Exercise 3

Working with Transitions

Below is a narrative paragraph from a story by the Russian writer Ivan Turgenev. Make a list of all the transitions of time that give order to the paragraph.

I went to the right through the bushes. Meantime the night had crept close and grown up like a storm cloud; it seemed as though, with the mists of evening, darkness was rising up on all sides and flowing down from overhead. I had come upon some sort of little, untrodden, overgrown path; I walked along it, gazing intently before me. Soon all was blackness and silence around—only the quail's cry was heard from time to time. Some small nightbird, flitting noiselessly near the ground on its soft wings, almost flapped against me and scurried away in alarm. I came out on the further side of the bushes, and made my way along a field by the hedge. By now I could hardly make out distant objects; the field showed dimly white around; beyond it rose up a sullen darkness, which seemed moving up closer in huge masses every instant. My steps gave a muffled sound in the air, that grew colder and colder. The pale sky began again to grow blue—but it was the blue of night. The tiny stars glimmered and twinkled in it.

▶ Writing the narrative paragraph step by step

To learn a skill with some degree of ease, it is best to follow a step-by-step approach so that various skills can be worked on one skill at a time. This will ensure that you are not missing a crucial point or misunderstanding a part of the whole. There certainly are other ways and steps to go about writing assignments, but here is one logical process you can use to get good results.

Steps for Writing the Narrative Paragraph

1. Study the given topic and then plan your topic sentence with its controlling idea. AND POINT.
2. List the sequence of events that come to your mind when you think about the story you have chosen.
3. Then choose the five or six most important events from your list.
4. Put your list in order.
5. Write one complete sentence for each of the events you have chosen from your list.
6. Write a concluding statement that gives some point to the events of the story.
7. Finally, copy your sentences into standard paragraph form.

Exercise 1 — Writing the Narrative Paragraph Step by Step

This exercise will guide you through the construction of a complete narrative paragraph. Start with the suggested topic. Use the seven steps above to help you work through each stage of the writing process.

Topic: Every family has a favorite story they like to tell about one of their members, often something humorous that happened to one of them. There are also crises and tragic moments in the life of every family. Choose a story, funny or tragic, from the life of a family you know.

1. Topic sentence: _____
   _____

2. Make a list of events.

   a. _____   f. _____
   b. _____   g. _____
   c. _____   h. _____
   d. _____   i. _____
   e. _____   j. _____

3. Circle the five or six events you believe are the most important for the point of the story.
4. Put your final choices in order by numbering each of them.
5. Using your final list, write at least one sentence for each event you have chosen.

   a. _____
   _____

Developing Paragraphs: Narration 247

b. _____
_____

c. _____
_____

d. _____
_____

e. _____
_____

f. _____
_____

g. _____
_____

6. Write a concluding statement. _____
_____
_____

7. Copy your sentences into standard paragraph form.

_____
_____
_____
_____
_____
_____
_____
_____
_____
_____
_____

_____

_____

_____

Exercise 2 Writing the Narrative Paragraph Step by Step

This exercise will guide you through the construction of a complete narrative paragraph. Start with the suggested topic. Use the seven steps on page 246 to help you work through each stage of the writing process.

Topic: Recount the plot of a book you have read recently or a movie you have seen within the last few weeks.

1. Topic sentence: _____

    _____

2. Make a list of events.

    a. _____   f. _____

    b. _____   g. _____

    c. _____   h. _____

    d. _____   i. _____

    e. _____   j. _____

3. Circle the five or six events you believe are the most important for the point of the story.

4. Put your choices in order by numbering them.

5. Using your final list, write at least one sentence for each event you have chosen.

    a. _____

    _____

    b. _____

    _____

    c. _____

    _____

    d. _____

    _____

    e. _____

    _____

Developing Paragraphs: Narration ▶ 249

    f. _____

    g. _____

6. Write a concluding statement. _____

7. Copy your sentences into standard paragraph form.

Exercise 3 — Writing the Narrative Paragraph Step by Step

This exercise will guide you through the construction of a complete narrative paragraph. Start with the suggested topic. Use the seven steps on page 246 to help you work through each stage of the writing process.

Topic: Tell a story that you have heard one of your parents tell about his or her past.

1. Topic sentence: _____
   _____

2. Make a list of possible supporting details.

   a. _____   f. _____

   b. _____   g. _____

   c. _____   h. _____

   d. _____   i. _____

   e. _____   j. _____

3. Circle the five or six details you believe are the most important for the point of the story.

4. Put your final choices in order by numbering them.

5. Using your final list, write one sentence for each detail you have chosen.

   a. _____
   _____

   b. _____
   _____

   c. _____
   _____

   d. _____
   _____

   e. _____
   _____

   f. _____
   _____

   g. _____
   _____

Developing Paragraphs: Narration ▶ 251

6. Write a concluding statement. _____

_____

_____

7. Copy your sentences into standard paragraph form.

_____
_____
_____
_____
_____
_____
_____
_____
_____
_____
_____
_____
_____
_____
_____
_____
_____

▶ On your own: writing narrative paragraphs from model paragraphs

The story of how you faced a new challenge

ASSIGNMENT 1: Write a paragraph telling the story of a day or part of a day in which you faced an important challenge of some kind. It could have been a challenge you faced in school, at home, or on the job. The following paragraph by the journalist Betty Rollin is an example of such an experience.

Model Paragraph

When I awoke that morning I hit the floor running. I washed my face, brushed my teeth, got a pot of coffee going, tightened the sash on my bathrobe, snapped my typewriter out of its case, placed it on the kitchen table, retrieved my notes from the floor where they were stacked in

Manila folders, unwrapped a pack of bond paper, put the top sheet in the typewriter, looked at it, put my head on the keys, wrapped my arms around its base and cried.

Ten suggested topics

1. The day I started a new job
2. My first day in history class
3. The day I began my first term paper
4. The day I tried to wallpaper my bedroom
5. The morning of my big job interview
6. Facing a large debt
7. Trying to reestablish a friendship gone sour
8. The day I started driving lessons
9. Coping with a death in the family
10. The day I faced a deadline

The story of an unpleasant fight or argument

ASSIGNMENT 2: Write a paragraph in which you tell the story of a fight or confrontation you either witnessed or became involved in. Choose an experience that left a deep impression on you. What are the important details of the incident that remain most clearly in your mind? The following paragraph is from Albert Halper's short story "Prelude."

Model Paragraph

But the people just stood there afraid to do a thing. Then while a few guys held me, Gooley and about four others went for the stand, turning it over and mussing and stamping on all the newspapers they could find. Syl started to scratch them, so they hit her. Then I broke away to help her, and then they started socking me too. My father tried to reach me, but three guys kept him away. Four guys got me down and started kicking me and all the time my father was begging them to let me up and Syl was screaming at the people to help. And while I was down, my face was squeezed against some papers on the sidewalk telling about Austria and I guess I went nuts while they kept hitting me, and I kept seeing the headlines against my nose.

Ten suggested topics

A confrontation between

1. A police officer and a guilty motorist
2. A teacher and a student
3. An angry customer and a store clerk
4. A frustrated parent and a child
5. A manager and an unhappy employee
6. A judge and an unwilling witness
7. A museum guard and a careless tourist
8. A politician and an angry citizen
9. A mugger and a frightened victim
10. An engaged couple about to break up

Developing Paragraphs: Narration ▶ 253

The beginning of a special relationship

ASSIGNMENT 3: Write a paragraph that tells the story of how you became close to another person. Select one particular moment when the relationship changed from casual friendliness to something deeper and more lasting. Perhaps you shared an experience that brought you together. The following paragraph is taken from Morley Callaghan's short story "One Spring Night."

Model Paragraph

Bob had taken her out a few times when he had felt like having some girl to talk to who knew him and liked him. And tonight he was leaning back good-humoredly, telling her one thing and then another with the wise self-assurance he usually had when with her; but gradually, as he watched her, he found himself talking more slowly, his voice grew serious and much softer, and then finally he leaned across the table toward her as though he had just discovered that her neck was full and soft with her spring coat thrown open, and that her face under her little black straw hat tilted back on her head had a new, eager beauty. Her warm, smiling softness was so close to him that he smiled a bit shyly.

Ten suggested topics

1. My relationship with a teacher
2. My relationship with a fellow student
3. A moment when I understood my clergyman in a new way
4. When I learned something new about a neighborhood merchant
5. When I shared an experience with a fellow worker
6. When I made friends with someone older or younger than myself
7. When my relationship with my brother or sister changed
8. The moment when my attitude about a grandparent changed
9. When a stranger became a friend
10. When a relationship went from bad to worse

You won't believe what happened to me today!

ASSIGNMENT 4: Tell the story of a day you found yourself in a difficult or frustrating situation. The following example is from Berton Roueche's short story "Phone Call."

Model Paragraph

I got out of the truck and got down on my knees and twisted my neck and looked underneath. Everything looked O.K. There wasn't anything hanging down or anything. I got up and opened the hood and looked at the engine. I don't know too much about engines—only what I picked up working around Lindy's Service Station the summer before last. But the engine looked O.K., too. I slammed down the hood and lighted a cigarette. It really had me beat. A school bus from that convent over in Sag Harbor came piling around the bend, and all the girls leaned out the windows and yelled. I just waved. They didn't mean anything by it—just a bunch of kids going home. The bus went on up the road and into the woods and out of sight. I got back in the truck and started it up again. It sounded fine. I put it in gear and let out the clutch and gave it the gas, and nothing happened. The bastard just sat there. So it was probably the transmission. I shut it off and got out. There was nothing to do but call the store. I still had three or four deliveries that had to be made and it was getting kind of late. I knew what Mr. Lester would say, but this was one time when he couldn't blame me. It wasn't my fault. It was him himself that told me to take this truck.

Ten suggested topics

1. When I ran out of money
2. When I ran out of gas
3. When I was accused of something I didn't do
4. When I was stopped by the police (or by some other authority)
5. When I was guilty of . . .
6. When something terrible happened just before a big date
7. When the weather didn't cooperate
8. When I locked myself out of the house
9. When I couldn't reach my family by phone
10. When my typewriter broke down the night before a paper was due

A memorable experience from childhood

ASSIGNMENT 5: Write a paragraph in which you remember a special moment from your childhood. The following example is from George Orwell's novel *Coming Up for Air.*

Model Paragraph

It was an enormous fish. I don't exaggerate when I say it was enormous. It was almost the length of my arm. It glided across the pool, deep under water, and then became a shadow and disappeared into the darker water on the other side. I felt as if a sword had gone through me. It was by far the biggest fish I'd ever seen, dead or alive. I stood there without breathing, and in a moment another huge thick shape glided through the water, and then another and then two more close together. The pool was full of them. They were carp, I suppose. Just possibly they were bream or tench, but more probably carp. Bream or tench wouldn't grow so huge. I knew what had happened. At some time this pool had been connected with the other, and then the stream had dried up and the woods had closed round the small pool and it had just been forgotten. It's a thing that happens occasionally. A pool gets forgotten somehow, nobody fishes in it for years and decades and the fish grow to monstrous sizes. The brutes that I was watching might be a hundred years old. And not a soul in the world knew about them except me. Very likely it was twenty years since anyone had so much as looked at the pool, and probably even old Hodges and Mr. Farrel's **bailiff** had forgotten its existence.

in England, a person who looks after a large estate

Ten suggested topics

1. The first time I went swimming
2. My first time on a roller coaster (or on another ride)
3. A frightening experience when I was home alone
4. My most memorable Halloween (or other holiday)
5. The best birthday party I ever had
6. My first bicycle (or car)
7. The greatest present I ever received
8. A memorable visit to a favorite relative
9. My first time traveling alone
10. The first time I went camping

14

Developing Paragraphs: Process

▶ **What is process?**

Process is the method that explains how to do something or that shows how something works. There are two kinds of process writing: **directional** and **informational**. A process that is directional actually shows you, step by step, how to do something. For example, if you want to show someone how to brew a perfect cup of coffee, you would take the person through each step of the process, from selecting and grinding the coffee beans to pouring the finished product. Instructions on a test, directions on how to get to a wedding reception, or your favorite spaghetti recipe are a few examples of the kinds of process writing you see and use regularly. You can find examples of directional process writing everywhere you look, in newspapers, magazines, and books, as well as on the containers and packages of products you use every day.

On the other hand, a process that is informational tells you how something is or was done. This is for the purpose of informing you about the process. For example, in a history course, it might be important to understand how a general planned his strategy during the Civil War. Of course, you would not use this strategy yourself. The purpose is for information.

The following paragraph describes the various steps the writer and public speaker Malcolm X went through in the process of his self-education. Notice that each step in the process is given in its proper sequence. Words such as *first, next,* and *finally* can be used to show that a writer is developing an idea by using process. In the paragraph that follows, the words that signal the *steps* or *stages* of the process have been italicized:

When Malcolm X was in prison, he became very frustrated because he could not express his thoughts in letters written to his family and friends. Nor could he read well enough to be able to get the meaning from a book. He decided upon a program to change this situation. *First,* he got hold of a dictionary along with some paper and pencils. He was astounded at how many words there were. Not knowing what else to do, he turned to the first page and *began* by copying words from the page. It took him the entire day. *Next,* he read what he had written aloud, over and over again. He was excited to be learning words he never knew existed. *The next morning,* he reviewed what he had forgotten and *then* copied the next page. He found he was learning about people, places, and events from history. This process *continued until* he had filled a tablet with all the A's and *then* all the B's. *Eventually,* Malcolm X copied the entire dictionary!

▶ Working with process: don't overlook any one of the steps

The writer of the process essay is almost always more of an authority on the subject than the person reading the essay. In giving directions or information on how something was done or is to be done, it is possible to leave out a step that you think is so obvious that it is not worth mentioning. The reader, on the other hand, does not necessarily fill in the missing step as you did. An important part of process writing, therefore, is understanding your reader's level of ability. All of us have been given directions that, at first, seemed very clear. However, when we actually tried to carry out the process, something went wrong. A step in the process was misunderstood or missing. The giver of the information either assumed we would know certain parts of the process or didn't stop to think through the process completely. The important point is that directions must be complete and accurate. Here is one further consideration: If special equipment is required in order to perform the process, the directions must include a clear description of the necessary tools.

Exercise 1   Is the Process Complete?

In each of the following processes, try to determine what important step or steps of information have been omitted. Try to imagine yourself going through the process using only the information provided.

Making Popovers

1. Do not preheat the oven.
2. Sift 1 cup of flour and ¼ teaspoon of salt into a mixing bowl.
3. Using another mixing bowl, combine the eggs, 1 cup of milk, and 1 teaspoon of melted butter.
4. Stir until well blended and smooth.
5. Lightly oil ovenproof glass custard cups.
6. Fill the cups a little more than half full.
7. Place the cups on a baking sheet and place in the oven.
8. Bake the popovers until done.

Missing step or steps: _____

_____

_____

_____

How to Use the Copying Machine

1. Open the top of the copier.
2. Position the paper you are copying on the glass surface.
3. Set the copier to the kind of copying you are going to do (light, normal, or dark).
4. Check the size of the paper. Most copiers have a setting for two sizes of paper.
5. Put your money into the copier machine.

Missing step or steps: _____

_____

_____

_____

Exercise 2 — Is the Process Complete?

In each of the following processes, try to determine what important step or steps of information have been omitted. Try to imagine yourself going through the process using only the information provided.

How to Install and Run an Air Conditioner

1. Clean the air conditioner's filter or replace it if necessary.
2. Clean the window frame by removing any loose dirt.
3. Make sure the air conditioner is tilted to allow excess water to drain off and to prevent buildup of any moisture in the unit.
4. Use caulking or other material to make the space between the air conditioner and the window airtight.
5. Place pieces of wood or metal in the window frame to prevent the weight of the air conditioner from forcing the window open.

Missing step or steps: _____

_____

_____

_____

How to Plan a Wedding

1. Make an appointment with the minister or other authority involved, to set a date for the wedding.
2. Discuss plans with both families as to the budget available for the wedding; this will determine the size of the party and where it is to be held.
3. Reserve the banquet hall as much as eight months in advance.
4. Choose members of the wedding party and ask them whether they will be able to participate in the ceremony.

5. Begin to choose the clothing for the wedding party, including your own wedding gown or suit.
6. Enjoy your wedding!

Missing step or steps: _____

_____

_____

_____

_____

_____

Exercise 3 — Is the Process Complete?

In each of the following processes, try to determine what important step or steps of information have been omitted. Try to imagine yourself going through the process using only the information provided.

How to Prepare for an Essay Exam

1. Read the chapters well in advance of the test as they are assigned.
2. Take notes in class.
3. Ask the teacher what format the test will take if the teacher has not described the test.
4. Get a good night's sleep the night before.
5. Bring any pens or pencils that you might need.
6. Arrive at the classroom a few minutes early in order to get yourself settled and to keep yourself calm.

Missing step or steps: _____

_____

_____

_____

How to Balance Your Checkbook with the Monthly Bank Statement

1. Put your returned checks in order by number or date.
2. Check them off in your checkbook, making sure the amount of each check agrees with each amount listed in your checkbook.
3. Subtract from your checkbook balance any amounts that are automatically deducted from your account (loan payments, for example).
4. Total up all the checks which have not been returned with your bank statement.
5. Add to your bank statement balance the amounts of deposits you made after the date on the statement.

6. The balance you get should agree with your checkbook balance.

(Do you see now why so many people cannot balance their checkbooks?)

Missing step or steps: _____

_____

_____

_____

_____

▶ Coherence in process: order in logical sequence

When you are working with process, it is important not only to make sure the steps in the process are complete; you must also make sure they are given in the right sequence. For example, if you are describing the process of cleaning a mixer, it is important to point out that you must first unplug the appliance before you actually remove the blades. The importance of this step is clear when you realize that a person could lose a finger if this part of the process were missing. Improperly written instructions could cause serious injuries or even death.

Exercise 1

Coherence in Process: Order in Logical Sequence

The following steps describe the process of refinishing hardwood floors. Put the steps into their proper sequence.

_____ Keep sanding until you expose the hard wood.

_____ Apply a coat of polyurethane finish.

_____ When the sanding is done, clean the floor thoroughly with a vacuum sweeper to remove all the sawdust.

_____ Allow the finish to dry for three days before waxing and buffing.

_____ Take all furnishings out of the room.

_____ Do the initial sanding with a coarse sandpaper.

_____ The edger and hand sander are used after the machine sanding to get to those hard-to-reach places.

_____ Put the second coat of polyurethane finish on the following day, using a brush or a roller.

_____ Change to a fine sandpaper for the final sanding.

_____ Any nails sticking out from the floor should be either pulled out or set below the surface of the boards before you start the sanding machine.

Developing Paragraphs: Process   ▸ 261

Exercise 2   Coherence in Process: Order in Logical Sequence

The following steps describe the process of moving a household. Put the steps into their proper sequence.

___3___ List the contents of every carton, including what room the carton should be brought to.

___5___ Seal the cartons a few days before moving with 2½-inch-wide heavy-duty gummed tape.

___4___ Before you seal the cartons, be sure no carton weighs more than fifty pounds.

___1___ About two months before the scheduled move, begin collecting boxes. Liquor stores are a particularly good source since their boxes are often cushioned and sturdy.

___7___ Allow young children on the day of the move to take with them one or two favorite toys for comfort.

___6___ The day before the move, make the beds with clean linen so the next morning you can roll up the bedclothes like a camp bedroll and have them all ready to put on the beds at the new home.

___2___ Also, buy a variety of thick felt-tip pens with which to mark the cartons.

Exercise 3   Coherence in Process: Order in Logical Sequence

The following steps describe the process of making a filing system that works. Put the steps into their proper sequence.

_____ When your mind begins to blur, stop filing for that day.

_____ Now label the file folder and slip the piece of paper in.

_____ Gather together all materials to be filed so that they are all in one location.

_____ Alphabetize your file folders and put them away into your file drawer, and you are finished for that session.

_____ Add to these materials a wastebasket, folders, labels, and a pen.

_____ Pick up the next piece of paper and go through the same procedure, the only variation being that this new piece of paper might fit into an existing file, rather than one with a new heading.

_____ Pick up an item on the top of the pile and decide whether this item has value for you. If it does not, throw it away. If it does, go on to the next step.

_____ Finally, to maintain your file once it is established, each time you consult a file folder, riffle through it quickly to pick out and throw away the dead wood.

_____ If the piece of paper is worth saving, ask yourself the question, "What is this paper about?"

Mastering the Paragraph

▶ **Transitions for process**

Writers of process, like writers of narration, usually order their material by time sequence. Although it would be tiresome to use "and then" for each new step, a certain number of transitions are necessary for the process to read smoothly and be coherent. Here is a list of transitions frequently used in process.

Transitions

the first step	while you are . . .	the last step
in the beginning	as you are . . .	the final step
to start with	next	finally
to begin with	then	at last
first of all	the second step	eventually
	after you have . . .	

Exercise 1 **Using Transitions to Go from a List to a Paragraph**

Select one of the six processes listed on pages 257–260. Change this list into a process paragraph that uses enough transitional devices so that the paragraph is coherent and flows smoothly.

_____
_____
_____
_____
_____
_____
_____
_____
_____
_____
_____
_____
_____
_____
_____
_____
_____

Developing Paragraphs: Process ▶ 263

Exercise 2 **Using Transitions to Go from a List to a Paragraph**

Select one of the six processes listed on pages 257–260. Change this list into a process paragraph that uses enough transitional devices so that the paragraph is coherent and flows smoothly.

_____
_____
_____
_____
_____
_____
_____
_____
_____
_____
_____
_____
_____
_____
_____
_____
_____
_____

Exercise 3 **Using Transitions to Go from a List to a Paragraph**

Select one of the six processes listed on pages 257–260. Change this list into a process paragraph that uses enough transitional devices so that the paragraph is coherent and flows smoothly.

_____
_____
_____

_____
_____
_____
_____
_____
_____
_____
_____
_____
_____
_____
_____
_____
_____
_____
_____
_____
_____

▶ Writing the process paragraph step by step

To learn a skill with some degree of ease, it is best to follow a step-by-step approach so that various skills are isolated. This will ensure that you are not missing a crucial point or misunderstanding a part of the whole. There certainly are other ways to go about writing an effective paragraph, but here is one step-by-step method you can use to get good final results. You will learn that writing, like most other skills, can be developed by using a logical process.

Steps for Writing the Process Paragraph

1. Write a topic sentence.
2. List as many steps or stages in the process as you can.
3. Eliminate any irrelevant points; add equipment needed or special circumstances of the process.
4. Put your list in order.
5. Finally, write at least one complete sentence for each of the steps you have chosen from your list.
6. Write a concluding statement that says something about the results of completing the process.
7. Copy your sentences into standard paragraph form.

Exercise 1   **Writing the Process Paragraph Step by Step**

This exercise will guide you through the construction of a complete process paragraph. Start with the suggested topic. Use the seven steps to help you work through each stage of the writing process.

Topic: How to lose weight

Perhaps no topic has filled more bookstores or magazine pages than the "lose ten pounds in two days" promise. The wide variety of diet plans boggles the mind. Here is your chance to add your own version.

1. Topic sentence: _____
   _____

2. Make a list of possible steps.

   a. _____   f. _____
   b. _____   g. _____
   c. _____   h. _____
   d. _____   i. _____
   e. _____   j. _____

3. Eliminate any items that are not appropriate.

4. Put your final choices in order by numbering them.

5. Using your final list, write at least one sentence for each step you have chosen.

   a. _____
      _____

   b. _____
      _____

   c. _____
      _____

   d. _____
      _____

   e. _____
      _____

   f. _____
      _____

Mastering the Paragraph

g. _____

6. Write a concluding statement. _____

7. Copy your sentences into standard paragraph form.

Exercise 2

Writing the Process Paragraph Step by Step

This exercise will guide you through the construction of a complete process paragraph. Start with the suggested topic. Use the seven steps to help you work through each stage of the writing process.

Topic: How to pick a college

Sometimes an individual goes through an agonizing process before he or she is finally seated in a college classroom. The factors that go into selecting a college can be extremely complicated. Give advice to a prospective college student on how to go about finding the right college.

1. Topic sentence: _____
   _____

2. Make a list of possible steps.

   a. _____   f. _____
   b. _____   g. _____
   c. _____   h. _____
   d. _____   i. _____
   e. _____   j. _____

3. Circle the five or six steps you believe are the most important.

4. Put your choices in order by numbering them.

5. Using your final list, write at least one sentence for each step you have chosen.

   a. _____
   _____

   b. _____
   _____

   c. _____
   _____

   d. _____
   _____

   e. _____
   _____

   f. _____
   _____

   g. _____
   _____

6. Write a concluding statement. _____
   _____
   _____

7. Copy your sentences into standard paragraph form.

_____
_____
_____
_____
_____
_____
_____
_____
_____
_____
_____
_____
_____
_____
_____
_____

Exercise 3 — Writing the Process Paragraph Step by Step

This exercise will guide you through the construction of a complete process paragraph. Start with the suggested topic. Use the seven steps to help you work through each stage of the writing process.

Topic: How to manage a budget

Imagine you are the expert who has been hired by a couple to help them sort out their money problems. They bring in a reasonable salary, but still they are always spending more than they earn.

1. Topic sentence: _____
   _____

2. Make a list of possible steps.

   a. _____   f. _____
   b. _____   g. _____
   c. _____   h. _____
   d. _____   i. _____
   e. _____   j. _____

3. Circle the five or six steps you believe are the most important.
4. Put your final choices in order by numbering them.
5. Using your final list, write one sentence for each step you have chosen.

   a. _____
   _____

   b. _____
   _____

   c. _____
   _____

   d. _____
   _____

   e. _____
   _____

   f. _____
   _____

   g. _____
   _____

6. Write a concluding statement. _____
   _____
   _____

7. Copy your sentences into standard paragraph form.
   _____
   _____
   _____
   _____
   _____
   _____
   _____
   _____

On your own: writing process paragraphs from model paragraphs

Directional: how to accomplish a physical task

ASSIGNMENT 1: Write a paragraph in which you describe the process of doing a physical task of some kind, or the process of doing a task in order to accomplish something else. For example, you might have learned how to antique an old piece of furniture in order to save money, or you might have learned how to drive so that you would be in a better position to get a job. The following paragraph, taken from Betty Smith's novel *A Tree Grows in Brooklyn*, describes the process of moving a piano at a time (around the turn of the century) when it was considered a major moving operation.

> Piano-moving in those days was a project. No piano could be gotten down those narrow steep stairs. Pianos had to be bundled up, roped, and hoisted out of the windows with an enormous pulley on the roof and with much shouting, arm-waving and brass-hatting on the part of the boss mover. The street had to be roped off, the policemen had to keep the crowds back and children had to play hooky from school when there was a piano-moving. There was always that great moment when the wrapped bulk swung clear of the window and twisted dizzily in the air for a moment before it righted itself. Then began the slow perilous descent while the children cheered hoarsely.

Ten suggested topics

1. How to move from one city to another
2. How to install your own telephone
3. How to install a stereo system
4. How to lay a carpet
5. How to make homemade ice cream
6. How to prepare a package for mailing
7. How to pack a suitcase
8. How to furnish an apartment inexpensively
9. How to wallpaper a room
10. How to care for a lawn

Informational: how something scientific works

ASSIGNMENT 2: Write a paragraph in which you describe a scientific process. You could tell how a simple radio works, or you could describe how a snake sheds its skin. The following paragraph gives a description of a modern scientific process that increases the world's supply of drinking water. After you have chosen a topic, look for specific information in encyclopedias, textbooks, or other sources to help you explain the process.

The Anse method of converting sea water to fresh water is a cheap and efficient way to produce drinkable water from the sea. First, you cover an area of water with a sheet of black plastic. Air-filled channels in the plastic keep it raised slightly above the water. Underneath this plastic is another sheet of plastic that floats on the water; this plastic has small holes that allow sea water to seep up between the two layers of plastic. The heat of the sun, striking the upper layer of the plastic, causes the water to evaporate, leaving the salt behind. The hot air, filled with water, is then forced through a pipe and into an underground collection chamber by wind that is channeled between the plastic sheets by air ducts built on top of the plastic. When the hot air enters the collection chamber, the water in the air condenses, leaving fresh water on the bottom of the submerged chamber. This fresh water can then be pumped out of the chamber and used.

Ten suggested topics

1. How leather is made
2. How metamorphosis happens
3. How an airplane flies
4. How stars are formed
5. How an eclipse occurs
6. How the human heart works
7. How a bee makes honey
8. How a camera works
9. How a piano works
10. How a book is produced

Directional: how to care for your health

ASSIGNMENT 3: Write a paragraph in which you give the major steps in some area of caring for your health, mentally or physically. Concern for health and physical fitness is enjoying great popularity, bringing in big profits to health-related magazines, health clubs, health-food producers, and sports equipment manufacturers. The following paragraph tells us how to get a good night's sleep.

The process of getting a good night's sleep depends on several factors. First, the conditions in your bedroom must be correct. Be sure that the room temperature is around sixty-five degrees and that the room is as quiet as possible. Next, pay attention to your bed and how it is furnished. A firm mattress is best and wool blankets are better than blankets made of synthetic material. In addition, pillows that are too soft can cause stiffness of the neck and lead to a poor night's sleep. Also, keep in mind that what you eat and how you eat are part of the process of preparing for bed. Do not go to bed hungry, but do not overeat, either. Avoid candy bars or cookies; the sugar they contain acts as a stimulant. Finally, do not go to bed until you are sleepy; do something relaxing until you are tired.

Ten suggested topics

1. How to plan a healthful diet
2. How to care for someone who is ill
3. How to plan a daily exercise program
4. How to choose a sport that is suitable for you
5. How to live to be one hundred
6. How to pick a doctor
7. How to make exercise and diet foods fun
8. How to stop eating junk food
9. How to deal with depression
10. How to find a spiritual side to life

Informational: how to accomplish an important task

ASSIGNMENT 4: Write a paragraph in which you show how an important task is accomplished. The task may be something that is frequently done in human society, or that occurs in the world of nature. The following paragraph, which describes how an insect builds a nest, is an example of this kind of process.

The insect known as the hunter wasp goes through a regular procedure when it builds a nest. First, it digs a small tunnel into the earth. Then it goes in search of a cicada, a large insect that resembles a cricket. After stinging and paralyzing the cicada, the hunter wasp brings it to the tunnel, lays an egg on the helpless insect, and seals the tunnel. The hunter wasp then leaves. When the egg hatches, it uses the cicada as a source of food.

Ten suggested topics

1. How cheese is made
2. How a piece of farm machinery works
3. How a school yearbook is produced
4. How people obtain a divorce
5. How Madame Curie discovered radium
6. How the ancient Egyptians built the pyramids
7. How a bill becomes a law
8. How penicillin was discovered
9. How Henry Ford mass-produced the automobile
10. How glass is made

Directional: how to write school assignments

ASSIGNMENT 5: Your writing in school takes many forms. Write a paragraph in which you show the process of writing a specific assignment related to school. The following paragraph, adapted from Donald Murray's *Write to Learn*, shows the several steps you need to keep in mind as you approach the writing of a term paper.

Doing a term paper involves both careful research on a topic and a methodical approach to the writing of the material. First, consult the important and up-to-date books and articles related to your subject. Next, find out the style of writing that your instructor wants; also find out details about length, organization, footnoting, and bibliography that will be part of the presentation of your paper. Then write a draft of the paper as quickly as you can, without using notes or bibliography; this will help you see your ideas and how they can be further developed. Before you go any further, review what you have written to see if you have begun to develop a point of view about your subject or an attitude toward your topic. Finally, write a draft of your paper that includes all of the important information about your subject, a draft that includes your footnotes and your bibliography.

Ten suggested topics

1. How to prepare an oral report
2. How to write a résumé
3. How to write a letter of application (for a school or for a job)
4. How to write a science experiment
5. How to write a book review
6. How to revise an essay
7. How to take classroom notes
8. How to take notes from a textbook
9. How to write a letter home, asking for money
10. How to write a story for the school newspaper

15

Developing Paragraphs: Comparison or Contrast

▶ **What is comparison or contrast?**

Comparison and contrast are two related methods of explaining subjects. When we use comparison, we emphasize the similarities between two subjects. When we use contrast, we emphasize the differences between two subjects. We sometimes use the word *comparison* to refer to both similarities and differences between people or things, but it is more exact to use *comparison* for similarities and *contrast* for differences. For example, if you were to write about twin sisters you know, and how close they are in appearance and personality, the similarities you would include would make up a comparison. On the other hand, if you wanted to emphasize some important differences between the two sisters, the result of your work would be a contrast.

We use comparison or contrast in a variety of ways every day. We put similar products side by side in the grocery store before we decide to buy one of them; we listen to two politicians on television and think about the differences between their positions before we vote for one of them; and we read college catalogues and talk to our friends before we make a final choice as to which school we should attend.

When we compare two items, we are able to judge which is better. In addition, when we use comparison we are able to see each individual item more clearly. For example, if you were trying to decide whether to buy a small computer or upgrade your typewriter, you should find someone who often uses typewriters and computers. This person could compare or contrast the two machines: show you the similarities or the differences. Today many people are trying to decide whether they would use the computer enough to justify the difference between the cost of a computer and the cost of a typewriter. If the person decides to buy a computer, then the comparison or contrast process begins again: finding out the similarities or differences among the many different makes and sizes. One must consider price, capability, servicing the machine, compatibility with other equipment, and clarity of the screen. Even the wisest shopper would find such a purchase a complicated procedure.

▶ Working with comparison or contrast: choosing the two-part topic

The problem with writing a good comparison or contrast paragraph usually centers on the fact that you now have a two-part topic. This demands very careful attention to the topic sentence. While you must be careful to choose two subjects that have enough in common to make them comparable, you must also not choose two things having so much in common that you cannot possibly handle all the comparable points in one paragraph or even ten paragraphs. For example, a student trying to compare the French word *chaise* with the English word *chair* might be able to come up with only two sentences of material. With only a dictionary to consult, it is unlikely that the student would find enough material for several points of comparison. On the other hand, contrasting the United States with Europe would present such an endless supply of points to compare that the tendency would be to give only general facts that your reader would already know. When the subject is too broad, the writing is often too general. A better two-part topic might be to compare traveling by train in Europe with traveling by train in the United States.

Once you have chosen a two-part topic that you feel is not too limiting and not too broad, you must remember that a good comparison or contrast paragraph should devote an equal or nearly equal amount of space to each of the two parts. If the writer is only interested in one of the topics, the danger is that the paragraph will end up being very one-sided.

Here's an example of a one-sided contrast:

> While American trains go to only a few towns, are infrequent, and are often shabby and uncomfortable, the European train is much nicer.

This example is a better written contrast that gives attention to both topics:

> While American trains go to only a few large cities, run very infrequently, and are often shabby and uncomfortable, European trains go to virtually every small town, are always dependable, and are clean and attractive.

Exercise 1   Evaluating the Two-Part Topic

Study the following topics and decide whether each topic is *too broad* for a paragraph, or whether it is *suitable* as a topic for a paragraph of comparison or contrast. Mark your choice in the appropriate space to the right of each topic.

Topic	Too Broad	Suitable
1. Australia and England	✓	
2. Indian elephants and African elephants		✓
3. California champagne and French champagne		✓

4. Wooden furniture and plastic furniture
5. Wood and plastic
6. Photography and oil painting
7. Heart surgeons and plastic surgeons
8. Taking photographs with a flash and taking photographs using available light
9. Doctors and lawyers
10. IBM computers and Apple computers

Exercise 2

Working with Comparison or Contrast

Each of these suggested comparison or contrast topics is followed by a more specific topic that has not been completed. Complete each of these specific topics by supplying details of your own. Each topic you complete should be one that you could develop as an example of comparison or contrast.

1. Compare two friends:

   My friend _____ with my friend _____.

2. Compare two kinds of coats:

   _____ coats with _____ coats.

3. Compare two kinds of diets:

   The _____ diet with the _____ diet.

4. Compare two kinds of floors:

   _____ floors with _____ floors.

5. Compare two kinds of entertainment:

   Watching _____ with looking at _____.

6. Compare two kinds of rice:

   _____ rice with _____ rice.

7. Compare two places where you can study:

   Studying in the _____ with studying in the _____.

8. Compare the wedding customs of two groups:

   What _____ do at a wedding with what _____ do at a wedding.

9. Compare two textbooks:

A textbook that has _____ with a textbook that contains _____.

10. Compare two politicians:

A local politician who _____ with a national politician who _____.

Exercise 3 — Working with Comparison or Contrast

Each of these suggested comparison or contrast topics is followed by a more specific topic that has not been completed. Complete each of these specific topics by supplying details of your own. Each topic you complete should be one that you could develop as an example of comparison or contrast.

1. Compare two kinds of popular board games people play:

Playing _____ with playing _____.

2. Compare two ways of looking at movies:

Watching movies on _____ with going to _____.

3. Compare two careers:

A career in _____ with a career as a _____.

4. Compare two ways of paying for a purchase:

Using _____ to buy something, with using _____ to buy something.

5. Compare two different life-styles:

Living the life of a _____ with living as a _____.

6. Compare two places to go swimming:

Swimming in a _____ with swimming in a _____.

7. Compare a no-frills product with the same product sold under a standard brand name (such as no-frills corn flakes with Kellogg's corn flakes):

A no-frills _____ with _____.

8. Compare two popular magazines:

_____ with _____.

9. Compare two hobbies:

Collecting _____ with _____.

10. Compare two kinds of tests given in school:

The _____ kind of test with the _____ kind of test.

▶ Coherence in comparison or contrast: two approaches to ordering material

The first method for ordering material in a paragraph or an essay of comparison or contrast is known as the **point-by-point method**. When you use this method, you compare a point of one topic with a point of the other topic. For example, here is a paragraph from Julius Lester's *All Is Well*. In the paragraph, the writer uses the point-by-point method to compare the difficulties of being a boy with the difficulties of being a girl:

> Now, of course, I know that it was as difficult being a girl as it was a boy, if not more so. While I stood paralyzed at one end of a dance floor trying to find the courage to ask a girl for a dance, most of the girls waited in terror at the other, afraid that no one, not even I, would ask them. And while I resented having to ask a girl for a date, wasn't it also horrible to be the one who waited for the phone to ring? And how many of those girls who laughed at me making a fool of myself on the baseball diamond would have gladly given up their places on the sidelines for mine on the field?

Notice how, after the opening topic sentence, the writer uses half of each sentence to describe a boy's situation growing up and the other half of the same sentence to describe a girl's experience. This technique is effective in such a paragraph, and it is most often used in longer pieces of writing in which many points of comparison are made. This method helps the reader keep the comparison or contrast carefully in mind at each point.

The second method for ordering material in a paragraph of comparison or contrast is known as the **block method**. When you use this approach, you present all of the facts and supporting details about your first topic, and then you give all of the facts and supporting details about your second topic. Here, for example, is another version of the paragraph you studied above, but this time it is written according to the block method:

> Now, of course, I know that it was as difficult being a girl as it was being a boy, if not more so. I stood paralyzed at one end of the dance floor trying to find the courage to ask a girl for a dance. I resented having to ask a girl for a date, just as I often felt foolish on the baseball diamond. On the other hand, most of the girls waited in terror at the other end of the dance floor, afraid that no one, not even I, would ask them to dance. In addition, it was a horrible situation for the girls who had to wait for the phone to ring. And how many of those girls who waited on the sidelines would have traded places with me on the baseball diamond?

Notice how the first half of this version presents all of the details about the boy, while the second part of the paragraph presents all of the information about the girls. This method is often used in shorter pieces of writing because with a shorter piece it is possible for the reader to keep the blocks of information in mind.

Looking at the above two paragraphs in outline form will help you see the shape of their development:

Point-by-Point Method

Topic sentence: "Now, of course, I know that it was as difficult being a girl as it was a boy, if not more so."

First point, first topic: "While I stood paralyzed at one end of a dance floor trying to find the courage to ask a girl for a dance . . ."

First point, second topic: ". . . most of the girls waited in terror at the other, afraid that no one, not even I, would ask them."

Second point, first topic: "And while I resented having to ask a girl for a date, . . ."

Second point, second topic: ". . . wasn't it also horrible to be the one who waited for the phone to ring?"

Third point, first topic: "And how many of those girls who laughed at me making a fool of myself on the baseball diamond . . ."

Third point, second topic: ". . . would have gladly given up their places on the sidelines for mine on the field?"

Block Method

Topic sentence: "Now, of course, I know that it was as difficult being a girl as it was a boy, if not more so."

First topic, points one, two, and three:

"I stood paralyzed at one end of the dance floor trying to find the courage to ask a girl for a dance. I resented having to ask a girl for a date, just as I often felt foolish on the baseball diamond."

Second topic, points one, two, and three:

"On the other hand, most of the girls waited in terror at the other end of the dance floor, afraid that no one, not even I, would ask them to dance. In addition, it was a horrible situation for the girls who had to wait for the phone to ring. And how many of those girls who waited on the sidelines would have traded places with me on the baseball diamond?"

You will want to choose one of these methods before you write a comparison or contrast assignment. Keep in mind that although the block method is most often used in shorter writing assignments, such as a paragraph, you will have the chance to practice the point-by-point method as well.

Exercise 1

Working for Coherence: Recognizing the Two Approaches to Ordering Material

Each of the following passages is an example of comparison or contrast. Read each paragraph carefully and decide whether the writer has used the point-by-point method or the block method. Indicate your choice in the spaces provided after each example. Also indicate whether the piece emphasizes similarities or differences.

1. Female infants speak sooner, have larger vocabularies, and rarely demonstrate speech defects. (Stuttering, for instance, occurs almost exclusively among boys.) Girls exceed boys in language abilities, and this early linguistic bias often prevails throughout life. Girls read sooner, learn foreign languages more easily, and, as a result, are more likely to enter occupations involving language mastery. Boys, in contrast, show an early visual superiority. They are also clumsier, performing poorly at something like arranging a row of beads, but excel at other activities calling on total body coordination. Their attentional mechanisms are also different. A boy will react to an inanimate object as quickly as he will to a person. A male baby will often ignore the mother and babble to a blinking light, fixate on a geometric figure, and, at a later point, manipulate it and attempt to take it apart.

_____ Point-by-Point _____ Block

_____ Similarities _____ Differences

2. Each man had, to begin with, the great virtue of utter tenacity and fidelity. Grant fought his way down the Mississippi Valley in spite of acute personal discouragement and profound military handicaps. Lee hung on in the trenches at Petersburg after hope itself had died. In each man there was an indomitable quality . . . the born fighter's refusal to give up as long as he can still remain on his feet and lift his two fists. Daring and resourcefulness they had, too; the ability to think faster and move faster than the enemy. These were the qualities which gave Lee the dazzling campaigns of Second Manassas and Chancellorsville and won Vicksburg for Grant.

_____ Point-by-Point _____ Block

_____ Similarities _____ Differences

3. I first realized that the act of writing was about to enter a new era five years ago when I went to see an editor at *The New Times.* As I was ushered through the vast city room I felt that I had strayed into the wrong office. The place was clean and carpeted and quiet. As I passed long rows of desks, I saw that almost every desk had its own computer terminal and its own solemn occupant—a man or a woman typing at the computer keyboard or reading what was on the terminal screen. I saw no typewriters, no paper, no mess. It was a cool and sterile environment; the drones at their machines could have been processing insurance claims or tracking a spacecraft in orbit. What they didn't look like were newspaper people, and what the place didn't look like was a newspaper office. I knew how a newspaper office should look and sound and smell—I worked in one for thirteen years. The paper was the *New York Herald Tribune,* and its city room, wide as a city block, was dirty and disheveled. Reporters wrote on ancient typewriters that filled the air with clatter; copy editors labored on coffee-stained desks over what the reporters had written. Crumpled balls of paper littered the floor and filled the wastebaskets—failed efforts to write a good lead or a decent sentence. The walls were grimy—every few years they were painted over in a less restful shade of eye-rest green—and the atmosphere was hazy with the smoke of cigarettes and cigars. At the

very center the city editor, a giant named L. L. Engelking, bellowed his displeasure with the day's work, his voice a rumbling volcano in our lives. I thought it was the most beautiful place in the world.

_____ Point-by-Point   _____ Block

_____ Similarities   _____ Differences

4. We went fishing the first morning. I felt the same damp moss covering the worms in the bait can, and saw the dragonfly alight on the tip of my rod as it hovered a few inches from the surface of the water. It was the arrival of this fly that convinced me beyond any doubt that everything was as it always had been, that the years were a mirage and there had been no years. The small waves were the same, chucking the rowboat under the chin as we fished at anchor, and the boat was the same boat, the same color green and the ribs broken in the same places, and under the floorboards the same freshwater leavings and debris—the dead helgramite, the wisps of moss, the rusty discarded fishhook, the dried blood from yesterday's catch. We stared silently at the tips of our rods, at the dragonflies that came and went. I lowered the tip of mine into the water, tentatively, pensively dislodging the fly, which darted two feet away, poised, darted two feet back, and came to rest again a little farther up the rod. There had been no years between the ducking of this dragonfly and the other one—the one that was part of memory. I looked at the boy, who was silently watching his fly, and it was my hands that held his rod, my eyes watching. I felt dizzy and didn't know which rod I was at the end of.

_____ Point-by-Point   _____ Block

_____ Similarities   _____ Differences

5. The streets are littered with cigarette and cigar butts, paper wrappings, particles of food, and dog droppings. How long before they become indistinguishable from the gutters of medieval towns when slop pails were emptied from the second-story windows? Thousands of New York women no longer attend evening services in their churches. They fear assault as they walk the few steps from bus or subway station to their apartment houses. The era of the medieval footpad has returned, and, as in the Dark Ages, the cry for help brings no assistance, for even grown men know they would be cut down before the police could arrive.

__X__ Point-by-Point   _____ Block

__X__ Similarities   _____ Differences

Exercise 2

Using the Point-by-Point and Block Methods for Comparison or Contrast

The passage below uses the block method to make its points of contrast. Rewrite the material using the point-by-point approach.

I first realized that the act of writing was about to enter a new era five years ago when I went to see an editor at *The New Times.* As I was ushered through the vast city room I felt that I had strayed into the wrong office. The place was clean and carpeted and quiet. As I passed long rows of desks, I saw that almost every desk had its own computer terminal and its own solemn occupant—a man or a woman typing at the computer keyboard or reading what was on the terminal screen. I saw no typewriters, no paper, no mess. It was a cool and sterile environment; the drones at their machines could have been processing insurance claims or tracking a spacecraft in orbit. What they didn't look like were newspaper people, and what the place didn't look like was a newspaper office. I knew how a newspaper office should look and sound and smell—I worked in one for thirteen years. The paper was the *New York Herald Tribune,* and its city room, wide as a city block, was dirty and disheveled. Reporters wrote on ancient typewriters that filled the air with clatter; copy editors labored on coffee-stained desks over what the reporters had written. Crumpled balls of paper littered the floor and filled the wastebaskets—failed efforts to write a good lead or a decent sentence. The walls were grimy—every few years they were painted over in a less restful shade of eye-rest green—and the atmosphere was hazy with the smoke of cigarettes and cigars. At the very center the city editor, a giant named L. L. Engelking, bellowed his displeasure with the day's work, his voice a rumbling volcano in our lives. I thought it was the most beautiful place in the world.

Developing Paragraphs: Comparison or Contrast   283

_____
_____
_____
_____
_____
_____
_____
_____
_____
_____
_____

Exercise 3   **Using the Point-by-Point and Block Methods**

Use the list below to write a comparison or contrast paragraph on life in the city compared with life in a suburban area. Review the list provided and add to it any of your own ideas. Omit any you do not wish to use. Then, selecting either the block method or the point-by-point method, write a comparison or contrast paragraph.

Topic sentence: If I could move back to the city from the suburbs, I know I would be happy.

The following points provide details that relate to living in the city and living in a suburban community:

Topic I *Advantages of the City*	*Topic II* *Disadvantages of the Suburbs*
A short ride on the bus or subway gets you to work.	Commuting to work in the city is often long and exhausting.
Men are as visible as women in the neighborhood.	Because they work in the city, few men are active in a suburban community.
Variety is more stimulating.	Sameness of people and streets is monotonous.
Families and single people.	Mostly families.
Local shopping for nearly everything.	Mostly highway shopping.
Mingle with people walking in the neighborhood daily.	Little walking, use cars to go everywhere.

Notice that the maker of this list centered only on the disadvantages of the suburbs in contrast to the city. No mention, for instance, has been made of crime. One could also present the contrast from the point of view of someone who prefers the suburbs.

_____

_____

_____

_____

_____

_____

_____

_____

_____

_____

▶ Working for coherence: using transitions

A number of words and phrases are useful to keep in mind when writing the comparison or contrast paper. Some of them are used in phrases, some in clauses.

My sister is just <u>like</u> me.

Like is a preposition and is used in the prepositional phrase "like me."

My sister is a good cook *as* is my mother.

As is a subordinate conjunction and is used in a clause with a subject and a verb.

Common Transitions

Transitions for Comparison	*Transitions for Contrast*	
similar to	on the contrary	though
similarly	on the other hand	unlike
like	in contrast with	even though
likewise	in spite of	nevertheless
just like	despite	however
just as	instead of	but
furthermore	different from	otherwise
moreover	whereas	except for
equally	while	and yet
again	although	still
also		
too		
so		

Developing Paragraphs: Comparison or Contrast ▸ 285

Exercise 1   Using Transitions in Comparisons and Contrasts

Each of the following examples is made up of two sentences. Read both sentences and decide whether the idea being expressed is one of comparison or contrast. Next, combine the two sentences by using a transition you have chosen from one of the above lists. Then write your new sentence on the lines provided. You may find you have to reword your new sentence slightly in order to make it grammatically correct. An example has been done for you.

    Mr. Johnson is a teacher.
    His wife is a teacher.

First you decide that the two sentences show a comparison. Then you combine the two by using an appropriate transition:

    Mr. Johnson is a teacher just like his wife.
    or
    Mr. Johnson is a teacher; so is his wife.

1. Dr. Rappole has a reputation for excellent bedside manners.

   Dr. Connolly is very withdrawn and speaks so softly that it is almost impossible to understand what he has said.

   Your combined sentence: _____
   _____
   _____

2. In the United States, interest in soccer has become apparent only in recent years.

   Soccer has always been immensely popular in Brazil.

   Your combined sentence: _____
   _____
   _____

3. Hemingway's book *Death in the Afternoon* deals with the theme of man against nature.

   The same writer's novel *The Old Man and the Sea* deals with the theme of man against nature.

   Your combined sentence: _____
   _____
   _____

4. Amy is carefree and fun-loving, with little interest in school.

   Janet, Amy's sister, is so studious and hard-working that she is always on the honor roll.

286 ◀ Mastering the Paragraph

Your combined sentence: _____

_____

_____

5. The apartment had almost no furniture, was badly in need of painting, and felt chilly even though I was wearing a coat.

   The other apartment was attractively furnished, had been freshly painted, and was warm enough so that I had to take off my coat.

   Your combined sentence: _____

   _____

   _____

Exercise 2

Using Transitions in Comparisons and Contrasts

First, identify each of the following examples as comparison or contrast. Then combine the two sentences by using a transition from the list on page 284. Finally, write your new sentence on the lines provided.

1. Phil Donahue's daytime talk show deals with current controversial issues that are of importance to society.

   Johnny Carson's *Tonight Show* gives people light entertainment in the evening.

   Your combined sentence: _____

   _____

   _____

2. Shakespeare's *Romeo and Juliet* is a famous love story that takes place in Italy.

   West Side Story is a modern-day version of Shakespeare's love story that takes place in New York City.

   Your combined sentence: _____

   _____

   _____

3. The French Revolution was directed by the common people.

   The Russian Revolution was directed by an elite group of thinkers.

   Your combined sentence: _____

   _____

   _____

Developing Paragraphs: Comparison or Contrast ▸ 287

4. Some scientists believe that dinosaurs became extinct because they ran out of food.

   Some scientists think that dinosaurs were victims of radiation from a meteor from outer space.

   Your combined sentence: _____

   _____

   _____

5. The Museum of Modern Art shows paintings, photographs, movies, and many other forms of twentieth-century art.

   The Metropolitan Museum of Art contains sculptures, paintings, and other forms of art that date from the beginning of recorded history.

   Your combined sentence: _____

   _____

   _____

Exercise 3

Using Transitions in Comparisons and Contrasts

First, identify each of the following examples as comparison or contrast. Then combine the two sentences by using a transition from the list on page 284. Finally, write your new sentence on the lines provided.

1. A ballet dancer trains for years in order to master all aspects of dancing.

   A football player puts in years of practice in order to learn the game from every angle.

   Your combined sentence: _____

   _____

   _____

2. The University of Chicago is a large urban university that has the resources of a big city as part of its attraction for faculty and students.

   Fredonia State College is a small rural college that has beautiful surroundings as part of its attraction.

   Your combined sentence: _____

   _____

   _____

3. Ice cream, a popular dessert for many years, has many calories and added chemicals to give it more flavor.

   Tofuti is a dessert made of processed soybeans that is low in calories and contains no harmful additives.

Your combined sentence: _____

_____

_____

4. Nelson Rockefeller gave much of his time and money for education and the arts.

   Andrew Carnegie set up a famous foundation to support learning and artistic achievement.

   Your combined sentence: _____

   _____

   _____

5. *A Soldier's Play* is a play that has a single setting for all of its action.

   A Soldier's Story, a film based on the play, is a movie that is able to use many different settings to present all of its action.

   Your combined sentence: _____

   _____

   _____

▶ Writing the comparison or contrast paragraph step by step

To learn a skill with some degree of ease, it is best to follow a step-by-step approach so that various skills are isolated. This will ensure that you are not missing a crucial point or misunderstanding a part of the whole. Of course, there are other ways to approach writing assignments, but here is one step-by-step approach you can use to achieve good results while at the same time learning how paragraphs can be developed through a logical process.

Steps for Writing the Comparison or Contrast Paragraph

1. Study the given topic, and then plan your topic sentence, especially the dominant impression.
2. List all your ideas for points that could be compared or contrasted.
3. Then choose the three or four most important points from your list.
* 4. Decide whether you want to use the point-by-point method or the block method of organizing your paragraph.
5. Write at least one complete sentence for each of the points you have chosen from your list.
* 6. Write a concluding statement that summarizes the main points, makes a judgment, or emphasizes what you believe is the most important point.
7. Finally, copy your sentences into standard paragraph form.

Exercise 1   **Writing the Comparison or Contrast Paragraph Step by Step**

This exercise will guide you through the construction of a comparison or contrast paragraph. Start with the suggested topic. Use the seven steps to help you work through each stage of the writing process.

Topic: Compare or contrast how you spend your leisure time with how your parents or a friend spends leisure time.

1. Topic sentence: _____
   _____

2. Make a list of possible comparisons or contrasts.

   a. _____ f. _____
   b. _____ g. _____
   c. _____ h. _____
   d. _____ i. _____
   e. _____ j. _____

3. Circle the three or four comparisons or contrasts that you believe are most important and put them in order.

4. Choose either the point-by-point method or the block method.

5. Using your final list, write at least one sentence for each comparison or contrast you have chosen.

   a. _____
   _____

   b. _____
   _____

   c. _____
   _____

   d. _____
   _____

   e. _____
   _____

   f. _____
   _____

   g. _____
   _____

6. Write a concluding statement. _____
_____
_____

7. Copy your sentences into standard paragraph form.
_____
_____
_____
_____
_____
_____
_____
_____
_____
_____
_____
_____
_____
_____
_____
_____
_____

Exercise 2 — Writing the Comparison or Contrast Paragraph Step by Step

This exercise will guide you through the construction of a comparison or contrast paragraph. Start with the suggested topic. Use the seven steps to help you work through each stage of the writing process.

Topic: Compare or contrast going to work with going to college immediately after high school.

1. Topic sentence: _____
_____
_____

Developing Paragraphs: Comparison or Contrast ▸ 291

2. Make a list of possible comparisons or contrasts.

   a. <u>DON'T MAKE AS MUCH MONEY</u>   f. <u>EASY TO PUT COLLEGE OFF</u>

   b. _____   g. _____

   c. _____   h. _____

   d. _____   i. _____

   e. _____   j. _____

3. Circle the three or four comparisons or contrasts that you believe are most important and put them in order.

4. Choose either the point-by-point method or the block method.

5. Using your final list, write at least one sentence for each comparison or contrast you have chosen.

   a. _____
   _____

   b. _____
   _____

   c. _____
   _____

   d. _____
   _____

   e. _____
   _____

   f. _____
   _____

   g. _____
   _____

6. Write a concluding statement. _____
   _____
   _____
   _____

7. Copy your sentences into standard paragraph form.

Exercise 3

Writing the Comparison or Contrast Paragraph Step by Step

This exercise will guide you through the construction of a comparison or contrast paragraph. Start with the suggested topic. Use the seven steps to help you work through each stage of the writing process.

Topic: Compare or contrast the styles of two television personalities (or two public figures often in the news).

1. Topic sentence: _____

2. Make a list of possible comparisons or contrasts.

   a. _____   f. _____
   b. _____   g. _____
   c. _____   h. _____
   d. _____   i. _____
   e. _____   j. _____

Developing Paragraphs: Comparison or Contrast ▸ 293

3. Circle the three or four comparisons or contrasts that you believe are most important and put them in order.

4. Choose either the point-by-point method or the block method.

5. Using your final list, write at least one sentence for each comparison or contrast you have chosen.

   a. _____

   b. _____

   c. _____

   d. _____

   e. _____

   f. _____

   g. _____

6. Write a concluding statement. _____

7. Copy your sentences into standard paragraph form.

▶ **On your own: writing comparison or contrast paragraphs**

Comparing two places

ASSIGNMENT 1: Write a paragraph in which you compare or contrast two places you know, either from personal experience or from your reading. The following paragraph, from James A. Michener's *Iberia,* contrasts Spain and Portugal as they appear to a person who has been to both places.

Model Paragraph

I am often asked to compare Portugal and Spain, and the simple truth seems to be that whichever of these two countries one visits first continues as his preference. No one can be more energetic in defense of a new-found land than the Englishman, Frenchman, or American who has visited Portugal first and then moved on to Spain: he loves the first and is never easy in the second. I discovered this when I traveled westward across Spain with an American couple who had worked for some years at our embassy in Lisboa, for it was touching to watch how apprehensive they were of all things Spanish and how their spirits revived the closer they got to their beloved Portugal. "We wouldn't feel safe drinking Spanish water, thank you. We've been all through Portugal and we've never seen villages as dirty as those in Spain. Doesn't anyone have paint in this country? The fact is, we feel safe in Portugal but in Spain you never know. Our police are so much better." As we approached the western border of Spain it became a question of whether we should take our lunch in Spanish Badajoz, which I preferred because of the great seafood zarzuela I knew was waiting, or press on to Portuguese Elvas, which lay just across the border. "Oh," my embassy friends said, "we'd never want to eat in a Spanish restaurant if a clean Portuguese one were nearby."

Ten suggested topics

Compare or contrast two places you have lived in, visited, or read about:

1. Two neighborhoods
2. Two towns or cities
3. Two vacation spots
4. Two states
5. Two countries
6. Two streets
7. Two schools
8. Two shopping areas
9. Two favorite (or least favorite) spots
10. Two regions with very different scenery and atmosphere

Comparing two cultures

ASSIGNMENT 2: Write a paragraph in which you compare two cultures, or an aspect of culture that may be observed in two societies. The following paragraph was written by Brenda David, an American teacher who worked with schoolchildren in Milan, Italy, for several years.

Model Paragraph

All young children, whatever their culture, are alike in their charm and innocence—in being a clean slate on which the wonders and ways of the world are yet to be written. But during the three years I worked in a school in Milan, I learned that American and Italian children are different in several ways. First, young American children tend to be active, enthusiastic, and inquisitive. Italian children, on the other hand, tend to be passive, quiet, and not particularly inquisitive. They usually depend on their parents to tell them what to do. Second, American children show their independence while their Italian counterparts are still looking to their parents and grandparents to tell them what to do or not do. Third, and most important to those who question the influence of environment on a child, the American children generally surpass their Italian schoolmates in math, mechanical, and scientific abilities. But American children are overshadowed by their Italian counterparts in their language, literature, art, and music courses. Perhaps the differences, which those of us at the school confirmed in an informal study, were to be expected. After all, what priority do Americans give to the technological skills? And what value do Italians—with the literature of poets and authors like Boccaccio, the works of Michelangelo, and the music of the world-famous LaScala opera at Milan—place on the cultural arts?

Ten suggested topics

Compare or contrast:

1. Mexican cooking with Chinese cooking
2. Marriage customs in Africa and in the United States
3. Attitudes toward women's roles in Saudi Arabia and in the United States
4. Folk Dancing in two countries

5. Raising children in Asia and raising them in the United States
6. Urban people with small-town people
7. The reputation of a place with the reality of the place as you found it
8. The culture of your neighborhood with the general culture of our society
9. The culture you live in now with the culture in which your parents were raised
10. Medical care in our society with the medical care of any other society

Comparing a place then and now

ASSIGNMENT 3: Write a paragraph in which you compare the appearance of a place you knew when you were growing up with the appearance of that same place now. The following paragraph compares a small city as it was some years ago and how it appeared to the writer on a recent visit.

Model Paragraph

As I drove up Swede Hill, I realized that the picture I had in my mind all these years was largely a romantic one. It was here that my father had boarded, as a young man of eighteen, with a widow who rented rooms in her house. Now the large old wooden frame houses were mostly two-family homes; no single family could afford to heat them in the winter. The porches which had once been beautiful and where people had passed their summer evenings had peeling paint and were in poor condition. No one now stopped to talk; the only sounds to be heard were those of cars whizzing past. The immigrants who had come to this country, worked hard, and put their children through school were now elderly and mostly alone, since their educated children could find no jobs in the small upstate city. From the top of the hill I looked down fondly upon the town built on the hills and noticed that a new and wider highway now went through the town. My father would have liked that; he would not have had to complain about Sunday drives on Foote Avenue. In the distance I could see the large shopping mall which now had most of the business in the surrounding area and which had forced several local businesses to close. Now the center of town no longer hummed with activity, as it once had. My town was not the same place I had known, and I could see that changes were taking place that would eventually transform the entire area.

Ten suggested topics

Compare or contrast a place as it appears now with how it appeared some years ago:

1. A barber shop or beauty salon
2. A house of worship
3. A local "corner store"
4. A friend's home
5. Your elementary school
6. A local bank
7. A downtown shopping area

8. A restaurant or diner
9. An undeveloped place such as an open field or wooded area
10. A favorite local gathering place

Comparing two approaches to a subject

ASSIGNMENT 4: Write a paragraph in which you compare two ways of considering a particular topic. The following paragraph compares two approaches to the art of healing—the traditional medical approach and the approach that involves less dependence on chemicals and more reliance on the body's natural defense system.

Model Paragraph

Natural healing is basically a much more conservative approach to health care than traditional medical practice. Traditional medical practice aims for the quick cure by means of introducing substances or instruments into the body which are highly antagonistic to whatever is causing the disease. A doctor wants to see results, and he or she wants you to appreciate the fact that traditional medicine is what is delivering those results to you. Because of this desire for swift, decisive victories over disease, traditional medicine tends to be dramatic, risky, and expensive. Natural healing takes a slower, more organic approach to the problem of disease. It first recognizes that the human body is superbly equipped to resist disease and heal injuries. But when disease does take hold or an injury occurs, the first instinct in natural healing is to see what might be done to strengthen that natural resistance and those natural healing agents so that they can act against the disease more effectively. Results are not expected to occur overnight, but neither are they expected to occur at the expense of the body, which may experience side effects or dangerous complications.

Ten suggested topics

Compare or contrast:

1. Retiring or working after age sixty-five
2. Owning your own business or working for someone else
3. Two views on abortion
4. Two attitudes toward divorce
5. Two political viewpoints
6. Your life-style today and your life-style five years ago
7. Working mothers and mothers who stay home
8. Buying U.S.-made products or buying foreign-made goods
9. Two attitudes on the "right to die" issue
10. Two attitudes toward religion

Comparing male attitudes and female attitudes

ASSIGNMENT 5: Some observers believe that males share similar attitudes toward certain subjects, while females seem to have a similar way of thinking on certain other topics. Other observers believe that such conclusions are nothing more than stereotypes and that people should not be divided in this way. The following paragraph reports that recent studies indicate a possible biological basis for some of the differences between males and females.

Model Paragraph

Recent scientific research has shown that differences in behavior between males and females may have their origins in biological differences in the brain. Shortly after birth, females are more sensitive than males to certain types of sounds, and by the age of five months a female baby can recognize photographs of familiar people, while a boy of that age can rarely accomplish this. Researchers also found that girls tend to speak sooner than boys, read sooner than they do, and learn foreign languages more easily than boys do. On the other hand, boys show an early visual superiority over girls and they are better than girls at working with three-dimensional space. When preschool girls and boys are asked to mentally work with an object, the girls are not as successful as the boys. In this case, as in several others, the girls are likely to give verbal descriptions while the boys are able to do the actual work in their minds.

Ten suggested topics

In a paragraph, compare what you believe are male and female attitudes on one of the following topics:

1. Cooking
2. Sports
3. The nursing profession
4. Child care
5. The construction trade
6. Military careers
7. A career in science
8. Hobbies
9. Friendship
10. Clothing

16

Developing Paragraphs: Definition, Classification, and Cause and Effect

▶ **What is definition?**

You define a term in order to explain its meaning or significance. The starting point for a good definition is to group the word into a larger category. For example, the trout is a kind of fish; a doll is a kind of toy; a shirt is an article of clothing. Here is a dictionary entry for the word *family*.

> **family** (fam′e -le, fam′le) *n., pl.* **-lies.** *Abbr.* **fam.** 1. The most instinctive, fundamental social or mating group in man and animal, especially the union of man and woman through marriage and their offspring; parents and their children. 2. One's spouse and children. 3. Persons related by blood or marriage; relatives; kinfolk. 4. Lineage; especially, upper-class lineage. 5. All the members of a household; those who share one's domestic home.

To what larger category does the word *family* belong? The family, according to this entry, is a kind of *social group*. Once the word has been put into a larger class, the reader is ready to understand the identifying characteristics that make it different from other members in the class. What makes a *trout* different from a *bass,* a *doll* different from a *puppet,* a *shirt* different from a *sweater*? Here a definition can give examples. The dictionary definition of *family* identifies the family as a married man and woman and their children. Four additional meanings provide a suggestion of some variations.

When you write a paragraph or an essay that uses definition, the dictionary entry is only the beginning. In order for your reader to understand a difficult term or idea, you will need to expand this definition into what is called **extended definition**. It is not the function of a dictionary to go into great depth. It can only provide the basic meanings and synonyms. Extended definition, however, seeks to analyze a concept so that the reader will have a more complete understanding. For instance, you might include a historical perspective. When or how did the concept begin? How did the term change or evolve over the years, or how do different cultures understand the term? You will become involved in the word's connotations. Extended definition, or analysis as it is sometimes called, uses more than one method to arrive at an understanding of a term.

The following paragraph, taken from *Sociology: An Introduction* by John E. Conklin, is the beginning of a chapter on the family. The author's starting point is very similar to the dictionary entry.

> In every society, social norms define a variety of relationships among people, and some of these relationships are socially recognized as family or kinship ties. A *family* is a socially defined set of relationships between at least two people who are related by birth, marriage, or adoption. We can think of a family as including several possible relationships, the most common being between husband and wife, between parents and children, and between people who are related to each other by birth (siblings, for example) or by marriage (a woman and her mother-in-law, perhaps). Family relationships are often defined by custom, such as the relationship between an infant and godparents, or by law, such as the adoption of a child.

The author began this definition by putting the term into a larger class. "Family" is one type of social relationship among people. The writer then identifies the people who are members of this group. Family relationships can be formed by marriage, birth, adoption, or custom, as with godparents. The author does not stop here. The extended definition explores the functions of the family, conflicts in the family, the structure of the family, and the special characteristics of the American family.

The writer could also have defined *family* by **negation**. That is, he could have described what a family is *not:*

> A family is not a corporation.
> A family is not a formal school.
> A family is not a church.

When a writer defines a concept using negation, the definition should be completed by stating what the subject *is:*

> A family is not a corporation, but it is an economic unit of production and consumption.
> A family is not a formal school, but it is a major center for learning.
> A family is not a church, but it is where children learn their moral values.

Exercise 1 — Working with Definition: Class

Define each of the following terms by placing it in a larger class. Keep in mind that when you define something by class, you are placing it in a larger category so that the reader can see where it belongs. Use the dictionary if you need help. The first example has been done for you.

> Chemistry is *one of the branches of science* that deals with a close study of the natural world.

1. Mythology is _____

2. Nylon is _____

Developing Paragraphs: Definition, Classification, and Cause and Effect ▶ 301

3. An Amoeba is _____

4. A Tricycle is _____

5. Cabbage is _____

6. Democracy is _____

7. Asbestos is _____

8. A Piccolo is _____

9. Poetry is _____

10. A University is _____

Exercise 2   **Working with Definition: Distinguishing Characteristics**

Using the same terms as in Exercise 1, give one or two identifying characteristics that differentiate your term from other terms in the same class. An example is done for you.

    Chemistry studies the structure, properties, and reactions of matter.

1. Mythology _____
   _____
   _____

2. Nylon _____
   _____
   _____

3. An Amoeba _____
   _____
   _____

4. A Tricycle _____
   _____
   _____

5. Cabbage _____
   _____
   _____

6. Democracy _____
   _____
   _____

Mastering the Paragraph

7. Asbestos _____
_____

8. A Piccolo _____
_____
_____

9. Poetry _____
_____
_____

10. A University _____
_____
_____
_____

Exercise 3

Working with Definition: Example

Help define each of the following terms by providing one example. Examples always make writing more alive. An example has been done for you.

Term: Chemistry

Example: Chemistry studies an element like hydrogen. This element is the simplest in structure of all the elements, with only one electron and proton; it is colorless, highly flammable, the lightest of all gases, and the most abundant element in the universe.

1. Mythology
_____
_____
_____

2. Friendship
_____
_____
_____

3. Philanthropist
_____
_____
_____

Developing Paragraphs: Definition, Classification, and Cause and Effect ▶ 303

4. Planet

_____
_____
_____

5. Gland

_____
_____
_____

6. Greed

_____
_____
_____

7. Volcano

_____
_____
_____

8. Patriotism

_____
_____
_____

9. Terrorism

_____
_____
_____

10. Equality

_____
_____
_____

Exercise 4   **Working with Definition: Negation**

Define each of the following by using negation to construct your definition. Keep in mind that such a definition is not complete until you have also included what the topic you are defining *is*.

1. A *disability* is not _____,

    but it is _____.

2. The *perfect car* is not _____,

    but it is _____.

3. *Drugs* are not _____,

    but they are _____.

4. *Freedom* is not CONFINEMENT ,

    but it is being able to do what you want .

5. A *good job* is not _____,

    but it is _____.

6. *Exercise* is not _____,

    but it is _____.

7. A *university* is not _____,

    but it is _____.

8. A *politician* is not _____,

    but he or she is _____.

9. The *ideal pet* is not _____,

    but it is _____.

10. A *boring person* is not _____,

    but he or she is _____.

Writing a paragraph using definition

Here is a list of topics for possible paragraph assignments. For each topic that you choose to write about, develop a complete paragraph of definition by using one or more of the techniques you have studied—class, identifying characteristics, example, and negation—as well as any further analysis, historical or cultural, that will help the reader.

Topics

1. Photosynthesis
2. Ecology

3. Coma
4. Football
5. Paranoia
6. Courage
7. Algebra
8. Democracy
9. Masculinity or femininity
10. Justice

▶ What is classification?

When you place items into separate groups, you are able to think more clearly about the groups you have created, and you are better able to understand individual items in each group. This is classification, a skill that helps you control information that you are given when you read and helps you control the way other people receive information that you give them when you write.

In order to classify things properly, you must always take the items you are working with and put them into *distinct categories,* making sure that each item belongs in only one category. For example, if you wanted to classify motorcycles into imported motorcycles, U.S.-made motorcycles, and used motorcycles, this would not be an effective use of classification because an imported motorcycle or a U.S.-made motorcycle could also be a used motorcycle. When you classify, you want each item to belong in only one category.

A classification should also be *complete.* For example, if you were classifying motorcycles into the two categories of new and used, your classification would be complete because any item can only be new or used. Finally, a classification should be *useful.* If you are thinking of buying a motorcycle, or if a friend is thinking of buying one, then it might be very useful to classify them in this way because you or your friend might save a great deal of money by deciding to buy a used machine.

The following paragraph is taken from Judith Viorst's essay "Friends, Good Friends—and Such Good Friends" and shows the writer classifying different kinds of friends.

> There are medium friends, and pretty good friends, and very good friends indeed, and these friendships are defined by their level of intimacy. And what we'll reveal at each of these levels of intimacy is calibrated with care. We might tell a medium friend, for example, that yesterday we had a fight with our husband. And we might tell a pretty good friend that this fight with our husband made us so mad that we slept on the couch. And we might tell a very good friend that the reason we got so mad in that fight that we slept on the couch had something to do with that girl who works in his office. But it's only to our very best friends that we're willing to tell all, to tell what's going on with that girl in his office.

In this paragraph, the writer gives us four distinct types of friends, beginning with "medium friends," going on to "pretty good friends" and "very good friends," and ending with "very best friends." Her classification is complete because it covers a full range of friendships, and of course it is useful because people are always interested in the types of friends they have—and the types of friends their friends have!

Exercise 1

Working with Classification: Finding the Basis for a Classification

For each of the following topics, pick three different ways that topic could be classified. An example has been done for you.

        Topic: Ways to choose a vacation spot

Basis for classification: By price (first class, medium price, economy), by its special attraction (the beach, the mountains, the desert, etc.), by the accommodations (hotel, motel, cabin, trailer)

1. **Topic:** Cars

    Ways to divide the topic: _____

    _____

2. **Topic:** Houses

    Ways to divide the topic: _____

    _____

3. **Topic:** Neighborhoods

    Ways to divide the topic: _____

    _____

4. **Topic:** Religions

    Ways to divide the topic: _____

    _____

5. **Topic:** Soft drinks

    Ways to divide the topic: _____

    _____

6. **Topic:** Dates

    Ways to divide the topic: _____

    _____

7. **Topic:** Floor coverings

    Ways to divide the topic: _____

    _____

8. **Topic:** Medicines

    Ways to divide the topic: _____

    _____

Developing Paragraphs: Definition, Classification, and Cause and Effect ▶ 307

9. **Topic:** Snack foods

    Ways to divide the topic: Healthy, uNHealthy, ~~sweet, salty~~ ~~Inexpinsive~~, expensive,

10. **Topic:** Relatives

    Ways to divide the topic: _____

Exercise 2

Working with Classification: Making Distinct Categories

First pick a basis for classifying each of the following topics. Then break it down into distinct categories. Divide the topic into as many distinct categories as you think the classification requires.

Keep in mind that when you divide your topic, each part of your classification will belong only to one category. For example, if you were to classify cars, you would not want to make *sports cars* and *international cars* two of your categories because several kinds of sports cars are also international cars.

1. Clothing stores

    Distinct categories:

2. Television commercials

    Distinct categories:

3. College sports

    Distinct categories:

4. Doctors

    Distinct categories:

5. Hats

    Distinct categories:

6. Courses in the English department of your college
   Distinct categories:

   _____ _____ _____

   _____ _____ _____

7. Pens
   Distinct categories:

   _____ _____ _____

   _____ _____ _____

8. Dances
   Distinct categories:

   _____ _____ _____

   _____ _____ _____

9. Mail
   Distinct categories:

   _____ _____ _____

   _____ _____ _____

10. Music
    Distinct categories:

    _____ _____ _____

    _____ _____ _____

Writing a paragraph using classification

Here is a list of topics for possible paragraph assignments using classification. As you plan your paragraph, keep in mind the following points. Is there some purpose for your picking the basis for your classification? (For example, will it help someone make a decision or understand a concept better?) Are you sure the classification is complete and that no item could belong to more than one category? Does the classification help to organize your material?

Topics

1. Parents
2. Governments
3. Dogs
4. Careers
5. Parties
6. Summer jobs
7. Movies
8. Classmates
9. Co-workers
10. Restaurants

When we use cause and effect, we are asking the basic question "Why?" about something. Children ask this question so often that they drive their parents crazy, but adults ask the same kinds of questions almost as often: Why do we have recessions? Why did my car break down just after I got it back from the garage? Why don't I ever win the lottery?

Some of the questions children and adults ask cannot be answered, but when causes or effects can be explained it is important to make a complete investigation and give the underlying causes or the long-term effects of what you are discussing. For example, if a plane crashed because it lost an engine in flight, the cause of the crash might be blamed on a mechanical failure. However, if it could be shown that the plane crashed because a mechanic did a sloppy job of attaching the plane's engines after a tune-up, then the real cause of the crash might be better described as a mechanic's failure.

Another important consideration when dealing with cause and effect is to be careful not to jump to conclusions. For example, if you find it hard to sleep every time you have worked late, the work itself may not be the reason. There could be another factor causing the problem. Were you also drinking coffee while you worked? A genuine cause-and-effect relationship is the result of a real connection between facts, and not simply coincidence.

Looking at a model paragraph: cause

The following paragraph discusses some of the causes of a widespread medical problem, the common headache.

Headaches can have several causes. Many people think that the major cause of headache is nervous tension, but there is strong evidence that suggests diet and environment as possible factors. Some people get headaches because they are dependent on caffeine. Other people may be allergic to salt, or they may have low blood sugar. Still other people are allergic to household chemicals including polishes, waxes, bug killers, and paint. If they can manage to avoid these substances, their headaches tend to go away. When a person has recurring headaches, it is worthwhile to look for the underlying cause, especially if the result of that search is freedom from pain.

Writing a paragraph using causes

Here is a list of topics for writing paragraphs dealing with cause. Use the above paragraph as your model. As you plan your paragraph, keep in mind that the writer of the paragraph on headaches was careful to note as many causes for headaches as possible. This gave the paragraph a sense of completeness. Your paragraph will also be successful if you include as many specific causes for your topic as possible.

Ten suggested topics

1. The causes of war
2. The causes of senility
3. The causes of social unrest in many countries
4. The causes of the teenage runaway problem
5. The causes of tax cheating

6. The causes of the feminist movement
7. The causes of drug abuse
8. The causes of divorce
9. The causes of prostitution
10. The causes of the backup in our legal system

Looking at a model paragraph: effect

The following paragraph by a student writer describes some of the effects on children when both parents in a family work.

> The most noticeable change for most families is that Mom is no longer home during the day—not there to fix hot lunches or to soothe scraped knees and bruised egos. So who does? The answer, unfortunately, often is "No one." Countless numbers of children have become "latchkey children," left to fend for themselves after school because there aren't enough dependable, affordable baby-sitters or after-school programs for them. Some children are able to handle this early independence quite well and may even become more resourceful adults because of it, but many are not. Vandalism, petty thievery, and alcohol and drug abuse may all be products of this unsupervised life, problems that society in general must deal with eventually. Some companies (although too few) have adapted to this changing life-style by instituting on-site childcare facilities and/or "flextime" schedules for working mothers and fathers. Schools have begun to provide low-cost after-school activities during the school year, and summer day camps are filling the need during those months.

Writing a paragraph using effects

Here is a list of topics for writing paragraphs dealing with effect. Use the above paragraph as your model. As you plan your paragraph, keep in mind that the writer of the model paragraph was careful to include both the short-term and the long-term effects on children whose parents both work. Your paragraph will also be successful when you are careful to include both the short-term and the long-term effects of the topics you have chosen.

Ten suggested topics

1. The effects of children on a marriage
2. The effects of a water shortage in the summer
3. The effects of unemployment on a family
4. The effects of having too much time on your hands
5. The effects of television on children
6. The effects of pornography
7. The effects of drunk drivers on our society
8. The effects of imported products on our economy
9. The effects of TV political commercials on how people vote
10. The effects of AIDS on our society.

PART III

Structuring the College Essay

17

Moving from the Paragraph to the Essay

When you learned to write a well-developed paragraph in Part II, you were creating the basic support paragraph for an essay. An essay is a longer piece of writing, usually five or more paragraphs, in which you can develop a topic in much more depth than you could in a single paragraph. This longer piece of writing is usually called a college essay, composition, theme, or paper. Such writing is an important part of almost every course, not only the English composition class.

You learned in Part II that the paragraph with its topic sentence and supporting details must have an organization that is both unified and coherent. The essay must also have these characteristics. Furthermore, since the essay develops a topic at greater length or depth, making all the parts work together becomes an added challenge.

▶ What kinds of paragraphs are in an essay?

In addition to the support paragraphs that you studied in Part II, the essay has two new kinds of paragraphs:

1. The **introductory paragraph** is the first paragraph of the essay. Its purpose is to be so inviting that the reader will not want to stop reading. In most essays, this introduction contains a **thesis statement**.
2. **Support paragraphs** (sometimes called body paragraphs) provide the evidence that shows your thesis is valid. An essay must have at least three well-developed support paragraphs. (You have studied these kinds of paragraphs in Part II.) One paragraph must flow logically into the next. This is accomplished by the careful use of transitional devices.
3. The **concluding paragraph** is the last paragraph of the essay. Its purpose is to give the reader a sense of coming to a satisfying ending, that everything has been said that needed to be said.

Before you begin the process of writing your own college essays, this chapter will prepare you to understand and work with these special essay features:

Thesis statement
Introductory paragraph
Transitions between body paragraphs
Concluding paragraph

▶ What is a thesis?

The **thesis** of an essay is a statement of the main idea of that essay. It is the statement of what you are going to explain, defend, or prove about your topic. It is usually placed at the end of the introductory paragraph.

▶ How to recognize the thesis statement

1. The thesis statement is a complete sentence. Students sometimes confuse a title for a thesis. Remember that titles are usually phrases rather than complete sentences.

    Title: The Advantages of All-Day Kindergarten

    Thesis: Schools should offer parents the option of an all-day kindergarten program for their children, not only for the benefit of the working mother but also because of the advantages for the children.

2. The thesis statement presents a viewpoint about the topic that can be defended or shown in your essay. Students sometimes think that a simple statement of fact can be a thesis. A fact, however, is either true or false. It is not a topic that is debatable. Such a sentence could not be the focus of an essay since there is no apparent purpose for providing the factual information.

    Fact: Nearly all kindergartens in the United States offer a half day of instruction.

    Thesis: Parents know there is more than one reason why most children at five years of age should only be in school for half a day.

_____ Practice _____

Read each of the following statements. If you think the statement is a fact, mark it with an *F*. If you think the statement is a thesis, mark it with a *T*.

_____ 1. In the United States, kindergarten is not compulsory.

_____ 2. Children should begin learning to read in kindergarten.

_____ 3. Putting a child into kindergarten before he or she is physically or emotionally ready can have several unfortunate effects on a child.

_____ 4. In some European countries, children do not begin formal schooling until age seven or eight.

314 ◀ Structuring the College Essay

Exercise 1   Recognizing the Thesis Statement

Identify each of the following as (1) a *title*, (2) a *thesis*, or (3) a *fact* that could be used to support a thesis.

____2____ 1. The personal interview is the most important step in the employment process.

____1____ 2. Looking for a job

____3____ 3. Sixty percent of all jobs are obtained through newspaper advertisements.

____2____ 4. The best time to begin a foreign language is in grade school.

____1____ 5. The importance of learning a foreign language

____3____ 6. In the 1970s, the number of students studying foreign languages declined dramatically.

____3____ 7. Most American doing business with Japan do not know a word of Japanese.

____1____ 8. Working and studying at the same time

____3____ 9. Many students in community colleges have part-time jobs while they are going to school.

____2____ 10. Working a part-time job while going to school puts an enormous strain on a person.

Exercise 2   Recognizing the Thesis Statement

Identify each of the following as (1) a *title*, (2) a *thesis*, or (3) a *fact* that could be used to support a thesis.

_____ 1. It is estimated that approximately 200 grizzly bears live in Yellowstone National Park.

_____ 2. The survival of grizzly bears in our country should be a top priority.

_____ 3. When bears are young cubs, there are twice as many males as females.

_____ 4. Only about sixty percent of bear cubs survive the first few years of life.

_____ 5. Bears, a precious natural resource

_____ 6. The average life span of a bear today is only five or six years.

_____ 7. The sad plight of the American grizzly bear

Moving from the Paragraph to the Essay ▸ 315

_____ 8. Five actions need to be taken to save the grizzly bear from extinction.

_____ 9. To save the grizzly bear, we need laws from Congress, the cooperation of hunters and campers, and an educated general public.

_____ 10. A decision to save the grizzly bear

Exercise 3   Recognizing the Thesis Statement

Identify each of the following as (1) a *title,* (2) a *thesis,* or (3) a *fact* that could be used to support a thesis.

_____ 1. Tons of ancient material have been taken out of Russell Cave.

_____ 2. The opening of the Cave is 107 feet wide and 26 feet high.

_____ 3. People lived in this cave more than nine thousand years ago.

_____ 4. Russell Cave in Jackson County, Alabama, is an important source of information about the ancient people in North America.

_____ 5. The way ancient people lived

_____ 6. All kinds of articles, from fish hooks to human skeletons, have been found in Russell Cave.

_____ 7. Learning about the diet of an ancient people of North America

_____ 8. An archaeologist discovers Russell Cave

_____ 9. The discovery of many artifacts in Russell Cave has changed some of the theories previously held about life in North America thousands of years ago.

_____ 10. Russell Cave is the oldest known home of human beings in the southeastern United States.

▸ Writing the effective thesis statement

An effective thesis statement has the following parts:

1. **A topic that is not too broad:** Broad topics must be narrowed in scope. You can do this by *limiting the topic* (changing the term to cover a smaller part of the topic), or *qualifying the topic* (adding phrases or words to the general term that will narrow the topic).

   Broad topic: Swimming
   Limited topic: Learning to float (Floating is a kind of swimming, more specialized than the term *swimming.*)

Qualified topic: Swimming two hours a week (The use of the phrase "two hours a week" narrows the topic down considerably. Now the topic concentrates on the fact that the *time* spent swimming is an important part of the topic.)

There are an endless number of ways to narrow a topic in order to make it fit into a proper essay length as well as make it fit your experience and knowledge.

2. **A controlling idea that you can defend:** The controlling idea is what you want to show or prove about your topic; it is your attitude about that topic. Often the word is an adjective such as *beneficial, difficult,* or *maddening.*

   Learning to float at the age of twenty, was a *terrifying* experience.
   Swimming two hours a week brought about a *dramatic change* in my health.

3. **An indication of what strategy of development is to be used:** (Often you can use words such as the following: *description, steps, stages, comparison, contrast, causes, effects, reasons, advantages, disadvantages, definition, analysis, persuasion.*)

   Although not all writers include the strategy in the thesis statement, they must always have in mind what major strategy they plan to use to prove their thesis. Professional writers often use more than one strategy to prove the thesis. However, in this book, you are asked to develop your essays by using one major strategy at a time. By working in this way, you can concentrate on understanding and developing the skills needed for each specific strategy.
   Study the following thesis statement:

   Although a date with the right person is marvelous, going out with a group can have many advantages.

Now look back and check the parts of this thesis statement.

General topic: Going out
Qualified topic: Going out in a group (as opposed to a single date)
Controlling idea: To give the advantages
Strategy of development: Contrast between the single date and the group date

Exercise 1

Writing the Thesis Statement

Below are four topics. For each one, develop a thesis sentence by (1) limiting or qualifying the general topic, (2) choosing a controlling idea (what you want to explain or prove about the topic), and (3) selecting a strategy that you could use to develop that topic. An example is done for you.

General topic: Senior citizens
a. *Limit or qualify the subject:*
   Community services available to the senior citizens in my town

b. *Controlling idea:*
   To show the great variety of programs
c. *Strategy for development* (narration, process, cause and effect, definition and analysis, comparison or contrast, classification, argument):
   Classify the services into major groups

Thesis statement:
The senior citizens of Ann Arbor, Michigan, are very fortunate to have three major kinds of programs available that help them deal with health, housing, and leisure time.

1. Miami (or another city with which you are familiar)

   a. Limit or qualify the subject

   _____

   b. Controlling idea

   _____

   c. Strategy for development (narration, process, cause and effect, definition and analysis, comparison or contrast, classification, or argument)

   _____

   Thesis statement:

   _____
   _____

2. Terrorism

   a. Limit or qualify the subject

   _____

   b. Controlling idea

   _____

   c. Strategy for development (narration, process, cause and effect, definition and analysis, comparison or contrast, classification, or argument)

   _____

   Thesis statement:

   _____
   _____

3. Shopping

   a. Limit or qualify the subject

   _____

b. Controlling idea

_____

c. Strategy for development (narration, process, cause and effect, definition and analysis, comparison or contrast, classification, or argument)

_____

Thesis statement:

_____

_____

4. The library

   a. Limit or qualify the subject

   _____

   b. Controlling idea

   _____

   c. Strategy for development (narration, process, cause and effect, definition and analysis, comparison or contrast, classification, or argument)

   _____

Thesis statement:

_____

_____

Exercise 2 — Writing the Thesis Statement

Below are five topics. For each one, develop a thesis sentence by (1) limiting or qualifying the general topic, (2) choosing a controlling idea (what you want to explain or prove about the topic), and (3) selecting a strategy that you could use to develop that topic. Review the example in exercise 1 (pages 316–317).

1. Television

   a. Limit or qualify the subject

   _____

   b. Controlling idea

   _____

   c. Strategy for development (narration, process, example, cause and effect, definition and analysis, comparison or contrast, classification, or argument)

   _____

Thesis statement:

_____

_____

_____

_____

2. Soccer (or another sport)

   a. Limit or qualify the subject

      _____

   b. Controlling idea

      _____

   c. Strategy for development (narration, process, example, cause and effect, definition and analysis, comparison or contrast, classification, or argument)

      _____

   Thesis statement:

   _____

   _____

   _____

   _____

3. Math (or another field of study)

   a. Limit or qualify the subject

      _____

   b. Controlling idea

      _____

   c. Strategy for development (narration, process, example, cause and effect, definition and analysis, comparison or contrast, classification, or argument)

      _____

   Thesis statement:

   _____

   _____

   _____

   _____

4. Guns

    a. Limit or qualify the subject

    _____

    b. Controlling idea

    _____

    c. Strategy for development (narration, process, example, cause and effect, definition and analysis, comparison or contrast, classification, or argument)

    _____

    Thesis statement:

    _____
    _____
    _____
    _____

5. Clubs

    a. Limit or qualify the subject

    _____

    b. Controlling idea

    _____

    c. Strategy for development (narration, process, example, cause and effect, definition and analysis, comparison or contrast, classification, or argument)

    _____

    Thesis statement:

    _____
    _____
    _____
    _____

▶ Ways to write an effective introductory paragraph

An introduction has one main purpose: to "grab" your readers' interest so that they will keep reading. There is no one way to write an introduction. However, since many good introductions follow the same common patterns, you will find it helpful to look at a few examples of the more typical patterns. When you are ready to create your own introductions, you can consider trying one of these patterns.

1. Begin with a general subject that can be narrowed down into the specific topic of your essay. Here is an introduction to an essay about a family making cider on their farm:

> The number of children who eagerly help around a farm is rather small. Willing helpers do exist, but many more of them are five years old than fifteen. In fact, there seems to be a general law that says as long as a kid is too little to help effectively, he or she is dying to. Then, just as they reach the age when they really could drive a fence post or empty a sap bucket without spilling half of it, they lose interest. Now it's cars they want to drive, or else they want to stay in the house and listen for four straight hours to The Who. That sort of thing.
>
> From Noel Perrin,
> "Falling for Apples"

Then comes the specific topic of this essay:

> There is one exception to this rule. Almost no kid that I have ever met outgrows an interest in cidering.

2. Begin with specifics (a brief anecdote, a specific example or fact) that will broaden into the more general topic of your essay. Here is the introduction to an essay about the role news plays in our lives.

> Let me begin with a confession. I am a news addict. Upon awakening I flip on the *Today* show to learn what events transpired during the night. On the commuter train which takes me to work, I scour *The New York Times,* and find myself absorbed in tales of earthquakes, diplomacy and economics. I read the newspaper as religiously as my grandparents read their prayerbooks. The sacramental character of the news extends into the evening. The length of my workday is determined precisely by my need to get home in time for Walter Cronkite. My children understand that my communion with Cronkite is something serious and cannot be interrupted for light and transient causes.
>
> From Stanley Milgram,
> "Confessions of a News Addict"

Then what follows is the topic of the essay, a topic that is larger than his own personal habits of watching and reading the news:

> What is news, and why does it occupy a place of special significance for so many people?

3. Give a definition of the concept that will be discussed. Here is the introduction to an essay about the public's common use of two addictive drugs: alcohol and cigarettes.

Our attitude toward the word "drug" depends on whether we are talking about penicillin or heroin or something in-between. The unabridged three-volume Webster's says a drug is "a chemical substance administered to prevent or cure disease or enhance physical and mental welfare" or "a substance affecting the structure or function of the body." Webster's should have added "mind," but they probably thought that was part of the body. Some substances that aren't drugs, like placebos, affect "the structure or function of the body," but they work because we *think* they're drugs.

From Adam Smith,
"Some American Drugs Familiar to Everybody"

4. Make a startling statement.

Man will never conquer space. Such a statement may sound ludicrous, now that our rockets are already 100 million miles beyond the moon and the first human travelers are preparing to leave the atmosphere. Yet it expresses a truth which our forefathers knew, one we have forgotten—and our descendants must learn again, in heartbreak and loneliness.

From Arthur C. Clarke,
"We'll Never Conquer Space"

5. Start with an idea or statement that is a widely held point of view. Then surprise the reader by stating that this idea is false or that you hold a different point of view.

Tom Wolfe has christened today's young adults as the "me" generation, and the 1970s—obsessed with things like consciousness expansion and self-awareness—have been described as the decade of the new narcissism. The cult of "I," in fact, has taken hold with the strength and impetus of a new religion. But the joker in the pack is that it is all based on a false idea.

From Margaret Halsey,
"What's Wrong with 'Me, Me, Me'?"

6. Start with a familiar quotation or a quotation by a famous person.

"The very hairs of your head," says Matthew 10:30, "are all numbered." There is little reason to doubt it. Increasingly, everything tends to get numbered one way or another, everything that can be counted, measured, averaged, estimated or quantified. Intelligence is gauged by a quotient, the humidity by a ratio, pollen by its count, and the trends of birth, death, marriage and divorce by rates. In this epoch of runaway demographics, society is often described and analyzed with statistics as with words. Politics seems more and more a game played with percentages turned up by pollsters, and economics a learned babble of ciphers and indexes that few people can translate and apparently nobody can control. Modern civilization, in sum, has begun to resemble an interminable arithmetic class in which, as Carl Sandburg put it, "numbers fly like pigeons in and out of your head."

From Frank Trippett,
"Getting Dizzy by the Numbers"

7. Give a number of descriptive images that will lead to the thesis of your essay. Here is the opening of a lengthy essay about the importance of sports in our lives.

> I cannot remember when I was not surrounded by sports, when talk of sports was not in the air, when I did not care passionately about sports. As a boy in Chicago in the late Forties, I lived in the same building as the sister and brother-in-law of Barney Ross, the welterweight champion. Half a block away, down near the lake, the Sullivan High School football team worked out in the spring and autumn. Summers the same field was given over to baseball and men's softball on Sundays. A few blocks to the north was the Touhy Avenue Fieldhouse, where basketball was played, and lifeguards trained, and behind which, in a softball field frozen over in winter, crack-the-whip, hockey, and speed skating took over. To the west, a block or so up Morse Avenue, was the Morse Avenue "L" Recreations, a combined pool hall and bowling alley. Life, in short, was games.

From Joseph Epstein,
"Obsessed with Sport:
On the Interpretation of a Fan's Dreams"

8. Ask a question that you intend to answer. Many essays you will read in magazines and newspapers use a question in the introductory paragraph to make the reader curious about the author's viewpoint. Some writing instructors prefer that students do not use this method. Check with your instructor for his or her viewpoint. Here is an example of such an introduction.

> Suppose there were no critics to tell us how to react to a picture, a play, or a new composition of music. Suppose we wandered innocent as the dawn into an art exhibition of unsigned paintings. By what standards, by what values would we decide whether they were good or bad, talented or untalented, successes or failures? How can we ever know that what we think is right?

From Marya Mannes,
"How Do You Know It's Good?"

9. Use classification to indicate how your topic fits into the larger class to which it belongs, or how your topic can be divided into categories that you are going to discuss. Here is how Aaron Copland began an essay on listening to music:

> We all listen to music according to our separate capacities. But, for the sake of analysis, the whole listening process may become clearer if we break it up into its component parts, so to speak. In a certain sense we all listen to music on three separate planes. For lack of a better terminology, one might name these: the sensuous plane, the expressive

plane, the sheerly musical plane. The only advantage to be gained from mechanically splitting up the listening process into these hypothetical planes is the clearer view to be had of the way in which we listen.

From Aaron Copland,
What to Listen For in Music

What *not* to say in your introduction

1. Avoid telling your reader that you are beginning your essay:

    In this essay I will discuss . . .

    I will talk about . . .

    I am going to prove . . .

2. Don't apologize:

    Although I am not an expert . . .

    In my humble opinion . . .

3. Do not refer to later parts of your essay:

    By the end of this essay you will agree . . .

    In the next paragraph you will see . . .

4. Don't use trite expressions. Since they have been so overused, they will lack interest. Using such expressions shows that you have not taken the time to use your own words to express your ideas. The following are some examples of trite expressions:

    busy as a bee

    you can't tell a book by its cover

    haste makes waste

▶ Using transitions to move the reader from one idea to the next

Successful essays help the reader understand the logic of the writer's thinking by using transitional expressions when needed. Usually this occurs when the writer is moving from one point to the next. It can also occur whenever the idea is complicated. The writer may need to summarize the points so far; the writer may need to emphasize a point already made; or the writer may want to repeat an important point. The transition may be a word, a phrase, a sentence, or even a paragraph.

Here are some of the transitional expressions that might be used to help the reader make the right connections.

1. To make your points stand out clearly:

the first reason	second, secondly	finally
first of all	another example	most important
in the first place	even more important	all in all
	also, next	in conclusion
	then	to summarize

2. To show an example of what has just been said:

> for example
> for instance

3. To show the consequence of what has just been said:

> therefore
> as a result
> then

4. To make a contrasting point clear:

> on the other hand
> but
> contrary to current thinking
> however

5. To admit a point:

> of course
> granted

6. To resume your argument after admitting a point:

> nevertheless
> even though
> nonetheless
> still

7. To call the reader's attention to your organization:

> Before attempting to answer these questions, let me . . .
> In our discussions so far, we have seen that . . .
> At this point, it is necessary to . . .
> It is beyond the scope of this paper to . . .

A more subtle way to link one idea to another in an essay is to repeat a word or phrase from the preceding sentence. Sometimes instead of the actual word, a pronoun will take the place of the word.

8. To repeat a word or phrase from a preceding sentence:

> I have many memories of my childhood in Cuba. These *memories* include the aunts, uncles, grandparents, and friends I had to leave behind.

9. To use a pronoun to refer to a word or phrase from a preceding sentence:

> Like all immigrants, my family and I have had to build a new life from almost nothing. *It* was often difficult, but I believe the struggle made us strong.

Exercise 1 — Finding Transitional Devices

Below are the first three paragraphs of an essay on African art. Circle all the transitional devices or the repeating words that are used to link one sentence to another or one idea to the next.

Like language and social organization, art is essential to human life. As embellishment and as creation of objects beyond the requirements of the most basic needs of living, art has accompanied man since prehistoric times. Because of its almost unfailing consistency as an element of many societies, art may be the response to some biological or psychological need. Indeed, it is one of the most constant forms of human behavior.

However, use of the word *art* is not relevant when we describe African "art" because it is really a European term that at first grew out of Greek philosophy and was later reinforced by European culture. The use of other terms, such as *exotic art, primitive art, art sauvage,* and so on, to delineate differences is just as misleading. Most such terms are pejorative—implying that African art is on a lower cultural level. Levels of culture are irrelevant here, since African and European attitudes toward the creative act are so different. Since there is no term in our language to distinguish between the essential differences in thinking, it is best then to describe standards of African art.

African art attracts because of its powerful emotional content and its beautiful abstract form. Abstract treatment of form describes most often—with bare essentials of line, shape, texture, and pattern—intense energy and sublime spirituality. Hundreds of distinct cultures and languages and many types of people have created over one thousand different styles that defy classification. Each art and craft form has its own history and its own aesthetic content. But there are some common denominators (always with exceptions).

▶ Ways to write an effective concluding paragraph

A concluding paragraph has one main purpose: to give the reader the sense of reaching a satisfying ending to the topic discussed. Students often feel they have nothing to say at the end. A look at how professional writers frequently end their essays can ease your anxiety about writing an effective conclusion. You have more than one possibility. Here are some of the most frequently used patterns for ending an essay.

1. Come full circle; that is, return to the material in your introduction. Finish what you started there. Remind the reader of the thesis. Be sure to restate the main idea using a different wording. Here is an example from the essay analyzing the meaning of news in our lives (page 321).

   Living in the modern world, I cannot help but be shaped by it, suckered by the influence and impact of our great institutions. *The New York Times, CBS* and *Newsweek* have made me into a news addict. In daily life I have come to accept the supposition that if *The New York*

Times places a story on the front page, it deserves my attention. I feel obligated to know what is going on. But sometimes, in quieter moments, another voice asks: If the news went away, would the world be any worse for it?

2. Summarize by repeating the main points. This example is from the essay on African art (page 326):

   In summary, African art explains the past, describes values and a way of life, helps man relate to supernatural forces, mediates his social relations, expresses emotions, and enhances man's present life as an embellishment denoting pride or status as well as providing entertainment such as with dance and music.

3. Show the significance of your thesis by making predictions, giving a warning, giving advice, offering a solution, suggesting an alternative, or telling the results. This example is from the essay on cidering (page 321):

   This pleasure goes on and on. In an average year we start making cider the second week of September, and we continue until early November. We make all we can drink ourselves, and quite a lot to give away. We have supplied whole church suppers. One year the girls sold about ten gallons to the village store, which made them some pocket money they were prouder of than any they ever earned from babysitting. Best of all, there are two months each year when all of us are running the farm together, just like a pioneer family.

4. End with an anecdote that illustrates your thesis. This example is from the essay on being obsessed with sports (page 323).

   When I was a boy I had a neighbor, a man who, after retirement, had a number of strokes. An old man and a young boy, we had in common a love of sports, which, when we met on the street, was our only topic of conversation. He once inspected a new glove of mine, and instructed me to rub it down with neat's-foot-oil, place a ball firmly in the pocket, wrap string tightly around the glove, and leave it like that for the winter. I did, and it worked. After his last stroke but one, he seldom left his house. Afternoons he spent in a chair in his bedroom, a blanket over his lap, listening to Cub games over the radio. It was while listening to a ball game that he quietly died. I cannot imagine a better way.

What *not* to say in your conclusion

1. Do not introduce a new point.
2. Do not apologize.
3. Do not end up in the air, leaving the reader feeling unsatisfied. This sometimes happens if the very last sentence is not strong enough.

▶ A note about titles

Be sure to follow the standard procedure for writing your title.

1. Capitalize all words except articles (*the, a, an*) and prepositions.
2. Do not underline the title or put quotation marks around it.
3. Try to think of a short and catchy phrase (three to six words). Often writers wait until they have written a draft before working on a title. There may be a phrase from the essay that will be perfect. If you still cannot think of a clever title after you have written a draft, choose some key words from your thesis statement.
4. Center the title at the top of the page, and remember to leave about an inch of space between the title and the beginning of the first paragraph.

18

The Writing Process

▶ **What is the process for writing a college essay?**

Writing is a craft. This means that a writer, no matter how good or how inexperienced, needs to follow a certain process in order to arrive at a successful product. Very few writers can "dash of" a masterpiece. We sometimes think that a person is "a born dancer" or "a born writer," but the reality is that the person has worked long hours for many years to achieve his or her level of skill.

Just as no two chefs or carpenters or painters approach their work in the same way, no two writers work in exactly the same way. In spite of this individuality, each writer goes through a surprisingly similar series of steps to reach the finished product.

Steps in the Writing Process

1. Getting the idea for developing a topic
2. Gathering the information (brainstorming, taking notes)
3. Selecting and organizing material
4. Writing the rough draft
5. Revising the rough draft (Some writers work on many, many drafts that they revise before they are satisfied.)
6. Writing the second draft
7. Proofreading
8. Preparing the final copy
9. Checking for errors

Following this process will help you produce your best writing. You will feel more in control since you will be working on one step at a time and not trying to do everything all at once. Careful preparation before writing and careful revisions after writing always pay off. You will see your initial idea change and develop into something much more detailed and organized than your first thoughts on the topic. Remember that writing, just like the other skills you develop in life, improves when you follow the same process used by those who have already been successful. If you take the time to practice using this process regularly, your writing will improve.

Many students believe that a writer somehow has a magical inspiration that allows him or her to sit down and produce the piece immediately. Although this very seldom happens, you may be lucky enough on occasion to have the exciting experience of being "turned on" to your topic, an experience in which the words flow easily from your pen. At such a time, you will feel how satisfying writing can be, for writing is a way to self-discovery. It is a method of finding within yourself the wealth of untapped ideas and thoughts that are waiting for expression.

▶ Understanding the writing process

Getting the idea

Usually a writer sits down to write knowing the general topic he or she wants to write about. You might have to write an essay on the two-party system in the United States for a history class. You might have to write a paper for psychology class on coping with stress. Maybe you are angry about a toxic waste site near your home, and you decide to write a letter to the newspaper. Perhaps your employer asks you to write a report to describe the ways in which productivity could be increased in your department. In all these cases, the topic is set before you. You do not have to say to yourself, "Now what in the world shall I write about?" Most students prefer to have a specific topic rather than have no direction at all. Furthermore, if the topic is of interest to you, your writing is much more likely to be interesting to your readers. When you enjoy your work, you will spend more time on it and use more of your inner resources.

Even though you will usually be assigned a particular topic or given a group of topics from which to choose, you will need to spend some time thinking of a possible approach that can make use of your experience or knowledge. In writing, this approach is called the "controlling idea." One of our students, for example, loved to play chess. He admitted to us in his senior year of college that he had tried to use his interest in and knowledge of this hobby to help him complete several of his college assignments. For an assignment in his psychology class, when the teacher asked for a paper titled "Stereotypes—Are They True?" he wrote about the characteristics of people who play chess. For a political science class, this same student discussed the importance of international games, including chess, of course. For a paper in his literature course, he wrote about four writers who used games in their writing to symbolize a struggle for power between two characters. You can see from these examples that this student was able to use his own special interests and knowledge to make his writing interesting for himself and undoubtedly interesting to the teachers who read his papers. Don't ever think that you have nothing to write about!

You should always keep in mind that your goal is to find an angle that will interest whoever is going to read your work. All writers write best about topics that are related to their own experience and knowledge. You cannot hope to interest the reader if the material does not first interest you! This chapter will guide you in this important step of searching for the approach or controlling idea that will work for you.

A student essay in progress: getting the idea for an essay

A student is asked to write a cause or effect essay about a social issue. She begins by making a list of possibilities for such an essay:

> The causes of children failing in school
> The effects of consumerism on the environment
> The effects of dishonesty in business
> The causes of couples choosing to have small families
> The effects of growing up in a large city
> The effects of a working mother on the family
> The effects of being an only child

Which one should she choose? She goes over the list of possibilities and realizes that she responds most directly to the topic of mothers who work. Here is a topic that she can easily identify with and a subject she feels she could write about objectively. Her own mother did not work while she herself was growing up, but today's economic pressures are making her think that she might have to become a second wage earner in her family. The topic appeals to her because she feels it is not only relevant to her own life, but it is a timely issue in today's society as well.

Gathering information

Once you have found a topic, you still have many choices to make. What is going to be your point about the topic? What angle or strategy will you use? You might choose to tell a story, give several examples or anecdotes to prove your point, define and analyze, or compare or contrast. In other words, you can choose from these several different strategies the one that best suits your knowledge or experience.

To make these choices, writers usually need to gather some information to find out what they have to work with. If the assignment calls for your own experience, you will not need to conduct outside research—in the library or in interviews, for instance—to get information. In such a case, you can begin with the technique known as **brainstorming**. Writers use brainstorming to discover what they already know and feel about a given topic.

When you brainstorm, you allow your mind to roam freely around the topic, letting one idea lead to another, even if the ideas seem unrelated or irrelevant. You jot down every word and phrase that pops into your mind when you think about your topic. Sometimes it helps to brainstorm with another person or a group of people. Since this list will only be for your own use, you can jot down single words, phrases, or entire sentences. Your thoughts will be listed in the order in which you originally think of them, or in some other order that makes sense to you. The important point about brainstorming is that it helps to stimulate your thinking on the topic, as well as gives you the opportunity to write down your first thoughts on the topic. Once you have some ideas jotted down on paper, you will begin to feel less anxious, and perhaps even pleasantly surprised that you have discovered so many possibilities for your essay.

A student essay in progress: brainstorming the topic

Topic: When a mother works

Approach (or controlling idea): The effects on an entire family when the mother works

economic pressures	trying to get through a normal workday
fatigue	strains on a marriage
housework on the weekends	fast food
children's activities	stress on everyone
needs of household during the daytime	no time to entertain
husband's new role	when someone gets sick
effects on society	cooking convenience foods at home
more income, more taxes	what women expect
children more mature	what employees expect
woman goes back to school	fathers with children on weekends

Selecting and organizing details

When you brainstorm, ideas come from your mind in no particular order, and you jot them down as they come. Your next step in the writing process is to give a sense of organization to these ideas. You do this when you place the results of your brainstorming in an order that helps you see a sequence of events, or logical order for the ideas. This need not be the final order, but it will help you plan an order for your first draft.

As you select and organize the details on your list, do not hesitate to cross out items you know you cannot use. This is an important part of the writing process at this stage. If you are careful in your choice of items, your essay will eventually have more, not less, to offer your reader.

A student essay in progress: organizing the material

The student writer strikes out the ideas that do not seem useful and then begins to group the other ideas that she can use. As she works with her words and phrases, she is considering what she should do with all this material. What she realizes is that she could write the essay in many ways: she could describe her own family situation, she could tell the story of one of her friends who went to work, or she could write a more objective analysis of the effects on families when mothers work. She decides to choose this last approach because she believes she could concentrate on items that apply to society as a whole and this would lead to a more objective essay. She also feels that this approach to the topic would allow her to use a wide variety of examples and this would make her writing more convincing.

She begins to work out an order to her material. Some instructors ask students to shape their material into an informal outline. Here is how this student outlined her material:

   I. **Introduction: Economy makes it necessary for most women to work.**
  II. **Effects on the families**
    A. Nobody home for the children
        1. No hot meals
        2. No sympathetic ear

  B. Nobody home to do daily errands or family chores
   1. Medical appointments
   2. Banking and other business
   3. Grocery shopping
  C. Dads helping more
   1. Household chores
   2. Child care
   3. Meal preparation
  D. Different eating habits
   1. Convenience foods
   2. Microwavable foods
III. Conclusion
  A. Dads might feel threatened
  B. Dads might feel resentful

  Notice how some of the ideas on the brainstorming list have been omitted or changed. This essay will focus on the effects on the family members when a woman works. The writer chooses to start with the children, then discusses family chores, dad's increased responsibilities, the meals, and finally the effects on the husband and father. Do you think this is a good working outline? Do you see any part of it that may be a problem?

Writing the rough draft

  After you have gone through the brainstorming process and you have organized the material into some kind of order, the time has come to write a rough draft. Some students write their drafts in the traditional way, using pen and paper. Others find it easier to compose directly on a word processor, correcting words, sentences, and even entire paragraphs as they go.

  A rough draft is just what its name implies, your first attempt to write your essay. The first attempt is "rough" because it will undoubtedly undergo many changes before it is finished: Parts may be missing, some paragraphs will probably lack sufficient detail, or some parts may be repetitious or inappropriate. Some sentences are likely to sound awkward and need to be rewritten later. The experienced writer expects all this and does not worry. All that you should try to accomplish in the rough draft is to let your mind relax and to get down on paper all of your initial ideas. These first ideas will provide the seeds that can be better developed later on.

  Armed with a first draft, you will now have something with which to work. No longer is there a blank paper staring you in the face. This accomplishment is a great relief to most writers, but remember, this is still the beginning!

A student essay in progress: the rough draft

When a Mother Works

1 The economy today has made it necessary for most women to work. What has been the effect?

2   The most noticeable change for most families is that Mom is no longer home during the day. She is not there to fix hot lunches or to soothe scraped knees and bruised egos.

3   Another effect of Mom's absence from the home is that businesses are discovering that she is no longer available to let meter readers in, accept furniture deliveries, take children to the doctor and dentist, or take care of banking needs. Just as many supermarkets have changed to a twenty-four-hour selling day, retail stores and service industries are beginning to realize that they must also adapt if they want to keep the working woman's business.

4   Even when Mom comes home in the evening, life is still not normal. Housecleaning is becoming a shared activity, when it gets done at all. Dad's duties are no longer confined to mowing the lawn and taking out the garbage, he is now expected to do lots of other things.

5   It's always a pleasure to see fathers taking their children out on weekends. Sometimes they are trying to give their wives a break, so they take the children out for a few hours or even for an entire day. This is a positive experience for the children, for they will remember these as happy hours spent with the exclusive attention of one parent.

6   So now we have Dad helping with the household chores and with the children. What about meals? Again, Dad may be asked to help out. But many men (and women) still feel the kitchen is the woman's domain. The idea that women belong in the kitchen is a popular one. Enter time-saving appliances, such as the microwave oven and convenience foods such as boil-in-the-bag frozen entrees. Mom simply doesn't have the time or the energy to prepare traditional meals. Instant meals are no longer considered a luxury and the food industry is cashing in on the demand. Even old standby items on the grocery shelves now proclaim that they are microwavable. A fact that is not hurting their sales one bit.

7   How does the family feel about Mom as a late bloomer? Dad may feel somewhat threatened, especially if he was raised to believe that a womans place is in the home. He may resent her working even more when the financial need is severe. Because he feels it announces to the world that he cannot provide for his family. In marriages that are not solid to begin with, this perceived loss of dominance by the husband may lead to divorce.

Revising the rough draft

If you have time, put aside your rough draft for a day or two. Then, when you reread it, you will look at it with a fresh mind. In this important revision stage, you should be concerned with how you have organized your ideas into paragraphs. At this point, do not worry about grammar, spelling, and punctuation.

Begin this important revision stage by asking these major questions:

a. Is the essay unified? Do you stick to the topic you have announced? Go through the essay and take out irrelevant material.

b. Do you repeat yourself? Look back over your essay to determine whether or not you have given the same information more than once. Even if you find you have used only some different words, you should delete the repetitious material.

c. Does the essay make sense? Can a reader follow your logic or train of thought? (Giving the rough draft to someone else to read will often answer this question for you.) If the essay is confusing to the reader, you must find out where it goes wrong and why. Sometimes when you read your writing out loud, you will hear a strange sentence or feel that one paragraph has leaped to some point that doesn't follow from the sentence before.

d. Are the paragraphs roughly the same length? If you see one sentence presented as a paragraph, you know something is wrong. Usually each paragraph should develop its point by the use of at least five sentences. Check through your essay. Do you need to change the paragraphing? You may need to develop one paragraph more fully, or a one-sentence paragraph may really belong with the paragraph that comes before or with the paragraph that follows.

e. Do you have all the types of paragraphs essential to an essay: the introduction with its thesis, at least three well-developed body paragraphs with transitional devices used to connect ideas, and a concluding paragraph?

f. Can you add more specific details? Most writing teachers agree that nearly every paper they read could be improved by adding more details, more descriptive verbs, and more sensory images to make the writing come alive.

g. Can you add dialogue or a quote from someone?

h. Could you make the introduction, conclusion, or title more creative?

A student essay in progress: revising the rough draft

Here is the same essay. This time marginal comments have been added by the student's writing instructor to aid in revision. No corrections of punctuation, spelling or grammar have been made yet. At this stage, the student should focus on the organization and content. As the student works with the text, she may correct some of the grammar errors when she rewrites, deletes, or adds material.

You might be able to think of a more catchy title.

When a Mother Works

1 The economy today has made it necessary for most women to work. What has been the effect?

Introductory paragraph needs more development. You might tell us more about the economy.

2 The most noticeable change for most families is that Mom is no longer home during the day. She is not there to fix hot lunches or to soothe scraped knees and bruised egos. *So who does? More development please!*

3 Another effect of Mom's absence from the home is that businesses are discovering that she is no longer available to let meter readers in, accept furniture deliveries, take children to the doctor and dentist, or take care of banking needs. Just as many supermarkets have changed to a twenty-four-hour selling day, retail stores and service industries are beginning to realize that they must also adapt if they want to keep the working woman's business. *good specific details*

4 Even when Mom comes home in the evening, life is still not normal. Housecleaning is becoming a shared activity, when it gets done at all. Dad's duties are no longer confined to mowing the lawn and taking out the garbage, he is now expected to do lots of other things. *What exactly does Dad do now?*

This ¶ is not relevant to this essay, is it? Omit it in your next draft or revise it.

5 It's always a pleasure to see fathers taking their children out on weekends. Sometimes they are trying to give their wives a break, so they take *Be more specific. Give examples.*

the children out for a few hours or even for an entire day. This is a positive experience for the children, for they will remember these as happy hours spent with the exclusive attention of one parent.

6 So now we have Dad helping with the household chores and with the children. What about meals? Again, Dad may be asked to help out. [But many men (and women) still feel the kitchen is the woman's domain. The idea that women belong in the kitchen is a popular one.] Enter time-saving appliances, such as the microwave oven and convenience foods such as boil-in-the bag frozen entrees. Mom simply doesn't have the time or the energy to prepare traditional meals. Instant meals are no longer considered a luxury and the food industry is cashing in on the demand. Even old standby items on the grocery shelves now proclaim that they are microwavable. A fact that is not hurting their sales one bit.

[Don't these two sentences say the same thing?]

7 How does the family feel about Mom as a late bloomer? Dad may feel somewhat threatened, especially if he was raised to believe that a womans place is in the home. He may resent her working even more when the financial need is severe. Because he feels it announces to the world that he cannot provide for his family. In marriages that are not solid to begin with, this perceived loss of dominance by the husband may lead to divorce.

[This ¶ presents another effect. It is not a conclusion.]

[In your concluding ¶, you might look to the future for more positive solutions or summarize all your points.]

Writing the second draft

If you have worked hard in revising the rough draft, you will be delighted with the improvements as you write the second draft.

Feedback is an important aid in each of the final stages of writing an essay. A good way to help yourself see your own work better is to put the writing aside for a few days, if you can. Then read what you have written aloud to someone else (or to yourself if no one else is available). You will be very surprised at the number of places in your writing where you will hear a mistake and make a change even as you read.

A student essay in progress: the second draft

Goodbye, Mom's Apple Pie

1 Inflation. Stagflation. Recession. No matter what you call the current state of our economy, virtually all of us have been touched by its effects. Rising prices and the shrinking dollar have made two-income families, once a rarity, now almost the norm. Besides fattening the family pocketbook (if only to buy necessities), how else has this phenomenon changed our lives?

2 The most noticeable change for most families is that Mom is no longer home during the day. She is not there to fix hot lunches or to soothe scraped knees and bruised egos. So who does? The answer, unfortunately, often is "No one." Countless numbers of children have become "latchkey children," left to fend for themselves after school because there aren't enough dependable, affordable babysitters or after-school programs for

them. Some children are able to handle this early independence quite well and may even become more resourceful adults because of it, but many are not. Vandalism, petty thievery, alcohol and drug abuse may all be products of this unsupervised life, problems that society in general must deal with eventually. Some companies (although too few) have adapted to this changing lifestyle by instituting on-site childcare facilities and/or "flextime" schedules for working mothers and fathers. Schools have begun to provide low-cost after-school activities during the schoolyear, and summer day camps are filling the need during those months.

3   Another effect of Mom's absence from the home is that businesses are discovering that she is no longer available to let meter readers in, accept furniture deliveries, take children to the doctor and dentist, or take care of banking needs. Just as many supermarkets have changed to a twenty-four-hour selling day, retail stores and service industries are beginning to realize that they must also adapt if they want to keep the working woman's business.

4   Even when Mom comes home in the evening, life is still not normal. Housecleaning is becoming a shared activity, when it gets done at all. Dad's duties are no longer confined to mowing the lawn and taking out the garbage. He is now expected to vacuum, wash dishes, bathe children, fold laundry—chores that no self-respecting man of a generation ago would have done. Has Dad's ego suffered? Maybe. But possibly, just possibly, his sense of being part of a family unit, not just the breadwinner and disciplinarian, has increased. Because he is now forced to deal with his children on a less exalted level, he may find that he is closer to them and they to him. Certainly, both parent and child will be affected by this more active fathering.

5   So now we have Dad helping with the household chores and with the children. What about meals? Again, Dad may be asked to help out, but many men (and women) still feel the kitchen is the woman's domain. Enter time-saving appliances, such as the microwave oven and convenience foods such as boil-in-the-bag frozen entrees. Mom simply doesn't have the time or the energy to prepare traditional meals, including apple pie and home-baked bread. Instant meals are no longer considered a luxury and the food industry is cashing in on the demand. Even old standby items on the grocery shelves now proclaim that they are microwavable, a fact that is not hurting their sales one bit. However, even with quickie meals Mom is sometimes just too tired to cook. At those times fast-food restaurants enjoy the family's business. They offer no fuss, no muss, and someone to clean up after the meal. And "clean up" the restaurants have. At a time when food prices were rising almost daily and supermarket sales were dropping, fast-food restaurants were enjoying even higher sales. Maybe part of the reason was that women were beginning to realize that their time was valuable too, and if food prices were high anyway, they reasoned, they might as well eat out and not have to spend their few precious hours at home in the kitchen.

6   How does the family feel about Mom as a late bloomer? Dad may feel somewhat threatened, especially if he was raised to believe that woman's place is in the home. He may resent her working even more when the financial need is severe because he feels it announces to the world that he

cannot provide for his family. Sometimes in marriages that are not solid to begin with, this perceived loss of dominance by the husband may even lead to divorce.

7   Yes, the two-income family has played havoc with our lifestyles but it hasn't been all bad. There are problems that must be solved, changes that are difficult to accept, priorities that must be rearranged. However, with increased pressure from the growing number of two-income families, these problems will be addressed. Hopefully, society in general and individual families in particular will find even better ways to deal with these changes regarding how we raise our children, how we care for our homes, and how we view our marriages and ourselves.

Proofreading

An important step still remains. You must check each sentence to see that the sentence is correct, including grammar, spelling, and punctuation. In the rush to get a paper in on time, this is a step which is often overlooked. If you take each sentence, starting with the last and going sentence by sentence back toward the beginning, you will be able to look at the sentence structure apart from the other aspects of the essay. Taking the time to look over a paper will usually result in your spotting several sentence-level errors.

At this point, you might want to correct errors of grammar, spelling, and punctuation in the first draft of the student essay (pages 333–334).

Preparing the final copy

Use 8½-by-11-inch paper.

Type on one side of the paper only.

Double-space.

Leave approximately 1½-inch margins on each side of the paper.

Do not hyphenate words at ends of lines unless you consult a dictionary to check how to divide the word into syllables.

Center the title at the top of the page.

Put your name, the date, and the title of your paper on a separate title page or on the back of the last page.

If you have more than one page, staple or clip them together so they are not lost.

Checking for errors

In many cases, your teacher will not accept handwritten work, and you will be expected to submit a paper produced on a typewriter or a word processor. Do not forget to proofread your work after it has been typed or printed; even if you have your paper typed for you, you are still responsible for errors. If there are not too many errors, you can make corrections neatly in ink on your typed or printed copy before handing it in.

19

Writing the Narrative Essay

At one time or another, you have found yourself in a situation where you have been nervous or uncomfortable. Perhaps you were overwhelmed by the rules and regulations of a large organization, or perhaps you were intimidated by a person who had authority over you at the time.

The essay you will write in this chapter will be a narrative essay, in which you will tell a story about yourself. Because the experience happened to you, you are the expert on the topic. As you read the model essay in this chapter, and as you study how a narrative essay is constructed, you will be preparing to write your own essay based on your personal experience.

▶ **Exploring the topic**

1. From your own observation, why do most students not want to speak in front of a class?

   _____
   _____
   _____
   _____

2. What type of person enjoys speaking in front of a class or large group?

   _____
   _____
   _____
   _____

3. How do you react when you are called upon to read in class or to make a presentation in front of a group?

_____

_____

_____

_____

4. When a person has been asked to do something and has not had time to prepare for it, the best thing to do is:

   _____ Ask to be excused, even if it is embarrassing

   _____ Try to do it, but be sure to explain that the results will not be good

   _____ Ask to do something else

   _____ Do it anyway just to get over with it, even if you look foolish

The model essay: Taylor Caldwell, "A Tale in the Classroom"

Taylor Caldwell (1900–1985) was a very successful writer of novels and books of nonfiction. She was born in England, but her family moved to the United States when she was six years old. The following selection, taken from her autobiography *On Growing Up Tough*, tells the story of one of her earliest experiences in her new country.

1 It was a Monday morning and Teacher smiled at us radiantly. (It did seem to cause her pain, but never mind.) She said, "Children, we are going to play a new game today! We call it "Sharing Our Week-End Experiences." That means you will all take turns telling all the rest of us what wonderful things happened to you on Saturday and Sunday, and what you did and thought, and where your parents took you, and what you said, and what you played. Won't that be fun!"

2 We kids stared at Teacher vacantly, and blinked. The old girl continued to beam at us encouragingly. Then she pointed to a little boy; "Tommy dear; do tell us what *you* did this wonderful spring week-end! And what your mama and papa talked about!" She had a notebook open and a pen poised.

3 Tommy rose sluggishly and blinked. "Well, uh," he said. "Saturday I skated. Sunday, we went to church. We, uh, had a big dinner. We all went to sleep. Then we went to the park and watched the airplane over the river. We came home and had some sandwiches, and then we went to bed."

4 Teacher wrote rapidly. "And what did you think about it all?" she cried.

5 Tommy considered. "I wished school was out. I wished it was summer, so I wouldn't have to go to school no more."

6 Teacher's pen flew. Her face became serious. She said, "Don't you like school, Tommy?"

7 Now, it is normal for healthy children to despise school with all their barbarian little hearts, and even young children suspect those mates who

declare they "love" school. They consider them either liars or fools out trying to attract the favor of Teacher. They are quite right, of course, and a thorough dislike for school was once accepted as quite natural among teachers, who probably hated it, too. But Teacher had been taught that a child was "in emotional difficulties" if he didn't like being tied to a desk all day and confined in a dreary space, while the sun shone outside invitingly.

8 "I hate school!" said Tommy, with powerful emotion, and we almost applauded.

9 Teacher's face was now really somber. She made several more notes, then called on a little girl. The child's recital was dull. So were the ones following. An ominous sleepiness began to overpower me. A delicious **inertia** was creeping over me, and a soft darkness, when Teacher's voice sharply awakened me. "Janet Caldwell! It is your turn to share."

the tendency to remain motionless

10 I stood up, crumpled as always, with my red hair over my face and in my eyes. I considered. The other kids had had uneventful week-ends, all seriously the same, and all tepid. Mine *could* have been gloriously different. Still, I hesitated. The British indoctrination of **reticence** had been pounded well into me at home and in British schools. Teacher fixed me with her hypnotic eye. "Well, well?" she said, with impatience. "Surely something happened at home, Janet, over the week-end that you can share with us."

silence; reserve

11 Kids, as a rule, have a pathetic belief in the **omniscience** of adults. I hadn't as yet discarded that belief, though it had begun to waver alarmingly when I was three. So, I considered that if Teacher wanted to know my experience it was quite all right to crank up a really good one for her. Hadn't I been taught that one was to obey one's superiors?

having total knowledge

12 In the two weeks I had been in that school I had already acquired a little notoriety among my innocent playmates, so that the half-dozing class came to attention and stared at me. This was both flattering and unnerving, but children love an audience. I brought the week-end experience into my inner eye and suddenly found it quite exciting, far different from the memoirs of my fellow-sufferers.

13 "On Saturday afternoon," I said, "Mama almost brained Papa with a frying pan, and then she threw a knife at him, and then he want out to the saloon and got drunk and didn't come home until Sunday morning. He didn't look well. He had a black eye. He told Mama it was worth it, and she hit him again. With the rolling pin, this time."

14 My schoolmates were enchanted. They laughed and clapped, and I preened. But Teacher was pale with horror. She said, in a hushed voice, "Your parents used violence on each other, Janet?"

15 I wasn't too certain what violence meant, but the sound of it seemed to fit the case. I nodded happily. "But Mama can hit harder," I informed the class, who applauded again (especially the little girls). "Mama can hit *very* hard," I went on, "though she's little. Papa's afraid of her, though sometimes he hits back."

16 Teacher folded her hands prayerfully on the desk. The kids looked at me with envy. What had their week-ends been in comparison with mine? Dullsville.

17 "Was your mother . . . er, drunk—too?" asked Teacher, almost whispering.

18   I considered. Now I come of two hard-drinking races and never will I lie and say that liquor never crossed Mama's lips. I didn't lie then, either. "Oh, Mama drinks, too," I said airily. "But I don't think they get drunk. They don't fall on the floor, like the men I see coming out of the saloons sometimes. They just fight."

19   I am sure I made a Prohibitionist out of Teacher on the spot. She closed the notebook as if it were the Book of Doom, and rested her hand upon it and gently bit her lip. She stared into space. She said, "Spelling books, children."

20   That was a come-down, of course. Later, Teacher asked me, in a hushed voice, to remain a few minutes after school. This was annoying. Mama had no patience with tardiness, and I had to wheel little Brother in the afternoons, and Mama took no excuses. After the other kids had left the room at two-thirty, Teacher drew me tenderly and slowly to her knee and gazed deeply and compassionately into my eyes.

21   "Tell me, dear," she said, "did you cry and tremble when your mother— did what she did to your father?"

22   I was astonished. "No," I said, "I thought she had killed Papa, at first." I was a little regretful. Not that I didn't have great affection for Papa, but murder is dramatic and children are eager for drama.

23   Teacher had begun to scribble in her notebook again, and for the first time a little apprehension touched me. Her pen was quite feverish. She said, "Janet, dear, didn't you just *shake* when you thought your Mama had killed your Papa?"

24   I thought this over, trying to remember. Hazy remembrance came to me. "Oh, I thought if she'd killed him she might be hanged, or something. Then he got up off the couch."

25   "Dear sweet Heaven," breathed Teacher. Her eyes were full of tears. She helped me on with my coat, something no adult had done since I had been three, and she took my hand and said bravely, "We really must talk to Mama."

26   Now apprehension rose to fear. I tried to pull my hand away. "Mama will *kill* me!" I exclaimed. Alas, as always, prudence came to me too late. And tears. I yelled with fright, seeing Mama's outraged face. "You made me tell the class!" I screamed at Teacher, "I didn't want to, but you made me!"

27   I had visions of police, and me in prison, iron doors clanging after me. Teacher had somehow pervaded my mind with criminality as well as terror. What had I done? I suddenly knew—too late, as usual—that Mama would not look kindly on my breach of reticence to entertain the class. How could I have forgotten that before my parents did battle they were careful to close doors and draw draperies?

28   I must have impressed Teacher with my terror, for she dived again for notebook and wrote something in it. This released my hand. I wanted to run for my life. And, believe me, I was sure it was my life. To this very moment the **trauma** of it remains with me; I never see Big Mommy in action or hear her voice in our suborned Press and on TV and in the mouths of politicians without that old feeling of sixty years ago, that feeling of imminent terror and despair, of absolute helplessness, and the desire to flee to some safe spot.

29   Teacher patted my shoulder. "All right, dear," she said. "Go home, alone. It will be all right." I fled, trembling and sweating with dread and with the sensation that I had escaped something terrible. I had. Temporarily.

a lasting emotional shock

Analyzing the writer's strategies

1. Most narratives do not have a formal thesis statement. Review the opening paragraph of the Taylor Caldwell selection. Even though there is no formal thesis statement, how do you know what the story will be about?
2. How does the writer use the teacher's way of speaking to the class to reveal the narrator's point of view?
3. At what points in the story were you most amused? Why?
4. What effect does the writer achieve by having her story told after the other students have made their presentations?
5. Select five or six adjectives or adverbs that are used to describe the teacher or her actions. Select five or six adjectives or adverbs that are used to describe the students or their actions. In each case, how does the writer's choice of words give a humorous tone to the story?

Suggested topics for writing

Choose one of the following topics and write a narrative essay of at least five paragraphs to develop that topic. Use the section that follows this list to help you work through the various stages in the writing process.

1. My worst classroom experience
2. A parent who would not listen
3. My first _____
4. When I tried to convince someone to hire me for a job
5. My experience with an aggressive salesperson
6. A day when nothing went right
7. A mix-up with a friend
8. Trouble at the office
9. A day that changed my life
10. A frustrating experience at a doctor's office
11. How my nervousness made matters worse
12. A perfect evening
13. The day I made a fool of myself
14. An embarrassing experience
15. The day I got a job

▶ Writing a narrative essay

Get the idea

Using the above list of fifteen topics, and/or using ideas of your own, jot down two or three different topics that appeal to you.

_____

_____

From this list of possibilities, select the topic you think would give you the best opportunity for writing. Which one do you feel strongest about? Which one are you the most expert about? Which one is most likely to interest your readers? Which one is best suited to being developed into a college essay?

Your next step is to decide what your controlling idea should be. What is the point you want to make about the experience? Was the experience humiliating, absurd, or hilarious?

Gather information (brainstorm or take notes)

Take at least fifteen minutes and jot down everything about your topic that comes into your mind. If your topic is one that you can easily share, brainstorm with other people who can help you think of additional material, including specific details or additional vocabulary words that you will be able to use to give your writing more accuracy, completeness, and depth. If you can, go to the spot where the story takes place and jot down some details, particularly the sensory images that you may have forgotten.

Select and organize material

Review your brainstorming list and cross out any ideas that you decide are not appropriate. Prepare to build on the ideas that you find promising. Put these remaining ideas into an order that will serve as your temporary guide. Keep in mind that in a narrative essay, the order is usually determined by chronology.

Some instructors may require you to work this material into an outline so you can see which ideas are subsidiary to the main points.

_____
_____
_____
_____
_____
_____
_____
_____
_____
_____
_____
_____
_____
_____
_____
_____
_____
_____
_____

Write the rough draft

At this point in your work, you should not feel that every phrase is set in final form. Many writers feel it is more important to let your mind be relaxed and allow the words to flow freely even if you are not following your plan exactly. Sometimes a period of "free writing" can lead you on to new ideas, ideas that are better than the ones you had in your brainstorming session. Keep in mind that you are free to add ideas, drop others, or rearrange the order of your details at any point. There are an infinite number of possibilities, so it is natural that you will make changes.

Structuring the College Essay

Revise

As you work on your rough draft, you may work alone, with a group, with a peer tutor, or directly with your instructor. Here are some of the basic questions you should consider at this most important stage of your work.

a. Does the rough draft satisfy the conditions for essay form? Are there an introductory paragraph, at least three well-developed paragraphs in the body, and a concluding paragraph? Remember that one sentence is not a developed paragraph. (One exception to this rule is when you have dialogue between two people, as you saw in the Taylor Caldwell section. Then each line of dialogue is written as a separate paragraph.)

b. Is your essay a narration? Does it tell a story of one particular incident rather than talk about incidents in general? Where does the action take place? Can the reader see it? What time of day, week, or year is it?

c. Have you put the details of the essay in a certain time order? Find the expressions that show the time sequence.

d. Can you think of any part of the story that is missing and should be added? Is there any material that is irrelevant and should be omitted?

e. Are there sentences or paragraphs that seem to be repetitious?

f. Find several places where you can substitute better verbs or nouns. Add adjectives to give the reader better sensory images.

g. Find at least three places where you can add details, perhaps even a whole paragraph that will more fully describe the person or place that is central to your story.

h. Can you think of a better way to begin or end?

i. Show your draft to at least two other readers and ask for suggestions.

Write the second draft

If you have worked hard in revising the rough draft, you will be delighted with the improvements as you write the second draft.

Feedback is an important aid in each of the final stages of writing an essay. A good way to help yourself see your own work better is to put the writing aside for a few days, if you can. Then read what you have written aloud to someone else, or to yourself if no one else is available. You may be very surprised at the number of places in your writing where you will hear the need for a change and indeed make changes even as you read.

Proofread

Check your second draft for:

misspellings	verb problems
fragments or run-ons	agreement
incorrect punctuation	parallel structure
consistency of voice, tense	

Prepare the final copy (See page 338.)

Check for errors (See page 338.)

20

Writing the Process Essay

It is your sister's birthday. You have bought her a gift that you must first put together. Carefully following the instructions, you try to assemble the item, but something is wrong. It does not work. Either you have not followed the instructions properly, or the instructions themselves are not clear. All of us have found ourselves in this situation at one time or another. It takes careful thought to write about a process. The writer must not assume the reader knows more than he or she is likely to know.

One of the most common examples of process writing that we use daily is the recipe. In order to be successful, a recipe must be accurate and complete. In the following selection, the late chef James Beard gives an unusually detailed recipe for making what he calls "Basic White Bread."

▶ Exploring the topic

1. Think of a time when you had to put something together, but you were not given good directions. What did you do?

   _____
   _____
   _____

2. When people write instructions or give directions, what do they usually neglect to keep in mind?

   _____
   _____
   _____

3. Recall a time when you had to explain a process to someone. You might have had to show someone how to get somewhere, or you might have had to write a detailed description of how you did a science experiment. What was the process? Was it hard to explain? Why or why not?

_____

_____

_____

4. What was your worst experience with trying to follow a process? You could have been trying to work something out yourself, or you could have been trying to follow someone else's directions. How did you overcome your difficulty?

_____

_____

_____

The model essay: James Beard, "Basic White Bread"

1   This is my idea of a good, simple loaf of bread—firm, honest in flavor, tender to the bite yet with a slight chewiness in the crust, and excellent for toast. The ingredients are just flour, water, salt, and yeast, with the addition of a little sugar. It is a recipe I use constantly, although I vary it from time to time, and . . . I think it will provide any beginner with the basic techniques of breadmaking. In fact, it is the one I have taught to my pupils through the years. Once you have mastered the procedures given here, you can go on to more complex recipes without difficulty.

2   First, proof the yeast, which means testing it to make sure it is still active. To do this, pour the contents of the package into ½ cup of warm water (about 100° to 115°), add the sugar, stir well, and set aside. After a few minutes the fermentation of the yeast will become apparent as the mixture swells and small bubbles appear here and there on the surface.

3   While the yeast is proofing, measure 3¾ cups unsifted flour into a two to three quart bowl with rounded sides. (Save the other ¼ cup flour for kneading, if necessary.) Add the tablespoon of salt and blend well. Pour approximately ¾ cup of warm water into the flour and stir it in with a wooden spoon or with your hands. Add the yeast mixture, and continue stirring until the ingredients are thoroughly blended and tend to form a ball that breaks away from the sides of the bowl. (If the dough is very stiff, add a tiny bit more water.) Transfer the dough to a lightly floured marble slab, bread board, or counter top.

4   Now begin the kneading process, which evenly distributes the fermenting yeast cells through the dough. There are several ways to knead, but I prefer this one-handed method: Sprinkle the dough lightly with flour and also flour your working hand. Push the heel of your hand down into the dough and away from you. Fold the dough over, give it a quarter turn, and push again with the hand. Continue the sequence of pushing, folding, and turning until it becomes a rhythmic motion. Knead until the dough no longer feels sticky and has a smooth, satiny, elastic texture, adding more

flour, if necessary; this will take anywhere from four to ten minutes, depending on the character of the flour and the warmth and humidity of the room. To test whether the dough has been kneaded enough, make an indentation in it with your fingers; it should spring back. Sometimes blisters will form on the surface of the dough and break, which is another sign that the kneading is sufficient.

5   When the dough has reached the consistency described above—with experience you will know what this means by the feel of it—it is ready for the first rising. (Rising allows the fermenting yeast to produce tiny bubbles of carbon dioxide, which stretches the gluten in the flour and thus leavens the bread.) First, rest the dough on the board for several minutes. Meanwhile, wash out the mixing bowl, dry it, and rub it with 1 to 1½ tablespoons of softened butter.

6   Place the ball of dough in the bowl, and roll it around so that it becomes completely coated with butter. (This will keep the surface from drying out and cracking as the dough rises.) Cover the bowl with a piece of plastic wrap or foil or with a towel and set it in a warm, draft-free place. (The term "draft-free" . . . is used because the yeast must be pampered with constant warmth to keep it active.) Find a protected corner or shelf, or use a cool oven. . . . Allow the dough to double in bulk, which will take about one to two hours.

7   It is difficult for a beginner to tell when dough has actually doubled in volume, but the increase is dramatically more than one might expect. You can get the idea best by pouring four cups of water into the empty bowl (before it has been greased) and then pouring in the same amount again, noting how high up the water comes. Fortunately there is another, surer test to show when the dough is properly risen. When it looks ready, simply make an indentation in it with two fingers. If the dough *does not* spring back, then it is ready. It will not hurt should it rise a little too much, but excessive rising will affect the flavor and texture of the finished bread. If for some reason you must prolong a rising, place the bowl of dough in the refrigerator to slow down the action of the yeast.

8   The dough must now undergo a second rising, which will take place in the baking pan. Thoroughly butter one or two heavily tinned loaf pans. Then remove the cover from the bowl and deflate the dough by pushing down into it with your fist. Transfer it to a floured board, knead it rather well for about three minutes, then pat it into a smooth round or oval shape. Let it rest for four to five minutes, then form it into a loaf about eight inches long and three inches wide. Lift it carefully, drop it into the loaf pan, and smooth it out.

9   Cover the loaf pan, as you did the bowl, and set it in a warm, draft-free place to double in bulk, at which point the loaf will have risen slightly above the edge of the pan. The second rising will take anywhere from 40 minutes to 1¼ hours, according to the warmth of the room and the way you have worked the dough. Don't rush the process, and watch the dough carefully. Meanwhile, set the oven for 400°.

10 There are various ways to treat the loaf before it goes into the oven. For this recipe, merely brush the dough with cold water, which helps to give the top a textured crust. Then, with a sharp knife make three diagonal slashes about ½ inch deep across the top of the loaf, both for a more professional look and to prevent cracking. Place the pan near the center of

the lower oven rack and set a timer for 35 minutes. Begin testing after that time, even though the total baking time may be as much as 50 minutes. To test, rap the top of the loaf with your knuckles. When done, it will sound hollow. Invert the loaf onto a towel held in one hand and test the bottom as well for that hollow sound. If it does not seem quite firm enough and needs only a little more baking, place the loaf directly on the oven rack to crisp the bottom, watching it carefully to prevent it from burning. If the test shows that the bottom is somewhat soft, slide the loaf back into the heated pan and return it to the oven to bake for five or six minutes more. Test the bottom again, and when firm enough, bake the unmolded loaf a few minutes for the final crisping. When completely baked, remove from the oven and set on a bread rack to cool.

11 After two or three hours the bread is good for slicing. When it is thoroughly cooled it can be stored in a plastic bag, in or out of the refrigerator, for several days. It also freezes well, and a frozen loaf, wrapped airtight, can be stored for a month. To reheat, remove from the freezer, wrap in aluminum foil, and heat in a 350° oven for about 20 to 40 minutes.

Analyzing the writer's strategies

1. What method did the writer use for the introduction?
2. What method did he use for the conclusion?
3. How many steps are there to the process as the writer described it?
4. Where, at each step of the process, does the writer give specific examples to make each part of his process clear?

Suggested topics for writing

Choose one or more of the following topics and write a process essay of at least six paragraphs to develop that topic.

1. How to get good grades in college
2. How to do well in a job interview
3. How to plan a budget
4. How to buy a used car
5. How to study for a test
6. How to choose the right college
7. How to redecorate a room
8. How to buy clothes on a limited budget
9. How to find the right place to live
10. How to make new friends

▶ Writing the process essay: how to . . .

Thousands of books and articles have been written that promise to help us accomplish some goal in life: how to start your own business, how to cook, how to lose weight, how to install your own shower, how to assemble a bicycle. In the essay you are about to write, you will have the opportunity to describe how you once went through a process to achieve a goal of some kind.

Get the idea

Using the above list of ten topics, and/or using ideas of your own, jot down two or three different topics that appeal to you.

_____
_____
_____
_____
_____

From these two or three topics, select the one that promises to give you the best opportunity for writing. Which one do you feel strongest about? Which one are you the most expert about? Which one is most likely to interest your readers? Which one is best suited to being developed into a college essay?

_____

Your next step is to decide what your controlling idea should be. What is the point you want to make about the process? Is the process tedious, useful, unpredictable, or complicated?

_____
_____
_____

Gather information (brainstorm or take notes)

Take at least fifteen minutes and jot down everything about your topic that comes into your mind. If your topic is one that you can easily share, brainstorm with other people who can help you think of additional material, including specific details or additional vocabulary words that you will be able to use to give your writing more accuracy, completeness, and depth.

_____
_____
_____
_____
_____
_____
_____

Select and organize material

Review your brainstorming list and cross out any ideas that you decide are not appropriate. Prepare to build on the ideas that you find promising. Put these remaining ideas into an order that will serve as your temporary guide. Keep in mind that in a process essay, the order and completeness of the steps are essential. Some instructors may require you to work this material into an outline so you can see which ideas are subsidiary to the main points.

Write the rough draft

At this point in your work, you should not feel that every phrase is set in final form. Many writers feel it is more important to let your mind be relaxed and allow the words to flow freely even if you are not following your plan exactly. Sometimes a period of "free writing" can lead you on to new ideas, ideas that are better than the ones you had in your brainstorming session. Keep in mind that you are free to add ideas, drop others, or rearrange at any point the order of your details. By reevaluating the logic of your ideas, you will undoubtedly make changes in content and approach.

Revise

As you work on your rough draft, you may work alone, with a group, with a peer tutor, or directly with your instructor. Here are some of the basic questions you should consider at this most important stage of your work.

a. Does the rough draft satisfy the conditions for essay form? Are there an introductory paragraph, at least three well-developed paragraphs in the body, and a concluding paragraph? Remember that one sentence is not a developed paragraph.
b. Does this essay show us how to do something specific?
c. Are the steps in the process in the correct order?
d. Is any step or important piece of information left out? Is any of the material included irrelevant?
e. Are there sentences or paragraphs that seem to be repetitious?
f. Find several places where you can substitute better verbs or nouns. Add adjectives to give the reader better sensory images.
g. Can you think of a better way to begin or end?
h. Does the paper flow logically from one idea to the next? Could you improve the paper with better use of transitional devices?
i. Show your draft to at least two other readers and ask for suggestions.

Write the second draft

If you have worked hard in revising the rough draft, you will be delighted with the improvements as you write the second draft.

Feedback is an important aid in each of the final stages of writing an essay. A good way to help yourself see your own work better is to put the writing aside for a few days, if you can. Then read what you have written aloud to someone else or to yourself if no one else is available. You may be very surprised at the number of places in your writing where you will hear a mistake and make a change even as you read.

Proofread

Check your second draft for:

misspellings

fragments or run-ons

incorrect punctuation

consistency of voice, tense

verb problems

agreement

parallel structure

Prepare the final copy (See page 338.)

Check for errors (See page 338.)

21

Writing the Comparison or Contrast Essay

Computer technology is advancing so rapidly that scientists are already discussing the possibility of creating what they call "artificial intelligence," a computer that will be able to duplicate the thinking process of the human mind. In fact, scientists in this country and abroad are now actively designing such a computer. In the following selection from his book *Please Explain,* science writer Isaac Asimov compares the workings of the modern computer and the workings of the human mind.

▶ **Exploring the topic**

1. What are some of the jobs that computers can already do better and faster than human beings can?

   _____

   _____

   _____

2. What are some of the jobs you have to do now that you would like a computer to do for you? How many of these jobs do you think a computer will take over in your lifetime?

   _____

   _____

   _____

3. Do you think a computer could ever be programmed to be as creative as the human mind?

_____

_____

_____

4. In your opinion, are there any dangers in the advanced computer technology we see all around us today?

The model essay: Isaac Asimov, "The Computer and the Brain"

1   The difference between a brain and a computer can be expressed in a single word: complexity.

having the characteristics of animals that produce milk for their young

2   The large **mammalian** brain is the most complicated thing, for its size, known to us. The human brain weighs three pounds, but in that three pounds are ten billion neurons and a hundred billion smaller cells. These many billions of cells are interconnected in a vastly complicated network that we can't begin to unravel as yet.

having complex parts

3   Even the most complicated computer man has yet built can't compare in **intricacy** with the brain. Computer switches and components number in the thousands rather than in the billions. What's more, the computer switch is just an on-off device, whereas the brain cell is itself possessed of a tremendously complex inner structure.

4   Can a computer think? That depends on what you mean by "think." If solving a mathematical problem is "thinking," then a computer can "think" and do so much faster than a man. Of course, most mathematical problems can be solved quite mechanically by repeating certain straightforward processes over and over again. Even the simple computers of today can be geared for that.

5   It is frequently said that computers solve problems only because they are "programmed" to do so. They can only do what men have them do. One must remember that human beings also can only do what they are "programmed" to do. Our genes "program" us the instant the fertilized ovum is formed, and our potentialities are limited by that "program."

6   Our "program" is so much more enormously complex, though, that we might like to define "thinking" in terms of the creativity that goes into writing a great play or composing a great symphony, in conceiving a brilliant scientific theory or a profound ethical judgment. In that sense, computers certainly can't think and neither can most humans.

7   Surely, though, if a computer can be made complex enough, it can be as creative as we. If it could be made as complex as a human brain, it could be the equivalent of a human brain and do whatever a human brain can do.

8   To suppose anything else is to suppose that there is more to the human brain than the matter that composes it. The brain is made up of cells in a certain arrangement and the cells are made up of atoms and molecules in certain arrangements. If anything else is there, no signs of it have ever been detected. To duplicate the material complexity of the brain is therefore to duplicate everything about it.

9   But how long will it take to build a computer complex enough to duplicate the human brain? Perhaps not as long as some think. Long before we

approach a computer as complex as our brain, we will perhaps build a computer that is at least complex enough to design another computer more complex than itself. This more complex computer could design one still more complex and so on and so on and so on.

10   In other words, once we pass a certain critical point, the computers take over and there is a "complexity explosion." In a very short time thereafter, computers may exist that not only duplicate the human brain—but far surpass it.

11   Then what? Well, mankind is not doing a very good job of running the earth right now. Maybe, when the time comes, we ought to step gracefully aside and hand over the job to someone who can do it better. And if we don't step aside, perhaps Supercomputer will simply move in and push us aside.

Analyzing the writer's strategies

1. An essay of comparison usually emphasizes the similarities between two subjects, while an essay of contrast emphasizes the differences. With this in mind, is the essay you have just read an essay of comparison or contrast?
2. Does the writer use the alternating method or the block method in writing this essay?
3. Does the writer provide an equal number of details that relate to both computers and the human brain?
4. Specifically, how does the writer demonstrate the complexity of a computer and the complexity of the human brain?

Ten suggested topics

Compare or contrast:

1. High school classes with college classes
2. Shopping in a mall with shopping in a downtown area
3. Two movies (the acting, the photography, the quality of the story)
4. A friend from your childhood with a present friend
5. Two items you have owned (cars, bicycles, radios)
6. Two stores that sell the same kind of merchandise
7. Two vacation spots
8. Two apartments or houses where you have lived
9. Watching television with reading a book
10. Cooking dinner at home with eating out

▶ Writing the comparison or contrast essay

Every time you go to the grocery story or look in your closet to decide what to wear, you are involved in making comparisons or contrasts. When you have to make a big decision in life, usually the problem involves weighing the advantages and disadvantages of one choice against the advantages and disadvantages of another choice. Should you go to college or get a job? Should you get married now or wait another year? Should you tell that person how upset you are by what he or she did? In all cases, you must compare the two choices to see which seems to be the better one. Making a decision is not easy, just as writing a good comparison or contrast essay is not easy. You have to consider two topics rather than one.

Get the idea

Using the list of ten topics, and/or using ideas of your own, jot down two or three different topics that are appealing to you.

_____

_____

_____

_____

From these two or three possibilities, select the topic you think would give you the best opportunity for writing. Which one do you feel strongest about? Which one are you the most expert about? Which one is most likely to interest your readers? Which one is best suited to being developed into a college essay?

Your next step is to decide what your controlling idea should be. What is the point you want to make about the comparison or contrast? Is your conclusion that one is better than the other?

_____

_____

_____

Gather information (brainstorm or take notes)

Take at least fifteen minutes to jot down everything about your topic that comes into your mind. If your topic is one that you can easily share, brainstorm with other people who can help you think of additional material including specific details or additional vocabulary words that you will be able to use to give your writing more accuracy, completeness, and depth.

_____

_____

_____

_____

_____

_____

_____

_____

Select and organize material

Review your brainstorming list and cross out any ideas that you decide are not appropriate. Prepare to build on the ideas that you find promising. Put these remaining ideas into an order that will serve as your temporary guide. Keep in mind that in a comparison or contrast essay, the order is important because it helps the reader to keep the points in mind. Use the block method or the point-by-point method. Some instructors may require you at this point to make an outline. This will help you see which ideas are subsidiary to the main points.

Write the rough draft

At this point in your work, you should not feel that every phrase is set in final form. Many writers feel it is more important to let your mind be relaxed and allow the words to flow freely even if you are not following your plan exactly. Sometimes a period of "free writing" can lead you on to new ideas, ideas that are better than the ones you had in your brainstorming session. Keep in mind that you are free to add ideas, drop others, or rearrange at any point the order of your details. By reevaluating the logic of your ideas, you will undoubtedly make changes in content and approach.

Revise

As you work on your rough draft, you may work alone, with a group, with a peer tutor, or directly with your instructor. Here are some of the basic questions you should consider at this most important stage of your work.

a. Does the rough draft satisfy the conditions for essay form? Are there an introductory paragraph, at least three well-developed paragraphs in the body, and a concluding paragraph? Remember that one sentence is not a developed paragraph. (One exception to this rule is when you have dialogue between two people, as you saw in the Taylor Caldwell essay. Then each line of dialogue is written as a separate paragraph.)
b. Did you use the point-by-point method or the block method?
c. What is the point of your comparison or contrast?
d. Is any important comparison or contrast left out? Is any of the material included irrelevant?
e. Are there sentences or paragraphs that seem to be repetitious?
f. Find several places where you can substitute better verbs or nouns. Add adjectives to give the reader better sensory images.
g. Can you think of a better way to begin or end?
h. Does the paper flow logically from one idea to the next? Could you improve the paper with better use of transitional devices?
i. Show your draft to at least two other readers and ask for suggestions.

Write the second draft

If you have worked hard in revising the rough draft, you will be delighted with the improvements as you write the second draft.

Feedback is an important aid in each of the final stages of writing an essay. A good way to help yourself see your own work better is to put the writing aside for a few days, if you can. Then, read what you have written aloud to someone else, or to yourself if no one else is available. You may be very surprised at the number of places in your writing where you will hear a mistake and make a change even as you read.

Proofread

Check your second draft for:

misspellings

fragments or run-ons

incorrect punctuation

consistency of voice, tense

verb problems

agreement

parallel structure

Prepare the final copy (See page 338.)

Check for errors (See page 338.)

22

Writing Persuasively

▶ What is persuasion?

So far, your purpose in various writing assignments in this text has been to describe, narrate, or explain by using various strategies of development. Still another purpose in writing is to persuade. **Persuasion** is the attempt to change the reader's present viewpoint, or at least to convince him or her that your viewpoint is a valid one. Every time you write a paper for a course, you are trying to persuade your teacher that what you are presenting is the correct view of the subject matter. You might want to show that Abraham Lincoln was a more calculating politician than most people believe, or you might want to prove that Charles Dickens used his travels in the United States as background material in several of his novels. As you approach such types of assignments, you need to be aware of each part of the persuasion process so that you will be able to use it effectively in your own writing.

You could view all writing as persuasion since one of the writer's main goals is always to get the reader to see, think, and believe in a certain way. However, **formal persuasion** follows certain guidelines. If you were ever a member of a high school debate team, you would have spent a good deal of time studying this special form. Learning to recognize techniques of persuasion and to use them in your own writing is the subject of this chapter.

▶ Guide to writing the persuasive essay

1. **State a clear thesis.** Use words such as *must*, *ought*, or *should*.

    > We should not ban all handguns.
    > The United States must reform its prison system.
    > All states should have the same legal drinking age.

2. **Use examples.** Well-chosen examples are the heart of any essay. Without them, the piece of writing would be flat, lifeless, and unconvincing. Providing a good example for each of your main points will help make a much stronger argument. Examples help your reader *see* what you are talking about.

3. **Use opinions from recognized authorities to support your points.** One of the oldest methods of supporting an argument is to use one or more persons of authority to support your particular position. People will usually believe what well-known experts claim. You should use carefully chosen experts to help make your position on a topic more persuasive. However, be sure that your authority is someone who is respected in the area you are discussing. For example, if you are arguing that we must end ocean dumping, your argument will be stronger if you quote a respected scientist who can accurately predict the consequences of this approach to waste disposal. A famous movie star giving the same information might be more glamorous and get more attention, but he or she would not be as great an authority as the scientist.

4. **Answer your critics in advance.** When you point out, beforehand, what your opposition is likely to say in answer to your argument, you will be writing from a position of strength. You are letting your reader know that there is another side to the argument you are making. By pointing out this other side and then answering its objections in advance, you are strengthening your own position.

5. **Point out the results.** Here, you help your reader see what will happen if your argument is (or is not) believed or acted upon as you believe it should be. You should be very specific and very rational when you point out results, making sure that you avoid exaggerations of any kind. For example, if you are arguing against the possession of handguns, it would be an exaggeration to say that "everyone is going to be murdered if the opposition's point of view is listened to."

The model essay: Dr. Howard Caplan, "It's Time We Helped Patients Die"

Howard Caplan is a medical doctor who specializes in geriatrics, that branch of medicine that deals with the care of older people. He is also the medical director of three nursing homes in Los Angeles, California.

As you read Dr. Caplan's essay, look for all of the elements of an effective argument. Where does the writer give his thesis statement? Where are his major examples? At what point does he use authorities to support his point of view? In addition, look for the paragraphs where he answers those who do not agree with him and be sure to find that section of the essay where he predicts the future of euthanasia. As you read the essay, do you see any weaknesses in the writer's argument?

a sac formed by the swelling of a vein or artery

a tumor made up of nerve cells

relating to a tube inserted through the nose and into the stomach

1 For three years, the husband of one of my elderly patients watched helplessly as she deteriorated. She'd burst an **aneurysm** and later had an **astrocytoma** removed from her brain. Early in the ordeal, realizing that she'd never recover from a vegetative state, he'd pleaded with me to pull her **nasogastric** tube.

2 I'd refused, citing the policy of the convalescent hospital. I told him I could do it only if he got a court order. But he couldn't bring himself to start such proceedings, although the months dragged by with no signs of improvements in his wife's condition. He grieved as her skin broke down and she developed terrible bedsores. She had to have several courses of antibiotics to treat the infections in them, as well as in her bladder, which had an indwelling catheter.

3   Finally I got a call from a lawyer who said he'd been retained by the family to force me to comply with the husband's wishes.

4   "I'm on your side," I assured him. "But you'll have to get that court order just the same."

5   I went on to suggest—though none too hopefully—that we ask the court to do more than just let the patient starve to death. "If the judge will agree to let her die slowly, why won't he admit that he wants death to happen? Let's ask for permission to give her an injection and end her life in a truly humane manner."

6   The lawyer had no answer except to say, "Aw, come on, Doc—that's euthanasia!"

7   Frankly, I'd have been surprised at any other reaction. Although most states have enacted living-will laws in the past decade, none has yet taken the next logical step—legalizing euthanasia. But I believe it's time they did. Ten years of practice in **geriatrics**[*that branch of medicine dealing with the problems of aging*] have convinced me that a proper death is a humane death, either in your sleep or being *put* to sleep.

8   I see appropriate patients every day in the extended-care facilities at which I practice. About 50 of the 350 people under my care have already ended their biographical lives. They've reached the stage in life at which there's no more learning, communicating, or experiencing pleasure. They're now simply existing in what is left of their biological lives.

9   Most of these patients are the elderly **demented**[*having lost normal brain function*]. A typical case is that of a woman in her 80s or 90s, who speaks only in gibberish and doesn't recognize her family. She has forgotten how to eat, so she has a feeding tube coming from her nose. She is incontinent, so she has an indwelling catheter. She can no longer walk, so she is tied into a wheelchair. She's easily agitated, so she gets daily doses of a major tranquilizer. Why shouldn't I, with the concurrence of her family and an independent medical panel, be allowed to quickly and painlessly end her suffering?

10 I think of another patient, a woman in her 50s, with end-stage multiple sclerosis, unable to move a muscle except for her eyeballs and her tongue. And younger patients: I have on my census a man in his early 40s, left an **aphasic triplegic**[*a person who has lost the ability to express or comprehend language, and who has paralysis of three limbs*] by a motorcycle accident when he was 19. For nearly a quarter of a century, while most of us were working, raising children, traveling, reading, and otherwise going about our lives, he's been vegetating. His biographical life ended with that crash. He can't articulate—only make sounds to convey that he's hungry or wet. If he were to become acutely ill, I would prefer not to try saving him. I'd want to let pneumonia end it for him.

11 Of my remaining 300 patients, there are perhaps 50 to 100 borderline functional people who are nearing the end of their biographical lives and—were euthanasia legal—would probably tell me: "I'm ready to go. My bags are packed. Help me."

12 Anyone who's had front-line responsibility for the elderly has been asked if there wasn't "something you can give me" to end life. Such requests are made by patients who clearly see the inevitability of their deterioration and dread having to suffer through it. For these people, there is no more pleasure, let alone joy—merely misery. They want out.

13 What is their fate? Chances are they'll be referred for psychiatric consultation on the grounds that they must be seriously depressed. The psychiatrist, usually decades younger than the patient, does indeed diagnose depression and recommends an antidepressant.

14 But if such patients lived in the Netherlands, odds are they'd get assistance in obtaining a release from the slow dying process to which our modern technology condemns them. While euthanasia is not yet legal there, it's openly practiced. On a segment of the CBS show "60 Minutes" not long ago, I heard a Dutch **anesthesiologist** describe how doctors in his country help 5,000 terminal patients slip away peacefully each year. Isn't that a promising indication of how well euthanasia would work in this country?

a medical specialist who administers anesthesia, or pain killers, to people about to undergo operations

15 I realize that there are those who vigorously oppose the idea. And there are moral issues to confront—how much suffering is too much, the one-in-several-million chance that a person given no hope of improving will beat the odds. But it's time for society to seriously reconsider whether it is immoral to take the life of someone whose existence is nothing but irreversible suffering. Euthanasia ought to be treated the same way the abortion issue has been treated: People who believe it a sin to take a life even for merciful reasons would not be forced to do so. What I'm pleading for is that doctors and their patients at least have the choice.

16 I doubt that we'll get congressional action on such an emotionally charged issue during my lifetime. Action may have to come at the state level. Ideally, legislatures should permit each hospital and each nursing home to have a panel that would approve candidates for euthanasia. Or it might be more practical to have one panel serve several hospitals and nursing homes in a geographic area. Made up of one or two physicians and a lawyer or judge, plus the attending doctor, the panel would assess the attending's findings and recommendations, the patient's wishes, and those of the immediate family. This would ensure that getting a heart-stopping injection was truly in the patient's best interests, and that there was no ulterior motive—for example, trying to hasten an insurance payout. Needless to say, members of the board would be protected by law from liability claims.

17 Then, if the patient had made it known while of sound mind that under certain circumstances he wanted a deadly substance administered, the process would be easy for everyone. But in most cases, it would be up to the attending to raise the question of euthanasia with the patient's relatives.

18 I'd start with those who've been part of the patient's recent life. If there are relatives who haven't seen the patient for years, it really shouldn't be any of their business. For instance, I'd try involving a son who's just kept in touch by phone. I'd say to him, "If you really want to stop this from happening, then you'd better come out here to see firsthand what's going on."

19 However, if he said, "Well, I can't really get away, Doctor, but I violently disagree," my answer would be, "Well, not violently enough. Everyone here can see what shape your mother's in. We're quite sure what she'd want if she could tell us, and we're going to help her."

20 Before any of this can happen, though, there's going to have to be widespread public education. The media will have to do a better job of discussing the issues than it has with living wills. Among my patients who are nearing death, there aren't more than a half-dozen with living wills attached to their charts. Patients' families often haven't even heard of them, and even when large institutions encourage families to get these things taken care of while the patient is still alert, it's hardly ever done.

21 Not knowing about living wills, unaware of no-code options, many families plunge their loved ones—and themselves—into unwanted misery. How many rapidly deteriorating patients are rushed from a nursing home

to a hospital to be intubated, simply because that's the facility's rigid policy? How many families impoverish themselves to keep alive someone who's unaware of himself and his surroundings?

22   For that matter, how many people themselves suffer heart attacks or ulcers—not to mention divorces or bankruptcies—from the stresses involved in working to pay where Medicare and Medicaid leave off?

23   Every day in my professional life, I encounter illogical, irrational, and inhumane regulations that prevent me, and those with whom I work, from doing what we know in our souls to be the right thing. Before high technology, much of this debate was irrelevant. There was little we could do, for example, when a patient **arrested**. And what we could do rarely worked. *died*

24   But times have changed. Now we have decisions to make. It helps to understand that many of the elderly infirm have accepted the inevitability—and, indeed, the desirability—of death. We who are younger must not mistake this philosophical position for depression. We need to understand the natural acceptance of death when life has lost its meaning.

25   About 28 percent of our huge Medicare budget is spent providing care during the last year of life. Far too little of that money goes to ensure that dying patients' last months are pain-free and comfortable. Far too much is wasted on heroic, pain-inducing measures that can make no difference. It's time to turn that ratio around—and to fight for the right to provide the ultimate assistance to patients who know their own fight to prolong life is a losing one.

Analyzing the writer's strategies

Because Dr. Caplan deals with a very sensitive subject, many people might find his position to be dangerous and even frightening. Even before we examine his essay, the title of the piece and the writer's medical background gain our attention. When a doctor writes on matters of life and death, we tend to pay more attention than we ordinarily might; the fact that Dr. Caplan works so closely with older people tends to give his views even more authority. For example, the facts and figures he gives in paragraphs eight and eleven go a long way towards strengthening his point of view. In addition, the writer uses both his own experience and his close observation of people in other countries to convince us that his stand on this controversial topic is the correct one.

The writer's position is also supported by the fact that he is so precise in paragraphs three to seven, when he deals with the law; almost from the beginning, Dr. Caplan is seen as a careful and caring professional. We notice too that in paragraphs twelve and thirteen he points out what happens when our present system operates and in paragraphs sixteen to eighteen he gives practical suggestions that would help put his own system into operation. Finally, we see that in paragraph fifteen he pays attention to the other side's arguments and then answers those same arguments.

It is clear that Dr. Caplan's argument is carefully written and complete; it has all of the parts needed for a good argument. After you have studied each part of the essay, can you find any weaknesses in the writer's presentation?

Exercise 1   Using Research Material to Write the Persuasive Essay

Several pieces of information on the controversial topic of mercy killing follow. Who should make the life-and-death decisions in such matters? Use

Writing Persuasively ▶ 371

this information as the basis for your own essay on the topic. You may choose to rely on as many facts as you want, or you may adapt the opinions to agree with your own way of thinking. As you study the list, try to decide in which of your paragraphs you could make use of several of these facts or opinions you have been given.

1. Henry Van Dusen, the head of Union Theological Seminary, and his wife committed suicide because they were both in ill health.
2. The idea of suicide has been rejected by society for many centuries.
3. Some societies discourage suicide by enacting strict laws against it.
4. Mercy killing is an act of charity when there is no hope that the sick person will ever enjoy a healthy life.
5. In the famous Karen Anne Quinlan case, when the life-support system was turned off, she remained alive for nearly ten years.
6. As our technical ability to extend life increases, the pressure on us to make life and death decisions will also increase.
7. "Suicide," the famous German poet Goethe said, "is an incident in human life which, however much disputed and discussed, demands the sympathy of every man, and in every age must be dealt with anew."
8. In 1962, Corrine van de Put was born without arms and with deformed feet. Eight days after she was born, her mother killed her.
9. If we had laws that encouraged mercy killing, we would not have the lives of such people as Helen Keller to show the world what handicapped people can do.
10. The general reaction to mercy killing will change as people realize that life should not always go on no matter what the cost may be.
11. In 1973 the American Medical Association stated that "mercy killing . . . is contrary to the policy of the American Medical Association."
12. The worst tragedy in life is to live without dignity.
13. "It is important for the morality of our society that 'the ultimate decision' be made only by a disinterested agent . . . of our society."—Dr. Mortimer Ostow
14. Years ago, people seldom spoke openly about suicide; now there are organizations that openly advocate it.
15. A very common form of mercy killing occurs when parents and doctors agree not to give retarded newborn children needed medical attention, eventually causing their deaths.

_____

_____

_____

_____

_____

_____

Several pieces of information on the controversial topic of gun control follow. Use this information as the basis for your own essay on the topic. You may choose to rely on as many facts as you want, or you may adapt the opinions to agree with your own way of thinking. As you study the list, try to decide in which of your paragraphs you would use each of the facts or opinions you have been given.

1. More than half of the people who kill themselves each year do so with handguns.
2. More than half of the murders committed in the United States each year are committed with handguns.
3. Robert Digrazia, the chief of police of Montgomery County, Maryland, states that "No private citizen, whatever his claim, should possess a handgun."
4. Anybody can purchase machine guns by mail order.
5. Half a million handguns are stolen each year.
6. There are forty million handguns in this country, and every year two and a half million more handguns are sold.
7. Since 1963, guns have killed over 400,000 Americans.
8. Thousands of people are killed or seriously injured every year because handguns are so easily obtained.
9. There are over 20,000 state and local gun laws on the books, but they are obviously ineffective.
10. It has been estimated that simply to track down and register all of the handguns in this country would cost four or five billion dollars.
11. Of eleven Boston policemen killed in the last twenty years, seven were killed with handguns, and of the seventeen policemen wounded by guns in the same period, sixteen were shot with handguns.
12. The state of California has a law which requires a jail sentence for a person who is convicted of a gun-related felony.
13. Senator Barry Goldwater of Arizona believes that gun education can actually reduce lawlessness in a community.
14. One small town in the United States has reacted to the controversy over handguns by passing a law that *requires* each adult in the town to own a handgun.
15. Members of the National Rifle Association often assert that people, not guns, kill people.

Responding to the writer's argument

Take a position either for or against one of the following topics and write an argumentative essay supporting your position. Use the "Guide to Writing the Persuasive Essay" (pp. 366–367) to help you construct your essay and to help you make sure you include all of the important points for a good argument.

1. All medical care should be free in our society.
2. Doctors should not be burdened by outrageously high malpractice insurance payments.
3. If a person wishes to commit suicide, for any reason, society should not try to interfere with that decision.
4. Doctors should always work to preserve life, but they must never cooperate in any effort to end a life.

5. New medical technology has created more problems than it has solved.
6. Permitting euthanasia would create a dangerous precedent that could easily lead to government sponsored murder of people it considers "undesirable."
7. People should always leave instructions (a living will) as to what should be done if they are terminally ill and are unable to respond to their surroundings.
8. A person's family has the responsibility to support decisions for life not death when a person is gravely ill, no matter how much money and effort it might cost that family.
9. In the case of a hopeless medical situation, no human being—including the person who is ill—has the right to make decisions that would lead to immediate death (euthanasia).
10. A husband or wife who helps a terminally ill spouse die should not be prosecuted by the law since the decision for euthanasia was made out of love, not from a desire to commit murder.

378 Structuring the College Essay

The model essay: Robert M. Curvin, "What If Heroin Were Free?"

One of the most serious problems in our society today is the widespread use of illegal drugs. Because the situation is so serious, different writers and observers have suggested several dramatic solutions. In the following essay Robert M. Curvin makes his proposal, which is revealed the moment we read his title. As you read the essay, keep in mind that it was originally published in a newspaper; the writer's paragraphs are shorter than they would be if he had chosen to do a more formal essay.

1   After years of more or less vigorous police action, American governments have failed to stop the importation, sale and use of heroin. As Leslie Maitland reported in last Sunday's Times, the latest wave of drug imports—from the opium fields of Afghanistan, Iran and Pakistan—is running high. So is the damage to addicts, families, neighborhoods. And so is the cost to society, on which addicts prey heavily to support their habit. Their search for the money for an ever more costly fix may be a major cause of street crime.

2   Isn't it time to try a wholly new, admittedly risky approach? Why not give addicts free heroin, and at least be rid of their crimes and the corruption spread by their suppliers?

3   An addict may need as much as $200 a day to support his habit. How much of that does he steal? Researchers at Temple University discovered recently that 243 heroin users in Baltimore committed more than 500,000 crimes over 11 years—an average of 200 crimes by each of them each year.

relating to punishment

4   The profits in the heroin trade are so great that no protective or **punitive** measures seem able to deter it. The dealers are experts at their work. They often provide free doses until a victim requires heroin more than food. Then comes the need to pay, and the victim often pays by agreeing to recruit other victims.

5   The Federal Drug Enforcement Administration has made numerous arrests of major drug dealers in the United States and abroad. But heroin still buys its way through. Local police forces are virtually helpless.

6   Methadone maintenance programs, which provide addicts with a free and less destructive narcotic than heroin, have allowed some of the victims to lead relatively normal lives. Yet as designed, these programs do not prevent thousands of new addicts from entering the criminal world of heroin every year.

7   In such desperate circumstances, it may be much more effective simply to supply addicts with the drug in exchange for their accepting medical and psychiatric help. A drug program run by governments or authorized private clinics should take much of the profit out of the heroin industry. The addicts thus removed from the illegal market would no longer have to support the habit, and the price to all others should decline.

8   Creating and supervising proper drug clinics would be expensive. But the heroin they give away, or the methadone substitutes if feasible, would cost a tiny fraction of what addicts now pay. The net saving to society could be huge.

9   Taking the profit out of heroin isn't a new idea. It has been tried in Britain, but in ways that cannot really instruct Americans. Besides, Britain's population is different, crime is less common and the criminal heroin system does not thrive there as it does in the United States.

10 The argument usually brought against giving heroin away is that society would thus sanction and allegedly encourage drug use. But if the humane treatment of addicts is the goal, it is at least arguable that a program of heroin support would help many more people than it would injure. And when society's potential benefits—lower crime rates, savings on law enforcement and a less fearful climate—are added to the balance, the case for official drug programs is greatly strengthened.

11 I do not pretend to know how best to manage a program of heroin support. What would be the minimum age for patients? What degree of addiction would qualify them for free doses? How to measure success and failure of such an experiment? And could an experiment run long in one

location

locale without attracting addicts from all over? The difficulties are obvious. But given the nation's record with heroin, the risks of a new approach seem more tolerable every day.

Analyzing the writer's strategies

Robert Curvin's essay was published ten years ago, but the subject he discusses is just as timely now. The drug problem continues to plague our society, and many of the solutions proposed over the years continue to be heard. In the essay, the writer's approach is businesslike and direct. After noting in the opening paragraph that the drug problem is only increasing, and after pointing out that even "vigorous police action" has not been able to stop the flow of drugs, the author comes right out with his solution, that we provide free heroin to addicts.

The writer's opening paragraphs are an excellent combination of evidence that convinces us of the size of the problem (he mentions that the drug problem has been going on for years and he lists three different countries that have supplied drugs to the United States) and convinces us of the author's sensible approach to the problem. He admits in paragraph two that his proposal is "admittedly risky," an admission that gives his argument an increased sense of fairness; the reader understands that a balanced approach is being presented. The writer's position is further strengthened by the very specific facts and figures contained in paragraph three: when we read how much a heroin addict needs every day, and how many drug-related crimes have been committed in the city of Baltimore alone, we are even more ready to seriously consider the writer's solution.

Throughout the essay, the writer directly and indirectly answers those who would disagree with him. For example, if one were to argue in favor of methadone programs rather than the distribution of free heroin, the author points out (in paragraph six) that such programs do not prevent the creation of many new addicts every year. A second indirect response to another point of view comes in paragraph eight, when Curvin admits that setting up "proper drug clinics would be expensive," but the "net saving to society could be huge."

The essay ends on a final note of fairness as the writer admits he does not have the answers to all the questions raised by the issue. He does, however, believe that if something is to be accomplished, we must risk a "new approach." After you have finished the essay, do you find that there are points the writer makes that do not convince you? What weak sections, if any, are there in his argument?

Exercise 1   Using Research Material to Write the Persuasive Essay

Below are several pieces of information on the controversial topic of violence in the movies and on television. To what extent is the violence we see in films and on television programs responsible for the degree of violence in our society? Use this information as the basis for your own essay on the topic. You may choose to rely on as many facts as you want, or you may want to adapt the different items of information to fit your way of thinking. As you study the list and plan your essay, try to decide in which of your paragraphs could you make use of the facts you have been given.

1. The National Coalition on Television Violence estimates that up to half of all violence in our country comes from the violent entertainment we are exposed to every day.

2. In 1984, violence in Hollywood movies contained an average of 28.5 violent acts per hour.
3. Hollywood spends over $300 million dollars each year advertising movies that are extremely violent.
4. Three Surgeons General of the United States have publicly declared that violence is a serious health problem that contributes to the violence and rape in our society.
5. Sixty-six percent of Americans interviewed think that violent entertainment increases crime in the streets.
6. The average viewer sees about 2,000 advertisements each year, advertisements intended to promote violent television programs.
7. The National Council on Television Violence (NCTV) has proposed that for every three advertisements for a violent movie or TV program, there should be one public message warning against TV violence.
8. Television violence has increased by 65 percent since 1980.
9. Mark Fowler, the former head of the Federal Communications Commission (FCC), stated openly that he did not want an investigation of the whole question of violence in the media.
10. Horror, slasher, and violent science fiction movies have increased from 6 percent of box office receipts in 1970 to 30 percent today.
11. In some years, more than half of the films produced by Hollywood have content that is intensely violent.
12. Over 900 research studies on violent entertainment give overwhelming evidence that violent films and other programs are having a harmful effect on the American people.
13. In 1983, the Department of Justice revealed that nearly all researchers on aggression agreed that there is a connection between violent entertainment and aggressive behavior in people.
14. A proposal has been made to require every cable TV company that offers violent movie channels to offer a nonviolent channel also.
15. One proposal has called for a federal movie-rating system that would cover the entire country but which would not censor movies.

Exercise 2

Using Research Material to Write the Persuasive Essay

Below are several pieces of information on the controversial topic of censorship and free speech. To what extent can a society permit its people to read, write, and say whatever they want? Use this information as the basis for your own essay on the topic. You may choose to rely on as many facts as you want, or you may want to adapt the different items of information to fit your way of thinking. As you study the list and plan your essay, try to decide in which of your paragraphs you could make use of the facts you have been given.

1. In Anchorage, Alaska, the *American Heritage Dictionary* has been banned from the schools.
2. In many American cities, you cannot publicly distribute leaflets or other literature without a permit.
3. In 1961, the American Nazi leader George Lincoln Rockwell was denied the right to speak in New York City, but the courts upheld his right to express his views.

4. Professor Ernest van den Haag, a famous psychoanalyst at New York University, has defined pornography as "whatever is blatantly offensive to the standards of the community."

5. Such literary works as D.H. Lawrence's *Lady Chatterly's Lover,* James Joyce's *Ulysses,* and J.D. Salinger's *The Catcher in the Rye,* have been denounced as pornographic.

6. The Supreme Court has stated that the government may prohibit materials that "portray sexual conduct in a patently offensive way."

7. In ancient Rome, the Censor was a powerful official who judged people's morals and who could even remove government officials from office.

8. The U.S. State Department denied an entry visa to the widow of Chile's president Salvador Allende because her scheduled speech to church groups in California was judged to be "prejudicial to U.S. interests."

9. *MS* magazine has been banned from a number of high school libraries because it was judged to be obscene.

10. The researcher and writer Gay Talese believes that we should not allow law enforcement officials "to deny pornography to those who want it."

11. Jerry Falwell, the founder of Moral Majority, has stated that "basic values such as morality, individualism, respect for our nation's heritage, and the benefits of the free-enterprise system have, for the most part, been censored from today's public-classroom textbooks."

12. In 1983, when the United States invaded the Caribbean island of Grenada, newspaper and television reporters were not told there would be an invasion. When they did find out, they were not permitted to go to the island and report on the invasion.

13. In 1982, the U.S. Supreme Court ruled that child pornography is not protected by the First Amendment because the prevention of sexual abuse of children is "a governmental objective of surpassing importance."

14. "In a free society each individual is free to determine for himself what he wishes to read . . . But no group has the right to take the law into its own hands and to impose its own concept of politics or morality upon other members of a democratic society."—from the "Freedom to Read" statement of the American Library Association.

15. Some psychologists believe that being able to enjoy pornography helps people deal with their frustrations without having to commit criminal or antisocial acts.

Responding to the writer's argument

Take a position either for or against one of the following topics and write an argumentative essay supporting your position. Use the "Guide to Writing the Persuasive Essay" (pp. 366–367) to help you construct your essay and to help you make sure you include all of the important points for a good argument.

1. Drug "kingpins" should face the death penalty if caught and convicted.
2. Marijuana has become so widely used in our society that it should be legalized.
3. Because so many drugs enter the United States from other countries, our government should send troops and other military supplies into those countries to stop the flow of drugs at the source.
4. The present generation of drug users is a lost generation. The only way to solve the drug problem is to educate today's children so that they will not fall into the same drug trap.
5. The solution to the drug problem is not to spend more federal funds, but rather to have towns and local neighborhoods fight drugs on the local level.
6. Taking drugs is no different than using alcohol; if you do not use drugs to excess, there is no real harm to the individual or to society.

7. Illegal aliens who are caught using or selling drugs should be deported immediately, with no chance for appeal.
8. Random drug testing in school, at work, or in a sports situation is a violation of people's basic right to privacy.
9. People who use drugs should never be treated as criminals. They are ill and need treatment, not persecution.
10. Any sports figure who is caught using drugs should be banned from all professional sports for life.

Writing the persuasive essay: additional topics

Choose one of the following fifteen topics and write an essay of at least five paragraphs. Use the five points discussed on pages 366–367 as a guide for your writing.

1. Write a strong thesis statement.
2. Provide examples for each of your reasons.
3. Use at least one authority to support your thesis.
4. Admit that others have a different point of view.
5. Indicate the results or predictions in the conclusion.

Plan your essay on scratch paper, and use the following lines to write your rough draft.

Essay topics

Argue for or against:

1. Legalized prostitution
2. Gambling casinos
3. Stricter immigration laws
4. Prayer in the public schools
5. Abortion
6. Tax exemption for religious organizations
7. Capital punishment
8. Single-parent adoption
9. Continuation of the manned space program
10. Females playing on male sports teams
11. Required courses in college
12. Tenure for teachers
13. Expense accounts for business people
14. Canceling a driver's license for drunk driving
15. Hunting for sport

_____

_____

_____

_____

_____

_____

_____

_____

23

From Photographs to Essays: *A Raisin in the Sun*

"Honey, you never say nothing new. I listen to you every day, every night and every morning, and you never say nothing new. So you would rather *be* Mr. Arnold than be his chauffeur. So—I would *rather* be living in Buckingham Palace."
(Ruth Younger in Act I of *A Raisin in the Sun*)

393

▶ Essay review: Lorraine Hansberry, *A Raisin in the Sun*

Lorraine Hansberry was an American writer whose play *A Raisin in the Sun* was the sensation of the 1959 Broadway theater season. The play, which tells of the struggles and triumphs of a black family living in Chicago, won the New York Drama Critics' Circle Award for that year, making Lorraine Hansberry the first black playwright to be so honored. Since its first success in New York, *A Raisin in the Sun* has been translated into over thirty languages and has been produced in such countries as France, England, and the Soviet Union. As Lorraine Hansberry's friend and fellow writer James Baldwin tells us, "never before, in the entire history of the American theater, had so much of the truth of black people's lives been seen on the stage."

The following scenes, taken from the film version of *A Raisin in the Sun*, show some of the problems and conflicts that challenge the Younger family, but which cannot shake its basic strength and endurance.

Walter Younger is a working man struggling to support his growing family. At the same time, he is trying to find a better place for them to live. He finds himself in conflict with his mother as to what he should do in life, and he also argues with her over what the family should do with a large amount of insurance money they have just inherited. Should they invest it in a liquor store, as Walter believes, or should they follow Mama's advice and use it as the down-payment on a house?

▶ Narrative, process, and comparison or contrast

The old expression "money comes between friends" could also include members of the same family who argue about money and how to use it. When we see Mama arguing with Walter Younger as to the best way to use the insurance money, we are watching two different generations express their conflicting fears and desires. Mama is older and more conservative; not only does she not want to waste the money, she wants a place where every member of her family can enjoy peace, stability, and the pride of ownership. Walter does not have the same outlook; he sees the chance to make a lot of money and to use that income to improve his family's situation. The way we handle money is often the result of how we have been raised, how old we are, how much responsibility we have at any point in our lives, and other factors that affect our thinking about money.

Using this theme from *A Raisin in the Sun,* write one or more essays on the following topics:

1. Write *a narrative essay* telling the story of what you did when you suddenly received money you had not expected. You might want to tell about your first paycheck, or when you received a gift of money and you were free to spend it as you pleased.

2. Write *a process essay* in which you describe how to make up a budget. What approach should a person take when trying to decide how to handle money? To what extent should a person in this situation depend on the experience or advice of others?

3. Write *an essay of comparison or contrast* on the subject of buying on credit or buying for cash. Remember that when you write a *comparison* essay you discuss the *similarities* between two things; when you write an essay of *contrast,* you point out the differences between two things. Also keep in mind that there are two ways to write an essay of comparison or contrast. In an essay of comparison, you could present all of the points about one subject and then all of the points about the other subject. This is called the *block method.* On the other hand, you could show one set of similarities between your two subjects before you go on to your next set of similarities. This is called the *alternating method.* The same two approaches are also used in constructing essays of contrast.

Mama uses part of the inherited money to make a down-payment on a house, and gives the rest of the money to her son. When Walter loses the money to a con man, he tells the family how he intends to replace it: The neighborhood association where they plan to move has offered Walter a large sum of money if he and his family will not move into their area. Here, to the family's dismay, Walter announces his intention to accept the offer.

▶ Cause and effect, comparison or contrast, and example

When we belong to any group, beginning with our own family, we are sometimes torn between our own needs and desires, and what is needed by the group as a whole. Walter Younger's decision to accept the money from the neighborhood association has resulted in a loss for his family; his personal ambitions have led to the end of his family's dream. The fact that he did not consult them before he made his decision adds to the tension of the situation. When we place our own desires above the needs of the group, we have to expect to pay the emotional price of that decision.

Using the theme suggested by this scene from the film, write one or more essays on the following topics:

1. Write *an essay of cause and effect* analyzing the effects of one family member's actions on the other members of that family. You might want to use a single family (perhaps your own) as the basis of your essay. As you provide your examples of what an individual family member can do that affects others in the family, be sure you deal with several members of the family, with the examples chosen to represent the range of possible effects.

2. Write *an essay of comparison or contrast* on the values held by single people and the values of those who are married. How do people's values change when they marry? In your essay, use examples of friends you have had who went through obvious changes when they married. As you plan your essay, keep in mind the two ways (the *block method* and the *alternating method*) of constructing a comparison or contrast essay.

3. Write *an essay of example* in which you discuss the many responsibilities of the head of a family. As you plan your essay, look for at least one opportunity to use an extended example. When you use an extended example, you are taking one of your supporting points and discussing it in more detail than any of your other points. Extended examples give depth and variety to a piece of writing.

400   Structuring the College Essay

At the last moment, Walter tells the neighborhood association's representative that he will not accept the money. The Younger family will move into the house they have chosen, after all.

▶ Argumentation

Most of us try to avoid confrontation whenever possible, but there are times in our lives when it cannot be avoided. Walter Younger stands up to the man from the neighborhood association because the situation has reached the point where only direct confrontation will make the issue clear. In this scene from the film, Walter Younger is calm, steady, and measured—the very opposite of the irritable and upset representative. How many confrontations have you witnessed where one of the people involved loses the argument because that person loses his or her temper?

Using the theme suggested by this scene from the film, write one or more essays on the idea of argumentation. As you plan your essay, keep in mind that a good argument begins with a clear statement of the problem, along with a clear announcement of your proposed solution. In addition to a number of specific examples to support your point of view, your argument should contain some mention of the other side's position, along with your response to that position. By giving the opposition's argument and answering that argument in advance, you will be making your own position even stronger.

Subjects for argumentation

1. It is better to live in an apartment rather than a private house.
2. If a family moves a great deal, the children are always harmed.
3. People should not have more than two children.
4. Everyone should be entitled to a free college education.
5. It is always better to have your own business rather than work for someone else.

At the new house, the entire Younger family gives Mama the gardening tools she has always dreamed of and which she will now be able to use. The family has at last found its rightful place, where each member can live and grow.

▶ Example, definition, and cause and effect

Everyone is part of one or more social groups. A person's membership in a group may be for a short period of time or it may be long-term. We are part of a college class for a single semester; we are part of our family unit for a lifetime. No matter how many groups we join and no matter how short our membership in any group may be, much of our identity depends upon this important part of our social lives.

Our degree of involvement in groups also changes as our needs change: a person may belong to a church for years, but only when that person joins the choir does he or she feel a part of that community; a parent may become deeply involved in local school issues, but when the children graduate from the school system and move on, the parent often does not have the same degree of interest.

This final scene from *A Raisin in the Sun* shows the Younger family at their new home, about to start a new and exciting part of their life together as a family. As we watch them present Mama with her gardening tools, we realize that soon each member of the family will be growing in different directions in the new neighborhood.

Using the theme suggested by *A Raisin in the Sun,* write one or more essays on the following topics:

1. Write *an essay of example* in which you provide a detailed analysis of the most serious threats to family life in our society today.

2. Write *an essay of definition* dealing with the roles of various members of a family. Use the various paragraphs of your essay to analyze how parents, children, grandparents, and even more distant relatives who live with a family, all have different roles in a family structure.
3. Write *an essay of cause and effect* in which you examine the causes of the high rate of divorce in our society, and the effects of divorce on both parents and children.

24

Writing under Pressure

▶ How to write well under pressure

Most people prefer to do their writing when they have the time to develop their subject, but it often happens that you do not have the chance to write and revise as you would like. Sometimes you have to write under pressure. For example, you may be given a last-minute assignment that must be done right away, or what is even more likely, you have to produce an in-class written examination for a course you are taking.

No matter what the circumstances, you want to be able to do the best writing you can with the time you are given. For example, if you are given an essay question for a final examination in a course, your first step should *not* be to begin writing. Instead, you should take a few moments to analyze the question you have been given. What does the question require you to do? Is there more than one part to the question? Does the professor want you to *define* a term or *compare* two historical figures or *narrate* the story of your search for the right part-time job? Furthermore, how many points is the question worth? How much time do you have to spend on the question?

Study the following sample essay question to determine exactly what is being asked for:

> What were the changes that contributed to the rise of the feminist movement in the 1960s in the United States? Be specific.

If this were one of five short essay questions on a final examination, the following answer would probably be adequate.

The feminist movement grew out of many changes happening in the 1960s in the United States. In 1961, the President's Commission on the Status of Women documented discrimination against women in the work force. The result of the Commission's report was a growing public awareness which soon led to the enactment of two pieces of legislation: the Equal

Pay Act of 1963 and the Civil Rights Act of 1964. In addition, the development of the birth-control pill brought the discussion of sexuality out into the open. It also lowered the birth rate, leaving more women looking to the world of work. A high divorce rate as well as delayed marriages further contributed to more women being concerned with feminist issues. Finally, in 1966 the National Organization for Women was formed and encouraged women to share their experiences with each other and to organize in an effort to lobby for legislative change.

Strategies for answering timed or in-class questions

1. Read the question again. How many points is it worth? Decide how much time you should spend answering it.
2. What is the method of development asked for?
3. From key words in the question, compose your thesis statement.
4. Answer the question using several specific details (include names and dates of important facts).
5. Check the question again to be sure all parts of the question have been answered. (A question can have more than one part.)

Answering an essay question correctly depends largely on the work you have done preparing for the test. To study for an essay exam, you should try to anticipate questions the teacher is likely to ask. Then prepare the information you need to have in order to answer these questions. Unlike the multiple-choice or true/false test, the essay examination requires that you have absorbed the material so well that you can give it back in your own words.

Frequently used terms in essay questions

Define: A definition is the precise meaning of a word or term. When you define something in an essay you usually write an *extended definition,* in which you select an appropriate example or examples to illustrate the meaning of a term.

Comparison or Contrast: When you *compare* two people or things, you point out the similarities between them. When you *contrast* two items, you point out the differences. Sometimes you may find yourself using both comparison and contrast in an essay.

Narration: Narration is the telling of a story by the careful use of a sequence of events. The events are usually (but not always) told in chronological order.

Summary: When you write a summary, you are supplying the main ideas of a longer piece of writing.

Discussion: This is a general term that encourages you to analyze a subject at length. Inviting students to discuss some aspect of a topic is a widely used method of asking examination questions.

Exercise 1   Methods of Development

Each of the following college essay questions deals with the single topic of computers. Use the above list of explanations to decide which method of development is being called for in each case. In the space provided after each question, identify the method being required.

1. Tell the story of the first time you encountered a computer. Did you first see a computer at school, at work, or in a friend's home? What was your reaction to this new technology? What did you learn about computers at this first encounter?

   Method of development: _____

2. Point out the similarities and differences between computer use in the home and at school. In how many ways are these uses similar? In how many ways are they different?

   Method of development: _____

3. Analyze the present role of computers in society.

   Method of development: _____

4. List and explain the uses of computers in school, at work, and at home.

   Method of development: _____

5. Write a condensed account of the history of computers, from the time they were invented up to the present day.

   Method of development: _____

Exercise 2 — Methods of Development / Parts of a Question

Each of the following questions is an example of an essay question that could be asked in different college courses. In the spaces provided after each question, indicate: (a) what method of development (definition, comparison or contrast, narration, summary, or discussion) is being called for; (b) how many parts there are to the question. This indicates how many parts there will be in your answer.

1. What does the term *sociology* mean? Include in your answer at least four different meanings the term *sociology* has had since this area of study began.

   Method of development: _____

   The different parts of the question: _____

   _____

   _____

2. Compare the reasons the United States entered the Korean War with the reasons it entered the Vietnam War.

   Method of development: _____

   The different parts of the question: _____

   _____

   _____

3. Trace the history of our knowledge of the planet Jupiter, from the time it was first discovered until the present day. Include in your answer at least one nineteenth-century discovery and three of the most recent discoveries that have been made about Jupiter through the use of unmanned space vehicles sent near that planet.

Method of development: _____

The different parts of the question: _____

_____

_____

4. Contrast baseball and soccer.

   Method of development: _____

   The different parts of the question: _____

   _____

   _____

5. Explain the three effects of high temperatures on space vehicles as they reenter the earth's atmosphere.

   Method of development: _____

   The different parts of the question: _____

   _____

   _____

6. What is the complete process of restoring the Statue of Liberty to its original condition? Include in your answer six different aspects of the restoration, from the rebuilding of the inside supports to the treatment of the metal surface.

   Method of development: _____

   The different parts of the question: _____

   _____

   _____

7. Trace the history of the English language from its beginnings to the present day. Divide the history of the language into at least three different parts, using Old English, Middle English, and Modern English as your main divisions.

   Method of development: _____

   The different parts of the question: _____

   _____

   _____

8. Discuss the events that led up to World War I. Be sure to include both the political and social problems of the time that directly and indirectly led to the war.

Method of development: _____

The different parts of the question: _____

_____

_____

9. Summarize the four theories that have been proposed as to why dinosaurs became extinct sixty-five million years ago.

    Method of development: _____

    The different parts of the question: _____

    _____

    _____

10. Define the term *monarchy* and discuss the relevance or irrelevance of this form of government in today's world.

    Method of development: _____

    The different parts of the question: _____

    _____

    _____

▶ Using the thesis statement in timed and in-class essay questions

One of the most effective ways to begin an essay answer is to write a thesis statement. Your thesis statement should include the important parts of the question and should also give a clear indication of the approach you intend to take in your answer. Writing your opening sentence in this way gives you a real advantage: as your professor begins to read your work, it is clear *what* you are going to write about and *how* you are going to treat your subject.

For example, suppose you were going to write an essay on the following topic:

> A woman president could handle the demands of the most stressful job in the country.

An effective way to write your opening sentence would be to write the following thesis sentence:

> I agree that a woman president could handle the demands of the most stressful job in the country.

The reader would then know that this was indeed the topic you had chosen and would also know how you intended to approach that topic.

Exercise 3

Writing Thesis Statements

Rewrite each of the following essay questions in thesis statement form. Read each question carefully and underline the important words or phrases in it. Then decide on the approach you would take in answering that question. An example has been done for you.

Essay question: How does one learn another language?

Thesis statement: The process of learning another language is complicated but usually follows four distinct stages.

1. Essay Question: Discuss Thorstein Veblen's theory of the leisure class.

   Thesis statement: _____

2. Essay Question: What are the effects of TV violence on children?

   Thesis statement: _____

3. Essay Question: Trace the development of portrait painting from the Middle Ages to today.

   Thesis statement: _____

4. Essay Question: What are the major causes for the economic crisis facing the African nations today?

   Thesis statement: _____

5. Essay Question: What have we recently learned from ocean exploration, and what remains to be done?

   Thesis statement: _____

6. Essay Question: Is it harmful or beneficial to adopt a child from one culture and raise that child in another culture?

   Thesis statement: _____

7. Essay Question: In what ways does the new Japan differ from the old Japan?

   Thesis statement: _____

8. Essay Question: What four countries depend on tourism for the major part of their national income and why is this so?

   Thesis statement: _____
   _____

9. Essay Question: What factors should a college use when judging the merits of a particular student for admission?

   Thesis statement: _____
   _____

10. Essay Question: What is Alzheimer's disease, its sequence of characteristic symptoms, and the current methods of treatment?

    Thesis statement: _____
    _____

Appendices

Understanding Your Basic Sourcebook: The Dictionary

▶ **The dictionary as a working tool**

A dictionary entry gives you a great deal of information about a word. Study the following dictionary entry for the word "gentle" and note the thirteen points of information that are contained in that entry.

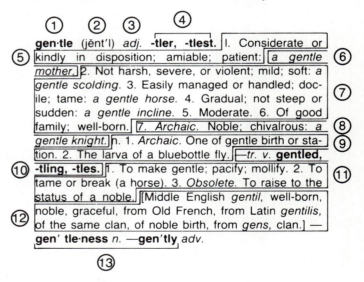

Information contained in dictionary entry for "gentle"

1. The spelling of the word, divided into syllables (capitalization and different spellings given here when necessary).
2. Pronunciation.
3. Part of speech.
4. The comparative and superlative forms of the word.

416

Understanding Your Basic Sourcebook: The Dictionary ▸ 417

5. First meaning.
6. An example, illustrating the first meaning.
7. Second, third, fourth, fifth, and sixth meanings, with examples as needed.
8. Seventh meaning, identified as "archaic."
9. Two noun meanings.
10. Transitive verb (a verb that takes a direct object). The entry gives the past tense, the present participle, and the third person singular of the present tense of the verb.
11. The three meanings of the verb, including an obsolete meaning.
12. The origin of the word, traced through more than one language.
13. Additional forms of the word.

Exercise 1

Understanding Dictionary Entries

Use your dictionary to answer each of the following questions. If your dictionary does not contain the information needed, use a more complete dictionary, which can be found in your school library.

1. What is the meaning of the word *catholic*? _____
2. From what language does the word *malaria* come? _____
3. What is a synonym for *transient*? _____
4. What is a *billabong*? _____
   _____
5. What are all the possible parts of speech for the word *home*? _____
   _____
6. What label does the dictionary give for the word *betwixt*? _____
7. How do you divide the word *tenacious* into syllables? _____
8. How do you pronounce the word *niche*? _____
9. What part of speech is the word *sometimes*? _____
10. Who was *Apollo*? _____

Exercise 2

Understanding Dictionary Entries

Use your dictionary to answer each of the following questions. If your dictionary does not contain the information needed, use a more complete dictionary, which can be found in your school library.

1. Who was Simón Bolívar? _____
   _____
2. What is a second way to spell the word *theater*? _____

3. What are four synonyms for the verb *contract*? _____

4. What is the origin of the word *companion*? _____

5. How do you pronounce the word *receipt*? _____

6. What is a second way to spell the word *councilor*? _____

7. *Cabbage* is slang for what common word? _____

8. What is the origin of the word *pajamas*? _____

9. How do you divide the word *magisterial* into syllables? _____

10. What are all the possible parts of speech for the word *solo*? _____

Exercise 3

Understanding Dictionary Entries

Use your dictionary to answer each of the following questions. If your dictionary does not contain the information needed, use a more complete dictionary, which can be found in your school library.

1. What are the possible parts of speech for the word *hustle*? _____

2. What is a second way to spell the word *judgment*? _____

3. Divide the word *crescendo* into syllables. _____

4. Where is *Timbuktu*? _____

5. What is the archaic meaning of the word *cute*? _____

6. What is the origin of the word *curfew*? _____

7. What is a second spelling for the word *color*? _____

8. What is the meaning of *hoi polloi*? _____

9. What are five synonyms for the word *sloppy*? _____

10. How do you pronounce the word *solder*? _____

One word, many meanings

A dictionary entry provides you with the many meanings that a single word may have. As you work with the entry for a word, you will see that each meaning uses the word in a different way.

Exercise 1

Using a Dictionary Entry to Find the Correct Meaning of a Word

Each of the ten sentences below contains the word *table*. In each sentence, find the correct definition for the meaning of the word *table* by referring to the dictionary entry that is provided for you. Write the definition under each sentence.

> **ta·ble** (tā′ bəl) *n.* Abbr. **tab.** 1. An article of furniture supported by one or more vertical legs and having a flat horizontal surface on which objects can be placed. 2. The objects laid out for a meal upon a table. 3. The food and drink served at meals; fare. 4. The company of people assembled around a table, as for a meal. 5. *Often plural.* A gaming table as for faro, roulette, or dice. 6. a. Either of the leaves of a backgammon board. b. *Plural. Obsolete.* The game of backgammon. 7. A plateau or tableland. 8. a. A flat facet cut across the top of a precious stone. b. A stone cut in this fashion. 9. *Music.* The front part of a stringed instrument, the **belly** *(see).* 10. *Architecture.* a. A raised or sunken rectangular panel on a wall. b. A raised horizontal surface or continuous band on an exterior wall; stringcourse. 11. *Geology.* A horizontal rock stratum. 12. In palmistry, a part of the palm framed by four lines. 13. An orderly written, typed, or printed display of data, especially a rectangular array exhibiting one or more characteristics of designated entities or categories. 14. An abbreviated list, as of contents; a synopsis. 15. A slab or tablet, as of stone, bearing an inscription or device. 16. *Plural.* A system of laws or decrees; a code: *the tables of Moses.* —**on the table.** Postponed or put aside for consideration at a later date. —**turn the tables.** To reverse a situation and gain the upper hand. —*tr. v.* **tabled, -bling, -bles.** 1. To put or place on a table. 2. To postpone consideration of (a piece of legislation, for example); shelve. 3. *Rare.* To enter in a list or table; tabulate. [Middle English, tablet, board, table, from Old French, from Latin *tabula,* board, list.]

1. The <u>table</u> of contents will give you some idea of what the book is about.

   _____

   _____

2. The <u>table</u> of the guitar was cracked.

   _____

   _____

3. They rode their horses across the table and up into the highlands.

4. Guests can always be sure of a delicious table when they are invited to one of Rosemarie's parties.

5. They tabled the tax reform bill.

6. The geologist took samples from the table of rock.

7. One of the legs on the table needs to be glued.

8. The tables were turned when the party in power lost the election.

9. On what page of the chemistry textbook will I find the table of the elements?

10. A list of the king's victories was inscribed on a table that was placed on the wall of the temple.

Exercise 2

Using the Dictionary to Find the Correct Meaning of a Word

Each of the ten sentences below contains the word *base*. In each sentence, find the correct definition for the meaning of the word *base* by referring to the dictionary entry that is provided for you. Write the definition under each sentence.

base (bās) *n.* Abbr. **b., B.** 1. The lowest or supporting part or layer; foundation; bottom. 2. The fundamental principle or underlying concept of a system or theory. 3. The fundamental ingredient from which a mixture is prepared; chief constituent: *a paint with an oil base.* 4. The fact, observation, or premise from which a measurement or reasoning process is begun. 5. *Sports.* A goal, starting point, or safety area; specifically, one of the four corners of a baseball infield marked by a bag or plate. 6. A center of organization, supply, or activity; headquarters. 7. *Military.* a. A fortified center of operations. b. A supply center for a large force. 8. *Architecture.* The lowest part of a structure, considered as a separate architectural unit: *The base of a column.* 9. *Heraldry.* The lower part of a shield. 10. *Linguistics.* A morpheme or morphemes regarded as a form to which affixes or other bases may be added. For example, in the words *filled* and *refill, fill* is the base. 11. *Mathematics.* a. The side or face of a geometric figure to which an altitude is or is thought to be drawn. b. The number that is raised to various powers to generate the principal counting units of a number system. c. The number raised to the logarithm of a designated number in order to produce that designated number. 12. A line used as a reference for measurement or computations. 13. *Chemistry.* a. Any of a large class of compounds, including the hydroxides and oxides of metals, having a bitter taste, a slippery solution, the ability to turn litmus blue, and the ability to react with acids to form salts. b. A molecular or ionic substance capable of combining with a proton to form a new substance. c. A substance that provides a pair of electrons for a covalent bond with an acid.

1. The politician told the crowd that they were the base of his support.

   _____

   _____

2. The umpire shouted that the player was out at first base.

   _____

   _____

3. I prefer make-up that has a water base rather than an oil base.

   _____

   _____

4. Belief in human progress was the base of all her way of thinking.

   _____

   _____

5. The base of the statue was made of solid marble.

6. A base will turn litmus paper blue.

7. The army returned, tired and dirty, to its base.

8. When you take away the prefix or the suffix of a word, you are left with the part of the word called the base.

9. The team was glad to be playing its championship game at its home base.

10. The formula for figuring out the area of a rectangle is to multiply the base by the height.

Exercise 3

Using the Dictionary to Find the Correct Meaning of a Word

Each of the ten sentences below contains the word *hand*. In each sentence, find the correct definition for the meaning of the word *hand* by referring to the dictionary entry that is provided for you. Write the definition under each sentence.

hand (hănd) *n.* Abbr. **hd.** 1. The terminal part of the human arm below the wrist, consisting of the palm, four fingers, and an opposable thumb, used for grasping and holding. 2. A homologous or similar part in other animals. 3. A unit of length equal to four inches, used especially to specify the height of a horse. 4. Something suggesting the shape or function of the human hand. 5. a. Any of the rotating pointers used as indexes on the face of a mechanical clock. b. A pointer on any of various similar instruments, such as on gauges or meters; a needle. 6. A printer's mark, **index** *(see)*. 7. Lateral direction indicated according to the way in which one is facing: *at my right hand.* 8. A style or individual sample of writing; handwriting; penmanship. **9.** A round of applause to signify approval; a clapping. **10.** Physical assistance; a help: *Give me a hand with these trunks.* **11.** *Card Games.* **a.** The cards held by a given player at any time: *a winning hand.* **b.** The number of cards dealt each player; a deal. **c.** A player or participant: *a fourth hand for bridge.* **d.** A portion or section of a game during which all the cards dealt out are played: *a hand of poker.* **12.** A person who performs manual labor: *a factory hand.* **13.** A person who is part of a group or crew. **14.** Any participant in an activity. **15.** A person regarded in terms of a specialized skill or trait. **16.** The immediacy of a source of information; degree of reliability: *at first hand.* **17. a.** *Usually plural.* Possession, ownership, or keeping: *The books should be in her hands by noon.* **b.** *Often plural.* Power; jurisdiction; care: *in good hands.* **c.** Doing or involvement; participation: *"In all this was evident the hand of the counterrevolutionaries"* (John Reed). **d.** An influence or effect; a share: *your professor's hand in your decision.* **18.** Permission or a promise, especially: **a.** a pledge to wed. **b.** A business agreement sealed by a clasp or handshake; word: *You have my hand on that.* **19.** Evidence of craftsmanship or artistic skill. **20.** A manner or way of performing something; emphasis; an approach: *A light hand with makeup.*

1. He moved the <u>hands</u> of the clock back to midnight.

   _____

   _____

2. The prince asked the Austrian for her <u>hand</u> in marriage.

   _____

   _____

3. You are in good <u>hands</u> at this hotel.

   _____

   _____

4. Give our performer another <u>hand</u> for her marvelous concert tonight.

   _____

   _____

5. The document will be in your <u>hands</u> before morning.

   _____

   _____

6. Let's deal one more hand before we quit.

7. I could see the fine hand of the jeweler when I examined the necklace.

8. The farm hand had become a member of the family.

9. I noticed his hand was nearly illegible.

10. At your right hand are all the reference shelves.

▶ Shades of meaning: denotation/connotation

Writing is a constant search to find the right word to express your thoughts and feelings as accurately as possible. For instance, if you were describing a young person under five years of age, you might choose one of these words:

> imp
> toddler
> preschooler
> child
> brat
> tot
> youngster

Some words are neutral. That is, they have no positive or negative associations besides the strict or very general dictionary meaning. Which word in the above list is strictly neutral or most general? If you chose *child,* you were correct. This strict dictionary meaning of a word is called the denotation of that word.

In writing, you do not always want to choose a strictly neutral word. When you want to be very precise, or when you want to give a flavor to your writing, you will choose a word that has further meanings associated with it. These meanings, which some words have apart from their strict definition, are called the connotations of a word.

For instance, if you had a job writing a brochure for a nursery school, you would probably use the word *preschooler.* If you were talking about a child who has just learned to walk, you might use the word *toddler,* which carries the association of a child toddling along. What word might a parent use to describe a child who is constantly getting into trouble? What word might an angry child use to describe a younger brother or sister who has just colored all over a favorite book?

The more experienced writer can find words that have the appropriate connotations. A good point to keep in mind is that the connotations of a word are not always the same for each person. Politicians know that if they want to get votes in a conservative area, they should not refer to their views as *liberal.* The strict dictionary meaning of *liberal* is "to favor nonrevolutionary progress or reform," certainly an idea that most people would support. However, when most people hear the words *liberal* or *conservative,* they bring to the words many political biases and experiences from their past: their parents' attitudes, the political and social history of the area in which they live, and many other factors that may correctly or incorrectly color their understanding of a word.

Choosing words with the right connotations is a powerful skill for your writing, one that will help your reader better understand the ideas you want to communicate. As your vocabulary grows, the challenge of writing will become easier because you will begin to discover all the shades of meanings that words can have.

Exercise 1

Working with Denotation

In each group of words below, circle the word that is the most neutral or general. Use your dictionary if you need to look up a word that might carry a specialized meaning.

1. a. slender   b. emaciated   c. lean   d. skinny   e. thin
2. a. cheap   b. inexpensive   c. underpriced   d. chintzy
3. a. active   b. frantic   c. energetic   d. hyperactive
4. a. unique   b. unusual   c. strange   d. remarkable
5. a. possessions   b. things   c. stuff   d. junk
6. a. zealous   b. committed   c. fanatical   d. devoted
7. a. enthralled   b. fascinated   c. enticed   d. interested   e. enchanted
   f. captivated   g. mesmerized   h. charmed
8. a. taste   b. devour   c. nibble   d. eat   e. gorge   f. gnaw   g. munch
9. a. clever   b. smart   c. cunning   d. shrewd
10. a. plump   b. flabby   c. dumpy   d. overweight   e. chubby   f. fat

Exercise 2

Working with Denotation

In each group of words below, circle the word that is the most neutral or general. Use your dictionary if you need to look up a word that might carry a specialized meaning.

1. a. cottage   b. mansion   c. house   d. estate   e. ranch
2. a. roan   b. horse   c. stallion   d. colt   e. mustang
3. a. sip   b. slurp   c. gulp   d. drink   e. swill

4. a. create   b. compose   c. build   d. design   e. make
5. a. nap   b. rest   c. sleep   d. doze   e. snooze
6. a. sag   b. slump   c. lower   d. droop   e. submerge
7. a. pleased   b. tickled   c. blissful   d. jubilant   e. gratified
8. a. stroll   b. meander   c. walk   d. stride   e. traipse
9. a. whisper   b. patter   c. murmur   d. mumble   e. talk
10. a. little   b. miniature   c. dwarfed   d. petite   e. puny

Exercise 3 — Working with Connotation

In each example below, a "neutral" word and its strict dictionary meaning are given along with several synonyms. Look up each synonym in the dictionary to find out the special association or additional meaning of the word.

1. **partner:** a person associated with another or others in some activity of common interest

   colleague _____

   _____

   confederate _____

   _____

   ally _____

   _____

   accomplice _____

   _____

   associate _____

   _____

2. **pity:** sorrow or grief aroused by the misfortune of another

   compassion _____

   _____

   commiseration _____

   _____

   sympathy _____

   _____

   condolence _____

   _____

empathy_____

_____

3. **burn:** to destroy with fire

scorch_____

_____

singe_____

_____

sear_____

_____

char_____

_____

parch_____

_____

4. **sad:** low in spirit

melancholy_____

_____

downhearted_____

_____

sorrowful_____

_____

doleful_____

_____

desolate_____

_____

Exercise 1   Having Fun with Connotation

Except for the underlined words, the following descriptions were contained in a travel advertisement for Puerto Rico. The underlined words need to be replaced by words that have richer associations. Write your own word choices in the spaces to the right. After you have supplied your own replacements, consult with your instructor to see what words the original advertisement used. Explain why your choice or the actual author's choice is richer in associations than the underlined word.

1. the bright city of new San Juan _____
2. the old gates of the city _____
3. to walk along the streets _____
4. the big fortress of El Morro _____
5. old-fashioned galleries _____
6. and busy cafes _____
7. where you can listen to artists _____
8. exciting casinos _____
9. excellent hotels _____
10. comfortable resorts _____
11. small restaurants _____
12. made by master jewelers _____

Exercise 2

Having Fun with Connotation

In this exercise you have the opportunity to think of words that are richer in associations than the neutral words that are underlined in the sentences below. Write your own word choice in the space to the right. Discuss with others in your class the associations you make with the words you have chosen.

1. I live in a house at the edge of town. _____
2. I walk home from work every night. _____
3. Usually the same person is always walking behind me. _____
   _____
4. She is always carrying a lot of stuff. _____
5. She looks as if she is very old. _____
6. She has marks all over her face. _____
7. Sometimes I try to talk to her. _____
8. She has such an unusual look in her eyes. _____
9. Sometimes I can hear her talking to herself. _____
10. At night when I am sitting in my favorite armchair, I often think of her and wish she could tell me the story of her life. _____

Exercise 3 — Having Fun with Connotation

The beginning of what might be a short story follows. Find a word richer in associations for each of the underlined words.

He had for many years been a <u>worker</u>① at an <u>office</u>②. Every morning he came in from the suburbs using <u>public transportation</u>③. At midday he had <u>some food</u>④ at a local <u>restaurant</u>⑤. His evenings were spent <u>walking</u>⑥ about the outskirts of the city. His liking for <u>music</u>⑦ brought him often to the concert hall. His subscription tickets seated him next to a very cultured looking <u>person</u>⑧. She wore such <u>nice</u>⑨ clothing. One such evening, she suddenly turned and <u>talked</u>⑩ to him.

1. _____
2. _____
3. _____
4. _____
5. _____
6. _____
7. _____
8. _____
9. _____
10. _____

▶ Words with special limitations

The dictionary uses several key terms to label a word that is limited in its use. Students often use some of these words incorrectly in formal writing. Such errors can be avoided by looking up any suspected word in the dictionary. The dictionary will tell you whether or not the word is appropriate. Here are the most frequently used labels.

Nonstandard: This label refers to any word or expression that is not generally accepted as educated speech or writing. For example:

> **ain't** (ānt). *Nonstandard.* Contraction of *am not.* Also extended in use to mean *are not, is not, has not,* and *have not.*

Informal: This label describes the language people generally use in conversation. Although this kind of English is more relaxed than written English, it is perfectly acceptable in everyday speech. For example:

> **hon·ey** (hŭn'ē) *n.*, pl. **-eys** 1. A sweet, yellowish or brownish, viscid fluid produced by various bees from the nectar of flowers and used as food. 2. A similar substance made by certain other insects. 3. A sweet substance, such as the nectar of flowers. 4. Sweetness. 5. *Informal.* Sweet one; dear. Used as a term of endearment. 6. *Slang.* Something remarkably fine. Often used with *of a.* —*tr. v.* **honeyed** or **-ied, -eying, eys.** 1. To sweeten with or as if with honey. 2. To cajole with sweet talk. —*adj.* Of or resembling honey. [Middle English *hony,* Old English *hunig.* . . .]

Slang: This label refers to the way a particular group of people uses special words or phrases, often with the intention of keeping the meaning to themselves. A characteristic of a slang word or expression is that it is often used only for a limited period of time and then is forgotten. For example:

> **fat·head** (făt' hĕd') n. *Slang.* A stupid person; a dolt.

Vulgar: This label describes words that are not acceptable in writing or conversation because of a strong social taboo against their use. For example:

> **crap** (krăp) *n.* 1. A losing throw of the dice in the game of **craps** *(see).* 2. *Vulgar.* Excrement. 3. *Vulgar Slang.* Nonsense. 4. *Vulgar Slang.* Something worthless. —*intr. v.* **crapped, crapping, craps.** *Vulgar.* To defecate. —**crap out.** 1. To make a losing throw in the game of craps. 2. *Slang.* To fail. ["Throw of dice," back-formation from *craps.* In other senses, Middle English *crappe,* residual rubbish, chaff, from Middle Dutch *crappe,* probably from *crappen,* to tear off.] **crap'py** *adj.*

Obsolete: The term *obsolete* indicates that at least one meaning of a word was commonly used at one time in the past, but that meaning is no longer used. For example:

> **dame** (dām) *n.* 1. A title formerly given to a woman in authority or to the mistress of a household. Now only used in expressions such as *Dame Fortune.* 2. A married woman; matron. 3. *Slang.* A woman; female. 4. *British.* a. *Archaic.* The legal title of the wife or widow of a knight or baronet. b. A title of a woman, equivalent to that of a knight. 5. *Obsolete.* A schoolmistress. [Middle English, from Old French, from Latin *domina,* feminine of *dominus,* master, lord.]

Archaic: Archaic language refers to old-fashioned words that were commonly used a long time ago, but now are no longer used at all. For example:

> **foot·pad** (foŏt′ păd′) *n. Archaic.* A highwayman or street robber who goes about on foot. [*Foot* + earlier *pad*, path, probably from Middle Dutch path. . . .]

Regional: Regional words and expressions are often used in a particular section of the country, but they are almost unknown outside of that area. For example:

> **gal·li·gas·kins** (găl′ ĭ-găs′kĭnz) *pl. n.* Also **gal·ly·gas·kins.** 1. Full-length, loosely fitting hose or breeches worn in the l6th and l7th centuries. 2. Any loose breeches. 3. *Regional.* Leggings. [Earlier *gallogascaine, garragascoyne,* perhaps from Old French *garguesque, greguesque,* from Old Italian *grechesa,* "Grecian breeches," . . .]

British: This label is for words that are commonly used in England and other countries where English is spoken, but are not used in the same way in the United States. For example:

> **guy** (gī) *n.* 1. *Informal.* A man; fellow. 2. *British.* One who is odd or grotesque in appearance or dress. 3. An effigy of Guy Fawkes, formerly paraded through the streets of English towns and burned on Guy Fawkes day. . . .

Foreign: This label is for words, and sometimes phrases, that have been borrowed from another language and used directly as English vocabulary. For example:

> **tou·ché** (to͞o shā′) *interj.* Used to express concession to an opponent for a point well made, as in an argument. [French, *touched,* indicating that one has been touched by the opponent's foil in fencing.]

Exercise 1 — Recognizing Words with Special Limitations

Each of the following sentences contains words that are inappropriate for formal writing. The dictionary labels such words as "informal" or "slang." Rewrite each sentence, changing every inappropriate word or expression to an acceptable word choice.

1. My old man gave me enough dough last night to take a chick to the flicks.

   _____

   _____

2. The fuzz finally caught the junkie and stuck the dude in the cooler.

   _____

   _____

432 ◀ Appendices

3. The sucker was conned by the guy he met in the street.
   _____
   _____

4. That kid has flunked every lousy French test because she always goofs off in class.
   _____
   _____

5. My older brother is swell, but my younger brother is a real creep; he's always bugging me.
   _____
   _____

6. Since I'm broke, my buddy will bring the grub.
   _____
   _____

7. I'll sack out for a while in this dump if it's okay with you.
   _____
   _____

8. I don't have the guts to level with my prof.
   _____
   _____

9. Her bum leg is driving her crazy.
   _____
   _____

10. Frank's box is awesome.
    _____
    _____

Exercise 2 Recognizing Words with Special Limitations

Each of the following sentences contains an italicized word that is an example of either *informal usage* or *slang*. Using your dictionary, look up each of the italicized words and write a more formal word choice in the space provided.

1. He worked with her for years, but he could never *cotton* to her way of doing

   things. _____

2. Many years after they dated, he told her he still had a *crush* on her. _____

3. As I was taking the exam, I became *rattled* by the sirens that went off every ten minutes. _____

4. We told our teacher that we really could not *dig* Shakespeare. _____

5. He wore a *classy* suit to the first dance of the school year. _____

6. The producers had high hopes for the movie, but all of the critics said it was a real *turkey*. _____

7. When the police arrested the gang, each member had some *hardware* that the police immediately confiscated. _____

8. They went to a *super* party last weekend. _____

9. After he answered the sergeant, all the other soldiers said it was a *gutsy* reply. _____

10. As she passed the scene of the accident, she heard one driver call the other a *nitwit*. _____

Exercise 3 Recognizing Words with Special Limitations

Each of the following sentences contains an italicized word. In the space after each sentence, choose whether the word should be labeled *nonstandard, informal, slang, vulgar, obsolete, archaic, regional,* or *foreign*. Use the dictionary to find the answers.

1. Don't give me any *jaw*. _____

2. The dealer told us that if we really wanted the car, it was going to cost us a few more *grand*. _____

3. I'm not sure if it's *gonna* rain tomorrow or not. _____

4. When he broke four plates in a row, I called him a *klutz*. _____

5. The messenger brought the news to the judge and, *anon* with joy, ran off to tell the villagers. _____

6. She wanted to save money, so she always brought her lunch to work in a poke. _____

7. When the child sneezed, the teacher said, *"Gesundheit!"* _____
_____

8. She *sure* was lucky to find that job. _____

9. They invited the whole neighborhood to the *burgoo,* which they had planned for months. _____

10. He decided not to buy the suit because he thought the style was too *passé.*
_____

B

Parts of Speech

Words can be divided into categories called **parts of speech**. Understanding these categories will help you work with language more easily, especially when it comes to revising your own writing.

▶ Nouns

A *noun* is a word that names persons, places, or things.

Common Nouns	***Proper Nouns***
officer	Michael Johnson
station	Grand Central Station
magazine	*Newsweek*

Nouns are said to be **concrete** if you can see or touch them.

> window
> paper
> river

Nouns are said to be **abstract** if you cannot see or touch them. These words can be concepts, ideas, or qualities.

> meditation
> honesty
> carelessness

To test for a noun, it may help to ask these questions.

▸ Can I make the word plural? (Most nouns have a plural form.)
▸ Can I put the article *the* in front of the word?
▸ Is the word used as the subject or object of the sentence?

Pronouns

A *pronoun* is a word used to take the place of a noun. Just like a noun, it is used as the subject or object of a sentence. Pronouns can be divided into several classes. Here are some of them:

Pronouns

Note: Personal pronouns have three forms depending on how they are used in a sentence: as a subject, object or possessive.

Singular	Subjective	Objective	Possessive
1st person	I	me	my (mine)
2nd person	you	you	your (yours)
	he	him	his (his)
	she	her	her (hers)
3rd person	it	it	its (its)
Plural			
1st person	we	us	our (ours)
2nd person	you	you	your (yours)
3rd person	they	them	their (theirs)

Relative Pronouns	Demonstrative Pronouns	Indefinite Pronouns
who, whom, whose	this	all, both, each, one
which	that	nothing, nobody, no one
that	these	anything, anybody, anyone
what	those	something, somebody, someone
whoever, whichever		everything, everybody, everyone

Adjectives

An *adjective* is a word that modifies a noun or pronoun. Adjectives usually come before the nouns they modify, but they can also come in the predicate.

> The *unusual* package was placed on my desk.
> The package felt *cold*.

Verbs

A *verb* is a word that tells what a subject is doing as well as the time (past, present, or future) of that action. Verbs can be divided into three classes:

1. **Action Verbs**

   > The athlete *runs* five miles every morning.
   > (The action takes place in the present.)
   > The crowd *cheered* for the oldest runner.
   > (The action takes place in the past.)

2. **Linking Verbs**

A *linking verb* joins the subject of a sentence to one or more words that describe or identify the subject.

> He *was* a dancer in his twenties.
> She *seemed* disappointed with her job.

> **Common Linking Verbs**
>
> | | |
> |---|---|
> | be (am, is, are, was, were, have been) | |
> | act | grow |
> | appear | look |
> | become | seem |
> | feel | taste |

3. ***Helping Verbs*** (also called "auxiliaries")

A *helping verb* is any verb used before the main verb.

▸ It could show the tense of the verb.

> It *will* rain tomorrow. (Shows future tense.)

▸ It could show the passive voice.

> The new civic center *has been* finished.

▸ It could give a special meaning to the verb.

> Anne Murray *may be* singing here tonight.

> **Common Helping Verbs**
>
> can, could
> may, might, must
> shall, should
> will, would
> forms of the irregular verbs *be, have,* and *do*

▸ Adverbs

An *adverb* is a word that modifies a verb, an adjective, or another adverb. It often ends in *-ly,* but a better test is to ask yourself if the word answers the question how, when, or where.

> The student walked *happily* into the classroom.

▸ The adverb *happily* answers the question "How?"
▸ It ends in *-ly,* and it modifies the verb *walked.*

> It will be *very* cold tomorrow.

▸ The adverb *very* answers the question "How?"
▸ It modifies the adjective *cold.*

> Winter has come *too* early.

▸ The adverb *too* answers the question "How?"
▸ It modifies the adverb *early.*

Here are some adverbs to look out for:

Adverbs of Frequency	Adverbs of Degree
often	even
never	extremely
sometimes	just
seldom	more
always	much
ever	only
	quite
	surely
	too
	very

▶ Prepositions

A *preposition* is a word used to relate a noun or pronoun to some other word in the sentence. The preposition with its noun or pronoun is called a prepositional phrase.

>The letter is *from* my father.
>The envelope is addressed *to* my sister.

Read through the following list of prepositions several times so that you will be able to recognize them. Your instructor may ask you to memorize them.

Common Prepositions

about	below	in	since
above	beneath	inside	through
across	beside	into	to
after	between	like	toward
against	beyond	near	under
along	by	of	until
among	down	off	up
around	during	on	upon
at	except	outside	with
before	for	over	within
behind	from	past	without

▶ Conjunctions

A *conjunction* is a word that joins or connects other words, phrases, or clauses.

▶ Connecting two words.

>Sooner *or* later, you will have to pay.

Connecting two phrases.

>The story was on the radio *and* in the newspaper.

▶ Connecting two clauses.

>Dinner was late *because* I had to work overtime at the office.

Conjunctions

Coordinating Conjunctions	*Subordinating Conjunctions*
and	after
but	although
or	as, as if, as though
nor	because
for (meaning "because")	before
yet	how
so	if, even if
	provided that
	since
	unless
	until
	when, whenever
	where, wherever
	while

Correlative Conjunctions

either . . . or
neither . . . nor
both . . . and
not only . . . but also

Adverbial Conjunctions (also known as "conjunctive adverbs")

To add an idea:	furthermore
	moreover
	likewise
To contrast:	however
	nevertheless
To show results:	consequently
	therefore
To show an alternative:	otherwise

▶ Interjections

An *interjection* is a word that expresses a strong feeling and is not connected grammatically to any other part of the sentence.

Oh, I forgot my keys.

Well, that means I'll have to sit here all day.

▶ Study the Context

Since one word can function differently or have different forms or meanings, you must often study the context in which the word is found to be sure of its part of speech.

The parent makes sacrifices *for* the good of the children.

In this sentence, *for* is a preposition.

The parent sacrificed, for the child needed a good education.

In this sentence, *for* is a conjunction meaning "because."

Exercise 1

Parts of Speech

In the sentences below, identify the part of speech for each underlined word. Choose from the following list:

a. noun
b. pronoun
c. adjective
d. verb
e. adverb
f. preposition
g. conjunction

_____ 1. The young man <u>pocketed</u> the change.

_____ 2. Unfortunately, he had a hole in his <u>pocket</u>.

_____ 3. He lost his <u>pocket</u> knife as well as his change.

_____ 4. Agatha changed her mind <u>rather</u> suddenly.

_____ 5. She slipped <u>quietly</u> out of the room.

_____ 6. Driving <u>fast</u>, she arrived home before her friend.

_____ 7. <u>Everyone</u> agrees with the basic concept.

_____ 8. <u>Between</u> you and me, I don't think the idea will work.

_____ 9. The young doctor tried to help the <u>victims</u> of the fire.

_____ 10. His hands were numb, <u>for</u> the air was frigid.

Exercise 2

Parts of Speech

Below are three words. Each word can function differently. Write sentences using the given words in the ways suggested. An example is done for you.

corrupt

Noun: The <u>corruption</u> of the local police caused a scandal.
Adjective: The entire force was not <u>corrupt</u>.
Verb: One individual <u>corrupted</u> two others.

1. spot

   Noun: _____

   Verb: _____

   Adjective: _____

   time

   Noun: _____

Verb: _____

Adverb: _____

3. like

Preposition: _____

Verb: _____

Adjective: _____

Adverb: _____

Exercise 3   Parts of Speech

In the following sentences, identify the part of speech for each underlined word. Choose from:

a. noun
b. pronoun
c. adjective
d. verb
e. adverb
f. preposition
g. conjunction

_____   1. Smiling cautiously <u>at</u> us, the child accepted the gift.

_____   2. The toy was <u>inexpensive</u>.

_____   3. Everyone was waiting for the <u>decision</u> of the committee.

_____   4. The director <u>looked</u> as if he had the answer.

_____   5. A <u>feeling</u> of anticipation was in the air.

_____   6. The manager is finishing his <u>monthly</u> report.

_____   7. <u>For</u> your own sake, eat a good breakfast.

_____   8. The authorities managed to capture the criminal, <u>but</u> they may not be able to convict him.

_____   9. Alisha is <u>seldom</u> late for class.

_____   10. This detective book is <u>thrilling</u> from beginning to end.

C

Distinguishing between Words That Are Often Confused

▶ **Words that sound alike: group I**

Practice inserting the correct word into each of the practice sentences. Mark the sets that give you trouble so you can return for further study.

       it's   contraction of "it is"
       its   possessive pronoun

1. _____ obvious that the car has lost _____ muffler.

2. The dog has no license, so _____ possible _____ owner doesn't care about the dog very much.

       they're   contraction of "they are"
       their   possessive
       there   at that place

3. When _____ in school, _____ parents work in the restaurant _____ on the corner.

4. Now that _____ living in the country, _____ expenses are not so great, so they might stay _____.

       who's   contraction of "who is"
       whose   possessive pronoun

Distinguishing between Words That Are Often Confused ▶ 443

5. _____ car is double-parked outside, and _____ going to move it?

6. _____ the pitcher at the game today, and _____ glove will he use?

    you're   contraction of "you are"
    your   possessive pronoun

7. When _____ a father, _____ free time is never guaranteed.

8. Please give me _____ paper when _____ finished writing.

    allowed *(verb)*   permitted
    aloud *(adv.)*   out loud

9. The sign told us we were not _____ to read _____ in the library.

10. She called _____ to him, and then she was _____ to go on the boat to speak with him.

    altar *(noun)*   an elevated place or table for religious rites
    alter *(verb)*   to change or adjust

11. The museum announced that it would not _____ the artist's famous painting of the Roman _____.

12. The architect decided to _____ her ideas of where the _____ should be placed.

    aural *(adj.)*   having to do with the ear or hearing
    oral *(adj.)*   having to do with the mouth or speech

13. The doctor's _____ report on my _____ examination was encouraging.

14. The _____ medicine I took helped my _____ condition clear up, and now I can hear much better.

    brake *(verb)*   to stop
    (noun)   a device used for slowing or stopping
    break *(verb)*   to smash, crack, or come apart

15. Because I had a good emergency _____ on my car, I was able to stop without _____ even a headlight.

16. When he had to _____ suddenly, he was grateful that his _____ in were in good condition.

    capital *(adj.)*   chief; major; fatal
    (noun)   leading city; money
    capitol *(noun)*   a building in which a legislature assembles

17. The senators met in Athens, the _____ of Greece, to discuss the question of _____ punishment.

18. If I could raise some _____, I would be able to make some _____ changes in my home.

19. Our class visited the state _____ when we saw our representatives meet in the _____ building itself.

   chord *(noun)* three or more tones sounded together; harmony
   cord *(noun)* a small rope of twisted strands; any ropelike structure; a unit of cut fuel wood

20. The lumberman would be cutting no more _____ of wood; his spinal _____ was badly injured in a car accident.

21. She couldn't play the _____ on the electric guitar because someone had unplugged the _____.

   close *(verb)* to shut
   clothes *(noun)* garments
   cloth *(noun)* fabric; a piece of material

22. Please don't _____ the closet door; I want to put away these _____ and this piece of striped _____.

23. I hurried to bring several yards of wool _____ to the tailor to make some new winter _____ for me; I knew he would _____ at five o'clock.

   coarse *(adj.)* rough; not fine; common or of inferior quality
   course *(noun)* direction or path of something moving; part of a meal; a school subject

24. I would have enjoyed the _____, but some of the students told _____ jokes during every class.

25. The captain was a very _____ man, but he could keep a ship on _____.

   complement *(noun)* something that completes or makes up a whole
   (verb) to complete
   compliment *(noun)* an expression of praise
   (verb) to give praise

Distinguishing between Words That Are Often Confused ▸ 445

26. She always wears clothes that _____ each other, but she never expects a _____.

27. I gave the artist a _____ when I told him that the colors in his painting _____ each other.

      fair *(adj.)*   unbiased; light color; free of clouds; promising; lovely
           (noun)   an exhibition; regional event; market
      fare *(noun)*   a charge for transportation

28. It was such a _____ day that he decided to save the bus _____ and walk.

29. I never thought it was _____ that Dad wouldn't let me go to the county _____.

      flour *(noun)*   the powder produced by grinding a grain
      flower *(noun)*   a blossom of a plant
           (verb)   to blossom

30. The child dropped the fresh _____ into his mother's bowl of _____.

31. After you put the _____ in a vase, sift the _____ for the cake.

      for *(prep.)*   directed to; in the amount of; on behalf of; to the extent of
      four *(noun, adj.)*   number
      forty: Notice that this number is spelled differently from *four, fourteen,* or *twenty-four.*
      fore *(noun, adj.)*   situated near the front

32. My uncle has _____ telephone books on his desk, one _____ every town in which he has lived.

33. The passenger walked to the _____ of the ship _____ a better view of the coastline.

      forth *(adv.)*   onward in time, place, or order
      fourth *(noun, adj.)*   number

34. He was the _____ one to walk _____ that morning.

35. She paced back and _____ in her _____ floor office.

        forward *(verb)*   to send on to another address
                    (adj.)   bold, progressive
                    (adv.)   moving toward the front
        foreword *(noun)*   introduction at the beginning of a book; preface

36. The editor thought that the _____ to the book was too _____.

37. Since the editor was anxious, I decided to _____ the manuscript at once and send the _____ later.

        grate *(verb)*   to shred; to annoy or irritate
              (noun)   a metal grill
        grateful *(adj.)*   appreciative
        great *(adj.)*   large; significant; excellent; powerful; skillful; first-rate

38. After I _____ the onions for dinner, I placed them on the _____ to get warm.

39. I am _____ that the landlord placed a _____ over the window for safety.

40. The _____ athlete was _____ for all the mail from her fans.

        knew *(verb)*   past tense of *know*
        new *(adj.)*   not old

41. Dan _____ yesterday morning that the car would need a _____ battery.

42. By the time she _____ that they had moved to a _____ town, it was too late to help them.

        know *(verb)*   to understand
        no *(adv.)*   a negative response
           (adj.)   not any; not one

43. They _____ there is _____ way to cross these mountains in the winter.

44. I am _____ artist, but I _____ what I like.

Exercise 1

Words That Sound Alike

Choose the correct word, and write it in the space at the right.

1. My family enjoys telling their dreams (allowed, aloud) at the breakfast table. _____
2. (It's, Its) not easy to know the meaning of our dreams. _____
3. (You're, Your) dreams may be interpreted differently depending on who does the interpreting. _____
4. (They're, Their, There) is no firm agreement about what all the various parts of a dream mean. _____
5. (Who's, Whose) to say that if I dream about eating a sundae it means that I'm frustrated? _____
6. People often dream they are falling (foreword, forward). _____
7. Does what we dream (altar, alter) the way we live in our waking hours? _____
8. In one dream, my old boyfriend was paying me a (complement, compliment). _____
9. In another dream, I was so rich I had enough (capital, capitol) to buy four race horses. _____
10. Of (coarse, course), before I had time to race them, I woke up. _____

Exercise 2

Words That Sound Alike

Choose the correct word, and write it in the space at the right.

1. The driver claimed her (brakes, breaks) had failed. _____
2. The bus (fare, fair) has been increased again. _____
3. He walked (foreword, forward). _____
4. He paced back and (forth, fourth). _____
5. After I (grate, great) the carrots, I will peel the potatoes. _____
6. I do not (know, no) the answers to the accounting problem. _____
7. I need whole wheat (flour, flower) to make this bread. _____
8. We always invite several guests (for, four) Thanksgiving dinner. _____
9. Stuffed trout is my favorite main (coarse, course). _____

10. (They're, Their, There) going to renovate the old village museum. _____

Exercise 3 — Words That Sound Alike

Edit the following paragraph for errors in word confusions. Circle each error and write each word correctly on the lines below the paragraph.

Wolfgang Mozart was the grate child star of the eighteenth century. At three years old, he could pick out cords and tunes on the piano. By for, he was composing at the piano. As a musical genius, Mozart had an extremely well-developed oral sense. When Mozart was only six, he and his sister played before the emperor in Vienna, the capitol of Austria. The empress paid Mozart a complement by having his portrait painted. Another gift was an embroidered suit of cloths. Mozart wrote a great deal of church music, and his compositions were so good that he seldom had to altar a note. He was not fully appreciated in his own day, so it is only fare that he enjoys worldwide fame today. You might be interested in reading a book of Mozart's letters which has been published in English. Be sure to read the forward.

_____   _____
_____   _____
_____   _____
_____   _____
_____

▶ Words that sound alike: group II

Here is a second set of words often confused because they sound alike. Find out how well you know these words by inserting the correct word into each of the practice sentences.

    pain *(noun)*   suffering
    pane *(noun)*   a panel of glass

1. When the child's arm went through the window _____, the _____ was not so bad as the sight of the blood.

2. The young father considered it a _____ to spend Saturday replacing the cracked window _____ on the sunporch.

    passed *(verb)*   the past tense of *to pass*—to move ahead
    past *(noun)*   time before the present
        (prep.)   beyond
        (adj.)   no longer current

Distinguishing between Words That Are Often Confused ▶ 449

3. I have spent the _____ few days wondering if I _____ the exam.

4. She walked _____ the old house thinking about her _____.

      patience *(noun)*   calm endurance; tolerant understanding
      patients *(noun)*   persons under medical treatment

5. The young doctor has not learned to have _____ with her _____.

6. All of the _____ in this understaffed hospital need a good deal of _____.

      peace *(noun)*   absence of war, calm
      piece *(noun)*   a portion, a part

7. Each person in the writing group wrote a _____ of the article on world _____.

8. We will have _____ at home only if everyone does a _____ of the housework.

      plain *(adj.)*   simple; ordinary; unattractive; clear
      (noun)   a flat, treeless land region
      plane *(noun)*   an aircraft; a flat, level surface; a carpenter's tool for leveling wood; a level of development

9. The _____ flew directly over the _____.

10. Although the man's features were very _____, his mind was on a higher _____ than the mind of his supervisor.

      presence *(noun)*   the state of being present; a person's manner
      presents *(noun)*   gifts
      (verb)   (third person singular) to introduce; to give a gift

11. The children claimed they felt Santa's _____ as they looked for their _____.

12. Each year the mayor always _____ an award as well as several lovely _____ to outstanding members of the community.

      principal *(adj.)*   most important; chief; main
      (noun)   the head of a school; a sum of money
      principle *(noun)*   rule or standard

13. The _____ lost his job because he would not compromise his

_____.

14. The _____ reason she had to see the bank clerk was to have the

terms of the loan explained to her, including the _____ and interest.

rain *(noun, verb)*		water falling to earth in drops
reign *(noun, verb)*		a period of rule for a king or queen
rein *(noun)*		a strap attached to a bridle, used to control a horse

15. The museum had on display a horse's bridle and _____ that dated

from the _____ of Henry the Eighth.

16. When it started to _____, he pulled the _____ tighter to
control the horse.

raise *(verb)*		to move upward; to awaken; to increase; to collect
(noun)		an increase in salary
rays *(noun)*		thin lines or beams of radiation
raze *(verb)*		to tear down or demolish

17. They are going to _____ that old building if the town cannot

_____ enough money to save it.

18. When he met his boss, he _____ the question of a _____ for
the new year.

19. The last _____ of the sun disappeared behind the hills, as the

woman who had _____ five children all by herself looked around

her farm with satisfaction.

sight *(noun)*		the ability to see; a view
site *(noun)*		the plot of land where something is located; the place for an event
cite *(verb)*		to quote as an authority or example

20. You do not have to _____ statistics to convince us of the impor-

tance of caring for our sense of _____.

21. They tried to convince her that the _____ was a good one for a

house, and they even began to _____ all kinds of evidence to prove

their point.

stair *(noun)*		one of a flight of steps
stare *(noun, verb)*		a fixed gaze; to look at insistently

Distinguishing between Words That Are Often Confused ▸ 451

22. Please don't _____ at the old woman who is sleeping on the _____.

23. She stood on the top _____ giving him a long, hard _____.

    stake *(noun)*   a post sharpened at one end to drive into the ground; a financial share
    (verb)   to attach or support in order to set the limits with a stake
    steak *(noun)*   a slice of meat, usually beef

24. She drove the last _____ into the ground, then built a fire and cooked a _____.

25. If you catch the vampire, feed him raw _____ and then drive a _____ into his heart.

26. The young man _____ out a claim for a _____ in the company.

    stationary *(adj.)*   standing still
    stationery *(noun)*   writing paper and envelopes

27. He bought the _____ from a clerk who said nothing and remained _____ all the time behind the counter.

28. The bus remained _____ for a few moments, so I quickly wrote a few sentences on my flowered _____.

    to *(prep.)*   in a direction toward
    to *(+ verb)*   the infinitive form of a verb
    too *(adv.)*   also; excessively; very
    two *(noun)*   number

29. It is _____ bad that the _____ of you cannot agree on anything.

30. I want _____ go _____ the movies, and I hope you do _____.

    vain *(adj.)*   conceited; unsuccessful
    vane *(noun)*   a plate of wood or metal, often in the shape of a rooster, that pivots to indicate the direction of the wind; the weblike part of a feather
    vein *(noun)*   a blood vessel; the branching framework of a leaf; an occurrence of an ore; a strip of color; a streak; a transient attitude

31. I saw a beautiful antique weather _____ from an old barn at an auction, and I made a _____ attempt to get it.

32. I could tell the old miner was _____ when he bragged endlessly about striking a rich _____ of silver.

33. It was a good thing the patient was not _____ because during the stress test every _____ stood out on his head.

    waist *(noun)*   the middle portion of a body, garment, or object
    waste *(verb)*   to use thoughtlessly or carelessly
           (noun)   objects discarded as useless

34. The inexperienced seamstress _____ a yard of material trying to cut out the pattern of a gown for her client with the large _____.

35. It is a _____ of time trying to get him to admit the size of his _____.

    wait *(verb)*   to remain inactive
    weight *(noun)*   the measure of the heaviness of an object

36. When you are _____ for something important, time can seem like a heavy _____.

37. I decided to _____ and see if the nurse would record my _____.

    weather *(noun)*   atmospheric conditions
    whether *(conj.)*   if it is the case that

38. _____ or not you choose Hawaii for your vacation, there is no argument that the _____ there is gorgeous.

39. We always listen to the _____ report _____ it's right or wrong.

    ware *(noun)*   an article of commerce
    wear *(verb)*   to have on
    where *(adv.)*   at or in what place

40. The peddler always _____ a tweed jacket as he sells his _____ on the street.

Distinguishing between Words That Are Often Confused

41. The salesperson was helpful after I explained _____ I intended to _____ the strange combination of clothes.

   whole *(adj.)*   complete
   hole *(noun)*   an opening

42. I am telling you the _____ story about the _____ in our new carpet.

43. The _____ problem about that dress was that moths had eaten a _____ in it.

   wood *(noun)*   the tough substance made from trees
   would *(verb)*   modal auxiliary

44. He _____ make the cabinets of solid _____ if he could afford it.

45. Helen said she _____ come if I _____ promise to be there.

   write *(verb)*   to form letters and words; to compose
   right *(adj.)*   conforming to justice, law, or morality; correct; toward a conservative political point of view
   (noun)   that which is just, morally good, legal, or proper; a direction; a political group whose policies are conservative
   (adv.)   directly; well; completely; immediately
   rite *(noun)*   a traditional, solemn, and often religious ceremony

46. Every American has the _____ to participate in the religious _____ of his or her own choosing.

47. You are probably _____; Isaac Asimov will continue to _____ books of science fiction.

48. Be sure to _____ this down: make a _____ turn at the first three lights and then a left at the next stop sign; we'll be _____ there as soon as we can.

   yoke *(noun)*   a harness fastening two or more animals together; a form of bondage
   yolk *(noun)*   the yellow of an egg

49. _____ are used to make many sauces.

50. They struggled under the _____ of slavery.

51. He unfastened the _____ from the oxen.

Exercise 1

Words That Sound Alike

Choose the correct word, and write it in the space at the right.

1. Deep in the (rain, reign, rein) forests of Central America stand the remains of the ancient Mayan civilization. _____
2. The Mayan Indians had a highly developed system of writing, and their knowledge of mathematics and astronomy was astounding (to, too, two). _____
3. The land was inhospitable, with its marshlands and dense forests; the (whether, weather) was hot and humid. _____
4. Their (hole, whole) economy was dependent upon the farmers. _____
5. The (principal, principle) crop was maize. _____
6. Without metal tools, wheeled vehicles, or beasts of burden, these people built great religious centers on several (cites, sights, sites). _____
7. Here they would (raise, rays, raze) sacred statues of stone called monoliths. _____
8. Hundreds of priests performed ceremonial (rights, rites, writes), including human sacrifices. _____
9. We do not (know, no) why this civilization mysteriously ended by A.D. 1000. _____
10. War seems unlikely since the Maya were essentially a people of (peace, piece). _____

Exercise 2

Words That Sound Alike

Choose the correct word, and write it in the space at the right. Then, on the lines provided, write sentences using each of the words you did not choose.

1. The emperor's (rain, reign, rein) was filled with wars and revolution. _____

   _____

   _____

2. We climbed to a higher point of the mountain to get a (cite, sight, site) of the valley. _____

   _____

   _____

3. I brought the meat back to the butcher because the (wait, weight) marked on the package was wrong.

4. The (principal, principle) crop of Southeast Asia is rice.

5. Even after the floats passed by, the children continued to (stair, stare) down the street.

6. The (pain, pane) was broken, and shattered glass lay on the floor.

7. Nutritionists feel that we should not eat too much (stake, steak) or other red meat.

8. Since she loved to read books on history, she knew a great deal about the (passed, past).

9. A (stationary, stationery) car was hit by a speeding motorcycle.

10. The pizzeria sells pizza by the (peace, piece).

Exercise 3   Words That Sound Alike

Edit the following paragraph for errors in word confusions. Circle the errors and write the correct word on the lines below the paragraph.

The magazine article sited three reasons why retired persons should consider moving to the South. Its a serious decision for senior citizens because they don't want to waist their limited amount of time, money, or energy. The first advantage is the mild climate. Older people lose patients with the cold and dark winter whether in the North. The days are to short, and they wish for the feeling of the warm raze of the sun. The yolk of shoveling snow and feeling chilled or isolated in the home makes winter a dreaded period to be endured. Another reason for moving to the South is that the cost of homes and other basic needs tends to be cheaper. Senior citizens are jumping on planes from all over the North and going to the South to have a look at what their missing.

_____   _____
_____   _____
_____   _____
_____   _____
_____   _____
_____   _____

▶ Words that sound or look almost alike

Some words are often confused with other words that sound or look almost the same. Learning to spell these words correctly involves a careful study of pronunciations along with meanings.

After studying each set for the spelling, pronunciation, and meaning, fill in the blanks with the correct word.

		Pronunciation	*Meaning*
1.	**accept** *(verb)*	a as in *pat*	to receive; to admit; to regard as true or right
	except *(prep)*	the first *e* as in *pet*	other than; but

I will buy all of the shirts _____ the blue one.

The judge refused to _____ the evidence the lawyer presented.

Please _____ my apologies for the delay.

Distinguishing between Words That Are Often Confused ▶ 457

		Pronunciation	*Meaning*
2.	**access** *(noun)*	a as in pat	a means of approaching; the right to enter or make use of
	excess *(noun)*	the first e as in pet	a quantity or amount beyond what is required

The secretary denied us _____ to her files.

My father had to pay an additional twenty-five dollars for his _____ baggage on the plane.

We heard that _____ to the valley would be difficult.

3.	**advice** *(noun)*	Pronounce -ice like the word *ice*.	opinion as to what should be done about a problem
	advise *(verb)*	Pronounce -ise like the word *eyes*.	to suggest; to counsel

I wish I had someone to _____ me.

The officer will _____ you of your rights.

She always gives her daughter good _____.

4.	**affect** *(verb)*	a as in *about*	*verb:* to influence
	effect *(noun)*	the first e as the	*noun:* result
	(verb)	i in *pit*	*verb:* to bring about a result

This medicine has several adverse side _____.

The new tax law will _____ the middle class.

The _____ of the earthquake in Mexico were disastrous.

5.	**allusion** *(noun)*	a as in *about*	an indirect reference
	illusion *(noun)*	the first i as in *pit*	a mistaken concept or belief

A fast elevator can give the _____ that one is not moving at all.

When the magician seemed to make his assistant hang in midair, everybody clapped at the _____.

I could tell the student was knowledgeable because of all her _____ to Shakespeare's plays.

		Pronunciation	*Meaning*
6.	**breath** *(noun)*	ea as the e in pet	noun: the air that is inhaled or exhaled in breathing
	breathe *(verb)*	the ea as the e in be	verb: to inhale and exhale air

Mouthwash promises to give you a fresh _____.

The skiier could see his _____ in the chilly winter air.

She told me to _____ deeply.

7.	**clothes** *(noun)*	o as the oe in toe	garments; wearing apparel
	cloths *(noun)*	o as the aw in paw	pieces of fabric

I will need three clean _____ to wash the windows.

Take warm _____ when you go camping next week.

When the family went away, they covered their furniture with large _____

8.	**conscience** *(noun)*	kŏn´shens (2 syllables)	recognition of right and wrong
	conscientious *(adj.)*	kŏn shē-en shes (4 syllables)	careful; thorough
	conscious *(adj.)*	kŏn´shes (2 syllables)	awake; aware of one's own existence

The thief gave himself up to the police because his _____ was bothering him.

She was not _____ when the ambulance came to take her to the hospital.

She had done nothing wrong, so she was able to give her testimony in court with a clear _____.

When the company hired a night watchman, they needed someone who was very _____.

9.	**costume** *(noun)*	o as in pot, u as the oo in boot	a special style of dress for a particular occasion
	custom *(noun)*	u as in cut, o as in gallop	a common tradition

It's the _____ every Halloween for children to wear _____.

Before you visit a foreign country, you should become familiar with its _____ so that you won't unknowingly offend anyone.

Distinguishing between Words That Are Often Confused ▸ 459

	Pronunciation	*Meaning*
10. **council** *(noun)*	*ou* as in *out*	*noun:* a group that governs
counsel *(verb)*		*verb:* to give advice
(noun)		*noun:* a lawyer; advice
consul *(noun)*	*o* as in *pot*	*noun:* a governmental official in the foreign service

The doctor gave the patient good _____.

I wrote to the American _____ to inquire about my visa.

Your faculty adviser will _____ you about what courses you should take.

The _____ met to discuss the new laws.

| 11. **desert** *(verb)* | di zurt´ *i* as in *pit* | to abandon |
(noun)	dez´ert the first *e* as in *pet*	barren land
dessert *(noun)*	di zurt´ *i* as in *pit*	last part of a meal, often a sweet

The teenagers _____ the old car on the side of the road.

She dreamed of a cruise to a _____ island.

We made a chocolate layer cake for _____.

The camel is an animal suited to the _____.

12. **diner** *(noun)*	*i* as the *ie* in *pie*	a person eating dinner; a restaurant with a long counter and booths
dinner *(noun)*	*i* as in *pit*	chief meal of the day

We went to the _____ for an inexpensive meal.

All I want for _____ is a salad.

The _____ asked the waitress for another cup of coffee.

| 13. **emigrate** *(verb)* | *e* as in *pet* | to go out of a country |
emigrant *(noun)*		someone who leaves a country to settle in another country
immigrate *(verb)*	the first *i* as in *pit*	to come into a country
immigrant *(noun)*		someone who enters a country to settle there

My parents _____ from Greece.

They _____ to the United States in 1948.

Most of the Irish _____ arrived here between 1900 and 1930.

		Pronunciation	*Meaning*
14.	**farther** *(adv.)* *(adj.)*	*a* as in *father*	greater physical or measurable distance
	further *(adv.)* *(adj.)*	*u* as in *urge*	greater mental distance; more distant in time or degree; additional
	(verb)		to help the progress of; to advance

I walked one mile _____.

She advised us to think _____ about the problem.

Let's not travel any _____ tonight.

15.	**local** *(adj.)*	loˊkel *a* as in *about*	relating or peculiar to a place
	locale *(noun)*	lo kalˊ *a* as in *pat*	a place, scene, or setting, as of a novel

While I am in the _____, I will visit my cousin.

Is there any interesting _____ news today?

The _____ is a small southern town in Tennessee.

16.	**moral** *(adj.)*	morˊal Pronounce the *a* as in *about;* the accent is on the first syllable.	*adj:* a sense of right and wrong
	(noun)		*noun:* the lesson of a story, fable, or event
	morale *(noun)*	mo ralˊ Pronounce the *a* as in *pat;* the accent is on the second syllable.	the attitude or spirit of a person or group of people

Mr. Jefferson felt a _____ obligation toward his neighbors.

The _____ of the prisoners is very low.

The _____ of the story is "Look before you leap."

Distinguishing between Words That Are Often Confused ▸ 461

		Pronunciation	*Meaning*
17.	**personal** *(adj.)*	per´son al Accent is on the first syllable	pertaining to a particular person
	personnel *(noun)*	per son nel´ Accent is on the third syllable	the people employed by an organization; an administrative division of an organization concerned with the employees

She went to the _____ office to discuss her problem.

Chico wouldn't tell us what his problem was; he said it was _____.

Most of the _____ at this company are well trained.

18.	**precede** *(verb)*	Pronounce the first *e* as the *i* in *pit*	to come before
	proceed *(verb)*	Pronounce the *o* as the *oe* in *toe*	to continue

When Stuart changed schools, his reputation _____ him.

You may now _____ through the intersection.

The chef will describe how you should _____ with the pastry.

19.	**quiet** *(adj.)*	qui´et *i* as the *ie* in *pie*, *e* as in *pet*	silence
	quit *(verb)*	*i* as in *pit*	to give up; to stop
	quite *(adv.)*	*i* as the *ie* in *pie*; the *e* is silent	somewhat; completely; truly

That woman is _____ a dancer!

Be _____ while she is performing.

She says she will _____ soon if she cannot find a job.

20.	**receipt** *(noun)*	Pronounce the first *e* as the *i* in *pit*, *ie* as the *e* in *be*; the *p* is silent.	a bill marked as paid; the act of receiving something
	recipe *(noun)*	Pronounce the first *e* as in *pet*, the *i* like the *a* in *about*, the final *e* as in *be*.	a formula for preparing a mixture, especially in cooking

Please give me your special _____ for boiled dumplings.

I cannot return the dress because I lost the _____.

Keep your _____ for tax purposes.

		Pronunciation	*Meaning*
21.	**special** *(adj.)*	spe cial	exceptional; distinctive
	especially *(adv.)*	Notice the extra syllable at the beginning.	particularly

He made several _____ trips to visit his father when he was in the hospital.

The father was _____ happy to see his son.

Now that he was so sick, they seemed to get along _____ well.

22.	**than** *(conj.)*	a as in *pat*	used to make a comparison
	then *(adv.)*	e as in *pet*	at that time; in that case

First he came home late; _____ he blamed me for the cold food.

This cake is sweeter _____ the one my mother makes.

I would rather try and fail _____ never try at all.

23.	**thorough** *(adj.)*	the first *o* as the *u* in *urge*, *ou* as the *oe* in *toe*	finished; fully done
	though *(adv. conj.)*	*ou* as the *oe* in *toe*	however; despite the fact
	thought *(verb)* *(noun)*	*ou* as the *aw* in *paw*	past tense of *to think*
	through *(prep)*	*ou* as the *oo* in *boot*	preposition used to indicate entrance at one side and exit from the other
	threw *(verb)*	Rhymes with *through*.	past tense of *to throw*

Thru is only an informal spelling for the word *through*.

He was deep in _____ when the doorbell rang.

When she walked _____ the door, he didn't recognize her

even _____ he had known her all his life.

Then she _____ him a set of keys and said, "You've made

such a _____ mess of everything. I'm _____!"

Distinguishing between Words That Are Often Confused

Exercise 1 — Working with Words That Sound or Look Almost Alike

Complete each of the following sentences by choosing the correct word.

1. She told the manager she would like very much to work in the _____ office of the company.
   (personal, personnel)

2. He told the police that his _____ mind could not recall what happened.
   (conscious, conscience, conscientious)

3. Northern Africa is becoming a vast _____.
   (desert, dessert)

4. The apartment was dangerous to live in because there was no _____ to a fire escape.
   (access, excess)

5. I met her after work at the _____, where we both joked with the owner and the waiters.
   (diner, dinner)

6. We decided it was not a good _____ for a store.
   (local, locale)

7. The snow is so deep I cannot walk any _____.
   (further, farther)

8. The magician gave the _____ of starting a fire on stage.
   (allusion, illusion)

9. The machine isn't working well even _____ it's new.
   (thorough, though, thought, through)

10. My father wears that clown _____ every Halloween.
    (custom, costume)

Exercise 2 — Working with Words That Sound or Look Almost Alike

Complete each of the following sentences by choosing the correct word.

1. It is _____ a place to take a vacation!
   (quiet, quite)

2. His case was so complicated that he knew he needed a lawyer's _____.
   (council, counsel, consul)

3. A weekend vacation is better _____ none at all.
   (than, then)

4. Please _____ my apologies for all the damage done to your car.
   (accept, except)

5. They had to _____ from their native country in order to find work.
   (emigrate, immigrate)

6. The captain tried to improve the _____ of his crew by showing them a movie.
   (moral, morale)

7. If you are going to wash the car, take several of the clean _____ from the bag under the sink.
   (cloths, clothes)

8. As she wandered in the desert, she had the _____ that there was a city in front of her.
   (illusion, allusion)

9. One _____ of the strike was an increase in the workers' salaries.
   (affect, effect)

10. Do not speak about the matter any _____.
    (further, farther)

Exercise 3 — Writing Sentences Using Words That Sound or Look Almost Alike

Write your own sentences using the following words.

1. special
   IT WAS A SPECIAL DAY

   especially
   THIS DAY WAS ESPECIALLY NICE FOR MY BROTHER

2. breath
   SHE TAKES MY BREATH AWAY

   breathe
   I NEED ROOM TO BREATHE

3. precede
   _____

   proceed
   _____

4. receipt
   _____

   recipe
   _____

5. advice
   _____

   advise
   _____

▶ Words that sound or look almost alike: *sit/set; rise/raise; lie/lay*

These six verbs are among the most troublesome verbs in English because each verb is similar in sound, spelling, and meaning to another verb. Since they are nearly all irregular verbs, students must be careful to learn to spell the principal parts correctly. The key to learning how to use the verbs *sit*, *rise*, and *lie* is to remember that these are actions the subject can do without any help; no other person or thing has to be included in the sentence. When you use the verbs *set, raise,* and *lay* in a sentence, the actions of these verbs are done to other persons or objects; these persons or things have to be included directly in the sentence. For example, when you use the verb *to sit,* all you need is a subject and a form of the verb:

> I sit.

However, when you use the verb *to set,* you need a subject, a form of the verb, and an object. For example:

> I set the glass on the table.

The subject *I* and the verb *set* are followed by the object *glass,* which is what the subject set on the table.

sit: to take a sitting position
never takes an object

set: to place something into position
always takes an object

Present: I *sit.*	I *set the glass* down.
Present participle: I *am sitting.*	I *am setting the glass* down.
Past: I *sat.*	I *set the glass* down.
Past participle: I *have sat.*	I *have set the glass* down.

Fill in each of the following blanks with the correct form of the verb *sit* or *set.*

I ___SET___ the table today.

I have ___SET___ the suitcases in your room.

I am ___SITTING___ in my favorite rocking chair.

She likes me to ___SIT___ by her bed and read to her in the evening.

rise: to stand up; to move upward
never takes an object

raise: to make something move up or grow
always takes an object

Present: I *rise.*	I *raise the flag.*
Present participle: The sun is *rising.*	I *am raising the flag.*
Past: He *rose* at eight o'clock.	I *raised the flag.*
Past participle: I *have risen* early today.	I *have raised the flag.*

Fill in each of the following blanks with the correct form of the verb *rise* or *raise.*

Last spring the manufacturers ___RAISED___ the prices.

Yesterday the prices of the magazines ___ROSE___ by a dime.

When I entered the room, the woman ___ROSE___ to greet me.

The woman ___RAISED___ her head when I entered the room.

The verbs *lie* and *lay* are easily confused because two of their principal parts have the same spelling. It takes concentration to learn to use these two verbs correctly.

lie: to recline
    never takes an object

lay: to put
    always takes an object

Present: I *lie* down.   I *lay the pen* down.
Present participle: I am *lying* down.   I am *laying the pen* down.
Past: Yesterday I *lay* down.   I *laid the pen* down.
Past participle: I have *lain* down.   I have *laid the pen* down.

The verb *lie* can also be a regular verb meaning "to tell an untruth." The principal parts of this verb are *lie, lying, lied, has lied.*

Fill in each of the following blanks with the correct form of the verb *lie* or *lay*.

I usually ___LIE___ down in the afternoon.

The auto mechanic is ___LYING___ under the car.

I can't remember where I ___LAID___ my keys.

The child has ___LIEN___ in the crib all afternoon.

This young man always ___LAYS___ the carpet in our house.

The witness ___LIED___ under oath when she was questioned.

Her coat ___LAY___ on the floor until I noticed it.

Exercise 1   Understanding *sit/set; rise/raise; lie/lay*

Fill in the blanks with the correct form of the verbs.

1. The cat has _____ in the sun all day.
    (lie, lay)

2. If you feel sick, ___LIE___ down on that bed.
    (lie, lay)

3. The elevator always _____ quickly to the tenth floor.
    (rise, raise)

4. The boss _____ her salary twice this year.
    (rise, raise)

Distinguishing between Words That Are Often Confused ▸ 467

5. The parents __LAID__ down the law when their son came home late.
   (lie, lay)

6. The carpenters __RAISED__ the roof when they remodeled the house.
   (rise, raise)

7. The dog __SITS__ up every night and begs for food.
   (sit, set)

8. Last week I _____ in front of my television set nearly every night.
   (sit, set)

9. I always watch the waiter _____ on a stool after his shift is done.
   (sit, set)

10. We have _____ a plate of cookies and milk out for Santa Claus every year since the children were born.
    (sit, set)

Exercise 2   Understanding *sit/set; rise/raise; lie/lay*

Fill in the blanks with the correct form of the verbs.

1. New apartment buildings are _____ in the city.
   (rise, raise)

2. When the baby-sitter arrived, the child's toys were _____ scattered all over the house.
   (lie, lay)

3. The moon has _____ behind the clouds all week.
   (lie, lay)

4. _____ those apples on the table, please.
   (Sit, Set)

5. My mother has _____ four children.
   (rise, raise)

6. The kitten _____ in the basket for three weeks.
   (lie, lay)

7. He _____ the cup to his mouth and drank.
   (rise, raise)

8. I will _____ and knead the bread dough.
   (sit, set)

9. The sun is _____ in the East.
   (rise, raise)

10. I _____ the bricks by the driveway yesterday.
    (lie, lay)

Exercise 3   Understanding *sit/set; rise/raise; lie/lay*

Fill in the blanks with the correct form of the verbs.

1. This year the price of food has _____ dramatically.
   (rise, raise)

2. Robert had _____ unconscious for several minutes before the
   (lie, lay)
   ambulance arrived.

3. Let's _____ here awhile and rest.
   (sit, set)

4. She came right home and _____ down.
   (lie, lay)

5. Please _____ the windows for some fresh air.
   (rise, raise)

6. I _____ my feet on American soil in 1983.
   (sit, set)

7. I had _____ at my favorite table.
   (sit, set)

8. The waiter, as usual, had _____ a reserved sign on the table
   (lie, lay)
   to save it for me.

9. The aroma of fresh bread _____ up from the table.
   (rise, raise)

10. I would probably have to _____ down after this meal.
    (lie, lay)

Exercise 4 — Understanding *sit/set; rise/raise; lie/lay*

Construct your own sentences using the following words correctly.

1. lie (to recline)

   _____

2. laying

   _____

3. set

   _____

4. rose

   _____

5. lain

   _____

6. lying

   _____

7. raised

   _____

8. laid

   _____

9. lay (to put)

_____

10. risen

_____

▶ Words that sound or look almost alike: *choose/chose; lose/loose; lead/led; die/dye*

These verbs are often misspelled because there is confusion about how to spell the vowel sounds of the verbs. Study the spelling of the principal parts below.

Present	*Present Participle*	*Past*	*Past Participle*
choose	choosing	chose	has chosen
lose	losing	lost	has lost
lead	leading	led	has led
die	dying	died	has died

▸ *Loose* is an adjective meaning "not tightly fitted." Remember, it rhymes with *goose*.

▸ *Lead* can also be a noun meaning a bluish white metal. Remember, it rhymes with *head*.

▸ *Dye* is another verb meaning "to color." Its principal parts are *dye, dyeing, dyed, has dyed*.

1. Fill in the blanks with the correct form of the verb *choose*.

    Yesterday I _____ Maggie for my lab partner.

    Today I _____ Jeff.

    He always _____ his friends for his partners.

2. Fill in the blanks with the correct form of the verb *lose*.

    Our team _____ the game Sunday.

    We always _____ when we play that team.

    Whenever she plays chess with her sister, she _____.

3. Fill in the blanks with the correct form of the verb *lead*.

    Yesterday, I _____ the students in singing our class song.

    Tomorrow I will _____ the students again.

    Have your ever _____ a group in singing?

4. Fill in the blanks with the correct form of the verb *die*.

    The sound of the train whistle is slowly _____ away.

The deer have _____ from lack of food.

Her hope _____ when she saw the empty mailbox.

▶ Words that sound or look almost alike: *use/used; suppose/supposed*

To use means *to bring or put into service; to make use of*.

  Present: I usually *use* my brother's bike to get to school.
  Past: Yesterday I *used* my father's car.

Used to means *accustomed to* or *familiar with*.

  I am not *used to* walking to school.
  I *used to* take the bus downtown, but now I get a ride with my neighbor.

To suppose means to *guess*.

  Present: I *suppose* he is trying.
  Past: I *supposed* he was trying.

A form of *to be* + *supposed to* means *ought to* or *should*.

  Waiters *are supposed to* be courteous.

Many people have difficulty knowing when to choose *used* and *supposed* in their writing because in speaking, the final *d* is often not clearly heard.

  Incorrect: I am *suppose to* be in school today.
  Correct: I am *supposed to* be in school today.

Fill in the blanks with the correct form of the verb *use* or *suppose*.

use or *used to*

  I always _____ a pen in English class now.

  I always _____ write with a pencil.

  Were they _____ studying several hours a day?

suppose or *supposed to*

  I am _____ help my sister today.

  I _____ I will have to help my sister tomorrow.

  I was _____ help her yesterday.

Distinguishing between Words That Are Often Confused ▸ 471

Exercise 1 — Using *choose, lose, lead, die, use,* and *suppose*

Fill in the blanks with the correct form of the verb.

1. I am _____ what courses to study next semester.
   (choose)

2. Last semester my friend _____ me to believe I would love astronomy.
   (lead)

3. He forgot to tell me I was _____ to have a good math background.
   (suppose)

4. Next semester I will be sure to _____ from the freshman-level courses.
   (choose)

5. I hope I won't _____ my scholarship.
   (lose, loose)

6. My father _____ last year, so I need financial support.
   (die)

7. I am _____ to working hard.
   (use)

8. I _____ every free moment to study now.
   (use)

9. I don't intend to _____ out on the honor role again.
   (loose, lose)

10. My counselor has _____ me to think about a career in the social sciences.
    (lead)

Exercise 2 — Using *choose, lose, lead, die, use,* and *suppose*

Fill in the blanks with the correct verb.

1. I am _____ to getting up at five o'clock in the morning.
   (use, used)

2. Napoleon _____ his troops to battle.
   (lead, led)

3. The young man was _____ a sweater when he was pickpocketed.
   (choose, chose)

4. Which course did you _____ to take?
   (choose, chose)

5. Some people have _____ a double life.
   (lead, led)

6. She will probably _____ her car because she is behind on her payments.
   (loose, lose)

7. I was _____ to work at the hospital today.
   (suppose, supposed)

8. Mozart was forgotten as he lay _____.
   (dying, dyeing)

9. Are we really _____ to eat this?
   (suppose, supposed)

10. They _____ me down the wrong corridor.
    (lead, led)

Exercise 3   Using *choose, lose, lead, die, use,* and *suppose*

Ten words in the following paragraph are underlined. If the word is used correctly, mark the answer blank with a C. If the word is used incorrectly, write the correct word choice.

Tomorrow we (1) chose partners for tennis. I hope I won't (2) loose every game this summer. Jennifer and Corey always (3) lead no matter whom they play. Jason's enthusiasm for the game seems to be (4) dieing. Like me, he also (5) loses every game he plays. He and I should (6) chose a sport we are better suited for. We both (7) use to do much more swimming in the summer. I (8) suppose we stopped because the pool fees doubled in price. Now we (9) use the tennis courts behind the elementary school for free. The town is (10) suppose to charge a fee, but nobody ever enforces the ruling.

1. _____   6. _____
2. _____   7. _____
3. _____   8. _____
4. _____   9. _____
5. _____   10. _____

D

Solving Spelling Problems

▶ **Learning to spell commonly mispronounced words**

Several common English words are often mispronounced or pronounced in such a way that the result is incorrect spelling. Below are sixty common words that are often misspelled. As you study them, be careful to spell each of the underlined syllables correctly.

I. The Common Omission of Vowels

1. Do not omit the underlined syllable with the *a:*

accident<u>a</u>lly	liter<u>a</u>ture
basic<u>a</u>lly	mini<u>a</u>ture
bound<u>a</u>ry	sep<u>a</u>rate
extraordin<u>a</u>ry	temper<u>a</u>ment
incident<u>a</u>lly	temper<u>a</u>ture

2. Do not omit the underlined syllable with the *e:*

consid<u>e</u>rable	math<u>e</u>matics
diff<u>e</u>rence	num<u>e</u>rous
fun<u>e</u>ral	scen<u>e</u>ry
int<u>e</u>resting	

   However, notice the following words in which the *e* should be omitted:

disaster	becomes	disast<u>r</u>ous
enter	becomes	ent<u>r</u>ance
hinder	becomes	hind<u>r</u>ance
hunger	becomes	hung<u>r</u>y
launder	becomes	laund<u>r</u>y
monster	becomes	monst<u>r</u>ous
remember	becomes	remem<u>br</u>ance

3. Do not omit the underlined syllable with the *i:*

   aspirin | family | similar

4. Do not omit the underlined syllable with the *o:*

   chocolate | humorous
   environment | laboratory
   favorite | sophomore

5. Do not omit the underlined syllable with the *u:*

   luxury | accuracy

6. Do not omit the underlined syllable with the *y:*

   studying

II. Omission of Consonants

1. **b**
   probably
2. **c**
   arctic
3. **d**
   candidate
   handkerchief
   supposed to
   used to
4. **g**
   recognize
5. **n**
   government
6. **r**
   February
   library
   surprise
7. **t**
   authentic
   identical
   partner
   promptly
   quantity

III. Common addition of a syllable:

athlete | athletic

IV. Common transposition of letters:

tragedy | perform
persuade | prefer

Exercise 1 — Words Commonly Mispronounced

Circle the correct spelling for each of the following words.

1.	seperate	seprate	separate
2.	probably	probaly	probly
3.	ardic	arctic	artic
4.	suprise	saprize	surprise
5.	tragedy	tradgedy	trajedy
6.	quantity	quantidy	quanity
7.	litrature	literature	literture
8.	hungery	hungary	hungry
9.	handsome	hansome	hansom
10.	favorite	faverite	favrite

Solving Spelling Problems ▸ 475

Exercise 2 — Words Commonly Mispronounced

Fill in each of the following blanks with an appropriate word from the list of commonly mispronounced words.

1. Benjamin Franklin began the free public _____.
2. The second month of the year is _____.
3. The federal _____ collects taxes.
4. Are these emeralds _____ or are they just glass?
5. Never go swimming alone; always have a _____.
6. The orchestra will _____ a Beethoven symphony.
7. Madame Curie was doing research in her _____ when she heard the news about the discovery.
8. Jessica and Jill are _____ twins.
9. He is never late; he arrives _____.
10. The _____ was made of Irish linen.

Exercise 3 — Words Commonly Mispronounced

Fill in the correct letters to complete the spelling of these words commonly mispronounced.

1. asp____in
2. disast____ous
3. fam____ly
4. ath____ete
5. math____matics
6. bound____ry
7. mini____ture
8. reco____nize
9. soph____more
10. use____to

▸ Learning to spell *ie* or *ei* words

Use this rhyme to help you remember how to spell most *ie* and *ei* words:

> *i* before *e*
> except after *c*
> or when sounded like *a*
> as in *neighbor* or *weigh*.

i before *e*

The majority of all the *ie* or *ei* words use *ie*.

believe   friend   yield
chief   shriek

except after c

ceiling	conceive	receive
conceit	receipt	

or when sounded like a

beige	reins	vein
eight	sleigh	

Once you have learned the rhyme, concentrate on learning the following groups of words that are the exceptions to this rhyme.

caffeine	leisure	ancient
codeine	seizure	conscience
protein	seize	efficient
		sufficient
neither	height	
either	Fahrenheit	
sheik	counterfeit	
stein	foreign	
their		
weird		

Exercise 1

ie and ei Words

Choose the correct combination of ie or ei in the following words.

1. sl_____gh
2. bel_____ve
3. s_____ge
4. v_____l
5. l_____sure
6. dec_____t
7. n_____ce
8. w_____ght
9. prot_____n
10. anc_____nt

Exercise 2

ie and ei Words

Choose the correct combination of ie or ei in the following words.

1. for_____gn
2. r_____ndeer
3. perc_____ve
4. f_____nd
5. br_____fcase
6. ach_____ve
7. misch_____f
8. rel_____ve
9. h_____ght
10. y_____ld

Solving Spelling Problems ▶ 477

Exercise 3

ie and ei Words

Choose the correct combination of *ie* or *ei* in the following words.

1. p_____ce
2. p_____
3. fr_____ght
4. n_____ther
5. n_____ghbor

6. dec_____ve
7. effic_____nt
8. rec_____pt
9. th_____f
10. Fahrenh_____t

▶ **Forming the plurals of nouns**

Almost all nouns can be made plural by simply adding *-s* to the singular form:

    girl   *becomes*   girls
    dinner   *becomes*   dinners

However, each of the following groups of words has its own special rules for forming the plural.

1. Words ending in -y:

In words ending in *-y* preceded by a *consonant*, change the *-y* to *-i* and add *-es*.

    la*dy*   *becomes*   lad*ies*
    ceremo*ny*   *becomes*   ceremon*ies*

Words ending in *-y* preceded by a *vowel* form their plurals in the regular way by just adding *-s*.

    d*ay*   *becomes*   days
    monk*ey*   *becomes*   monkeys
    vall*ey*   *becomes*   valleys

────────── Practice ──────────

In the spaces provided, write the plural form of each of these singular nouns:

    turkey   _____
    candy   _____
    play   _____
    Gypsy   _____
    delivery   _____

2. Words ending in -o:

Most words ending in *-o* preceded by a consonant add *-es* to form the plural.

he*ro*	*becomes*	hero*es*
pota*to*	*becomes*	potato*es*
ec*ho*	*becomes*	echo*es*

However, musical terms or names of musical instruments add only *-s*.

pia*no*	*becomes*	piano*s*
so*lo*	*becomes*	solo*s*
sopra*no*	*becomes*	soprano*s*

Words ending in *-o* preceded by a *vowel* add *-s*.

pat*io*	*becomes*	patio*s*
rad*io*	*becomes*	radio*s*
rod*eo*	*becomes*	rodeo*s*

Some words ending in *-o* may form their plural with *-s* or *-es*.

memen*to*	*becomes*	memento*s*	or	memento*es*
pin*to*	*becomes*	pinto*s*	or	pinto*es*
ze*ro*	*becomes*	zero*s*	or	zero*es*

If you are uncertain about the plural ending of a word ending in *-o*, it is best to use the dictionary. The dictionary gives all the endings of irregular plurals. If no plural form is given, you know the word will form its plural in the regular way by adding only *-s*.

Practice

In the spaces provided, write the plural form of each of these singular nouns:

banjo _____

stereo _____

torpedo _____

studio _____

embargo _____

3. Words ending in -ch, -sh, -s, -x, and -z:

For words ending in *-ch, -sh, -s, -x,* and *-z,* add *-es.*

witch*es*	dress*es*	buzz*es*
dish*es*	tax*es*	

Solving Spelling Problems ▶ 479

———————————— **Practice** ————————————

In the spaces provided, write the plural form for each of these singular nouns:

quiz   _____

success   _____

flash   _____

box   _____

peach   _____

4. **Words ending in -fe or -f:**

   Some words ending in *-fe* or *-f* change the *f* to *v* and add *-es*. You can hear the change from the *f* sound to the *v* sound in the plural.

wi*fe*	*becomes*	wi*ves*
lea*f*	*becomes*	lea*ves*

   Other words ending in *-fe* or *-f* keep the *f* and just add *-s*.

sheri*ff*	*becomes*	sheri*ffs*
belie*f*	*becomes*	belie*fs*

   Again, you can hear that the *f* sound is kept in the plural. Some words can form their plural either way. If so, the dictionary will give the preferred way first.

———————————— **Practice** ————————————

In the spaces provided, write the plural form of each of these singular nouns:

hoof   _____

scarf   _____

tariff   _____

chief   _____

self   _____

5. **Foreign words:**

   Some words borrowed from other languages keep the plurals from those other languages to form the plural in English.

cris*is*	*becomes*	cris*es*
phenomen*on*	*becomes*	phenomen*a*
alumn*us* (masc.)	*becomes*	alumn*i*
alumn*a* (fem.)	*becomes*	alumn*ae*
alg*a*	*becomes*	alg*ae*

6. **Compound nouns:**

   Compound nouns make their plurals by putting the -s on the end of the main word.

brother-in-law	*becomes*	brother**s**-in-law
passer-by	*becomes*	passer**s**-by

7. **Irregular plurals:**

   Some nouns in English have irregular plurals.

Singular	*Plural*
child	children
deer	deer
foot	feet
goose	geese
man, woman	men, women
moose	moose
mouse	mice
ox	oxen
sheep	sheep
tooth	teeth

Exercise 1 — Forming the Plurals of Nouns

Using the rules you have learned, make the following words plural.

1. puppy   _____
2. mother-in-law _____
3. tooth   _____
4. cameo   _____
5. phenomenon   _____
6. loaf   _____
7. match   _____
8. mix   _____
9. enemy   _____
10. bag   _____

Exercise 2 — Forming the Plurals of Nouns

Using the rules you have learned, make the following words plural.

1. attorney   _____
2. watch   _____

3. tempo   _____

4. letter   _____

5. library _____

6. echo   _____

7. glass   _____

8. deer   _____

9. hypothesis _____

10. ratio   _____

Exercise 3   **Forming the Plurals of Nouns**

Using the rules you have learned, make the following words plural.

1. woman   _____

2. company _____

3. calf   _____

4. alumnus _____

5. address _____

6. ox   _____

7. wish   _____

8. melody   _____

9. zero   _____

10. key   _____

▶ **Should the final consonant be doubled?**

The answer to this question involves the most complicated spelling rule. However, the rule is well worth learning because once you know it, you will suddenly be able to spell thousands of words correctly.

In order to understand the rule, remember first the difference between vowels (*a, e, i, o, u,* and sometimes *y*) and consonants (all the other letters in the alphabet).

The problem in spelling occurs when you want to add an ending that begins with a vowel such as *-ed, -er, -est,* or *-ing*. Sometimes the word will double the last letter before adding an ending:

trap + ing = trapping   The fur traders spent their time tra*pp*ing animals.

Sometimes the word will *not* double the last letter before adding the ending:

turn + er = turner   He dropped the pancake tur*n*er.

How do you know when to double the final consonant?

Rule for Doubling One-Syllable Words

Double the final consonant of a one-syllable word when adding an ending that begins with a vowel only if the last three letters of the word end with a consonant-vowel-consonant combination.

Since *rap* in the word *trap* is a consonant-vowel-consonant combination, this one-syllable word will double the final consonant when adding an ending beginning with a vowel. Since the last three letters *urn* in the word *turn* are a vowel-consonant-consonant combination, this one-syllable word does not double the final consonant when adding an ending beginning with a vowel.

Study the list of words that follows. For each of these one-syllable words, determine whether or not the word will double the final consonant when adding an ending beginning with a vowel.

One-Syllable Word	Consonant-Vowel-Consonant Combination?	Double?	Add -ing Ending
dr*a*g	yes	yes	drag*g*ing
dr*ai*n	no	no	drai*n*ing
slip			
crack			
broil			
win			

NOTE: In words with *qu* like *quit* or *quiz*, think of the *qu* as a consonant. (The *u* does have a consonant *w* sound.) quit + ing + qui*tt*ing

---
Rule for Doubling Words of More than One Syllable

For words of more than one syllable, the rule adds one more condition: If the first syllable is accented in the newly formed word you do not double the final consonant.

pre fer´ + ed = pre ferred´
but
pre fer´ + ence = pref´ er ence

(The accent has changed to the first syllable.)

Try these two-syllable words.

con *trol´* + ing = _____

hu*m´ or* + ous = _____

Study the list of words that follow. For each of these words of more than one syllable, determine whether or not the word will double the final consonant when adding an ending beginning with a vowel.

com *pel´* + ed = _____

dif´ *fer* + ence = _____

de *sign´* + er = _____

be *gin´* + ing = _____

Exercise 1

Doubling the Final Consonant When Adding Endings That Begin with Vowels

Decide whether or not to double the final consonant when adding the endings to the following words.

	Word		*Ending*	*New Word*
1.	bit	+	-en	_____
2.	oc cur´	+	-ence	_____
3.	cen´ ter	+	-ing	_____
4.	pre fer´	+	-ed	_____
5.	pre´ fer	+	-ence	_____
6.	thin	+	-er	_____
7.	trans fer´	+	-ed	_____
8.	sail	+	-ing	_____
9.	ex cel´	+	-ent	_____
10.	o mit´	+	-ed	_____

Exercise 2

Doubling the Final Consonant When Adding Endings That Begin with Vowels

Decide whether or not to double the final consonant when adding the endings to the following words.

	Word		Ending	New Word
1.	stop	+	-ed	_____
2.	com mit´	+	-ee	_____
3.	com mit´	+	-ment	_____
4.	big	+	-est	_____
5.	e quip´	+	-ed	_____
6.	tap	+	-ing	_____
7.	suc ceed´	+	-ing	_____
8.	hid	+	-en	_____
9.	lis´ ten	+	-er	_____
10.	god	+	-ess	_____

Exercise 3 — Doubling the Final Consonant When Adding Endings That Begin with Vowels

Decide whether or not to double the final consonant when adding the endings to the following words.

	Word		Ending	New Word
1.	soul	+	ful	_____
2.	for got´	+	en	_____
3.	rag	+	ed	_____
4.	ben´ e fit	+	ed	_____
5.	wrap	+	er	_____
6.	plan	+	ing	_____
7.	fi´ nal	+	ize	_____
8.	trans mit´	+	er	_____
9.	wed	+	ing	_____
10.	sup port´	+	ive	_____

▶ Words ending in y

1. When a *y* at the end of a word is preceded by a consonant, change *y* to *i* and add the ending.

Word		Ending		New Word
carry	+	er	=	carr*ier*
merry	+	ment	=	merr*iment*
funny	+	er	=	_____
busy	+	ness	=	_____
vary	+	es	=	_____

Exceptions: Do not change the *y* to *i* if the ending starts with an *i*. In English we seldom have two *i*'s together.

stu*dy*	+	ing	=	stud*ying* not studiing
rea*dy*	+	ing	=	_____

Some long words drop the *y* when adding the ending. You can hear that the *y* syllable is missing when you pronounced the word correctly.

milita*ry*	+	ism	=	milita*rism*
accompa*ny*	+	ist	=	_____

2. When *y* at the end of a word is preceded by a vowel, do *not* change the *y* when adding the ending. Simply add the ending.

sur*vey*	+	s	=	sur*veys*
enj*oy*	+	ment	=	_____

Exercise 1 — Adding Endings to Words That End in y

Add endings to the following words, being sure to change the *y* to *i* wherever necessary.

1. key + s = _____
2. lonely + ness = _____
3. cry + ing = _____
4. cry + s = _____
5. pray + er = _____
6. cray + fish = _____
7. monkey + ing = _____
8. beauty + ful = _____
9. theory + es = _____
10. ceremony + al = _____

Exercise 2 — Adding Endings to Words That End in y

Add endings to the following words, being sure to change the y to i wherever necessary.

1. day + care = _____
2. carry + ing = _____
3. mercy + ful = _____
4. valley + s = _____
5. category + ize = _____
6. bury + ed = _____
7. bury + ing = _____
8. ally + es = _____
9. chimney + s = _____
10. try + ed = _____

Exercise 3 — Adding Endings to Words That End in y

Add endings to the following words, being sure to change the y to i wherever necessary.

1. easy + ly = _____
2. marry + age = _____
3. attorney + s = _____
4. hurry + ing = _____
5. destroy + er = _____
6. baby + ish = _____
7. baby + ed = _____
8. lucky + est = _____
9. story + es = _____
10. monopoly + ize = _____

▶ Is it one word or two?

There is often confusion about whether certain word combinations should be joined together to form compound words. Study the following three groups of words to avoid this common confusion.

These words are always written as one word:

another	everything	playroom
bathroom	grandmother	schoolteacher
bedroom	nearby	southeast, northwest, etc.
bookkeeper	nevertheless	roommate
cannot	newspaper	yourself
downstairs		

These words are always written as two words:

a lot	living room	high school
all right	no one	good night
dining room		

These words are written as one or two words depending on their use:

all ready *(pronoun and adj.)*   completely prepared
already *(adv.)*   previously; before

He was _____ there by the time I arrived.

I have _____ read that book.

We were _____ for the New Year's Eve party.

all together *(pronoun and adj.)*   in a group
altogether *(adv.)*   completely

Our family was _____ at Thanksgiving.

I am _____ too upset to concentrate.

Have you gathered your papers _____?

all ways *(adj. and noun)*   every road or path
always *(adverb)*   on every occasion

Be sure to check _____ before you cross that intersection.

She tried _____ she could think of before she gave up on the problem.

She _____ figures out the homework.

any one *(adj. and pronoun)*   one person or thing in a specific group
anyone *(indef. pronoun)*   any person at all

Did _____ ever find my gloves?

She will talk to _____ who will listen to her.

I would choose _____ of those sweaters if I had the money.

every one *(adj. and pronoun)*	every person or thing in a specific group
everyone *(indef. pronoun)*	all of the people

_____ of the books we wanted was out of stock.

_____ was so disappointed.

_____ of the workers disapproved of the new rules.

may be *(verb)*	might be
maybe *(adv.)*	perhaps

The news broadcast said that there _____ a storm tomorrow.

If it's bad, _____ I won't go to work.

_____ my car won't start.

Exercise 1

One Word or Two?

Fill in the blank in each of the following sentences by choosing the correct word to complete that sentence.

1. The blue rug looks beautiful in the white _____.
   (bed room, bedroom)

2. The room is usually occupied by _____, but she is not
   (grandmother, grand mother)
   here right now.

3. She has _____ left for a winter vacation.
   (all ready, already)

4. Last night we called her _____, and we sang "Happy
   (all together, altogether)
   Birthday" over the phone.

5. We _____ remember her birthday, no matter where we
   (all ways, always)
   are.

6. _____ likes to be remembered on special days, partic-
   (Every one, Everyone)
   ularly a birthday.

7. Next year, _____ all the members of the family will be
   (may be, maybe)
   able to celebrate her birthday with us.

8. If she _____ come to us, we will drive up and surprise
   (cannot, can not)
   her.

9. Most families have members who do not live _____.
   (near by, nearby)

10. _____, we can keep in touch by letter, phone, or visits.
    (Never the less, Nevertheless)

Exercise 2

One Word or Two?

Fill in the blank in each of the following sentences by choosing the correct word to complete that sentence.

1. When you rent a place to live, you must ask _____ (yourself, your self) several important questions.

2. First, you have to make sure the _____ (living room, livingroom) is big enough for your needs.

3. Next, if you plan to have people over for dinner very often, you might need a _____ (dining room, diningroom).

4. If _____ (anyone, any one) in your family is going to stay with you, you have to take that into account.

5. If you are going to rent a house, think of the advantages of having a _____ (bathroom, bath room) on the first floor.

6. When there are several young children in a family, having a _____ (play room, playroom) is an important consideration.

7. Also, where will you spend most of the time in your house—will you be in the upper rooms or _____ (down stairs, downstairs)?

8. _____ (No one, Noone) ever has enough space.

9. Finally, after you have thought about what you hope to find, consider what percent of your salary you _____ (maybe, may be) paying for rent.

10. If the rent is too high, you might want to consider looking for a _____ (roommate, room mate).

Exercise 3

One Word or Two?

Fill in the blank in each of the following sentences by choosing the correct word to complete that sentence.

1. A major problem facing _____ (a lot, alot) of people these days is how to get a good education and how to get a good job.

2. Some people would like to look for a job right after they graduate from _____ (high school, highschool).

3. _____ should make a quick decision about this, since
    (No one, Noone)
   it will have a long-term effect on one's life.

4. If you want to be a _____, you will have to have a
                      (book keeper, bookkeeper)
   certain amount of college education in addition to specific training.

5. It is certainly _____ to take off a year to think about
                   (all right, alright)
   your future plans.

6. If often happens that one of the best sources of advice is a
   _____ you had in high school.
   (school teacher, schoolteacher)

7. A further career consideration is the area of the country where you would
   like to live—the _____, for example.
                    (South West, Southwest)

8. _____ important point about a career is whether or
   (Another, An other)
   not it will be in demand five or ten years from now.

9. One way to get some good information about the best jobs now and in the
   future is to carefully read the _____ for details on
                                   (newspapers, news papers)
   economic trends.

10. In the end, such important decisions about education and career depend
    on _____ you can find out about them.
       (every thing, everything)

▸ Spelling 200 tough words

Word list 1: silent letters

b	*h*	*p*
crum*b*	ex*h*ibit	*p*neumonia
clim*b*	r*h*etoric	*p*sychology
de*b*t	r*h*ythm	*s*
dou*b*t	sc*h*edule	ai*s*le
	l	i*s*land
c	co*l*onel	debri*s*
indi*c*t	*n*	*t*
d	autum*n*	depo*t*
knowle*d*ge	colum*n*	lis*t*en
We*d*nesday	condem*n*	mor*t*gage
		w
		ans*w*er

Word list 2: double letters

acc**i**denta**ll**y	a**rr**angement	nece**ss**ary
a**cc**o**mm**odate	co**mm**i**tt**ee	o**cc**asiona**ll**y
a**cr**o**ss**	exa**gg**erate	po**ss**e**ss**ion
a**nn**ual	fina**ll**y	prefe**rr**ed
a**pp**arently	guarant**ee**	questio**nn**aire
reco**mm**end	su**gg**est	tomo**rr**ow
su**ccee**d	su**mm**arize	wri**tt**en *but* wri**t**ing
su**cc**e**ss**		

Word list 3: *-able* or *-ible*

-able

Usually, when you begin with a complete word, the ending is *-able*.

    acceptable   agreeable

These words keep the *e* when adding the ending:

peaceable	manageable
noticeable	knowledgeable

These words drop the *e* when adding the ending:

conceivable	indispensable
desirable	inevitable
imaginable	irritable

-ible

Usually, if you start with a root that is not a word, the ending is *-ible*.

audible	irresistible
compatible	permissible
eligible	plausible
feasible	possible
illegible	sensible
incredible	susceptible
inexhaustible	tangible

Word list 4: *de-* or *di-*

de-	*di-*
decide	dilemma
decision	dilute
delinquent	discipline
descend	discuss
describe	disease
despair	disguise
despicable	dispense
despise	dispute
despite	dissent
despondent	divide

destructive division
develop divine
device

Word list 5: the -er sound

Most words ending with the -er sound are spelled with -er, as in the words *prisoner, customer,* and *hunger.* Words that are exceptions to this should be learned carefully.

-ar	*-or*
beggar	actor
burglar	author
calendar	bachelor
cellar	doctor
dollar	emperor
grammary	governor
pillar	humor
polar	labor
similar	motor
vulgar	neighbor
-ur	professor
murmur	sailor
-yr	scissors
martyr	

Word list 6: -ance or -ence

Most words with the -ence sound at the end are spelled -ence. Here are a few examples:

audience   intelligence
correspondence   presence
excellence   reference
existence

Learn these exceptions:

-ance
allowance   nuisance
ambulance   observance
appearance   resistance
assistance   significance
attendance   tolerance
balance   *-ense*
dominance   license
guidance   *-eance*
ignorance   vengeance

Word list 7: problems with s, c, z, x, and k

absence	criticize	medicine
alcohol	ecstasy	muscle
analyze	emphasize	prejudice

auxiliary
awkward
biscuit
complexion
concede
consensus

especially
exceed
exercise
fascinate
magazine

recede
sincerely
supersede
vacillate
vicious

Word list 8: twenty-five demons

acquire
argument
benefit
cafeteria
cemetery
category
conquer
corroborate
courageous

extremely
frightening
grateful
inoculate
judgment
lightning
ninety
ninth

occurred
occurrence
privilege
ridiculous
secretary
truly
until
village

E

Capitalization

Many students are often confused or careless about the use of capital letters. Sometimes these students capitalize words without thinking, or they capitalize "important" words without really understanding what makes them important enough to deserve a capital letter. The question of when to capitalize words becomes easier to answer when you study the following rules and carefully apply them to your own writing.

▶ **Ten basic rules for capitalization**

  1. *Capitalize the first word of every sentence.*
  2. *Capitalize the names of specific things and places.*

Specific buildings:

  I went to the Jamestown Post Office.
   but
  I went to the post office.

Specific streets, cities, states, countries:

  She lives on Elam Avenue.
   but
  She lives on the same street as my mom and dad.

Specific organizations:

  He collected money for the March of Dimes.
   but
  Janice joined more than one club at the school.

Specific institutions:

  The loan is from the First National Bank.
   but
  The loan is from one of the banks in town.

Specific bodies of water:

> My uncle fishes every summer on Lake Chautauqua.
> *but*
> My uncle spends every summer at the lake.

3. *Capitalize days of the week, months of the year, and holidays. Do not capitalize the names of seasons.*

> The last Thursday in November is Thanksgiving Day.
> *but*
> I cannot wait until spring.

4. *Capitalize the names of all languages, nationalities, races, religions, deities, and sacred terms.*

> My friend who is Ethiopian speaks very little English.
> The Koran is the sacred book of Islam.

5. *Capitalize the first word and every important word in a title. Do not capitalize articles, prepositions, or short connecting words in the title.*

> *For Whom the Bell Tolls* is a famous novel by Ernest Hemingway.
> Her favorite short story is "A Rose for Emily."

6. *Capitalize the first word of a direct quotation.*

> The teacher said, "You have been chosen for the part."
> *but*
> "You have been chosen," she said, "for the part."

NOTE: *for* is not capitalized because it is not the beginning of the sentence in quotation marks.

7. *Capitalize historical events, periods, and documents.*

> The American Revolution
> The Colonial Period
> The Bill of Rights

8. *Capitalize the words north, south, east, and west when they are used as places rather than as directions.*

> He comes from the Midwest.
> *but*
> The farm is about twenty miles west of Omaha.

9. *Capitalize people's names.*

Proper names:

> George Hendrickson

Professional titles when they are used with the person's proper name:

| Judge Samuelson | *but* | the judge |
| Professor Shapiro | *but* | the professor |

Term for a relative (like *mother, sister, nephew, uncle*) when it is used in the place of the proper name:

I told Grandfather I would meet him later.

NOTE: terms for relatives are not capitalized if a pronoun, article, or adjective is used with the name.

I told my grandfather I would meet him later.

10. Capitalize brand names.

Lipton's Noodle Soup	but	noodle soup
Velveeta Cheese	but	cheese

Exercise 1 — Capitalization

Capitalize wherever necessary.

1. The italian student got a job in the school cafeteria.
2. Our train ride through the canadian rockies was fabulous.
3. The author often made references in his writing to names from the bible.
4. A student at the university of delaware was chosen for the national award.
5. My uncle's children always have a party on halloween.
6. I met the president of american telephone and telegraph company last friday at a convention in portland, oregon.
7. In 1863 president Lincoln wrote his famous emancipation proclamation.
8. My niece said, "why don't you consider moving father south if you hate the winter so much?"
9. The united auto workers voted not to go on strike over the new contract.
10. A very popular radio program in the east is called a prairie home companion.

Exercise 2 — Capitalization

Capitalize wherever necessary.

1. Every tuesday the general visits the hospital.
2. On one level, the book *the lord of the rings* can be read as a fairy tale; on another level, the book can be read as a christian allegory.
3. The golden gate bridge in san francisco may be the most beautiful bridge in the world.
4. She is the sister of my french teacher.
5. I've always wanted to take a trip to the far east in spring.
6. The kremlin houses the soviet government and is located in moscow.
7. I needed to see dr. Madison, but the nurse told me the doctor would not be in until next week.
8. He shouted angrily, "why don't you ever arrive at your history class on time?"

9. The scholastic aptitude test will be given on january 18.
10. While yet a teenager growing up in harlem, james Baldwin became a baptist preacher.

Exercise 3 — Capitalization

Capitalize wherever necessary.

1. The lawyer's office is located on south pleasant street.
2. My uncle lives farther south than grandmother.
3. I'd like to move to the south if I could find a job there.
4. The well-known anthropologist Margaret Mead was for many years director of the museum of natural history in new york city.
5. The constitution of the united states was signed in constitution hall on september 17, 1787.
6. Sculptor John Wilson was commissioned to create a bust of the late rev. Martin Luther King.
7. The money will be funded partly from the national endowment for the arts.
8. I read the magazine article in *newsweek* while I was waiting in the dentist's office yesterday.
9. The tour took the retired teachers above the arctic circle.
10. Many gerber baby foods no longer have sugar and salt.

F
Irregular Verbs

▶ **Principal parts of irregular verbs**

	Simple Form	*Past Form*	*Past Participle*

1. Principal parts are the same.

Simple Form	Past Form	Past Participle
beat	beat	beat or beaten
bet	bet	bet
burst	burst	burst
cast	cast	cast
cost	cost	cost
cut	cut	cut
fit	fit	fit
hit	hit	hit
hurt	hurt	hurt
let	let	let
put	put	put
quit	quit	quit
read	*read	*read
rid	rid	rid
set	set	set
shut	shut	shut
split	split	split
spread	spread	spread
wet	wet	wet

2. The simple present form and the past participle are the same.

Simple Form	Past Form	Past Participle
come	came	come
become	became	become

*Pronunciation changes.

Simple Form	Past Form	Past Participle

3. The past form and past participle are the same.

bend	bent	bent
lend	lent	lent
send	sent	sent
spend	spent	spent
build	built	built
creep	crept	crept
keep	kept	kept
sleep	slept	slept
sweep	swept	swept
weep	wept	wept
feel	felt	felt
leave	left	left
meet	met	met
deal	dealt	dealt
mean	meant	meant
bleed	bled	bled
feed	fed	fed
flee	fled	fled
lead	led	led
speed	sped	sped
cling	clung	clung
dig	dug	dug
spin	spun	spun
stick	stuck	stuck
sting	stung	stung
strike	struck	struck
swing	swung	swung
wring	wrung	wrung
win	won	won
lay (to put)	laid	laid
pay	paid	paid
say	said	said
sell	sold	sold
tell	told	told
bind	bound	bound
find	found	found
grind	ground	ground
wind	wound	wound
bring	brought	brought
buy	bought	bought
fight	fought	fought
think	thought	thought
seek	sought	sought

Simple Form	Past Form	Past Participle
teach	taught	taught
catch	caught	caught
have	had	had
sit	sat	sat
hear	heard	heard
hold	held	held
shoot	shot	shot
stand	stood	stood

4. All forms are different.

Simple Form	Past Form	Past Participle
draw	drew	drawn
fall	fell	fallen
shake	shook	shaken
take	took	taken
bear	bore	borne
swear	swore	sworn
tear	tore	torn
wear	wore	worn
blow	blew	blown
fly	flew	flown
grow	grew	grown
know	knew	known
throw	threw	thrown
begin	began	begun
drink	drank	drunk
ring	rang	rung
shrink	shrank	shrunk
sink	sank	sunk
sing	sang	sung
spring	sprang	sprung
swim	swam	swum
bite	bit	bitten (or bit)
hide	hid	hidden (or hid)
drive	drove	driven
ride	rode	ridden
stride	strode	stridden
rise	rose	risen
write	wrote	written
break	broke	broken
choose	chose	chosen
freeze	froze	frozen
speak	spoke	spoken
steal	stole	stolen
weave	wove	woven

Simple Form	Past Form	Past Participle
get	got	gotten
forget	forgot	forgotten
give	gave	given
forgive	forgave	forgiven
forbid	forbade	forbidden
do	did	done
eat	ate	eaten
go	went	gone
lie (to recline)	lay	lain
see	saw	seen

Exercise 1

Irregular Verbs

Supply the past form or the past participle for each verb in parentheses.

1. We _____ four trout in the stream.
   (to catch)
2. The burglar _____ up the fire escape.
   (to creep)
3. The audience _____ when the singer attempted the high notes.
   (to flee)
4. The pipe _____ yesterday; we are waiting for a plumber.
   (to burst)
5. He has _____ aimlessly around the city for several hours.
   (to ride)
6. The firefighters _____ down the ladder.
   (to slide)
7. The elevator _____ quickly to the tenth floor.
   (to rise)
8. She had _____ her job before the baby was born.
   (to quit)
9. The pond was _____ enough for ice skating.
   (to freeze)
10. He had washed and _____ out all his clothes in the bathtub.
    (to wring)

Exercise 2

Irregular Verbs

Read the following paragraph and find all the mistakes in irregular verbs. Write the correct forms below.

    Mr. Weeks, an alumnus of our university, had gave a large sum of money to the school just before he died. A committee was choosen to study how the money should be used. Each member thunk about the possibilities for several weeks before the meeting. Finally, the meeting begun in late November. Each member brung his ideas. One gentleman felt the school should improve the graduate program by hiring two new teachers. Another committee member layed down a proposal for remodeling the oldest dormitory on campus. Janice Spaulding had a writen plan for increasing the scholarships for deserving students. A citizen unexpectedly swang open the door and strode into the room. She pleaded with the school to provide more programs for the community. After everyone had spoke, the committee was asked to make a more thorough study of each project.

1. _____   6. _____
2. _____   7. _____
3. _____   8. _____
4. _____   9. _____
5. _____ 10. _____

Exercise 3   Irregular Verbs

Supply the past form or the past participle for each verb in parentheses.

1. We _____ in the lake last summer.
   (to swim)

2. The director _____ a solution to the problems.
   (to seek)

3. The family _____ bitterly over the death of the child.
   (to weep)

4. The clerk _____ the clock before going home.
   (to wind)

5. The door seemed to be _____.
   (to stick)

6. The dog _____ itself as it came out of the water.
   (to shake)

7. The youth _____ he was telling the truth.
   (to swear)

8. Yesterday, the food had _____ on the table all day without
   (to lie)
   being touched.

9. My friend _____ her first child in a taxicab on the way to the
   (to bear)
   hospital.

10. The hosts _____ their guests to drink in their home.
    (to forbid)

Index

abstract noun, 14, 435
action verb, 23-24, 436
active voice, 129-130
adjectives
    definition of, 13, 436
    use of commas with, 135
adverbial conjunctions
    list of, 54, 439
    used to combine sentences, 53-58
adverbs
    definition of, 26
    of frequency, 438
    of degree, 438
agreement
    subject-verb, 97-101
    pronoun-antecedent, 101-107
antecedent
    pronoun agreement with, 101-107
        ambiguous, 103-104
        missing, 103-104
        repetitious, 103-104
apostrophe, 140-143
    to form contractions, 141
    to form plurals, 141
    to form possessives, 140-141
appositive phrase
    definition of, 21
archaic usage, 431
argumentation, *see* persuasive writing
Asimov, Isaac, "The Computer and the Brain," 359-360
auxiliary verbs, *see* helping verbs

"Basic White Bread," (Beard), 350-352
Beard, James, "Basic White Bread," 350-352
brainstorming, 331-332
British usage, 431

Caldwell, Taylor, "A Tale in the Classroom," 340-343
capitalization, 494-497
cause and effect, paragraphs of, 309-310
    definition of, 309
    model paragraphs, 309-310
    suggestions for writing, 310
classification, paragraphs of, 305-308
    definition of, 305
    finding basis for, 306-307
    making distinct categories, 307-308
    model paragraph, 305
    suggestions for writing, 308
clause
    dependent, 65
    independent, 48, 65
    restrictive and nonrestrictive, 73
coherence
    in comparison or contrast, 278-288
    in description, 218-224
    in narration, 236-243
    in process, 260-261
collective noun, *see* group noun
colon, 145-146
combining sentences
    using coordination, 48-64
    using subordination, 65-81
comma
    between adjectives, 135
    after adverbial conjunction, 53
    with coordinating conjunction, 48, 135
    in dates and addresses, 134
    around interrupters, 136-137
    after introductory words, 136
    around nouns in direct address, 137
    in numbers, 138
    with quotations/dialogue, 138
    with relative clauses, 73-74, 137

with series, 134–135
    with subordinating conjunction, 66, 136
comma splice, 82
common noun, 14, 435
comparison or contrast essays, 358–365
    model essay, 359–360
    suggested topics, 360
comparison or contrast paragraphs, 274–298
    definition of, 274
    block method, 278–284
    model paragraphs, 294–298
    order, 278–284
    point-by-point method, 278–284
    steps for writing, 288
    suggestions for writing, 295–298
    transitions, 284–288
    two-part topic, 275–278
complex sentence
    definition of, 65
    how to construct, 65–81
compound sentence
    definition of, 48
    how to construct, 48–64
"Computer and the Brain, The," (Asimov), 359–360
conclusions, writing, 326–327
concrete noun, 14, 435
conditional, 130
conjunctions, 438–439
    adverbial
        list of, 54, 439
        used to combine sentences, 53–58
    coordinating
        list of, 49, 439
        pairs of, 49, 98, 439
        used to combine sentences, 48–53
    correlative, 49, 439
    definition of, 438
    list of, 439
    pairs of, 49, 98, 439
    subordinating
        list of, 66, 439
        used to combine sentences, 66–71
conjunctive adverb, see adverbial conjunction
connotation, 424–429
contractions, 141
conversation, fragments in, 29–30
coordinating conjunctions
    list of, 49
    meaning of, 49
    used to combine sentences, 49–53
coordination
    definition of, 48
    with an adverbial conjunction, 53–58

with a coordinating conjunction, 48–53
with a semicolon, 58–60
Curvin, Robert M., "What If Heroin Were Free," 379–380

dangling modifier, 112–114
dash, 146
definition, paragraphs of, 299–305
    class, 299–301
    definition of, 299–300
    distinguishing characteristics, 299–302
    example, 302–303
    model of, 300
    negation, 304
    suggested topics for writing, 304–305
denotation, 424–426
dependent clause, 65–69
    definition of, 65
description, paragraphs of, 205–233
    dominant impression, 205–211
    model paragraphs, 230–233
    order, 218–224
    sensory images, 211–218
    steps for writing, 224
    suggested topics for writing, 230–233
dictionary, use of, 416–434
    connotation, 424–429
    denotation, 424–426
    entries, understanding of, 416–418
    limitations or labels, 429–434
    meanings of a word, 419–424
direct address, 137
direct object, 14
Diary of Anne Frank, The, 1–9
doubling final consonant, 481–484

"Epidemic of Fear, An," (Hyde and Forsyth, M.D.), 195–197
essay tests, taking, 407–413
    terms used in, 408
    parts of, 408–411
essay writing, 312–413
    concluding paragraph, 312, 326–327
    introductory paragraph, 312, 320–324
    process of, see writing process
    support paragraphs, 312
    thesis statement, 313–320
    titles, 328
    transitions, 324–326

foreign words, use of, 431
fragments
    in conversation, 29–31
    correcting fragments, simple sentences, 32–33

Index

correcting fragments, complex sentences, 152–159
  definition of, 31
Frank, Anne, *The Diary of Anne Frank,* 1–9
freewriting, 8–9
fused run-on, 82

gerund phrase, 35
group nouns, 98–99

Hansberry, Lorraine, *A Raisin in the Sun,* 393–406
helping verbs, 25–27, 437
hidden subjects, 20–22
homonyms, *see* sound-alikes
Hyde, Margaret O. and Elizabeth H. Forsyth, M.D., "An Epidemic of Fear," 195–197

indefinite pronouns, 15, 98, 436
independent clause, 48, 65, 67–69
  definition of, 65
infinitive phrase, 35
informal usage, 430
interjections, 439
introductions to essays, 312, 326–327
irregular verbs, 118–122, 498–502

joining ideas, *see* combining sentences
Journal writing, 1–9

linking verbs, 24–25, 436–437

modifiers
  misplaced, 112–114
  dangling, 112–114

narrative essay, 339–348
  model essay, 340–343
  suggested topics for writing, 343
narrative paragraphs, 234–255
  definition of, 234
  model paragraphs, 251–254
  order, 236–243
  steps for writing, 245–251
  suggested topics for writing, 252–255
  transitions, 243–245
nonstandard English, 429
nouns
  abstract, 14, 435
  collective, *see* group
  common, 14, 435
  concrete, 14, 435
  group, 99
  in direct address, 137
  plurals of, 477–481
  proper, 14, 435
noun phrase, 34, 435

obsolete usage, 430

paragraphs, 170–310
  definition of, 170
  controlling idea, 180–185
  length of, 170
  standard paragraph form, 170–172
  supporting details, 189–204
  topic sentence, 172–180
  see also cause and effect, classification, comparison or contrast, definition, description, narration, process
parallelism, 107–112
parentheses, 146
participial phrase, 34–37
participles, past and present, 34
parts of speech, 435–441
  adjective, 13, 436
  adverb, 26, 437–438
  conjunction, 48–53, 53–58, 66–71, 438–439
  in context, 439
  interjection, 439
  noun, 14, 99, 137, 435, 477–481
  preposition, 17, 438
  pronoun, 15, 72–77, 98, 101–107, 436
  verb, 23–28, 97–101, 118–122, 129–130, 436–437, 498–502
passive voice, 129–130
perfect tenses, 127–129
person, consistency of, 103
persuasive writing, 366–392
  definition of, 366
  essay topics, 390
  guidelines for writing, 366–367
  model essays, 367–370, 379–380
  using research material, 370–379, 381–389
phrases
  definition of, 34
  identifying, 34–37
plural nouns, 477–481
prepositional phrases
  definition of, 16, 34
  finding the subject in sentences with, 16–20
  and subject-verb agreement, 16–20
prepositions
  list of, 17, 438
process essay, 349–357
  model essay, 350–352
  suggested topics for writing, 352
process paragraphs, 256–273
  definition of, 256

model paragraphs, 270–273
order, 260–261
steps for writing, 264
suggested topics for writing, 270–273
transitions, 262–264
process, writing, *see* writing process
pronouns
and antecedent agreement, 101–107
demonstrative, 15, 436
indefinite, 15, 98, 436
list of, 436
personal, 15, 436
relative, 15, 72–77, 436
proper noun, 14, 435
punctuation
colon, 145–146
comma, 48, 53, 66, 73–74, 134–140
dash, 146
parentheses, 146
quotation marks, 143–144
semicolon, 53–60, 144–145

quotation marks, 143–144

Raisin in the Sun, A, (Hansberry), 393–406
regional usage, 431
relative pronoun
combining sentences with, 72–77
and punctuation, 73–77
list of, 15, 72
run-on sentences, 82–96, 152–168
different kinds of, 82
guide for correcting, 83

semicolon, 53–60, 144–145
sentence
agreement, subject-verb, 97–101
combining, 48–64, 65–81
comma splice, 82
complex, 65
compound, 48
coordination, 48–64
definition of, 12
finding subjects and verbs, 12–28
fragment, 29–47
fused run-on, 82
run-on, 82–96
simple, 65
subordination, 65–81
thesis statement, 313–320
topic sentence, 172–180
slang usage, 430
sound-alikes, 442–472

spelling, 473–493
doubling final consonant, 481–484
ie or ei words, 475–477
mispronounced, 473–475
one word or two, 486–490
plurals of nouns, 477–481
words ending in y, 484–486
subjects
and agreement with verbs, 97–101
finding in a sentence, 13–22
with appositive phrases, 21
with commands, 21
with prepositional phrases, 16–20
with there, 20
hidden, 20–22
identifying, 13–15
subjunctive, 130–131
subordination, 65–81
subordinating conjunctions
list of, 66
function of, 66
support, paragraphs of, 312
supporting details, 189–204

"Tale In the Classroom, A" (Caldwell), 340–343
tense
consistency of, 123–124
present and past perfect, 127–129
sequence of, 125–127
testtaking, essay, 407–413
thesis statement
definition of, 313
how to write, 315–320
in essay questions or tests, 411–413
titles, 328, 313–315
topic sentence, 172–180
transitional words and phrases
in comparison and contrast, 284
in essays, 324–326
in narration, 243–245
in process, 262

underlining, 144

verbs
action, 23–24, 436
active voice, 129–130
and agreement with subject, 97–101
auxiliary, *see* helping
be, forms of, 99
conditional, 130
do, forms of, 99
finding in a sentence, 23–28

helping, 25–27, 437
    list of, 25, 437
identifying, 23–27, 436–437
infinitive phrase, 35
irregular, 118–122, 498–502
linking, 24–25, 436–437
    list of, 24, 437
passive voice, 129–130
past perfect tense, 127–129
participial phrase, 34
past participle, 34
present perfect tense, 127–129
sequence of tenses, 125–127
shift in verb tense, 123–125
subjunctive, 130–131
tense consistency, 123–125
verb phrase, 34

voice, 129–130
vulgar usage, 430

"What If Heroin Were Free," (Curvin), 379–380
writing process, steps in, 329–338
    brainstorming, 331–332
    checking for errors, 338
    gathering information, 331–332
    getting idea, 330–331
    preparing final copy, 338
    proofreading, 338
    rough draft, revising, 334–336
    rough draft, writing, 333–334
    second draft, writing, 336–338
    selecting and organizing details, 332–333